THE
RUNNING
MATE

THE
RUNNING
MATE

A Novel by
Joe Klein

Chatto & Windus
LONDON

Published by Chatto & Windus 2000

First published in the United States by The Dial Press in 2000

2 4 6 8 10 9 7 5 3 1

Copyright © Machiavelliana, Inc. 2000

Joe Klein has asserted his right under the Copyright, Designs
and Patents Act 1988 to be identified as the author of this work

First published in Great Britain in 2000 by
Chatto & Windus
Random House, 20 Vauxhall Bridge Road,
London SW1V 2SA

Random House Australia (Pty) Limited
20 Alfred Street, Milsons Point, Sydney,
New South Wales 2061, Australia

Random House New Zealand Limited
18 Poland Road, Glenfield,
Auckland 10, New Zealand

Random House (Pty) Limited
Endulini, 5A Jubilee Road, Parktown 2193, South Africa

The Random House Group Limited Reg. No. 954009
www.randomhouse.co.uk

A CIP catalogue record for this book
is available from the British Library

ISBN 0 7011 6966 4

Papers used by Random House are natural,
recyclable products made from wood grown in sustainable forests;
the manufacturing processes conform to the environmental
regulations of the country of origin

Printed and bound in Great Britain by
Clays Ltd, Bungay

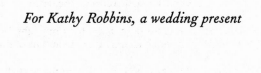

For Kathy Robbins, a wedding present

Author's Note

———

Apologies in advance to Benazir Bhutto, who makes a cameo appearance in an entirely fictional situation here. None of the other characters should be mistaken for actual people; and none of the events described herein ever happened, although the Republicans did do quite well in the congressional elections of 1994.

But women *are* politics.

—*Talleyrand*

PROLOGUE

————

[i]

The event at the Elks Club ended at dusk and they headed west, into the countryside. She was surprised by the drama of the terrain—the rolling hills were steeper than she'd expected, and perfectly proportionate; the chocolate soil fresh and fecund. The sun was setting between pilasters of clouds, which were less delicate than the casual coastal puffs she was used to; they were bigger, heavier, like the heroic thuds of mashed potato that had been deposited on their plates at the Elks. And yet, the sunset colors were as subtle as the clouds were dramatic; no pollution-induced fuchsias out here. There were streaks of canary and tangerine rising to a robin's-egg blue, then fading into a navy night.

"Great sky," she said.

"Why?" he asked.

Why? She turned to him, wrinkling her brow.

"I just want to see what you see," he explained. She brushed a hand along his cheek, which was sandpapery with early evening stubble.

"All you have to do," she said, "is look more slowly."

Just past dark they stopped at a picket fence, at the end of a long dirt road, after endless, rolling miles of corn and soy. Straight ahead was a simple white farmhouse, overilluminated by halogen crime lights; there was a red barn to the right, and corn all around. The senator slid open the minivan door and jumped out.

"I need to talk to you," he said, taking her by the wrist and, gently but firmly, leading her along the driveway path. She resisted, in part a visceral response to being tugged, but also a consequence of her khaki skirt, which was long and cumbersome. She was also wearing a white silk blouse and navy espadrilles—he didn't much like the espadrilles, but that was part of her allure: she challenged his predispositions.

He yelled a greeting—"Hey, Tom!"—in the general direction of an elderly, heavyset man in coveralls, who was ratcheting himself, with some difficulty, out of the rocking chair on the porch. "Take it easy, Tom," he quickly added, "we'll be right with ya," and he pulled her abruptly to the left, into the corn—several rows in, so no one could see them, although the lights from the house and the campaign minivan threw competing, smoky shadows through the leaves and tassels. He stopped, turned, put his hands on her shoulders; she sensed their unevenness in the dark—the right hand strong; the left a shadow of a presence.

"Okay," Charlie Martin exhaled. "Okay. . . . Will you marry me?"

"*Marry* you?" Nell Palmerston was suddenly breathless—and laughing. "Uhhh . . . no?" She was, she realized, imitating her daughter, for whom every statement was a question.

"'Uhhh . . . no?'" He imitated her imitation, expecting a response. But she was too stunned to say anything. *"No?* As in, for real—no?" Actually, he wasn't surprised. A simple yes would have been astonishing, perhaps even slightly disappointing. Nothing was ever simple with Nell. He knew he'd have to work at this. "Why the hell not?"

"Because," she said, catching her breath, "you're in campaign mode."

"Oh, come on," he said, trying to see her through the tasseled shadows, "I don't know what that *means.*"

"Yes you do," she said. "At least, I hope you do. I mean, if you didn't—that would really be pathetic."

"I'm in the middle of a campaign," he acknowledged. "So what?" He was having trouble reading her in the dark. It was hard enough reading her when he could see her.

"You're completely caught up in this thing."

"Well, what did you think—"

"I didn't think," she said. "Sometimes I have a problem with that."

"Oh, come *on,*" he said. "You knew. You think I invited you out here to help with the haying?"

"Well." She played a bit, regaining her balance. "Rhymes with haying . . ." He didn't laugh, and now she was disappointed: he didn't want to play? He wanted a serious response?

"I guess I wasn't expecting the onstage-all-the-time part of it," she tried. "I mean, it's Saturday and we were out there all day—and tomorrow's Sunday, and we have to do it all day then, too. . . . And my role: comatose devotion, perpetually amazed by your brilliance. Two days of it, and my face hurts from smiling. When do we go to the beach? I'd settle for a lake.

I saw a lake today. People were swimming." She smiled and dropped an arm over his shoulder. "Can't we go campaigning in a lake? It looked so nice. We drove right past it, on our way to where? The Fort Ditty-Bop Burrito Festival? Or was it the Firehouse Bazaar in Grove Corners?"

"It was the Fort Dantrobet Burrito Festival," he said, "and if you were having such an awful time, why did I have to wipe the salsa off your chin and drag you away from those women you were yakking with?"

"Well, they were quilt makers," she explained.

"Ohhhh, I see: *quilt* makers." He debated whether to tell her that it just wasn't politic to get so deeply embedded in a conversation on the hustings: the rest of the crowd might feel slighted. It was a detail of implementation, and he didn't want to force her political education; she'd learn the ropes at her own speed. Or so he hoped. He returned to Topic A. "So, is this a permanent no or just a provisional one?"

"Is it going to be a standing offer, or a one-shot deal?"

"I don't know," he said. "What do you think?"

"I'm guessing it's somewhere in between," she said. "A provisional standing offer. You're too proud to make it permanent and—I'd guess—too reasonable to make it a one-shot deal."

"Can we negotiate? Should I try again? You want a knee?" he offered.

"Seriously?" she asked, chuckling—she had a wonderful, unexpected chuckle; her laughing voice was deeper than her speaking voice. "A knee? As in, down on one knee?"

"Absolutely . . . not really. I've given you all the corn I could muster," he said. "I put a lot of thought into this, proposing to you here."

It was sort of fabulous. Looking straight up, she could see a brilliant night sky, with the same sliver of moon the cow jumped over in nursery rhyme books. The rich, damp smell of the soil was intoxicating.

Charlie could see her eyes now, calm and gray-green, and her coarse tangle of blond hair; Nell could see his mouth, but not his eyes, and that was a disadvantage. She had fallen in love with his eyes. He was holding her hand; he kissed the inside of her wrist. She touched his hair, which was thick and black, tending toward gray, rather aesthetically, at the temples. "I'll bet this is where you used to take all the girls," she said, "haying."

He did like a good cornfield. He'd thought about corn all the time in Vietnam, especially when he'd pass through a stand of bamboo—bamboo creaked in the wind; corn swished. Corn was so much more delicate, and benign. The thought of a midsummer cornfield, undulating over the hills, had always made him homesick. In Vietnam, he'd sometimes found himself drifting here, to Uncle Tom and Aunt Leah's place, just outside of Fort Jeffords—the corn backed up to the edge of their yard on all sides. And so he'd brought Nell to Tom and Leah's, to propose to her in the middle of their cornfield, after the last event of the day: a broasted chicken dinner with the Fort Jeffords Future Farmers of America at the Elks Hall.

Nell thought the dinner was indescribably exotic. They had been served white bread and margarine, along with the chicken, mashed potatoes, and way overcooked canned vegetables—and apple pie with slices of processed cheese melted on top. She had also been tickled by the idea that there was such a thing as *Future* Farmers: she had always imagined farmers to be part of the past, like coopers or blacksmiths. But there they were, these incredibly earnest and soon-to-be-overweight kids, talking about hybrids and genetics, and none of them wearing overalls. Nell hadn't thought about plant genetics since high school biology. She tried to remember the name of the monk who'd done the experiment with fruit flies—was it Gregor Mendel, or was he the Kafka character? She was going to ask Charlie, but he seemed so busy, asking intricate questions about the vagaries of modern agronomy, listening intently to the Future Farmers, joking—flirtatiously. Politics, as far as she could tell, involved an awful lot of flirting.

Charlie's plan was they would spend the night at Tom and Leah's— something he hadn't done since childhood—after he proposed and she'd accepted. He had imagined himself and Nell coming down the stairs Sunday morning, his arm around her waist, newly engaged. There would be Leah's famous cinnamon buns. They would go to church, of course; you have to go to church in the middle of a campaign (usually, you have to go to several churches). But he knew a rowdy apostolic congregation outside of town—great music. It would be more midwestern exotica. He wanted to show her all of it, see how she reacted. He loved watching her see things.

A cellular phone in the distance. "Hey, Senator," shouted Mustafa, his driver. "Headquarters. They got the numbers from tomorrow's *R-W.*"

Nell sighed. "See?" she said. "Campaign mode."

"Fuck campaign mode," he said softly—but intensely, just above a whisper. "You think I'm asking you to marry me for the sake of *appearances?* I'm asking you to marry me because you are . . ." He struggled for something clever, and failed. "The most . . . interesting person I know."

" 'Interesting'?" She laughed.

"This isn't funny," he said, but, of course, he knew it had to be. "All right: I'm asking you to marry me because . . . Well, what are you going to wear to church tomorrow?" During the day, when the sun had been hot, she'd worn a spectacular wide-brimmed straw hat with a white nylon mesh band that flowed down her back, and Jackie O sunglasses—with the khaki suit, she looked as if she were on a safari photo shoot for some fashion magazine. Plainly, she hadn't been born to do politics. But he loved having her there, and he was still pretty much amazed that she finally had agreed to come out from New York—although she did affect his ability to concentrate on the business at hand. Then again, she'd only been traveling with him for two days. This—Nell working his turf, living his life—was still new, for both of them. He had hoped she'd find his world as . . . charming as he'd found hers; well, maybe not *as* charming. He was hoping she'd find it tolerable.

"What does my Sunday best have to do with anything?" she asked.

"You're the first woman I've ever been with where I'm even thinking about it," he said. "You make everything—"

"Groovy?"

"Wild thing," he said, making the connection. "You make my heart sing." Truly a great rock lyric; he'd never focused on it before. Simple, elegant, perfect. She made his heart sing. "Hey, you want to go dancing?" he asked. "Then we won't be in campaign mode."

"Dancing?" He'd used this tactic before, shifting gears on her, proposing an outlaw getaway—dancing, usually. They had danced, on occasion; but they'd never actually gone dancing.

"We're about forty-five minutes from the Crescent Lake Casino, where Mom met Dad. Saturday night, they'll have some old-fart band, or maybe square dancing, or polkas," he said. "C'mon, let's go."

"You just want to hear the numbers," she said mischievously. "You want to get me out of the cornfield, so you can take the phone call and hear the numbers. You're not even interested in getting me to marry you anymore."

"Bull shit," he said, making them two words. "That's a done deal. You're going to marry me, sooner or later." He snaked an arm around her waist, nuzzled her neck, went woozy at her smell. "But right now," he said, "we're going dancing."

"I do hope it's square dancing," she replied, reaching down, squeezing the back of his thigh. "I'll be able to ask the caller something I've always wondered about: is do-si-do short for something? And what about allemande left—is that a reference to El Alamein? And—"

"Senator!" Mustafa shouted. "You comin' or what?"

"Coming!" Charlie Martin said. Nell rolled her eyes.

Mustafa was leaning against the van. He was, Nell thought, a strange specimen: a tall, middle-aged black man who chain-smoked Virginia Slims, thin and angular except for an incongruous potbelly. He handed Charlie the phone.

"Who?" Charlie asked.

"Aunt Mary."

It made sense. Mary Proctor ran his home-state office. She knew all the pooh-bahs at the *Register-World*. She'd have their poll numbers first.

"So okay, Mary," he said. "Cut to the chase. What's the story?"

"You're behind. Only a couple of points, margin of error," she said. "But behind."

"To that little turd?" he said. "No fucking way."

"As my granddaughter would say," Mary said, "way."

[ii]

One of the first things Nell Palmerston had noticed in the den of the Martin family home in Des Pointe—everyone just called the place "Oak Street"—was a laminated copy of a *Life* magazine article from June 1968: "A Hero Comes Home." And there he was: young, skinny, black hair closely cropped, left hand heavily bandaged, but smiling . . . and those eyes. Even in black and white, they were deadly, she thought: almost feminine. In real life, they were a very dark but vivid ceramic blue—like Delft china—each with a perfectly etched aurora of crow's-feet, which made it seem as if he were perpetually on the brink of a smile, even when he was angry. They were calm, kindly, long-lashed eyes, unexpectedly benign; Charlie Martin's best feature. Without them, his face would have seemed irreparably harsh and masculine, slightly pockmarked: a good face for a soldier or a ballplayer, much too severe for a politician. The eyes made politics possible.

Nell found herself drawn repeatedly to the *Life* story, which hung on plywood paneling surrounded by family photos. The photos dominated the room—not just photos of the hero-politician son, but of the hero-politician mother, and the charming accordion-playing dad. The den was the most lived-in room of the house, containing what appeared to be the family's three most significant pieces of furniture: the console television, Charlie's father's La-Z-Boy recliner and a spinet piano; there was also a couch, side tables and lamps—undistinguished, department store early-American style—and bookcases filled with Book-of-the-Month Club selections. The Martins didn't seem to be very conscious of physical appearances; there was no visual coherence to the place. In a way, the absence of attention to design was as jarring to Nell as the all-consuming presence of politics.

There was a lot to assimilate in the *Life* magazine spread, even though it was only two pages long. Indeed, the story seemed as exotic to Nell, and as deeply American, as the Future Farmers had. She remembered studying issues of *Life* in the orthodontist's office back in the sixties, the same way other people flipped through *National Geographic*—it was a form of anthropology: the photo-fantasy of an utterly foreign people, strong and happy and unencumbered by irony. And yet, in this case, the blandness of the words and photos seemed off-key—a harbinger of the end of innocence, the end of *Life*: this story was about a return from Vietnam. Charlie was beautiful but painfully thin, reluctant and haunted. One photo was of a parade, with the hero standing in an open car, tentatively waving with his good right hand. Another was of Charlie being given the key to the city by a big-boned prairie woman with a sweet, small face—the caption said: "Captain Martin receives the key to the city from his mother, Mayor Clarice Campbell Martin." His smile was a wince.

Another photo, captioned: "First Family of Des Pointe." There was Charlie, arm in arm with "his wife, Johanna"—a very serious-looking young woman with rimless eyeglasses and an acute, back-to-the-barricades sort of beauty. Nell remembered that look—great skin, high cheekbones, blazing eyes: those girls had been truly intimidating in college (but not since). Charlie and Johanna were flanked by the hero's "colorful" parents, Clarice and Buzz Martin. They were Mutt and Jeff: Buzz was as thin and casual as Clarice was sturdy. He was wearing shades, and a thin dark tie, and he was smiling—with his left eyebrow raised mischievously. The caption described him as "a local musician."

According to the text, written in a style Nell found clumsy and yet comforting, Charlie was a "much-decorated Marine," just released from the Philadelphia Naval Hospital, where he'd been treated for wounds suffered in a land mine explosion southwest of Danang. Asked about the "recent large-scale protests against the war in Washington," Captain

Martin said, "I'm not going to criticize that. Everyone has a decision to make about this war, and it's possible to come to different conclusions. My heart is with the grunts, the guys I served with—we need to give them all the support we can."

The mayor, however, was more forthcoming: "My son lost most of a hand. For what? I thought we could use this year's Memorial Day parade to honor Charlie's sacrifice, and to honor all the other boys who are doing their patriotic duty. But I think Lyndon Johnson should spend a day—maybe this day, Memorial Day—emptying bedpans in the ward where they had Charlie in Philly, and then I'd like to see what he'd be saying about this war."

The "feisty" mayor, "a former social worker and community activist," had run a "grassroots" campaign against the "infamous Petunia Social Club" political machine in 1966 and "won a narrow victory, much to everyone's surprise."

But most of the article was about Charlie Martin, who had been awarded two silver stars in Vietnam. "Local Democrats are already talking up the possibility of a political career for young Martin. 'He's a natural,' said Patrick Dunn, chairman of the state Democratic party. 'He's the kind of kid who, soon as you meet him, you think: this guy's going to be president some day.' "

"Bobby Kennedy died the week that came out," Charlie said, coming up behind Nell, the evening after she had rejected his marriage proposal.

"I remember," she said.

"Where were you?"

"In Paris . . ."

"Negotiating with the Vietnamese? The Paris Peace Talks?"

"Negotiating with Chanel," she said. "For a summer job."

"As a model?"

"Too weird-looking, too irregular," she said. "I was a kid. I was willing to work for free . . . and, it turned out, the price was right. The family thing didn't hurt, either."

The family thing: Charlie always had to be reminded that she was distantly related, on her father's side, to the British royals. Nell found this endearing, and a bit exasperating: most of the other men in her life had been a bit too impressed by her lineage. It was an advantage she'd been able to use on them, one that Charlie wouldn't allow, stone Democrat that he was. It was nice to be loved for one's own attributes, Nell thought, but it was also nice to have advantages.

"The 'family thing' didn't hurt you, either," she said. "You went into the family business . . . 'the kind of kid who could be president some day' . . ."

He snorted. "That was just politics," he said. "Patsy was making a peace offering to Mom. He was a creature of the Petunias, the machine's state chairman. He was making nice, hoping she wouldn't come after him, too. Funny thing is, it worked. Pat was a labor guy, and the meat packers were big in Des Pointe in those days. He and Mom found they had more in common than not. . . ."

"Yeah, but everyone—including you—believed it, the president stuff. In fact, you still do," she said.

"I'm still licking my wounds from last time," he said. "It's probably why this guy is giving me a tussle now. . . . Anyway, I've got to check in with Patsy Dunn. And, sweetie"—he paused theatrically—"tonight's the night. You want to come along, have a meal with him?"

"Do I have a choice?" she asked, with a smile. "Aren't there any more Future Farmers, or Former Farmers, we can chat up?"

"You'll like Pat," he said. "I promise."

"Where do we find him?" she asked. "Will there be more Wonder Bread?"

"At the Petunia Social Club, of course," he said. "And don't be so proud of your cultural disadvantages: Wonder Bread builds strong bodies twelve ways."

"From what I've seen," she said, moving toward him, nuzzling his ear and whispering, "that could only be true if you define strength as fat."

"You are cruel to my people," he said, snaking an arm around her waist.

* * *

The Petunia Social Club Restaurant wasn't the real Petunia Social Club: that had been a speakeasy and whorehouse down on the Flats, near the east bank of the Brown River, which flowed through Des Pointe on its way to the Mississippi. Charlie had always loved the Flats—several blocks of redbrick factory and warehouse buildings, just like St. Louis or any other real city. The meatpacking plants had been there, and the whorehouses that serviced the meat packers: Des Pointe had been a wild town in the Petunia days, an era that had lingered until the advent of the

Clarice Martin Democrats in the mid-1960s. Now the Flats had been "restored," just as similar neighborhoods throughout urban America had been: lots of exposed brick, and T-shirt shops, and restaurants where the waiters told you their names and carried the menu on a blackboard. The new Petunia Social Club was just such a place, with some nice sepia photos of old Des Pointe on the walls—meat packers in bloodstained aprons, stone-faced farmers coming to town in the wagons, members of the Petunia machine in bowlers, painted ladies. And Patrick Dunn could usually be found there, too.

He sat in a rear booth—his unofficial office—nursing a tap beer, far from the crowd of young professional this-and-thats at the bar busy picking one another up.

"Dr. Demento," Charlie said, giving Dunn a brisk hug, "this is Nell Palmerston. She's the granddaughter of a duke. Nell, this is Patsy Dunn. He's the son of a duchess."

"Thought you were going to say, he's the son of a bitch, Chas," Pat said. "That'd be true, too. Pleased to meet you, ma'am."

Nell noted that Charlie had used her lineage. It had been a joke, but he'd used it, which was slightly disappointing—and slightly not: advantage Nell. She also noted that Patsy Dunn was perhaps the most handsome bald man she'd ever met. He had strong, straight features and clear, Windex-blue eyes—did startling eyes come with the territory out here? she wondered—and he held his age well, nothing stooped or cloudy about him, though he was well into his seventies. He was wearing a navy Polo golf shirt; he didn't have the slightest hint of a potbelly.

Patsy's booth came equipped with a red-checked tablecloth and oversized everything: napkins, plates, utensils; the waiter brought an oversized loaf of bread (white, though furiously grainy) on a board, with an oversized bread knife to cut it. Nell ordered a vodka on the rocks, and was presented with enough alcohol to level a Cossack; Charlie was brought at least sixteen ounces of diet Coke.

"Dunnsie actually grew up here," Charlie explained, "in the Flats."

"Mother was in the entertainment business—middle management," Patsy said. "This wasn't so cute and fancy then. Smelliest place in the world—blood and cow dung. That's why they put it on the east side, so the proper folks, like Clarice Martin and all, wouldn't get the whiff."

"No one ever accused Buzz of being proper," Charlie reminded him.

"We'd see Charlie's dad from time to time in the old days," Patsy explained. "He'd come play the piano for a poke at Sarah Miller's, which was where my mother worked. I always said, Clarice—Charlie's mom—couldn't reform Buzz, so she reformed the rest of us instead. Ruined the local economy. We used to get farm boys and cowboys from all over the Upper Plains, patronizing our local institutions."

"Didn't do much for the tax base," Charlie said.

"But it promoted social stability," Pat replied, thankful that Charlie had turned out to be something more than Clarice's son—she'd been a hard woman, cold as Utah in a blizzard, a revisitation of the Women's Christian Temperance Union. Charlie had a filial weakness for reform, but it was leavened by a healthy respect for human frailty—Buzz's legacy, no doubt. Truly, a felicitous combination in a senator, Patsy thought. "The Flats saved a lot of marriages," he explained to Nell. "Safety valve. After all Clarice did to wreck that, I'd say it was simple justice that the boy's getting bit in the ass by the Righteous Lad now."

"Oh, right," she said to Dunn. "Mr. Muffler." Charlie had told her about his rich young challenger, but the descriptions hadn't done Leland Butler justice. For one thing, Charlie hadn't mentioned that Butler was extremely good-looking. Not her type, to be sure: blond, bland, over-scrubbed, a distant cousin of Troy Donahue—Nell found that she was still thinking in *Life* magazine–era terms—or the King family. But handsome, in an American way. "It was the King family, wasn't it?" she asked.

"What was?" Charlie said, laughing at the out-of-left-field non sequitur, a very Nell-ish thing—and nodding at Dunn, as if to say: isn't she a stitch?

"Those milk-fed dray horse girls who sang with Lawrence Welk," Nell said. "Back when."

"The Lennon Sisters, I think," Pat offered.

"And . . . so?" Charlie asked, happily bemused.

Patrick Dunn sat back, watched, evaluated: an oddball, this Nell—a throwback, like the rich girls in the movie comedies when he was a kid, during the Depression: she had a touch of Carole Lombard, but wilder hair.

"Lee Butler reminds me of them," she said. "He's good-looking for a goody-goody."

"A goody-goody, but not a prude," Dunn said. "That's the part that gives me the itch. He's six ways righteous, and yet he's got this *Saturday Night Live* sense of humor—and the leather jacket, and riding his motorcycle around the state. It doesn't fit."

"Patsy, you're too damn old for *Saturday Night Live*," Charlie said.

"You're the one who's lookin' old right now, Senator," Patsy shot back.

"I haven't seen his ads yet," Nell said. She'd only seen Butler once, in fact, silent footage of him campaigning, picnics and town square festivals, on the evening news. "It's been nonstop stumping since I got here."

"He's not running ads right now," Charlie said.

"You said he had clever ads." She looked at him, perplexed.

"That was before," Charlie began to explain. It had been two years since the first Muffler Man spots, starring Leland Butler, had appeared on local television—reappeared, actually—and become something of a phenomenon. Lee Butler was the grandson of the original Muffler Man, Jackson Butler, who had been a constant presence on the air when Charlie was growing up.

"Nell, this guy's grandfather was like—he was a Des Pointe institution," Charlie said. "He did birdcalls. He'd do contests: guess the birdcall and win a free lube job . . . He wore a straw boater and a bow tie. He'd say, 'Wanta hear a funny noise?' and he'd put his hands up to his mouth like this." Charlie started, then stopped—he didn't like doing obvious things with his hands. "Well, you know what bird callers do . . . And then he'd say, sort of singsong, 'Dat's a *fun*-ny *noise.*' "

Nell cracked up. She'd never heard of Jackson Butler, of course; but it was clear that this was one of Charlie's ancient talents—a perfect Muffler Man impersonation. The senator was pleased with himself. Nell saw him, fleetingly, as a child—the sort of kid who didn't need to do impersonations to be popular, but did them anyway. "I mean, you can imagine what it was like when we were kids," he said. "Everyone did a Muffler Man, 'Dat's a *fun*-ny *noise.*' Right, Patsy?" Dunn was laughing now. "And then he'd say, 'But you don't want your car making *fun*-ny noises. So come on down to Butler Muffler.' That was the grandfather. . . . So what's your guess, Patsy?" Charlie said, returning to business. "What do you think he'll throw at us? Did you hear what they're doing to McGreevey in Ohio? They're running spots that morph him into Jack Stanton. You think they can do that to me?"

"Dunno. It's a worry," Dunn said, but he didn't sound too worried. He had more immediate concerns. He was worried about his candidate. He needed Charlie to be more focused, less in love. Patsy watched the senator across the table, without being too obvious about it—which wasn't hard, because Charlie couldn't keep his eyes off Nell. This was astonishing: Charlie Martin had always been the guy who'd been ogled—men and women, didn't make a difference, they couldn't take their eyes off him. The change in Charlie was potentially more perplexing than the

Lee Butler challenge: Pat Dunn searched his memory and tried to remember if he'd ever been involved in a campaign with an infatuated candidate before—drunks, yes; thieves, far too often; cads, of course. But smitten? Never. Politicians weren't built like that. They were loved, not vice versa. He wondered if the craziness of the past few years had softened Charlie, made this head-over-heels tumble inevitable. Or was it just this particular woman?

She wasn't beautiful, certainly not in a straightforward midwestern way. But she was undeniably attractive—she had one of those arch, eastern, long-nosed, sophisticated looks: the sort of look a lot of midwestern folks didn't understand, or like much if they did. And she was clever, which was not good at all—a liability at best in politics, and quite possibly a disaster.

Charlie excused himself, and Nell immediately asked, "So, how much trouble are we in here, Mr. Dunn?"

"Hard to say," Patsy said. "Won't know until the campaign really gets rolling, although Butler's off to a good start. We're bringing in a consultant, New York fella named Morey Richardson." He looked at Nell as if she might know the man. She didn't. "First time we've ever done that. But he's had experience with these goofball sort of candidates—you know, rich guys running for the first time, TV and radio celebs. Anyway, Richardson says there's no handbook. Can't tell what you're up against until you're up against it. Some of them, you hit them and they fall down. Some of them, you hit them and they fall down and then they get back up and knock your block off."

"And what happens to Charlie when this guy swings at him?" she asked. "Does he fall down, too?"

"Been thinking a lot about that," Dunn said. "Thing about Charlie, he's never had a tough race, never really had to slug it out. First time he ever got clocked was the presidential campaign. And that sent him spinning. I don't know if he's recovered yet. You've seen more of him the past year than I have, what do you think?"

"I don't know very much about politics," she said. "All I know is, he looks at me and he sees me—exactly who I am. . . . Patsy, we've been so damn happy these past few months. It's, like, shocking. I think our senator is in a state of shock. Me too. I mean: Here I am . . . like, *duuuhhhh*." She circled her index finger next to her forehead, meaning—what?—Pat wasn't quite sure. Either that she was crazy to have come out there, or crazy about Charlie. Maybe both. "Anyway, I don't want to lose what we have. I don't know if I can watch him become someone else, the tough guy you want for this campaign. Or worse, get pummeled by—"

Charlie was back, a waiter in tow. Instead of going through the specials, the waiter looked over at Dunn, who said, "I'd say two and a half. Salad and potatoes. Madame," he asked Nell, trying to be continental, "you like your steak rouge or rose?"

"Steak?" she said with a shudder. "Oh, well." And then she gleamed wickedly across the table at Patrick Dunn: "*Saignant . . .* bloody."

"She's a difficult woman, Charles," Patsy said. "About time you found one. This is good steak, Ms. Palmerston. Medium red, son," he said to the waiter.

"Oh, by the way: it's not Ms. Palmerston," Nell said. "It's Mrs. Belligio."

"You're still married?"

"Not really, but I have kids and they have his name, so I keep it, too, to cut down the confusion at school."

"And what are your intentions toward our good senator?"

This was a direct, formal and rather startling question. Charlie glared at Dunn. Nell didn't want to take it seriously, and Pat saw that. "We—"

"Are living in sin, in the middle of a campaign," the old man said lightly, but not really. So that's the agenda, she thought.

"Hey, Dunnsie, cool it," Charlie said. "We are not living in sin. She's just visiting. Anyway, we're grown-ups."

"Would that the voters were," Dunn said.

Nell looked at Patsy. There was no anger, or outrage, or exasperation. He seemed perfectly calm.

"This is none of their business," Charlie said firmly. "When have they ever cared before?"

It was true: Charlie's rather gaudy social life had always been a public titillation, but never an issue. He was a hero, a veteran—and veterans received special dispensation: they were *assumed* to have warrior libidos. But the Washington press was treating politicians differently now; Pat wondered if the Des Pointe press might be induced, in a tough campaign, to follow suit.

"Mr. Dunn, are you saying you think that our private life will be"—Nell paused—"public business?"

"I don't know," Patsy said. Overwrought salads arrived in huge wooden bowls. "The lad here is the most popular politician in the history of this state . . . at least, that's how they always introduce him at rallies, and I worry that he has come to believe it."

"I'm out here every weekend, I'm working my tail off—"

"Finally," Dunn said coldly. "You weren't around much the past six months."

"Every other week," Charlie said.

"Seemed like less."

"Well," Charlie conceded. He had been spending a fair amount of time in New York, with Nell, the past six months.

"Nell, Lee Butler has been a celebrity in this state for the past two years, and he's got some powerful friends," Dunn said. "Chas, you saw what gunnies did with the crime bill?"

"Fuck the gunnies," Charlie said.

"Easy for you to say," Patsy said, then looked over at Nell, who was trying to follow, but having trouble: they were speaking Greek.

"I'm opposed to crime," Nell offered. "Is that okay?"

"Well, if you were *really* opposed to crime, you'd also be opposed to the Crime Bill," Patsy said. "At least, that's the argument."

"Okay, I'll bite," she said. "How does supporting the Crime Bill make you against crime? And who, by the way, are the gunnies?"

"The National Rifle Association," Charlie said, and realized that Nell had only a vague idea who the NRA was. "The gun lobby. They attacked my Crime Bill position in a series of newspaper ads—Muffler Boy didn't have to raise a finger. They hate the bill because of a few gun-control provisions we snuck in."

"And that's worrisome?" Nell asked. "You'd think the gunnies were doing you a favor."

"You'd think," Charlie said. "Back in New York, they might be. And maybe here, too, when we get on the air in the fall—unfortunately, we don't have any 'independent' groups like the NRA to run ads for our side. At least, not on that issue."

"Maybe I could be an independent group, like the NRA," she offered. "We could call it the American Swimwear Institute and Foundation—AS-*IF*, for short."

"Nell designs bathing suits," Charlie explained proudly.

"And are you planning to address the other issues in this campaign?" Patrick Dunn asked her, attempting her ironic style.

"Are you kidding?" She rolled her eyes. "I'm going to zip my lip." She zipped it with her hand and threw away the key. Patsy decided that he liked her, which made it all so much worse. She had grit, unlike some of the sheer lookers Charlie had trotted out over the years; she had edges.

He was happy for Charlie, but worried—and then angry at himself for being worried: What was so wrong about the kid, finally, having a life?

"And what will you do if some of our enterprising reporters ask your opinion about this or that?" Patsy asked.

"I will hand them a petunia and send them to you," she said. "Charlie, they're not going to ask me—" She stopped, thought a moment. "But of course they are. Aren't they, Mr. Dunn?"

[iii]

On Monday mornings when he was home, Charlie Martin would hold a press conference in Des Pointe for local reporters. If the Senate was in session, he'd fly back to Washington in the afternoon. The week of Nell's visit, however, he'd made an election year decision to stay home—it was a noncompulsory week for senators who had races: no major votes were scheduled. "You sure ISTEA isn't coming up this week?" Charlie asked Hilton Devereaux, his communications director, as they headed to the state capitol in the campaign minivan.

Nell stared out the window: Des Pointe wasn't nearly as exotic as the surrounding countryside. It had some nice Victorian and prairie-style homes on the west side, where Charlie's family lived, but downtown was generic—nondescript glass curtain-wall buildings (although, in a concession to the stark winters, some of the buildings were connected by enclosed, mezzanine-level walkways). After a few blocks of semihigh density, downtown dribbled off into vacant parking lots. The state capitol stood about a half mile in the distance like a mirage, on a hill next to the Brown River. It was surrounded by a cluster of state office buildings, which seemed to have been built in thirty-year intervals—in the 1930s and 1960s, with the excavation for the inevitable 1990s edition just begun nearby. The capitol itself was a late Victorian masterpiece with a curious Eastern Orthodox onion dome. Charlie would meet the press, picturesquely, on the granite steps outside, with the golden dome—recently regilded, a consequence of the booming nineties—in the background.

"What is Iced Tea?" Nell asked. Dinner with Pat Dunn had convinced her that she should try to learn the lingo.

"It's the transportation bill," Charlie said, with a bit of an edge.

"Why is it called Iced Tea?" she asked, catching the testiness.

"Because . . . because it's an acronym," Charlie said. He could never remember what it stood for. "What are we gonna have from the peanut gallery this morning?" he asked Hilton abruptly.

"Hog lots, topsoil and pesticides," the press secretary replied, turning to Nell: "Remember *Oklahoma!*? Remember 'the farmer and the cowboy should be friends'? Now it's the farmer and the environmentalist. . . ."

"Which side are we on?" Nell asked. There were all these issues.

"We take a *nuanced* position," Hilton said, with raised eyebrow. He was mortally droll, languorously stringy, a homosexual from Mississippi. "It's super-responsible. It just isn't very explicable. Senator, that's sort of our modus operandi, isn't it? Impenetrably worthy?"

Hilton's presence was one of the things Nell loved about Charlie: he sought out irregularity; he appreciated irony. He was impatient with people who were too respectful, too willing to do his bidding, too timid to get up into his face—she'd seen it time and again at social occasions in New York and Washington. He liked to be provoked. He would create conversational skirmish lines, challenge and probe and fence with all comers—it was how he learned. This was a wonderful quality in a handsome man, but an odd one in a politician (those she'd met with Charlie, at least, seemed tepid, cautious, determinedly banal). The testiness in his voice that morning was the first time she'd ever heard him the slightest bit taut. She took his hand, stroked it, sending a message: she wouldn't always be difficult. She would try to read his moods, learn his business.

"What else, you think?" he asked Hilton, reciprocating her message with a slight squeeze.

"Horse race, of course. The *R-W* poll. They'll want your version of 'the only poll that counts is on election day. . . .' "

"What if I say," Charlie said, "if this poll is accurate, and it probably is, I can't believe how *thick* the people of this state are?"

"That'll work," Hilton said.

A clot of reporters, four television cameras, several radio sorts, campaign spies, malingering office workers and a smattering of the bizarre, special-pleading human driftwood who hang around every statehouse greeted Senator Martin on the glary, late-morning capitol steps. Nell and Hilton blended into an octet of Martin supporters—a couple of state senators and assembly members, county chairpeople, all of whom seemed to be sweating. She reached into her bag for the sunglasses, but Hilton stayed her arm as she moved to put them on: okay, okay—shades bad, squinting good. But why? "*You're* wearing sunglasses," she whispered to

Devereaux, who was otherwise safely in uniform: blue blazer, button-down shirt and striped tie, chinos and Top-Siders.

"I am not you," he said. "Every last one of those reporters is going to be checking you out."

"Why?" But she knew why.

"Because you're bonking the senator."

Charlie was easy at the microphone. First question to Mike Ryan of AP: reaction to the poll?

"Well, we've got a long way to go, haven't we?" Charlie said. Then he gave them all a smile. "You want me to give you 'The only poll that counts is on election day'? That's true, of course. But I do think this poll is an indication of some real questions that folks have: they don't like the way things are going in Washington. Well, okay. Let's talk it over. But in the end, I'm confident they'll decide I've been working hard on the things they care about."

"Senator, have you ever been behind in a poll before?"

"Didn't you cover that presidential campaign we had two years ago?"

"I mean, a statewide poll."

The answer was no, but Charlie didn't want to admit that. He didn't want to avoid it, either. "I hope it'll prove a fleeting phenomenon."

On to topsoil and hog lots and pesticides. Charlie fenced and danced, and explained his position in excruciating detail. Nell watched the reporters taking notes and not taking notes. She found herself quite impressed by them: they were asking serious technical questions about topsoil loss, and tree-planting programs, and PCBs in the runoff, and fecal matter from the feedlots—and Charlie was firing right back at them: how did he find the time to keep all that stuff in his brain and still be a human being?

Finally, a television guy who looked like a young male model read a question from a slip of paper he pulled from his notebook. "Blake Dornquist from KFYR—*News Nine*," he introduced himself. "Your opponent said yesterday, in an exclusive interview with *News Nine* that will air tonight, that you had an 'alternative lifestyle' and that voters should be concerned, not only with how you vote, but how you live."

"No kidding!" Charlie said lightly, as if he were answering another question about topsoil. "Well, first of all, I didn't hear Mr. Butler say it and I'll grant him the right to have been misquoted. But . . . if he did say it, what on earth do you suppose he meant by it? He thinks I shouldn't be dating?" Charlie asked with a smile. He actually seemed to be enjoying this; he certainly didn't seem to take the accusation very seriously.

"Well, I guess—" the male model said.

"He means," said Bob Hamblin of the *Register-World,* "that your social life, and that of your staff, should be fair game."

Nell felt Hilton flinch: they were both in the same boat.

"Do *you* think that, Bob?"

"Doesn't matter what I think, Senator," Hamblin said. "I just report what you guys do to each other."

"But it does matter," Charlie said, getting serious. Nell had never seen him publicly serious before; he seemed to slow down, become more thoughtful. He spoke softly—the opposite of his conversational skirmish style. "Let's think about it a minute," he continued. "What if I turned it around on you? Now, I know you and Gracie have a great marriage, and three terrific kids—but what if you were a guy who wasn't married, or who had an 'alternative' lifestyle, whatever that is: you think it would be any business of mine? Or of your readers? I'm sure you have a few nontraditional sorts over there at the *R-W.* Should we have footnotes after your bylines for 'lifestyle' choice, list them down at the bottom of the story: reporter X once had an abortion, reporter Y once paid for an abortion, reporter Z did some cocaine back in the seventies, reporter W is born-again and a teetotaler?"

"We're not on the public payroll," Bob Hamblin said.

"But you're doing the public's work," Charlie said, coming right back at him—amiably, though. "I could argue—since abortion, sadly, is likely to be a part of this campaign—that there should be full disclosure: the public has a right to know whether a person who reports on such an important issue ever had to make a personal decision on that issue . . . but I'm not gonna do that. Because I believe there are lines we shouldn't cross. I don't care if my opponent watches kung fu movies in his spare time, or cheats on the golf course—or on his wife, for that matter. None of my business. I think we get into pretty dangerous territory when we start fishing those waters. I expect Mr. Butler and I will have enough differences on the public's business, without having to get into how we butter our toast. Next question."

Hilton whispered to Nell, "That probably wasn't very good for us, but I loved it."

"How could it be bad?"

"Stick around," he said. "Personal stuff always turns bad. And I'm not so sure that the working press likes to be confronted that way."

When the press conference ended, a few innocuous questions later, Charlie chatted informally with reporters. "You should come out on the road with us," he said to Bob Hamblin.

"You'll be sick of me before this is done," Hamblin said.

"I'm sick of you already," Charlie replied. "Your middle kid okay?"

"Thank God for special ed, Senator," he said. "He's catching up."

Nell was transfixed by this, the intimacy, the ease of the transaction—much more so than she'd been during the technical parts of the press conference, when her mind had wandered: the topsoil talk had gotten her thinking again about how this was the farthest she'd ever been from an ocean in midsummer. She missed the smell of salt and suntan oil; she missed thinking about bathing suits and cover-ups, and seeing who was wearing what at Bridgehampton. A woman approached her. "Hello," she said. "Caroline Adams from the *R-W*."

"Hello," said Nell, not introducing herself.

"You're traveling with the senator?" the reporter asked, working at informality.

"Yes." Even. Pleasant.

"Well, I was wondering if you'd be willing to let me interview you," Caroline Adams said. She was a plain girl, badly dressed—a yellow blouse with a Peter Pan collar, battleship-blue-gray slacks. "Are you having fun?"

"Oh, yes," Nell said. "But why would anything I'd have to say be noteworthy?"

"People in this state have been fascinated with Charlie Martin for a long time," Adams said. "They've watched him grow up, they've been through a lot with him. They're interested in who he's dating."

Hilton approached, nick of time. "Now, Caroline, you're looking spiffy this fine Monday morning," he said. "Where you been the last couple of weeks?"

"Oh, foolin' around—Dutch festival up at Speights. Amazing, the artwork you can do with soybeans and corn kernels," she said, with a grimace. "I was just asking Miss Palmerston if she'd be willing to have a cup of coffee or lunch with me. . . ."

"Well, you heard how the senator feels about his private life," Hilton said, very friendly.

"But I don't know how you feel," she said to Nell.

Nell smiled benignly—a reaction she had inferred from Hilton.

"Look, I'm sorry," Caroline said to her. "My editors think you're a story."

"I'm a person," Nell said. "Not a story."

"I mean," Adams said, "you may want to get your side of the story out."

"My side of the story?" Nell asked, trying to control her irritation: how could there be *another* side to the story?

"There's no evil intent," Adams said. "The society page runs profiles of wives and . . . friends of our elected officials all the time. By the way, I have one of your swimsuits."

"Really?" Nell tried to imagine what sort of body this plain girl had; she seemed long-waisted. She was about to ask which suit, and where Adams had bought it—Nell didn't think she had any outlets in Des Pointe—but she saw Hilton giving the "Don't ask!" signal with his eyes.

"I got it in St. Louis."

"Really?" She wondered which store.

"You're very talented," Adams said. "Do you design them yourself?"

"Thank you." Nell was jogged back to reality by the compliment, and withdrew into blandness. "Yes I do, design them myself."

Charlie was with them now. "Hi, Adams. Working the girlfriend angle?"

Caroline shrugged. "Your opponent is," she said.

"Dating is an alternative lifestyle?" Charlie asked. Nell sensed Hilton's concern: Charlie had made his statement, he shouldn't push his luck. "Does that mean *you* have an alternative lifestyle, Adams?"

"Senator, we'd better—" Hilton tried.

"A reluctant alternative to marriage," Adams said, with a smile. "Look, I'm sure most of the reporters here—and most of our editors—agree with you about this, but you have to help us out a little."

"No, I don't," he said, glancing over at Nell.

"There are a lot of cluckers out there," she said.

"I haven't heard any. And I have to go now, Adams, and listen to the noncluckers' problems, and see if we can do something about them," he said. "We've got a Garden Club lunch in Otweegum, and then I'm gonna visit Sam Leason over at the Pike County *Dispatch,* and hit a few fire houses, and then wander east and do shift change at the Ford plant in Port Sallesby. Busy day, huh? You want to come along with us? Don't have room in the van, but you can travel along behind."

"Can I speak with Ms. Palmerston?"

"What does she say about that?" Charlie asked.

"She hasn't said."

"I'm sure you would be entirely fair," Nell said. "But I don't want a story written about me."

"It's going to be written," Caroline Adams said. "The only question is whether you cooperate or not."

"We have to go," Hilton said.

"I'll be right behind you," Caroline Adams said.

"You had to invite her along?" Nell said, back in the van.

"She was coming anyway," Charlie said. "What do you think, HD? Talk or balk?"

"Talk, I guess," Hilton shrugged.

"Do I get a say in this?" Nell asked.

"You get ultimate say, my love," Charlie said. "I just wanted you to hear Hilton on the subject, before you decide."

"Why talk, Hilton?" she asked, disappointed: the Des Pointe Hilton was different from the Washington Hilton. He was distant, distracted: a working Hilton. She turned to Charlie: "I came out here to be with *you*. Not to be a public spectacle."

"I *am* a public spectacle," he said coolly. "It's what I do. I'm sorry." Nell wondered about the coolness. She wondered if he was still smarting from the rejection of his marriage proposal. On the other hand, living a life in which reporters were as common a presence as deliverymen was just the sort of thing she'd always tried to avoid; her parents had been far too public with their various and sundry debauches—and then there were her British cousins, who lived on the media equivalent of Devil's Island.

"Nell," Hilton said, "you say no, it becomes a Big Story. You say yes, you shmooze her a little, charm her, and you can draw the line on anything really personal. Most reporters aren't killers. They're embarrassed to ask the personal questions. They ask because they have to, and they're relieved when you put up the stop sign. The biddies will read it in the lifestyle section, and they'll say, Oh, she may be from New York, but she's not so bad. End of story. Think of it as publicity for your company."

"And you want me to do this?" she asked Charlie.

"I'll go with whatever you decide," he said. Clever. Charlie, good cop; Hilton, bad cop.

"I don't know," she said. "All right. But you be there with me," she said to both of them.

"One other thing," Hilton said. "We probably should stop by Oak Street and get you changed."

"What's wrong with this?" she flared. She was wearing a navy-blue sundress with a halter top and a very full skirt; it was modestly cut, but her shoulders were bare. "I was thinking Kim Novak in *Picnic*," she said, plaintively but playfully, taking the edge off.

"Think Auntie Em in *The Wizard of Oz*," Hilton said. "Where there's a women's page reporter, a photographer is likely to follow. Do you have like a plain blue suit?"

"You want me to dress like him?" She nodded at Charlie. "And won't Lois Lane notice that we stopped at Oak Street for me to change?"

"She may," Hilton said. "She may even note it in the story. But you don't want to be photographed sexy or fashion-forward. If you don't want to be a story in this campaign, we're gonna have to work at it."

On Wednesday morning, after reading the *Register-World*—where the story had appeared on the front page, before jumping, improbably, to the lifestyle section—Nell had absolutely nothing to say.

"You want to talk about it?" Charlie asked.

"No," she said. "Later."

"It's not so bad," Hilton said.

It was excruciating.

THE SENATOR'S ROYAL CRUSH
By Caroline Adams, *staff reporter*

Senator Charles C. Martin has a new camp follower.

The 51-year-old bachelor, who has "squired" some of the world's most glamorous women through the corridors of power, unveiled his latest conquest on the campaign trail this week: Arabella "Nell" Palmerston Belligio, a New York fashion designer—who is blond, 42 years old, a distant cousin of the British Royal Family and the divorced mother of two.

But the designer, a jet-setter who crafts expensive and revealing swimsuits, also seems to be specializing in a new line of cover-ups. When asked the nature of her relationship with the senator over coffee at Mae's Café in Port Sallesby, she said: "I don't like to talk about my private life."

Her private life has been quite public since she arrived in Des

Pointe last week, and took up residence in the senator's Oak Street home. She has been out on the campaign trail with Senator Martin each day, a very striking fixture in the Martin entourage. "It's been fun," she said. "But I have to be careful. The food at all these barbecues and pancake breakfasts and broasted chicken dinners is so good that I'll have to start dieting."

Local political pros questioned Senator Martin's decision to flaunt his very active social life during a difficult political campaign. "After what happened to him back in '92," said one distraught Democrat, "you've got to wonder if he has a death wish."

Martin was accused of fondling a campaign worker in the waning days of his failed presidential campaign that year, an accusation he denied at the time. In the past, the once-divorced politico has squired country music diva Natalie Dilley, flame-haired movie star Susan Whitworth and local photojournalist Anne Hellstrom, among others.

Senator Martin refused to discuss his relationship with Mrs. Belligio. "I think she's fabulous," he said. "I'd hope the public would be more interested in how I'm going to represent them than in who I'm dating. I've built a record of service. The people of this state know I work overtime for them."

But the senator's social life may well become an issue in the coming campaign against colorful, conservative muffler magnate Leland Butler. "It's arrogance on Martin's part," said a gleeful Republican. "He's been in office for so long, he thinks he can get away with anything—but the public is getting a little tired of his parade of tootsies. . . ."

Mrs. Belligio, a shy and dignified woman, is the daughter of Nigel Palmerston—of the famed, eccentric Darbyshire family—and Susannah Coxley of South Carolina, heiress to the Coxley Power fortune.

And on, and on, and on. A jet-setter who "crafts" swimsuits? A country music *diva*? Flame-haired? God. The interview at Mae's Café had gone well, she thought. The questions had been 97 percent pleasant. But none of the questions, or her answers, had made their way into the story, except the "I don't like to talk about my private life" line, and that awful business about the food.

She stewed all day, angry at herself—and at Charlie, and at Hilton, for pushing her into the interview. And at herself, again: it would have been quite a different story if she had agreed to marry him, which was obviously what he'd been expecting. Then it would be "Bachelor Senator to Settle Down." But she couldn't do that. Not yet. She was frightened, suddenly, by how little she knew about him, about his life. She knew Charlie had gotten around—she remembered seeing a picture of him with the actress, Susan Whitworth, in *Vogue* or *W* (his eyes, she'd thought, even then, were far more interesting than Whitworth's dress)—but she hadn't known that he was *famous* for getting around, and the notion that she'd be seen as just the latest installment in a long line of "tootsies" was way beyond unimaginable.

"*Why* didn't you help more?" she pleaded that night, back in his Oak Street bedroom, which was the Des Pointe version of a loft: a big room over the garage, separated from the rest of the house. It had campaign posters on the walls—for Kennedy, George McGovern, Jimmy Carter . . . and in an unobtrusive corner, a red and black "Charlie Martin for Congress," with a remarkable picture of him: long-haired in the seventies, smiling, sleeves rolled, shaking hands. "You're a politician," she said, trying to keep her eyes off the poster. "You must have seen it coming."

"Some things are unavoidable," he said, plopping down in his black leather reading chair, loosening his tie. His white shirt seemed excessively white. "You take the hit and move on. And I gotta tell you, this isn't so bad."

"It's awful," Nell said, thinking, he really doesn't understand.

"She tried to be nice," he said. "She called you 'shy and dignified.' "

"She got that wrong, too," Nell said. "I mean, what *right* does she have?— She doesn't know anything about me."

"Only the First Amendment," Charlie said, leaning back. "Look, here's how it works. She got those juicy blind quotes and had to go with them: the hot news in the story was the political gossip about me. That's what put it on the front page. The Republican shot was to be expected, but I'd love to know who the 'distraught Democrat' was. I've got it narrowed down to about three—I'll know next time I look them in the eye."

"I don't know," she said, standing over him. He seemed more interested in figuring out who the "distraught Democrat" was than in talking to her.

"It's newspaper stuff." He looked up at her, furrowed his brow. "It's bullshit. I know the folks out here. They like to know who I'm going out with. It's a vicarious kick. But they don't cast their votes on it. Muffler Boy doesn't understand the difference between curiosity and prudery. They're curious. They're not prudes. They voted for Stanton, and he was messing around while married."

"But you must have known this would happen," she said, exasperated. "Why didn't you tell me?"

"I thought," he started, "you—"

"I would marry you?" she said. "A campaign ploy to end the Charlie Martin Tootsie Show?"

"Nell, for chrissakes," he said, his eyes softening, saddening, looking up at her. "You know better than that." And then his eyes hardened. "Anyway, why the fuck won't you marry me? We both had to jump off a cliff to get here—"

"You make me do crazy things," she said, sitting on the edge of the bed. It was a guy's bed. It didn't have a headboard. "This was a bad move, Chas. Bad timing. Premature."

"No, it wasn't," he said. He sat beside her on the bed. He took her chin in his hand, kissed her gently. "It was time. Nell, you've gotta admit, we make a pretty okay team," he said softly.

"But not as candidate and candidatrix," she said, pulling away, standing up, clearing her head—the kiss had been spectacularly soft, not a *guy* kiss: it had been about essential things, not sex. How did he know to do that? Did it come from the same place as his politics? "I don't like this public stuff."

"What about the Future Farmers—"

"Oh, come on, Charlie: I'm not cut out for it," she said, hands on hips. "That should be painfully obvious by now. I'll embarrass you."

"Never. You may drive me nuts, but you'll never embarrass me," he said, folding his hands between his knees, stretching and thinking, Well, maybe. It would be too easy for people to read her lack of interest in politics as disdain for it.

"Charlie," she said slowly, tentatively, "is being a senator worth all this bother? I mean, what does it matter now anyway? What's at stake? I've been here a week, and I can't for the life of me figure out what this election is *about*. The farmers are so rich that half of them migrate to Florida for the winter. The air is clean, compared to New York. The topsoil may be eroding, but surely they can find someone else to deal with that. . . ."

"Look," he said, raising his voice, standing up, taking her by the arms. "Stop. This is what I do. I'm a United States senator. End of topic."

"Charlie," she said, with a wistful smile. "I love you, but the unexamined life is not worth living *with*."

"Whew," he said, dropping back down into the armchair. "You don't really think I haven't thought about . . . You wouldn't have come this far . . . and, by the way, I also do this because life won't always be so good for the folks and I don't trust a callow dilettante asshole jerk like Lee Butler to make the right decisions when things go bad."

"I came this far because the guy I knew back East knew *me*," she said sadly. She saw that she'd hurt him. "But you're a different guy out here— not completely, but sort of . . . What on earth am I trying to say? I don't even want to think about all those people who are going to be staring at me tomorrow, the way they did today. And I'm certainly not going to bring the kids into a situation like this—where their mother is a 'story.' Are they going to be 'stories,' too? No way. I'm out of here. . . ."

"No, you're not," he said, reaching out for her, but she pulled away. "You may think you are, but we're in this— You ever see the movie with Walter Brennan, took place in the Everglades, and at one point he says to—I don't even remember who the leading man was. But he says, 'You're stuck in Okefenokee for good, bub.' "

"Sorry, Charlie," she said, moving to the closet, fishing for her suitcase. "I'm out of here."

He followed her, took her by the waist, kissed the top of her shoulder and whispered, "No, you're not. Even if you do walk out that door, you'll be back. And if you don't come back, I'll go find you. I swear I will."

"Oh, Charlie. Honestly." She put down the suitcase, and turned to him. He was giving her the crinkly eye; she sighed. "Oh, for God's sake— say something, so I can dispute it. . . ." But he didn't say anything. He just looked at her—and she saw the same thing that Pat Dunn had seen: a once-in-a-lifetime look. "Oh, all right, I'll . . ."

He kissed her then, before she had a chance to decide whether to say "marry you" or "stay."

"What?" he asked. "You'll what?"

"Stay, for a while."

VIETNAM

———

1

———

I think our senator is in a state of shock," Nell had said, and Patrick Dunn had trouble imagining that: Charlie Martin shocked by love; shocked by anything.

Once, early in the 1980s, Dunn had traveled to Washington with then-congressman Martin. Their plane hit an air pocket—or, perhaps, something more drastic—and plummeted about ten thousand feet in a matter of seconds, the oxygen masks popping down, screams and groans and panicked glances from the passengers. It was as if the sky had simply vanished beneath them. The middle-aged man sitting across the aisle, a study in hawklike executive composure till then, lunged over and latched on to the congressman's arm. At which point, Charlie turned to Patrick Dunn—slowly, it seemed; in slow motion—and smiled slightly, his eyes dead calm.

Then, an upward whoosh—like a balsa wood glider caught by a breeze, only more extreme than that: you could feel the metal straining, creaking against the mortal pressure of gravity, a colossal exertion—until finally, blissfully, the plane was righted, and stable once more. The pilot apologized, said something about "a little" turbulence. The stewardesses replaced the oxygen masks. The passengers relocated their stomachs, laughing and chattering—a community, suddenly; the executive retrieved his vagrant hand, apologized and, shedding his attaché case, chatted about other near-misses and weird aeronautic occurrences; he'd been an air traffic controller at Tan Son Nhut during the war. In the end, everyone applauded as the pilot executed an utterly miraculous and perfectly routine three-point landing and then they tripped, light-footed and grateful, into the terminal.

From time to time, Pat or Charlie would laugh and reminisce about the close call. People still came up to Charlie and said, "Hey, Senator, I was on that plane with you, the one that almost crashed." But Pat never asked about the most memorable part of it—that smile. He assumed it was a warrior reflex; Charlie had been trained for such moments, trained not just to be calm but to welcome the challenge of adversity. Pat thought his protégé's nonchalance was reassuring, but also slightly terrifying: the absence of fear wasn't a terrific quality in a politician. The most success-ful practitioners, if not always the best, were born cautious. On the other hand, here was a guy who would never lose his head, who might have the courage to do something memorable with his career.

And then Charlie seemed to lose his head. And not just over Nell. The decision to run for president had been precipitous, and the failure of that campaign had initiated a very un-Martin-like period of uncertainty. Over time, Pat came to realize that Charlie's bout of severe turbulence was a far more purposeful phenomenon than standard postdefeat dis-combobulation. It was a measured reaction to a political environment that was being pulled in opposite directions, becoming more noxious and also more sterile as the century staggered home. Charlie was con-ducting an experiment in reckless calm: he wanted to see if public life could be made habitable.

*   *   *

As late as two weeks before the New Hampshire primary, the Martin presidential campaign had almost seemed hot. *The Boston Globe* said he was gaining momentum. The polls had him sneaking into double digits. There was a motorcade, including a bus full of reporters, some of whom were beginning to question the standard party pooh-bah wisdom about the senator's campaign: that Charlie was running for president an elec-tion cycle too soon.

But Governor Jack Stanton had snuffed the Martin moment and he'd done it in the most maddening fashion possible—unintentionally: the press evaporated when the tabloid stories hit. The Stanton scandals over-whelmed everything. The week before the primary, Pat Dunn and Char-lie's press secretary, Jim Drake, and the rest of the inner circle scuffled to come up with a creative way for their candidate to avoid the cruelest of political fates—irrelevance. They had to get him back in the news. The only way to do it, of course, was to trash Stanton. But Charlie wasn't buy-ing. Stanton had been arrested protesting the war twenty-five years ear-lier. He'd had an affair with his wife's hairdresser. These were not, to

Charlie's mind, mortal sins. "Am I supposed to pretend I'm shocked?" he asked. "Are you shocked, Dunnsie?"

Finally, after much prodding, the senator agreed to raise the "character" question in the final New Hampshire debate. He wasn't very good at it. "You've got to wonder, after all this," he'd said, halfheartedly, "if Jack Stanton is, um, damaged goods." He immediately felt foolish, smarmy; a cad—the sort of politician he sneered at when he saw them on television, the sort who rehearsed and market-tested and polled a phrase like "damaged goods" before he went public with it. Someone like Jack Stanton. "Don't you ever, *ever*," he said to Patsy afterward, quietly, "ask me to do something like that again."

He would go down proud. He would disappear in a drizzle of press releases about defense spending and farm subsidies. "You know, Dunnsie," he said on the road to Manchester near the end of the campaign, "the truth is"—he laughed, overcome by toxic giddiness—"the truth *is*, the guy who really got screwed by the Happy Hairdresser—was me."

And then, when New Hampshire was over, Charlie didn't know what to do next. He lacked the proper vocabulary for losing. In Vietnam, battles were rarely won or lost: you were ambushed, you called in air strikes, the enemy disappeared. But air strikes were not an option after New Hampshire. He didn't have the money or the desire to pummel his opponents. He stood at arm's length from the defeat, whimsically disoriented—still that calm smile, after the plane scare—unable to clear the battlefield.

At first, he tried to organize—to lead—his way past the humiliation (that was what he'd done in Vietnam, too). But there wasn't much to organize: no resupply, no fresh troops; most of his volunteers—the press had said they were the best-*looking* college students assembled by any candidate—went home after New Hampshire. Ten days passed. He lost more primaries. He did so with charm and grace; he refused to mope. Not even his closest friends could penetrate his reinforced bunker of good cheer.

And then, on the Monday before the Colorado, Maryland and Georgia elections, Pat Dunn advised him—by phone, and for the third time—to throw in the towel. "Before you say no," Patsy said, "you want to know the damages?"

"Okay . . . no." Then, initiating diversionary action—because he really didn't want to hear the unbelievably depressing number that Pat was about to unload on him—Charlie said, "Look, Dunnsie, I know I've been wearing this one out, but if I can get Stanton one-on-one somewhere, I'll nail him—I'm sure of it."

"Charlie." Patrick Dunn knew two things: Charlie was right, and Charlie was wrong. They might well beat Stanton one-on-one, if they ever got the chance. But the campaign was too broke and battered to ever get the chance. Charlie's complaint was a cliché: the death rattle of the mortally wounded candidate. Pat guessed Charlie knew that, too.

"Hey, I've finished ahead of each of these guys *somewhere*," Charlie said now, with a laugh, trying to charm him. "If I can beat them all in the same place at the same time, I'm back in it."

"Name that state." Dunn sighed into his telephone, a message sigh.

"The one I'm driving through right now—Colorado."

Indeed, at that very moment Senator Martin was entering Colorado Springs in not exactly triumphant fashion, in a sky-blue Dodge Aries— the sort of car that county governments purchase for use by building inspectors and tax assessors. He was being chauffeured by a chunky blond college student named Martha Something-or-other, who had been thoughtfully provided by the local Democratic party organization and who represented the sum total of Charlie's campaign entourage as they chugged into a Colorado Springs dulled by massive but unthreatening prairie-putty clouds.

The traveling staff had been laid off after South Dakota. The last to go was Jim Drake, the press secretary, hired away by the House majority leader, William Larkin. Drake announced his departure as he and Charlie were landing in extremely modest commercial fashion—a United commuter flight, the money for chartered planes long gone—at Stapleton Airport in Denver four days earlier. "C'mon, Ducky," Charlie said, "you're backsliding. No one goes from the Senate to the House."

"Larkin's leadership," Drake replied as the small plane landed and began to taxi toward the terminal. "And he's got this weird reputation: he'll actually talk things over with staff before he opens his mouth."

"Will he let you have a ponytail?"

"I'm cutting it off," he said. "Look, Senator. There comes a time . . ." He shook his head, unbuckled his seat belt. "I'll give you two weeks' notice, if you want, but the campaign doesn't have the money to pay me— and I'd like to take a few days off before starting the rest of my life, and anyway, there's a Continental to Dulles in forty-five minutes."

"Aw, c'mon, Ducky—"

"Larkin probably won't be calling me 'Ducky,' either," he said. "I'm *really* going to miss that."

Drake had carefully avoided looking his boss in the eye throughout the conversation, but he knew the deal wouldn't be closed—the senator wouldn't believe him—until he cleared that hurdle. "I'm going to miss you, Senator," he said, as evenly as he could, turning to Martin. "You can call on me anytime, but—"

"But you think I'm history," Charlie said, probing.

"Shit," Drake said. "I don't know *what* you are—except a . . ."

". . . A?" the senator said, playfully. ". . . Eh?"

"A really great boss. Would you please stop making this hard on me?"

And now Charlie was drifting through the usual triple-canopy tangle of golden arches, flying tires, Chevrons, color tiles and carpet stores: the Great American Anywhere. Colorado wasn't a different state. It was the same old state. It had the same old Americans—the people who were *his* people back home, but strangers here. They didn't know diddly about him, and weren't motivated to learn. He would lunch with the Lions in Colorado Springs. If he was lucky, there might be a reporter from the local paper—maybe a camera crew from the local TV.

"Charlie?" Pat Dunn knew his candidate had drifted.

"Yeah?" the senator replied. "Guess I just got caught up in all the excitement I'm generating out here in Colorado."

Dunn snorted. "You seen the polling? You *owe* points. How are the crowds?"

"Encouraging," he said, using an official voice.

Pat laughed. This was progress; the senator was acknowledging the futility, maneuvering himself toward splashdown. "Look, kid, here's what we've done. We shut down the Washington and Des Pointe campaign offices. Donna's quietly doing what needs to be done—scheduling and so forth—out of your Senate office. Won't be much. Oskar's prepared to run a similar skeleton operation for you in Florida, if you make it past tomorrow, which, I might add, every last one of your friends—the people who know and love you best in the world—hope you won't."

"Where did you get the polling from?" Charlie asked. Dunn realized he'd been foolish to bring it up. "We're not paying for it anymore, are we?"

"Rathburn got it from Mike Coleman. You know where Mike gets it."

"Yeah, they're all lining up with Stanton now, aren't they?" Charlie said, wistfully. "All my pals, except Linc—and he'd go, too, if they asked. Well, maybe not. . . . How come Linc didn't call me himself? He never hesitates to reach out and touch someone when the news is grim."

"He said you would probably be in your bullshit, macho, snake-eating mode," Pat said. "He said he didn't have the stomach to watch you mangle yourself again. . . . He said you could call him if you were ready to think about getting sane."

"'Mangle' myself? He said that?" Charlie glanced over at Martha, who was pretending not to be listening, but she shot a quick look at his hand—which had most of a thumb and a delicate, perfectly formed index finger, but not much else: shiny smooth roseate scar tissue stretched tight over uneven stumps of knuckles.

"Yeah, he did," Pat said. This was, he realized, the first time in twenty years of friendship that Charlie's injury had ever come up—directly—in conversation. The senator never talked about it. That Linc would even mention it was drastic, that Dunn would repeat what Linc had said was truly unprecedented—a form of shock therapy Pat immediately regretted. "I liked the 'snake-eating' part," he said, trying to move to safer turf. "We had snails in my war, not snakes. The only snake we had was Hitler."

"It's gruntspeak for special forces," Charlie explained. "Linc thinks it makes him authentic."

"Charlie," Pat tried, "one thing you Vietnam guys should've learned over there is when to bail."

"I'm bailing from this phone call right now, partner," the senator said. "Roger and out. . . . No, Patsy, wait a minute."

Martha had pulled into a Ramada: dull redbrick, white plantation house columns—a ridiculous riff on Tara, a strange and ancient marketing conceit. More of the Great American Anywhere. The prospect of another sad motel room drenched in sticky-sweet disinfectant had, he realized, produced an insight of stunning clarity: it was over. His race was run. And thank God: Having it over would be good. There were things to do.

"Charlie?" Dunn had sensed the change in tone.

"Dunnsie, even if I won tomorrow—"

"Yes?"

"I'm—" The senator looked over at his driver. He didn't want to announce the end of his presidential campaign in front of a stranger. "Pat, let me call you back in a few minutes."

His mind was suddenly filled with tasks: he would have to get the Senate Caucus Room for an official resignation fandango on Wednesday morning. He would call Don O'Brien, the majority leader, and let him know the party was over. He'd catch up on his committee stuff—maybe he'd go straight off to Russia, check out the missile reduction program that he'd proposed and then dragged through a recalcitrant Congress (a historic diplomatic triumph that apparently meant nothing, not a thing, to residents of the Great American Anywhere). He needed to get inside, get to a private phone, end his campaign, start the rest of his life.

"Do we have a room here?" he asked Martha, who seemed startled by the sudden burst of energy.

"What do you *mean?*" She looked at him, terrified.

"Excuse me?"

She was staring at his hand. What on earth . . . ?

"Marsha," Charlie said, "you didn't actually think I was asking if you wanted to *do* anything—"

"Martha!" she said, embarrassed—or angry, or something. He remained clueless, slightly irritated, not quite there (indeed, still mostly preoccupied by the exhilaration of his decision). He wondered: was this misunderstanding, or whatever it was, somehow his fault? Had he been flirty? In all the flesh-pressing and simulated hail-fellow horse flop of the campaign, he'd begun to worry that he was losing track of the basic grammar of human interaction. He'd been performing so relentlessly for so many months, he couldn't always remember what his face was doing.

And now her eyes were filling with tears. He figured he should try to comfort her, get her to calm down, stop this nonsense.

He made a mistake then, reaching over with his good right arm—he didn't want to frighten her with his left hand—to touch her shoulder. But she was turning toward him, and his hand brushed her breast—he pulled it back lightning fast, but not nearly fast enough. *"Get your hands off me!"* she screamed, and he reflexively leaped from the car, and she, remarkably, drove off with his cell phone and luggage and the assorted detritus of what official Washington had once thought was a "promising" campaign for the presidency of the United States.

Standing in front of the Ramada several hours later, having almost allowed himself to be "encouraged" by the smatterings of appreciation that his standard stump speech had elicited from the Lions, having shaken—

but not stirred—every available hand, Charlie Martin found himself dragooned into a moment with the inevitable Flip Hunstiger of KGAA, or some such station, and his hulking hippie cameraman, Lars, and thinking—thinking hard—about how he was going to get himself to Denver without a driver, while Flip tried to position him for the shot: "Okay, Senator, now, d'ya mind standing over by the Ramada sign welcoming you . . . ?"

"Now, there's a brilliant idea," Lars scoffed. He had long, greasy blondish hair and was wearing a Hawaiian shirt and one of those khaki, multipocketed combat photographer's vests.

A completely ridiculous situation, Charlie thought. He had made all the necessary phone calls and arrangements ending this phase of his life—except for the most immediate arrangement. He had called Dunnsie and told him about his decision to quit. He'd also told him about the Martha incident. In retrospect, Pat would kick himself for not focusing more on the latter—but he couldn't imagine Charlie ever finding himself in a seriously awkward situation with a woman. Far more important, he was thrilled that his candidate had finally agreed to stop the bleeding.

"Dunnsie," Charlie said, laughing. "It's a lovely irony: My campaign is over, but I don't know how to get out of town."

"You'll announce it when?"

"Wednesday, Senate Caucus Room."

"Okay, we'll want to start planning the press part, especially with Drake gone," Dunn said. "Hamblin's gonna want an exclusive."

Bob Hamblin of the *Register-World* had been the world's greatest Charlie Martin expert for the past few months—an occasional guest on *MacNeil/Lehrer* and *Nightline*—and he'd be bitter now, forced to fade into sullen localness. There were so many details to work out. Pat assumed Charlie would arrange the Colorado Springs exit strategy with Donna Mendoza, his Washington chief of staff. And Charlie did call Donna, telling her he was getting out of the race, setting up the arrangements for a farewell press conference. He called Don O'Brien, the Senate majority leader—but Don wasn't in. He called his friend and campaign finance chairman, Oskar Millar, in Florida; he tried to reach Lincoln Rathburn. . . .

But he hadn't remembered to arrange a ride out of town. It was, Charlie realized belatedly, yet another way running for president had caused him to lose touch with reality. In a campaign, *staff* has responsibility for moving the candidate around. He hadn't had to think about travel arrangements for more than six months. Once this silly local TV interview was over—his last as a presidential candidate—he'd find a phone, call Washington, have them advance him a rent-a-car or something. Actually, he was exhilarated by the novelty of a drive, alone, to Denver, with the radio turned as loud as he could bear it—if he could ever liberate himself from Hunstiger and the Fellini of the Foothills, who was now down on his knees, practicing his shot, shooting from below.

"Hey, guys?" Charlie asked, allowing a slight edge into his voice. "You think we could do this?"

"Okay, okay . . . Senator, you ready?" Flip asked.

At which point, a sky-blue Dodge Aries pulled up—and for just the slightest hint of an instant, Charlie Martin was hopeful: Martha had gotten herself together and was back, ready to take him on to Denver—except that it wasn't Martha getting out of the car, but a tall, solidly built man, with a craggy western look including longish, neatly trimmed sideburns turning gray. He was wearing a white pharmacist's jacket ("Pharm-Land" was embroidered on the pocket) and a string tie and snakeskin boots, and he was saying—almost rhythmically, as he was striding, "How *dare* you? Who do you think you *are*? What gives you the *right*?"

He stopped directly in front of Charlie, about six inches too close for comfort, ruining the composition of Lars's shot, among other things. "You Washington guys think you can get away with any darn thing," he elaborated, with a country music catch in his voice, as Lars scurried to get a better angle.

Charlie Martin softened his eyes reflexively, tried to go political, turn on the charm. "You must be Martha's—"

"Father," he said.

"Hey, look, I don't know what she said, but—"

Stars. No, not stars. An illumination round; searing white phosphorus fireworks. Charlie didn't even feel the man's fist, except for the metal of his cheesy pharmacology school class ring, and his face didn't hurt nearly so bad as the back of his head, which cracked against the doorstep, or the curb, or something. . . .

He tried to regroup, but lost track of time and place. He drifted back to the last time he'd been hurt badly. He had been knocked flat that time, too; but not quite flat on the ground—knocked more precariously, on a sharp incline, the side of a paddy dike. He remembered staring into the sun, squinting, sweat and mud and maybe blood in his eyes, with his feet higher than his head somehow, his head down in the squish at the base of the dike—with an enormous weight on him. The weight turned out to be Richie Radio, who had been blown back on top of him, the field radio smashing into Charlie Martin's nose, his face; and there were other problems, too. But those had only been physical problems and Charlie hadn't realized their severity, at least not immediately (the things that hurt most—his face, for example—had been hurt the least). No real pain at all, in fact, right then. The pain and constant, almost hilariously incandescent, discomfort came later. No, in those first moments, Charlie had studied his situation with an odd, detached curiosity: he had just experienced something amazing. He had been blown back—how far? Five, ten yards, maybe? Wow. He could barely focus on the most obvious things, like Richie Radio, who had shielded him—well, most of him, except for a few extremities, particularly his left hand—and who had caught most of the toe-popper in his groin and gut, and was now worse than dead: dead and on top of Charlie, twitching uncontrollably, as if his ganglia had short-circuited; he felt Richie fibrillating from a distance, at the edge of his awareness. Charlie didn't know how many others had been blown up. He wanted to talk about it, though. He wanted to compare notes with the guys. He was thrilled when Spazio—Spaz, the Spazmaster—leaned in over him: the Spaz always had a lateral take on everything, always saw Vietnam as stone strange as it was. But he was looking at Charlie now, terrified. "Sir," he said, "I found the, uh—your, uh—the finger with, uh, the wedding ring. . . ."

"Spaz," said Corporal Solomon Purifory, a majestic African-American farmer from the Virginia mountains. "Spaz, put a fucking lid on it."

"Right. Sorry, sir," he said to Charlie. And he began to cry. And Charlie loved him, and he loved Purifory, and Richie—who had been rolled off him, now—and the others. They were brothers. They were with him. There was a medic. There was morphine.

And now, through the haze, he could hear Flip Hunstiger saying in his best professional voice, "Senator, can you tell me what happened?"

"Flip, you're interviewing me?" he said, working to sit up. "You've got to be kidding."

"Senator, what impact will this incident have on your campaign?"

2

———

Oskar Millar heard about Charlie Martin's disaster during batting practice. He was sitting in his front-row box at Clearwater, having just been wheeled in from the parking lot—through the outfield, along the warning track—by his usual ballpark chauffeur, an ancient redneck groundskeeper named Lowell, who insisted on the honor even though Millar was always accompanied by his private security detail. Oskar loved and dreaded this daily processional, which took place during the month each spring that his beloved Phillies camped near his Dunedin home: it put him in close proximity to the ballplayers, who saluted him with hats and bats (and inevitably asked for stock tips), but the welcome came at the price of being something of a public curiosity—although the ballpark was fairly empty when he arrived each day, the satisfying crack and thwapp of balls hit and caught echoing through the vacant stands.

The phone call from Pat Dunn came just as Oskar was settling into his box at dusk—a favorite time of day, after the American markets had closed and before the Asian markets opened. He switched on the multi-screened television and computer console the Phillies had allowed him to install so he could keep up with the latest financial news.

"You watching CNN?" Dunn asked.

"What? Trouble?"

"Our boy. A doozy this time. . . ."

Oskar Millar had met and befriended Charlie Martin in 1967, on the amputee ward at the Philadelphia Naval Hospital—a friendship considered something of a miracle by the staff. Oskar was the hardest of hard cases, spectacularly truncated just below the waist and flagrantly antisocial. He sat, staring out the window in the dayroom, fending off all comers with his titanic scowl and an occasional, iambic "GET . . . the FUCK . . . a-WAY!"

And yet, Charlie blithely slipped the forbidding ramparts, as if he hadn't noticed the glower. He simply walked over one day, just after he'd arrived and scoped out the ward, and invited Oskar to play a game of APBA baseball, the most complicated and statistically authentic board game of the precomputer age. Oskar was stunned by the direct approach, especially from someone as confident and self-possessed as this newcomer seemed to be, someone who had no earthly reason to seek out the aggravation of an Oskar Millar outburst. He found himself agreeing to a game—reflexively, before he knew what he was doing—and soon was lost in the contest. He had always loved baseball: the infinite measurability of it. For an hour, he forgot everything, where he was and why, and how his mother had fled at the sight of him and not yet come back, and how the amp ward smelled, the screams and groans. The next day, he wheeled himself over to Charlie and said, "Hey, you want to—?"

"Absolutely," Charlie said.

As the weeks passed, Oskar transformed their daily game into an ever more elaborate ritual, creating teams, a league, a schedule. He kept statistics, not just on the basics like batting averages, but also some really arcane stuff, statistics he invented. Soon he and Charlie began to develop other games. Everything became a contest, some of them quite ridiculous—guessing the proportion of carrots to peas on their dinner trays, the proportion of cars to trucks on South Market Street. Inevitably, this led them to the stock market. They gave themselves an imaginary thousand dollars each, and bought portfolios.

Years later, when Oskar Millar's success in the market had become legendary, there was speculation that he had found a mystery formula, or that he had cheated somehow. The Securities and Exchange Commission, the FBI and the Internal Revenue Service, among others, investigated him and found nothing untoward. But Charlie Martin could have told them that (and he did, when visited, occasionally, by agents of the various agencies). There was no magic to it—only information, market analyses, annual reports, which Oskar began to accumulate, and memorize, and categorize in great gobs while they were still on the amp ward in Philly. Information, obsession . . . and fury: Oskar lived to prove the rest of the world foolish. He disdained the wisdom of the moment, bet the tortoise and prospered—slowly at first, then torrentially.

In the beginning, Charlie persuaded the orderlies to requisition a small bookcase and a desk for his new friend. These were placed in the corner of the dayroom, which became Oskar's office. He was there before dawn most mornings, clicking a number-two pencil between his stubby teeth, chasing theories down narrow statistical corridors, sharpening pencils—he had a bundle of them—and writing, in a tiny, precise accountant's hand, filling a shelf of loose-leaf binders he stored in his bookcase. He was there most evenings, when the rest of the ward—including Charlie—depressed itself by watching Mary Tyler Moore in pedal pushers on reruns of *The Dick Van Dyke Show*. His first major killing was in gold, which he bought at thirty-five dollars an ounce and sold at $350 just after he was released from the hospital.

"How did you know it was going to be deregulated?" Charlie asked him.

"The stupid fucking war," Oskar scoffed, taking no pleasure in his triumph. "Lyndon inflated the shit out of the currency."

Oskar was flattered by the lavish quality of Charlie Martin's attentions, so casually bestowed. Charlie's eyes never drifted south, the way everyone else's did—even the orderlies and the other amps were shocked by the severity of Oskar's situation. Martin not only refused to acknowledge the deficits, he focused immediately upon the considerable assets that remained. Eventually, it occurred to Oskar that this might be a marketable skill—a singular talent that Charlie Martin had, a singular talent significantly underutilized. "Charlie," he finally said one day as they packed away the APBA equipment. "I am sick of being surrounded by life's losers. It's time you taught these guys how to win something."

"Me, huh? Right."

Oskar, dark eyes under dark bushy eyebrows, tried to stare at Charlie Martin with the same casual intensity that Charlie routinely focused on him. But he was too self-conscious about it. He thought about the sight of himself staring—with his square head and square body, a cube atop a box; the loss of his legs had made him more symmetrical and apelike, his arms hung longer than his legs. He relinquished the stare, glanced down—encouraging Charlie to look where his legs had been. "You saved my life," he said. "You can save theirs."

"Get lost," Charlie replied, embarrassed, refusing to look. "I didn't do anything. I hounded you into playing a board game."

"Why me?"

"You looked smart. I envied your anger. I was bored."

"And now I'm bored," Oskar confessed. "You're making me feel guilty about playing the damn game. I'm sick of living with all these self-pitying slugs. So here's the deal: organize them. If those fuck-brained college kids can march in the streets and get what they want, think of the leverage we'd have. A bunch of hero gimps protesting? The local news might be interested in that. You could get whatever you want."

"Except the things we really want," Charlie said.

"Stow that shit." Oskar was surprised by the breach of etiquette. "I thought this was a No Mope zone."

"That's only because pain is relative," Charlie cracked back, quickly retreating from the moment of self-pity. "No way to quantify it. Just think, Oz—if we could've figured a way to quantify pain . . ."

"The most convincing whiner would've won," Oskar said. "It would have been counterproductive. We would have been like the rest of them."

"Yo, Oz," Charlie said. "We are like the rest of them. We're just better at self-delusion." (In fact, Oskar and Charlie had competed in the one injury-related area they could quantify: medication—they'd raced to see who could go cold turkey first; Charlie had won, painfully.)

"Charlie," Oskar said. "You're underemployed. You need vocational therapy. You need to organize these gimps. Protest something. Pick some idiot cause. Organize them. Let the blown-up fuckers win something for a change."

Hence, ICED. Ice Cream Every Day. Instead of ice cream once a week, on Sunday. Instead of Jell-O, or pudding, or the yellow cake that tasted like wax paper. Ice cream every day. Charlie drew up the petition. They all signed it; given the circumstances, some of the signatures were rudimentary. It was a ridiculous protest and, obviously, it had very little to do with ice cream. It had to do with getting ripped apart, and coming together again: the amp ward's manifest, and grotesque incompleteness, gave it power over the witlessly complete and unsuffering authorities.

The Navy acted like the Navy, and ignored the petition. So Charlie called Tom Snyder—who later went on to quirky notoriety as a network talk show host, but was then a young anchor at KYW—and he snuck onto the ward with a hidden camera in a satchel; the real dramatic cases, the triple amps, the faceless, were tricked out with protest signs. Oskar had an "ICED would be Nice" sign on his wheelchair. It made for very dramatic television. The brass tried to come down on Martin; they mentioned court-martial. They sent a Marine colonel to work him over.

"You're threatening unit cohesion," the colonel said. "You're trivializing the military. How do you think it sounds to civilians, Ice Cream Every Day?"

"Sir," Charlie replied, "with respect, I don't give a flying fuck. And this unit is about as cohesive as it can get."

Oskar was right. They did have a lot of leverage. A local ice cream company stationed a pushcart on the ward, and started a job-training program for military gimps. And Oskar had been right about Charlie, too: he was good at making trouble. So, back in Philadelphia, they'd given each other a life. Charlie gave Oskar the stock market; Oskar restored Charlie's natural tendency to lead—and he also gave his friend financial security.

When he left the hospital, Oskar staked Charlie to a real ten-thousand-dollar investment, which proceeded to grow by an average of 23 percent annually over twenty-five years, a portfolio that Millar continued to manage as a "blind trust" when Charlie entered politics, and had a real salary and money to invest for the first time. Oskar also served de facto as the finance chair of the various Charlie Martin campaigns—de facto because Oskar rarely did anything directly, and never did anything publicly. His company was named Fairmont Equities, for no apparent reason except its surpassing blandness; he accepted investments only from combat veterans, friends of friends who had served in Vietnam. He never gave speeches or granted interviews. Indeed, he seemed to grow more reclusive as the Millar empire entered a period of exponential growth in the late 1970s, while the rest of the world was stagnating. Suddenly, everyone—the press, the money managers, the politicians—wanted to get close, know more. Oskar would have none of it. He wasn't neurotic about his solitude; he just wasn't very interested in other people, at least not the nonfiduciary aspects of their lives. He had only been photographed a few times, from a distance. When he did go out into the world, he was accompanied by a significant but unobtrusive security detail: stray fans seeking autographs or stock tips at the Phillies games in Clearwater would find themselves politely but firmly rebuffed by a pair of middle-aged former Marines quietly sitting in the box behind Millar's. (Oskar only employed disabled combat veterans: his lawyers, doctors, stock analysts, household staff—every one of them had received a purple heart.)

He and Charlie didn't see each other often. They communicated by phone, and only when there was something to say; Oskar didn't chat. But he made sure to call the night of the Colorado Springs incident.

"So, you okay?" he growled, when he reached Charlie in Washington just past midnight.

"Awesome."

"What are you going to do now?"

"Dunno."

"I were you, I'd have the hick arrested for assault and battery, get myself a neck brace and sue his ass," Oskar said.

"Real men don't sue," Charlie said. He sounded distant and empty—but reflexively cheerful, depressingly so, like a talented telephone sales solicitor.

"Oh, that's right. I forgot," Oskar replied. "Real men seduce Neanderthal campaign pastries."

"Fuck you, Oz," he insisted. "She went dinky-dau on me. I don't know what happened."

"You don't know what happened? That makes you unique in America."

After Oskar had received the phone call from Pat Dunn, he'd watched the cataclysm unfold on the minitelevisions in his Clearwater box. The Martin story led the evening news on all the networks. The Colorado Springs videotape was broadcast over and over, often in slow motion. The girl's name was Martha Schollwengen; her father was a honcho with the Colorado Springs Democratic party. Later, heading back to Dunedin, Oskar listened with disgust to several professional Vietnam vets yammering on talk radio: Charlie Martin probably was suffering from posttraumatic stress disorder. Oskar was incensed. There was a whole world of opinions out there, all of them dumb. Back home, more opinions: he watched a panel discussing "campaign date rape" on *Nightline*. And there were the late-night network comedy shows. David Letterman gave the top ten reasons why Democrats like Charlie Martin and Jack Stanton were so horny. (Number 8: they really like to press the flesh.) On *The Tonight Show,* Jay Leno rubbed his hands together and said, "Either of these guys is elected and gets his finger on the button—you gotta be thinking: which button?"

"You catch the stuff on the tube?" Oskar asked Charlie.

"No." Charlie didn't want to see or hear any of it. The enormity of the embarrassment was incomprehensible, paralytic.

"It sucks," Oskar said.

"I'm sure," Charlie replied. "Oz . . ."

And Oskar, sensing the reason for the hesitation, did an unprecedented thing: he encouraged Charlie to let it out. "Go ahead," he said, for perhaps the first time in his life.

"Oz, this is worse than Philly, worse than the boonies," Charlie said. "I did it to myself."

"You said nothing happened."

"I put myself in that position. I should have deep-sixed the campaign two weeks ago," Charlie said. "And now, I'm tabloid dog meat—I'm a fucking scandal. Me and Stanton and all the fucked-up movie stars and serial killers. We're all the same. Fodder. Interchangeable. I'm better known for *this* than for getting the Russkies to disarm. I mean, Oz, how do you show your face?"

"Dunno," Millar said, stumped. The situation was well beyond foreign to him. "You alone there?"

"Totally," Charlie said. He had bunkered down in his D.C. flat, which was something of a first: the place had always been an afterthought, a weeknight billet (weekends were usually spent back home, being a politician). It was large and glass and horizontal, on the sixth floor of an undistinguished horizontal glass building on New Mexico Avenue. It was, in fact, yet another motel room, although it did have a few amenities. He could ride his stationary bike, listen to CDs.

"So?" Oskar asked.

"So?"

"So what are you fucking doing?"

"I'm on my bike, listening to James Brown," Charlie said.

"And what are you going to do?" Oskar asked again.

"Hey!" Charlie tried. "I'm gonna have a funky good time. . . ."

"Seriously."

"Seriously seriously?" Charlie said. "Every talking head—every last nimrod inhabitant of Mediapolis—assumes I actually felt up that girl. I mean, did you hear one of them say, 'Why would he do a thing like that? Maybe he didn't do it. Maybe she's a dipstick'? Of course not. And you want me to be serious? Fuck that, man. Fuck them all. I'm gonna maintain radio silence. I say anything, I just feed the beast."

"Not good," Oskar said. "Not you. Think some more. Smile. Reload."

"Ozwaldo, I'm going to sleep," Charlie said, refusing to play. "Or try to. Or something. See ya."

Oskar figured the thing to do now—first thing in the morning—would be to organize a rescue party, a small core of on-site advisers who could help Charlie through the next few days. This would have to be done subtly, and it would not be pleasant duty. He knew he would have to deal with the Lords of the Delta—the small circle of noncombatant striped-pants pinwheels Charlie had met in the Saigon Embassy during his years as a military attaché, before he airmailed himself into the boonies. To Oskar's dismay, they had all remained friends, more or less, ever since. And the very first call would have to be to Lincoln Rathburn, who was Charlie's closest friend in that group: Linc was a Hoosier who aspired to aristocracy, perfect-looking, too blond to be real (even in late middle age), and perfectly educated—as all the Lords had been, exemplary young men with brilliant futures in government. After Saigon, they'd spent the next thirty years trying to recover from the damage the war had caused their glide paths. Now each new presidential election brought the hope, for Lincoln Rathburn and the others, that they would finally be elevated by a new administration to their rightful places at the center of foreign policy decision-making.

Rathburn, who lived in New York but was always somewhere else, was in London that day, doing—well, it was never easy for Oskar to understand what Linc was doing: he was a lawyer-diplomat, with the emphasis on the latter. He had clients, but they tended to be countries or companies; he never actually handled cases. He was, Oskar figured, the white shoe lawyer equivalent of Joe Louis in his later years, when the champ had been employed as a "greeter" in a Las Vegas casino. His handshake alone was assumed to produce profits.

"Have you talked to him?" Linc asked. "How is he?"

"You haven't? How the fuck do you think he is?"

"I can't call him now," Linc explained. "It would seem like piling on."

"Yeah?"

"He knows I thought running for president was wrong."

"So when do you think you'll resume the friendship?" Oskar asked.

"Oskar, you—" Linc considered tactical anger, then decided that, given Millar's emotional bluntness, it was better not to even try. "Charlie has the greatest talent for leadership of anyone I've ever known."

That was one of the things Oskar couldn't stand about Rathburn: the overripe Olympian pronouncements of the obvious. "I guess the question is," Linc now mused, "how completely do leadership ability and political talent intersect? I mean, are they the same thing? An interesting question, don't you think?"

"For a symposium," Oskar said. "Right now, I have a different question: what can we do for him without hurting his pride too much?"

"Send in Sherpas," Rathburn said, getting down to it—and Oskar had to admit the son of a bitch was right. "If you and I or Pat Dunn showed up on his doorstep tonight, he'd have to put on his happy face. He'd get stubborn; he'd find ways not to listen to us. But somebody had better help him work through the next few days. What's the girl's next move?"

"Dunno," Oskar said. "But I'll see if I can handle that end."

"He had to be crazy."

"Linc, you actually believe he mashed her?" Oskar snorted. "When was the last time Charlie Martin had to force himself on a woman? More like vice versa."

"Mike Coleman should go over there," Linc said, picking the best organized and least ego-afflicted of the Lords.

"All right," Oskar conceded. "Anyone else?"

"I have a better question," Linc said. "What's the agenda?"

"Stop the bleeding," Oskar said. But Rathburn, the asshole, had hit the nail once more.

*   *   *

"You know what this reminds me of . . . and boy, do you look like shit," Mike Coleman said when he showed up at Charlie Martin's apartment at dusk the next day. Mike was a detail man, a genius staff guy; a corporate lawyer now. He had always been small, gruff, unprepossessing, notable mostly for the most severe flattop in Saigon outside of the military: a haircut lovingly maintained, the front row waxed upright like a picket fence across his forehead. He had surrendered the 'do reluctantly; thirty years later, it was still a crew cut, but the front and sidewalls were no longer so flashy, and the hair was now a black-gray tweed. He handed Charlie his overcoat.

"Thanks a lot. . . . And okay, I'll bite: what does 'this' remind you of?"

"The last time you got yourself all fucked-up, back in Vietnam."

"Great to see you, too, Mike."

"No, think about it," Coleman said. "Careless gallantry. Unnecessary risk. . . . Is there anything you can do about that eye?"

"There wasn't much to do with gallantry in Colorado Springs," Charlie said. "Carelessness, I'll concede."

But Mike was right. Charlie's decision to patrol with Bravo Company—filling in for Lieutenant Sam Frost, walking the paddy dike behind Richie Radio—had been the combat equivalent of traveling alone with Martha Schollwengen: an idiot risk, not his job, something a captain left to subordinates, but a risk Charlie took because—because he always assumed he'd be able to handle any eventuality, because the grunts would be

happy to see him out there: being out with his men was what a real soldier did.

"You want something to drink?" Charlie asked.

"Water," Coleman said. "Straight up."

Charlie retrieved a tall, clear glass of water from the kitchen. He admired the perfect austerity of it.

"So, Charles, what now?" Mike asked, having arranged himself on the
couch, a yellow legal pad and pen at the ready on the coffee table. Charlie took this as a rhetorical question and chose not to answer. "You want
to sit down or something?" Charlie was standing helplessly in the middle
of the room, unsure of where to plant himself—a pathetic state of affairs
in his own apartment. "You're making me nervous."

Charlie slumped down on the floor, his back against the console television, and reconnoitered Mike, who was settling into a chunky, jowly
and rather distinguished middle age. His utter sanity, the steadiness of
his gaze, was his most appealing physical characteristic. At the same time,
Mike's job hadn't changed at all: he was still Gideon Reese's assistant, just
as he'd been in the political section of the Saigon embassy. Only now
they were running Jack Stanton's foreign policy. Mike had made it clear
from the start, in his absolutely no-bullshit way, that he thought Charlie's
presidential run was premature, and he would not support it, but that he
would remain a friend and he would be there to help—as a conduit to
Stanton, at the very least. "So, Miguel," he asked, genuinely interested,
"what would you do?"

"Get back on the horse," Mike replied. "Go back to work."

"Work?" Charlie said. "It's an election year. Nothing's happening. I can
go back, walk through appropriations and stuff, but nobody's going to be
up for any fun battles this year—what do I do with the rest of my mind?"

"You could cool it," Mike said. "Take a break."

"A vacation? Sheesh."

"How about a committee junket—some Armed Services boondoggle?"
Mike said. "It's your specialty, right? You could go make sure the Russkies
are actually destroying the warheads. Or you could go to someplace
really inconvenient, someplace painful and worthy—Chechnya, maybe.
Make yourself useful. Come back and brief Stanton on it."

"Stanton?" Actually, a real vacation suddenly sounded not so bad, a lot
better than a junket: Charlie wondered, idly, why he never took them.
His recreation was always hinged on a speech, a meeting, a fact-finding
thing—the appearance of business in a leisure setting.

"We can think that out later," Mike said. "First, let's deal with the tough part."

"The tough part?" Charlie snorted. "You'd better brief me on precisely which part that is."

"The next few days," Mike said evenly. "Figure out what advice you'll be least unlikely to follow, and save your ass."

The doorbell. "Who's that?" Mike asked, rolling his eyes. Charlie shrugged, and went to the door. A large slab of a human back in a scruffy, wrinkled tan London Fog raincoat darkened the doorway: Sylvester Parkinson, Chairman of the House Armed Services Committee, shouting into his cell phone. "It's important, goddammit!" Parkinson screamed. "Bruce, he's major. He's huge. If he's asking for another look at it, you make sure he gets it—oh, hi, Chuck, excuse me—Bruce, you ask the Air Force to give it a review. All right? Do it. Bye."

"Sly, what the—?"

"Char-lie!" he said, spreading his arms wide, enveloping the senator in a bearhug. This was truly weird. Sly Parkinson on a mercy call. Sly had never visited his apartment before; but then, neither had Mike—or very many other people, for that matter. "I brought these," Sly said, handing the senator a bag of Quarter Pounders. "I figured you wouldn't be cooking."

"Sly, what the hell are you doing here?"

"Had an interview up at NBC," Parkinson said. He was a big mess of a man with thinning white hair and a short, sharp nose too thin to hold his eyeglasses, which he'd push back with an inverted thumb even when they didn't seem to need pushing back. "Figured I'd drop by. Friends know when to say when." He saw Charlie wasn't buying this at all. "Okay, okay. Linc called. Said you might want some company. Hey, Mike . . . Mr. Wonderful sure looks like shit, doesn't he? Great shiner, Chas. Have a cheeseburger," he added, tossing his raincoat over a chair. Sly was still wearing makeup from the television gig; he looked more vivid than usual.

"Sly, I—" Charlie was touched by Parkinson's visit, and embarrassed by it, and infuriated by it. Was he now officially pathetic?

Sly had never actually served in Vietnam, but he'd been one of Robert McNamara's whiz kids and showed up in Saigon on occasion. Charlie and Linc had adopted him, taking him out on the town when he accompanied the secretary of defense on his in-country tours. In return, Parkinson would give them the latest gossip from Washington. And then Sly and Charlie had found themselves thrown together once more, in

Congress of all places. They became renegades together on the House Armed Services Committee. Their shared Vietnam frustration led to passionate discussions about how to build a killer force to fight little wars in a world where big wars were unthinkable; and those conversations led to something approaching friendship.

"Just in time, Sly," Mike said. "Charlie's going to tell us what happened."

"Why? What difference does it make?" Charlie asked.

"Because you're not going out to meet the press tomorrow without a script. You understand? No silly-ass-Charlie-Martin-flying-by-the-seat-of-your-fucking-pants-because-it's-more-honest-to-be-spontaneous. Too much is at stake. The rest of your career. That's why."

"He's right, Chas," Sly said, pulling a large bag of small carrots from his attaché case and popping one in his mouth.

"Dare to be dull?" Charlie asked.

"You bet," Mike replied. "So, let's start from the beginning. What happened?"

He told them. Parkinson shook his head and whistled. "What a waste," he lamented. "As Shakespeare once said, 'More's the pity to take the hit and get no nooky.' "

"You're not forgetting anything?" Mike asked.

"There isn't anything to forget," Charlie said. "Nothing happened."

"I love it," Sly said, consulting his watch and popping another carrot.

"Firing at three-minute intervals, Slick?" Charlie asked.

"Yup. Twenty an hour is about sixty calories. You do it every other hour, three hours a day. No-fat breakfast. You don't eat lunch. You exercise. Wash down the carrots with a ton of water. Who knows? It could work." Sly was an object lesson in what happens to high school defensive linemen when they start indulging their senses. He'd been able to subdue an incredible amount of military data, but not much else in life. In recent years, he'd had a string of extramarital adventures and heart attacks; the former, fleeting; the latter, mild. Sooner or later, he'd have one or the other that would be cataclysmic—although the prospect of a Stanton presidency was having a remarkably salubrious effect on him: Sly desperately wanted to be secretary of defense. But he understood he had to clean up his act. "Been working on my discipline, getting in shape. Learning to love hunger," he added now, laughing at himself. "Charlie, could you get rid of those damn cheeseburgers before I go nuts?"

"Sly, could you put a fucking lid on it?" Mike Coleman said as Charlie took the McDonald's sack into the kitchen. "Or better still: you got any thoughts about how to finesse this?"

"Where ya doin' the press conference?" Sly asked.

"A zoo. Anyplace I do it will be a zoo," Charlie said, then glanced at Mike. "Okay, the Senate Caucus Room. Noon tomorrow."

"Then what?" Sly asked.

"I don't know."

"Go home."

"Why?"

"Because it's home. What are you gonna do here this week? We're in recess." Actually, Sly had turned out to be a pretty fair politician. He was one of those happy, huggy public pols who specialized in constituent service, a culinary populist who never left a kielbasa uneaten at a Pulaski Day picnic in his New Jersey district.

"Okay, I go home," Charlie agreed. "Pat Dunn'll be happy. I'll do home-state press."

"Guys. Can we slow down just a little bit?" Mike said. "Before we get on with the rest of Charlie's life, can we think about what he should say tomorrow? Sly?"

"Sheesh," Sly said, consulting his watch, popping another carrot. "Tough one. Charlie goes, Nothing happened. The press goes, So why did the father punch you out? Charlie goes, There was a misunderstanding."

"The press goes, Ha-fucking-ha," Charlie said.

"She was distraught," Sly tried again. "She was a devoted Martin worker, saw the campaign going down the tubes, she burst into tears, Charlie tried to comfort her. . . ."

"That sounds plausible." Charlie scowled. "I'm sure she'll agree with that scenario."

"Sly," Mike Coleman said, "would you get up there and say that?"

Silent Sly. "Maybe we should call an expert," Mike said.

"Like who?" Charlie asked.

"You're out of the race," Mike said. "Maybe we could get one of the Stanton guys to help—Richard Jemmons or Arlen Sporken. I'll make a call."

"Oh, please," Charlie said. He stood up. "Enough of this." But he didn't stop Mike, who went to the bedroom to make his call.

"Look, Chuckie, I better run," Parkinson said, more antsy than usual, discomforted by the personal nature of the situation. "You want me to stand there with you tomorrow?"

"Nah. Thanks, big guy. This is my show."

"You sure?" Sly said, putting on his coat.

"Hey, Sly, thanks for coming by." And for leaving so quickly.

"Well, I was in the neighborhood," Parkinson said, draping an arm around Charlie's back. "And I was sort of hoping it would be a juicier story."

Charlie let him out, then stood in the hallway, lost; he thought about the Senate Caucus Room. He'd never dreaded the press, the way most of his colleagues did. He'd always been able to handle reporters. But things had turned snipey toward the end of the campaign—and now he would have to explain the inexplicable. There was only one way to do that: head-on. He would tell his story and take the hit.

"Charlie," Mike said, poking his head into the room, "I've got Jack Stanton on the phone. He wants to talk to you."

He went to the bedroom, picked up the phone, paced with it. "Hi, Jack," he said. "How's it going?"

"You okay?" Stanton asked.

"Peachy," Charlie said. "This is some screwed-up world. . . . I'm sorry that you've been getting some of the blow-back from my adventures."

"May have cost me Colorado, according to the first-wave exits," Stanton said, "but that's okay. We won big in Georgia."

Charlie had almost forgotten that this was election day. "Jack, if you were me, what would you do?"

"Depends," he said. "Did you have relations with the girl?"

"No! That's why it's so crazy, Jack. I didn't lay a h-h—well, I did put my hand on her. . . ."

"In a romantic way?"

"No! I mean, have you seen her?"

"Big knockers, it looks like," Stanton said. "I can usually tell from the hang of the shoulders, even from photographs. I pride myself on that."

"Oh, Christ, Jack—" But this sure was strange: a locker room Jack Stanton, one of the guys. It was clear that he no longer considered Charlie Martin the competition.

"Why on earth were you with her alone?" Stanton asked. Charlie's silence signified that he didn't want to admit that it was because he was in the midst of a macho, snake-eating, pigheaded unwillingness to do the obvious thing: fold his tent and go home. Indeed, at that moment, Charlie felt the juices again: he still wanted to beat Jack Stanton somewhere.

"Charlie, my man, don't you know the Rule of Three?" Stanton asked. "It's like, basic. In a campaign, you never, ever travel alone. You always need a third person, a witness. Anybody can claim any damn thing on you, you don't have a witness. And if you do have a witness—the right kind, of course—you can deny any damn thing. It's Politics 101."

"I skipped 101," Charlie said. "They put me in advanced placement."

"Yeah: war hero," Stanton said. "They'll give you a lot of running room when you're a war hero. I always envied all the fun you were havin' out in Hollywood and all. I couldn't get away with that."

Charlie resisted the temptation to say: That's right, asshole, you're *married.*

"For the record," Stanton continued, "only things *I* do alone in a campaign are the three S's."

"The three S's?" Charlie asked, thinking: he couldn't mean the old college dorm three S's.

He did.

"What about phone calls?" Charlie asked.

"Phone calls, too. It's an innovation. I've only just started doin' it since the shit started flying, especially if I do a phoner with the press. I got Henry listening in right now—right, Henry?"

"Hello, Senator—sorry about the mess," Henry Burton said.

"You could've told me he was on," Martin said, medium hot.

"Sorry, Charlie," Stanton said. "So what you gonna do now?"

"Dunno," Charlie said, finally putting two and two together, realizing that Mike had asked Stanton to let one of his campaign guys help him think this through and Stanton had said no. "Hey, Jack," Charlie said, "I never really had you looking over your shoulder, did I?"

"Well, there were a couple of days there in New Hampshire—"

"Really?"

"Nawww," he laughed. What a guy.

3

Charlie Martin had never read the book about the different stages of grief. He experienced four: disbelief, blind anger, fetal position and flight. On Wednesday, when he returned to his office after announcing the end of his campaign—a curiously peripheral act: most of the hotshot reporters were off with the surviving presidential candidates in Florida—Charlie succumbed to the senatorial equivalent of fetal position. He lay flat on his back, on the battered old leather couch from his grandfather's law office in Fort Jeffords, thinking about other, more hopeful times in the Senate Caucus Room: he had announced his presidential candidacy there, just as John and Robert Kennedy had—their campaigns were considered "premature," too. Back in 1987, his baptism as a serious player had taken place in that room, with a "quiet, searing" opening statement at the Iran-Contra hearings, or so it had been described by Mary McGrory in *The Washington Post*, who added, "Does anyone doubt that this young man will lead the nation one day?"

Charlie loved his office, which was located on the second floor of Russell, the oldest of the three Senate office buildings. He'd decorated the reception area in basic grain—lovely black-and-white photos of corn and wheat and sunflowers by Anne Hellstrom, whom he'd dated for a while on weekends in Des Pointe. There was a long, narrow hallway, with closets and cubicles for several dozen staff members (several dozen more were relegated to back office buildings and the Armed Services Committee space). His inner sanctum had the leather couch, two wing chairs and a marble fireplace, as well as his desk. The walls were covered with rural scenes by home-state artists; Charlie rotated the paintings from year to year, sending the old ones back to the Midwest, bringing a fresh set in—there were plenty of home-state artists, and his staff made sure that each relevant local newspaper received word that Silas Barnham or Beatrice Button had a landscape hanging in Senator Martin's office. And now he stared at a cold, lonely blue winter scene—by a dairy farmer named Fred Dienst—as he listened to his chief of staff, Donna Mendoza, rattling off the coordinates of his disaster. "You're lucky it happened the day before the election," she said. "Limited the damage some. Too bad they got you on camera. Would've been a nonevent without that."

"They missed me on camera," he said. "They got jostling and blue sky."

"The handheld with you flat on your dumpkin was pretty memorable," she said.

Donna had been with him both Senate terms. She had come with the office, working her way up from receptionist to administrative assistant (which, in the Congress, is what you call a chief of staff) for his predecessor, Roger Pullman—who had recommended her, eloquently for Roger: "She's a grown-up." That she was, and more. Charlie figured Donna had been great-looking, in a bronze, slightly chubby kind of way, back in the sixties. Now she had the Nurse Blazer look, which was what women in Washington did to themselves when they wanted to be taken seriously: Ferragamo pumps, off-white stockings, a blue blazer with a gold pin—some form of eagle was appropriately patriotic and prim—which was worn with everything, dresses and blouses (subdued shades, subdued prints) and skirts (no higher than the knee). Women in Washington dressed about as creatively as men in Washington did.

Donna was the widow of Master Sergeant Luke Mendoza of Tucumcari, who had been blown away by a rocket-propelled grenade while assaulting a tree line in I Corps, the same general area where Charlie had been wounded. That was something he and Donna had in common. There was a lot, however, they didn't: she had raised a boy and a girl by herself. They were grown now; Donna was in danger of becoming a grandmother.

"So," she sighed. She was sitting at Charlie's desk, with several manila folders in front of her, with her reading glasses on. "I've divided the list into categories: interview requests—although most of the A-list is gone now—messages from constituents, messages from colleagues, messages from friends and contributors, speaking engagements canceled . . ."

"Canceled?"

"Well, you're no longer going to be the featured speaker at the Des Pointe League of Women Voters annual dinner, or . . ."

"Okay, okay." he said.

"On the interview request list," Donna continued. "Does Lanny Scott count as one of the Lords, or one of the press?"

"Both, I guess . . . why?"

"They've got a new feature on the evening news at ABC. 'The Story Behind the Story.' He wants to inaugurate it with a piece about you—going back to your days together in Vietnam, talking about the heroism and the stress . . . apparently, they dug out some old footage of you at the Philadelphia Naval Hospital. He said it'll be basically sympathetic, getting at why you did what you did—"

"Fuck no."

"Okay," Donna said, "but you can't mess around on the home-state press. Hamblin wants an exclusive."

"The sky is blue," he replied. "How much of this do we have?"

"More than you can begin to imagine," said Donna. "We had a lot to catch up on before your phantom grope, or whatever it was. You want some comic relief? Here's my own personal favorite."

"Shoot."

"It's an invitation from the Des Pointe Battered Women's Shelter."

"No kidding."

"You want me to read or summarize?" Donna asked, pulling a fax from her pile. He waved his left hand, a whoop-de-doo motion with his index finger: whatever. "Well," she said. "They're very appreciative of the help you've given them in the past—and, it says here, they believe that you're not the sort of man to abuse women, certainly not chronically—and so they want to give you the opportunity to redeem yourself by explaining your side of the story, and apologizing, if necessary, at their annual fundraising dinner next November. And they have several suggestions about where you might go for therapy before then."

"Jesus," Charlie said. "I got a whole lifetime of this ahead of me?"

"I doubt it," Donna said. "Things fade."

"Not in a world with Nexis." He could run for president in the year 2008, win, establish national health care, repel an alien invasion—and it would still be there, in his obituary: "President Martin, who once was decked by a Colorado pharmacist who believed the then-senator had groped his daughter during the 1992 presidential campaign, won the Nobel peace prize in . . ."

Rosemary Buffa, gatekeeper of the inner sanctum, poked her head in the door: "Senator, Mrs. Thurston on the phone. Second time today."

Charlie nodded, and Donna exited: Lynn Thurston was the custodian of his Washington social life. He'd been dreading this moment.

"Oh, Charlie, Charlie are you okay?" Lynn leaped in as soon as he said hello—and then, before he could say anything more, "I've just had the most terrible scene. Lunch at the Occidental with Sally. She asked if you had taken leave of your senses, and I got very angry and said, 'Sally, you know damn well that's not Charlie.' And she said, 'Well, what did happen?' And I had to say that I didn't know. That we hadn't talked. And she gave me a look, and I did the worst possible thing—I began to . . . weep a little. I was so angry with myself. I just up and left. It was awful."

"I'm so sorry, Lynn," Charlie said. "I should have called you last night. But I was so bummed."

"Well, I assumed you'd be depressed—"

"You didn't throw anything at her?" Charlie interrupted, hoping Lynn would have the sense not to attempt a glutinous, therapeutic intervention. "A bruschetta or something?"

"Char-lie," Lynn said. "I was embarrassed."

"I know. I'm sorry." Lynn was a good soul, and a good soldier.

"I just hate what everyone is saying." She sighed. And, of course, Lynn would know what "everyone" was saying. She spent far too many evenings raising funds for liberal campaigns and causes—although Charlie was always surprised, and quite pleased, that she managed not to be callused by such antic sociability. She wasn't hard, in the Capital way. She was from Oregon, and seriously Scandinavian in looks and demeanor; a stoic, not a cynic, and a very acceptable dinner date. They were an extremely plausible public couple; privately, they were careful with each other—casually affectionate and friendly, not quite enraptured even when intimate. And so this was a delicate moment.

He could ask her, What *is* everyone saying? But he didn't care to hear the specifics (and, of course, he could guess the general outlines). Or he could confide in her—tell her what had happened in Colorado Springs, confess embarrassment, allow her to comfort him. Charlie shuddered at the thought: he'd owe Lynn then. He'd owe her more affection than had been their practice, a deeper level of devotion than he was prepared to give.

"They're probably saying I'm—"

"No, not really," she said, cutting him off, mercifully, before he disparaged himself. "No one who knows you takes the Colorado business seriously They just think it was a particularly messy end to a sloppy campaign. Apparently, that's unforgivable."

"They're right," he said, wondering if no one really cared about the girl, or if Lynn was just being kind. He was mortified by her loyalty.

"They're wrong," Lynn scolded, "and we're going to show them." Indeed, she had a resuscitation campaign planned. "We are not going to act as if you're some sort of pariah. I am taking you in hand. There's a book party for Arthur Schlesinger at Kay Graham's tomorrow. And this weekend there's an Environmental Defense Fund ball at the Corcoran."

"Lynn, no. I can't." She was proposing party penance, the stiffest of sentences, the opposite of the solitary confinement he craved. He would have to be civil, controlled, implicitly contrite. He wondered if Lynn was wily enough to understand the subtle brilliance of such punishment. "Actually," he added. "I'm going away for a bit."

He was flat on the couch again when Donna returned. "Hey, D, what would you say to me getting lost for a while?"

"I would say no. Absolutely not," she replied reflexively. "Lynn wring you out or something?"

"No. Worse. She wants me to socialize."

Donna laughed. "Tough love, huh? Beltway boot camp."

"Why the hell *can't* I get lost?" he asked, sitting up. "I'm gonna miss a vote on the National Furniture Day proclamation or something?"

"How lost?" The boss did need a vacation, although Donna was shocked he'd admit that. A sign of health, perhaps. "How long?"

"Pretty damn lost. Not sure how long."

"If you disappear now, people are going to think—"

"Yeah, I know," he said, swiveling, lying back down. "That I'm guilty of something. Lynn's point exactly. But the hell with that. I'm gonna take a WTF on that. I've got one coming after all this, right?"

"There are those who'd argue that the last six months have been one long WTF," Donna said.

"There are those who'd argue that I need some time off, clear my head, after being so useless for so long," he replied, lifting himself up with his elbows and craning his neck around to give Donna a poor-little-me look. She peered at him over her reading glasses: she liked the poor-little-me look—the boss wasn't being pathetic, he was riffing on being pathetic. He could certainly use a breather. There was no danger he'd fall off the map: he'd be gone for two days, think of some brilliant scheme—she remembered his last one: vaccination vans distributing candy and balloons in the ghettos, staffed by premed students on summer break—and then he'd be right back, making her life miserable . . . and more fun than it had ever been with Roger Pullman (or with Luke Mendoza, for that matter).

"So, where?" she asked.

"Thailand," he said, surprising himself—although it did make sense from a WTF perspective: he had a history of being successfully irresponsible in Thailand. He'd gone to Bangkok for R&R in 1967, the last time he was in the process of being seriously defeated. He wasn't thinking about going to Bangkok now, of course. He was thinking about the beach resort Corporal Larry Kenny operated down the Malay Peninsula. Kenny had been sending Christmas postcards for years—the place had thatched roof cottages on the beach, hammocks, rum drinks. It was hard to get more lost than that.

"Surely," Donna said, "there must be an easier way to get laid."

"I'm not going there to get—"

"Getting laid and setting up a sweatshop are the only reasons why anyone goes to Thailand," Donna said, "and I'm sure, given the past few days, most people will assume that of all the possible places in the world to go, you haven't chosen this particular spot for the air quality."

"Most people won't know that I'm there," he said. "In fact, no one will."

"And if they find out?"

"Tell them I'm on a fact-finding mission."

"I hope the facts aren't communicable," Donna said. "You couldn't go to Tahiti instead?"

"No." Although Tahiti didn't sound bad, either.

"You better call Buzz," Donna sighed.

"I'll do better than that," he said. "Des Pointe is on the way to Thailand, sort of. I could go via DP, do the local press with Dunnsie—then Frisco, Narita, Bangkok—I think Kenny said you take a hydrofoil down the coast from there. Could you check it out? I'll take the four o'clock to Chicago, surprise Buzz and Edsy in DP tonight. Call Proctor, have her set up some press things."

"You're sure about all this?" Donna sighed.

"Of course not," Charlie said, coming around the desk, standing behind her, squeezing her shoulder and kissing her on top of the head. "But don't worry, *muchacha*—"

"*'Muchacha'?*" Donna said. "It's *señora* to you, buster."

* * *

"Hey, Pop, how's it going?" Charlie said, pushing through the unlocked front door of the Oak Street house that night.

"Free and easy," Buzz crooned, from his usual spot in the den.

"Better than Brie and freezy." The senator completed their signature hello. Buzz hadn't known what Brie was the first time Charlie tried the line on him—but he laughed when he learned it was runny French cheese that tasted a little like cardboard, and they served it at all the best cocktail parties in Washington, which were, indeed, frosty occasions.

"Brie and freezy's better than grim and greasy," Buzz sometimes said, in that wonderful, reedy crooner's tenor—a voice that was born to be broadcast from a heartland bandstand. But he knew better than to try that after the events of the past few days.

"You look in serious need of a toddy," he offered instead, putting aside the newspaper, getting up from his La-Z-Boy, giving his son a kiss on the cheek—the same sweet, casual kiss he'd always given Charlie at bedtime when he was a child, on those occasional evenings when Buzz was around at bedtime. When Buzz had a gig, he'd kiss Charlie much later, when he got home; Charlie remembered the late-night, reassuring smell of whiskey breath, although he wasn't sure his mother had found it very reassuring. "You want your usual fancy stuff? Edsy's getting her beauty rest."

"Thanks, Pop," Charlie said, surveying the place. He hadn't been home in months, but it seemed forever: the campaign had distended time. Nothing much had changed—the family pictures on the spinet, the gig pictures on the walnut plywood walls, the saggy bookcase filled with Mom's old favorites: Dorothy Day, Dr. Tom Dooley, William L. Shirer, Theodore H. White, all the John Gunther books—Popular Nonfiction Central.

Buzz returned from the kitchen with a brandy for Charlie and a Seagram's V.O. for himself—Charlie loved the fact that the old man still drank rye, that most unfashionable of blends. He sat on the lumpy brown couch with the crocheted afghan throw splayed across the back, as it had always been. "So how's life in Squareadelphia?" Buzz asked, plopping down into the La-Z-Boy. He was still tall and thin, but he'd gone gray—

and didn't look so much like Dennis the Menace's father as he once had; although he did wear thick black-rimmed glasses all the time now.

"Grim and greasy, Pop," Charlie said. "I blew it."

"I ever tell you 'bout the yokel who popped me one in Omaha?" Buzz asked. "Said I was makin' google-eyes at his damsel the whole first set—"

"This was like in ought-eight?" Charlie was tickled by the brilliance of his father's diversionary action.

"More like ought-not," he said. "See, I had been making google-eyes at the lady. She moved like a breeze. She had one of those, what do you call them—chiffon?—dresses, like a peach color and matching shoes, and sweet stems, let me tell you . . . and I could see she had caught what we were doing, caught our drift. Fact, I started moving the music along with her . . . nudgin' the boys where she was going. It happened sometimes, you find someone in the crowd who's diggin' it and you let them lead you a little. Let them select the tunes, too, at least the ones you think they're gonna want to dance to—boys'd get a little ripped over that, me screwing with the set . . . but where was I? Oh, yeah: set's over. I'm puttin' my squeezer on the stand, leanin' over, and this boy comes over and says, 'You makin' eyes at my lady, accordion boy?' That's what he called me, and I gotta say, it ticked me off and so I said, 'That's what they're there for—'"

"Did you mean your eyes or the girls?"

"The girls, but it could've worked both ways, now that I think of it," he said. "Anyway, he popped me. Didn't see it comin'. Wouldna' got close if I hadn't been leanin' down, but he popped me a good one, knocked me back into Vern's sax stand, bent the horn. . . . Vern had to fill with his licorice stick, second set."

"And you? The show must go on?"

"Cramped my style a little. Trouble landin' high C with a headache. Couldn't sing falsetto on 'Stardust.' Got the girl, though."

"Mom know about that?"

"This was before your mother—but, you know, Clarice was wearing one of those chiffon dresses and diggin' our chops just the same as that other girl, the night we met at the Crescent Lake Casino. That girl in the peach dress was like a—what do you call it, a premonition?—of your mom."

"Thanks, Pop." Charlie figured the old man had riffed it on the spot, just to make him feel better: a clear jolt of classic Buzz. Of course, if the story was true, it probably hadn't happened before Clarice. Everyone in the family assumed Buzz never stopped being a sucker for girls in chiffon dresses. But Charlie appreciated the effort: it was about as direct an acknowledgment of his predicament as he was likely to get from his father. Buzz had never been big on heart-to-hearts; Charlie's mother, the mayor, had been tasked all the usual father-and-son topics.

"Early for Edwina to be shagging a break," Charlie offered, slipping into Buzz's idiom. "She okay?"

"Pretty swell, for an old bag." Edwina had been married to Milky Flancik, the trumpet player; Buzz made the move on her just after Charlie's mother died, with Milky still in mid-drool at the Meadows Nursing Home. Within weeks, they had set up light housekeeping together, right there in the house on Oak Street—which had been Clarice's house, part of her inheritance from Judge Campbell. The haste had been unseemly, and it was the talk of the West Side Senior Center. But Buzz had never really bought into middle-class values—he'd always been a hayseed hipster—and Charlie was, in truth, relieved: Edwina would take care of him (although Charlie did wonder, given the speed of the move, how long it had been in the works). Clarice had always been far more interested in doing good than in looking after Buzz; it was a marriage of inconvenience, the sort that wouldn't last in Charlie's generation.

Clarice and Milky were long gone now; but Buzz and Edwina had never bothered to tie the knot, probably because he had never bothered to ask. And Edwina was okay for a trumpet player's wife: they tended to be flashy and trashball. She still had a weakness for scalloped scoop-cut dresses when she went out (she had kept her figure, proportionally; everything was just a bit thicker now)—but she did dote on Buzz. To Edsy Flancik, he would always be the leader of the Buzzards, and a step up. To Charlie's mom, he had been a lifelong salvage operation—a sacrifice lovingly performed at first, and then less so, one of her many good works, but not exactly what she'd been looking for, or deserved.

"Any gigs?" Charlie asked. Buzz Martin and the Buzzards were still in operation, though down to a trio now: Vern O'Donnell still handled the reeds, and Harlan Weeks was sitting in as the umpteenth drummer.

"We got an Elks in Proctor on the twenty-third, and a couple of Gazebo shots when the summer comes around," Buzz said. "Hey, you been diggin' this Kenny G?"

"I've heard him."

"Been thinking about moving one of his cuts into the Canadian Sunset medley." Buzz had always been a great one for medleys: it had been a car game when they were kids—match three songs by lyrics or, more fun, by musical pattern—the Canadian Sunset medley had always been a clarinet thing. "It's Vern's big turn," he said. "Remember? 'Canadian Sunset,' 'Stranger on the Shore'—"

"You think Vern's got the wind left for that, Pop?"

"I fill for him a little on the synthesizer—"

"No shit—very high-tech."

"You know it," Buzz crooned. "I got it up in the bedroom. You can play it sitting in bed, damn thing's just a keyboard. Usin' it a lot now. You can play it standing and face the crowd—that was always the bum deal with the piano: had to play it sideways, couldn't look at the folks. Nothing better than the piano, musically, of course. It's a lordly thing. Beats the old squeezer, hands down. But you could squeeze facing the folks. Farmers loved it, too. And I could make it swing a little, sometimes. . . . I'm thinkin' about getting a sequencer when Harlan goes—but it's cold, empty stuff. I like the feel of a live trap set behind me, even if it's just barely alive."

"Harlan's in bad shape?" Charlie asked, marveling at how Buzz could talk about what he wanted to talk about.

"You ever hear an arthritic drummer? Bump and groan."

"Pop, you—you sound pretty good. I—"

Buzz was silent, waiting, offering nothing.

"Pop, how's this business playing out there? 'M I on the hit parade?"

"Well, Edsy says there was a lot of clucking on the checkout line," he said. "And I hear the Muffler Man put you in the Hall of Fame."

"He's still around?"

"The grandson. He's running the company now. Goes on the TV, just like his grandpa did, only different. Wears the American flag tie. Does these ads about things that need to be muffled. This week, it's you."

"Me, huh?"

"Yeah." Buzz was clearly uneasy with this topic. "You can see it tonight. He's usually on just after the news, before Leno."

"Pop, I'm gonna take a breather," Charlie said. "You remember me talking about Corporal Kenny, the guy who became a hippie and never came back from Thailand? He's got a hotel down the coast."

"You once sent me a postcard from Thailand," he said. "You were on recreation, or whatever they called it—"

"R and R." They hadn't had R & R in Buzz's war. And not much action, either: the old man had been a Supply Corps clerk in Hawaii, after Pearl Harbor.

"Great name. Bangkok," the old man mused. "Pretty much describes it, right? Wonder if anyone ever used it in a lyric."

"Could've rhymed it with 'limp sock,'" Charlie said.

"Girl I never forgot . . . Bangkok, forget me not," Buzz crooned.

"Not bad," Charlie said. Buzz was one of the great two-phrase song-writers. Never found a bridge he could cross, though. "Pop—"

"Don't forget your galoshes," Buzz said, cutting Charlie off at the pass before he did something stupid like try to explain the Schollwengen business, or tell him how bad he hurt, or ask advice.

"Thanks, Pop—I won't do anything you wouldn't do," he said, donating a straight line to Buzz's favorite charity.

"Leaves you lots of running room," Buzz said, with a gentle smile, raising himself stiffly from the La-Z-Boy. "EGBDF, right?"

EGBDF: the lines of the treble clef. Buzz had taught him to read music before his mother had taught him to read words, and it all started with EGBDF: Every Good Boy Does Fine.

"Night, son," Buzz said, giving him another of those odd kisses. Two in a night: Charlie realized that the old man must have been pretty upset by the recent events.

Perhaps the most generous thing a parent can do for a male teenager is give him a room with a separate entrance. Buzz and Clarice had done that for Charlie, clearing out the space above the garage, installing a bathroom and an outdoor staircase for easy access. It was a two-car garage, so there was lots of room. Charlie had lived there for most of his life, except for the few years after Vietnam when he was over in East Des Pointe, serving "the community" with Johanna Lecoutre Martin, his first and only wife, a woman whom Oskar Millar once said had brought do-goodism to a new level: too-goodism.

Charlie had upgraded the place over the years, adding a TV, computer, fax machine, Exercycle and king-sized bed. But it was still a teenager's room, in spirit—although the senator was usually too exhausted on the weekend nights that he stayed there, after long days of politicking, to notice or think twice about the idea that he was nearing fifty years of age and still, in effect, living at home.

He called Mary Proctor, while clicking around the local cable system.

He half listened as Mary suggested an elaborate cross-state implicit-apology tour; Charlie promised he'd think about doing one after his vacation. He said good-bye just as the news was ending.

And there it was: a handsome fellow with startling blond hair and a good voice—deeper, more authoritative than his appearance would lead you to expect—in a blue sportscoat with an American flag tie: "Hey, folks, it's Lee Butler of Butler Muffler with another edition of 'Things That Need to Be Muffled.'" He was standing in front of a slide of a Butler Muffler shop—Charlie had seen the cherry red plastic signs all over the Great American Anywhere, especially the Midwest.

"This week we have a new inductee into our Muffler-Worthy Hall of Fame," Butler said. He was easy with the camera; he knew not to work it too hard. Pretty professional; very impressive. Butler was clean-cut, but also clever; innocent and sarcastic simultaneously. Impossible not to watch.

And then there was tape of the most awkward moment of Charlie Martin's resignation press conference, just after he'd insisted that nothing untoward had happened with Martha Schollwengen. An elderly woman reporter had asked, "You're asking us to believe that nothing happened?"

"Well, there was obviously a misunderstanding. . . ."

Which was where the ad began, with the Muffler Man providing commentary: "That's right. Our own Senator Charlie Martin . . . who's been out running for president instead of doing the job he was elected to do. But you have to give ol' Charlie credit. Works hard, groping for answers to our nation's problems . . ."

And then, sound again, Charlie saying—clumsily, very clumsily it seemed now: "There was no malicious or provocative action on my part—and I'm sorry if Miss Schollwengen misperceived any action on my part." Then Lee Butler, close up and deadpan: "Too bad we don't have a full line of Butler mufflers."

Then a freeze-frame of Charlie Martin at the press conference with a crude drawing of a red muffler, the same color as a Muffler Man sign, covering his mouth—and a red glove covering his right hand (thank God, Charlie thought, it was his right hand) as he pointed out into the audience, soliciting a question.

"But," the Muffler Man concluded, "we can do for your car what we can't do for your country. Stop in at your local Muffler Man car care center tomorrow and help make America a nicer, quieter place."

The next morning, as they were making the Des Pointe media rounds in Charlie's official minivan, Dunn asked, "So, you see Muffler Boy's ad?"

Charlie looked at him evenly. "Patsy, it scared the shit out of me."

Dunn was amazed, as always, by Charlie's self-deprecating candor. But this admission wasn't credible—it was too easy, too casual. And Charlie had never admitted anything resembling fear before. Then again, maybe this was how a snake-eater admitted fear: fearlessly. "You? Scared?"

"Totally freaked, frozen on the bed, my stomach somewhere around my toes," Charlie said. "Y'know, after the press conference, I thought maybe the worst was over." Wishful thinking: his humiliation had been a passing media squall; the big story, the presidential campaign, had gone elsewhere. But the Butler ad ended that; it seemed a very personal sort of assault—a direct challenge on his home turf. "In the boonies, in the amp ward, there were always the other guys to think about, always something to do. Last night, there was nothing to think about but me. And I'm not much fun to think about these days."

"So what did you do?"

"Well, the first thought was busywork. Proctor wants me to take a cross-state jaunt. I called Donna, told her to cancel my plane tickets."

Dunn whistled. "So you're staying?"

"Nah, Donnzo talked me out of it," Charlie said, smiling. "She said, 'You're freaked over a guy who sells mufflers? Two months from now, he'll need a tax break and want to be your best friend.' "

"She's probably right," Pat said. "Although Mary's probably right, too."

"But Donna's a better psychologist than Proctor," Charlie said. In fact, Donna had proposed that he take a shorter, less ambitious vacation. Florida, maybe. The magic words: Charlie Martin never did anything less ambitious. If he was going away, he would go as far away as he possibly could.

"So," Dunn asked. "You're going?"

"As soon as we get done with illuminating the locals," Charlie said, with a sigh, "I will give peace a chance."

4

—————

Middle of the night, seriously jet-lagged. Middle of the day back home. Charlie lay on the bed in his overchilled room, channel-surfing. He'd traveled halfway around the world and gone nowhere: just another hotel, complete with CNN. This one was nicer than those he'd endured during the campaign: a big Sheraton, not a motel—muted gray-mauve carpet and matching, deeper mauve bedspread and drapes; Chinese-style bamboo prints on the walls. There was a floor-to-ceiling window; it faced the river, which seemed the only Asian thing left in Bangkok, a mucky chaos of ships and skiffs. There was high-rise con-struction on both banks; the scaffolding appeared rickety and was co-cooned in green canvas, Western banality about to burst forth—the city was in the midst of a reverse metamorphosis, from butterfly to cater-pillar.

Charlie found a Courvoisier in the minibar, settled back in his bed and wondered if he were being overly nostalgic: had Bangkok ever been a butterfly? He wasn't sure. He didn't remember much about how Bangkok looked in 1967; he remembered other things. The girls in Pat-pong, of course. But breathing had been memorable, too, breathing without fear—a tingly phenomenon, like regaining the use of a leg after it had fallen asleep. The ability to inhale and exhale freely, after months of constant trepidation, was unexpected and intoxicating.

He remembered the faces of the other soldiers on the plane out of Danang. He didn't know any of them, but that didn't make a differ-ence—they had far more in common than not: they had all seen too much and this was a moment they'd been dreaming about for months. They shucked their ancient warrior faces midair, transforming them-selves into adolescents again, slapping on aftershave, breaking out

Hawaiian shirts and cigars. They were gloriously, unapologetically, transcendently horny when they hit the ground.

Charlie accompanied several of them—fellow Marines; he couldn't remember their names, only their extravagant swagger—to a joint where the girls wore American college T-shirts and short-shorts and flip-flop sandals; his girl had a Cornell T-shirt and she leaned casually, collegiately, elbow on the bar, long black hair falling over her eyes, laughing and chatting, asking about America. "Why they call it hot dog, Joe?" She shouted in his ear, competing with the Rolling Stones. "Why they call it jukebox?"

He sipped his Courvoisier, fully dressed on his bed, and debated whether to risk a walk over to Patpong. He had heard that the district had become less exotic, more touristy. There was a night market now; souvenirs—T-shirts, wallets, fake Rolexes—were sold outside the sex clubs. He was curious, but he couldn't go; a stroll through Patpong was politically, and morally, untenable. There was no such thing as innocent naughtiness anymore, if there ever had been. In 1967, he'd been a kid, not much older than the girls; now he was old enough to be their grandfather—and now he knew that many of them were there involuntarily, dragooned from villages all over Asia (he wondered if that had been true in 1967: they'd seemed so happy, so free).

He clicked his way through the late-night TV options. Jack Stanton worked southern crowds on CNN. There was week-old NBA basketball on the sports channel. The latest Rolling Stones video was on Asian MTV, which was appropriate: for Charlie, the Stones would always be part of Bangkok. They sounded the same, but they looked ancient, ridiculous; Mick Jagger was still flailing his arms and pooching his lips, but now he seemed an aged, wizened Mick Jagger impersonator. There was a gorgeous young Chinese announcer on MTV—she chattered in Mandarin, switched effortlessly into Valley Girl: "The Red Hot Chili Peppers, very cool—from the city of angels . . . Ellayy . . . they're up next with, uh-huh, uh-huh . . . 'Under the Bridge.' "

Click. Elvis on TNT. Not just Elvis, but Elvis as an Arab? Actually, a relatively young Elvis as an American movie star in Saudi Arabia, pretending to be an Arab in order to escape from—assassins? Amazing. He was singing now. What was this movie?

And then Charlie clicked onto the hotel's service channel: trips to the boonies were on offer. Terraced chartreuse paddies of new rice, phlegmatic water buffalo, peasants in cone hats, haunting lute music. He drifted off, and found himself deep in the dull horror of the plane back to Danang after R&R. A different group of guys, same faces. All of them hung over on oxygen and other things, the tenseness and anger and absurdity reclaiming them. Two rows back, a boy sat staring out the window, tears streaming. No one said a word. How many would get blown away that first day back because they weren't paying sufficient attention? How many would take out their frustrations on the natives? Had he been thinking of the girl in the Cornell T-shirt, or of Johanna, or of cornfields, when Richie Radio took the step? And who or what had Richie been thinking about? He was blown back, sliding down, crashing heavily like a log falling through a watercourse. . . .

And up. The phone was ringing. He glanced at his suitcase, not yet unpacked—and knew it never would be. Sorry, Corporal Kenny. Bad idea. This was far too serious a part of the world for a vacation.

The phone: it was, of course, Lincoln Rathburn. Linc was bound to track him down. They hadn't spoken in more than a week, their longest radio silence in thirty years. "Have you contracted anything serious yet?" Linc asked, in his nasal, edgeless baritone, a butter knife of a voice.

"Maybe a cold. The Asians have gone berserk over air-conditioning, it seems." He clicked back to the Elvis movie. "Hey, an Elvis where he's an Arab?"

"*Harum Scarum,*" Rathburn said. Linc didn't exactly know *everything*, but he knew lots of things—and allowing him to show off early in the conversation might spare Charlie some hurt down the road. "But he's only pretending to be an Arab. And isn't Mary Ann Mobley in that one?"

"Is she a dark, bland, interchangeable early sixties sort with big hair?"

"A former Miss America," Lincoln said, "from Mississippi, if memory serves. And I always thought she was . . . sultry."

"God, you're such an asshole," Charlie observed. "I thought it was Annette Funicello, or something."

"I don't know that Elvis ever worked with Annette." Linc had the ability to sound equally grave discussing nuclear proliferation or schlocky date movies of the sixties. "So," he said. "It's three in the morning. You're in your room, watching an Elvis movie. Does this mean that you've already made a fool of yourself with some pathetic bar girl, or are you building up to that—or maybe you're in the process?"

Linc also had the ability to always know what time it was everywhere in the world. "Oh, that's right," Charlie said, annoyed by Rathburn's condescension. "I forgot: you always worked the high end of the Asian female market."

"You know that's not true," Linc replied, with some heat.

"Gotcha," Charlie said. Rathburn was rumored—unfairly, he'd always insisted—to have been linked romantically with Madame Nhu. It was, in a way, Charlie Martin's fault: back in '65, they'd been up on the roof of the Caravelle one evening, watching the war with some of the press guys—Linc morose, still trying to figure out a way to move Washington toward sanity at a moment when everyone else was coming to the conclusion that it was probably futile. There were times for being morose and serious, and knocking back 33's at dusk on the Caravelle roof wasn't one of them. So Charlie said, "Linc, you haven't had a smile on your face since Madame Nhu left town."

He looked up, startled. Had Charlie gotten close to something?

"What?" he said.

"Just kidding." Charlie shrugged. But everyone else there—Lanny Scott was a young ABC correspondent, fresh in town; Nick McMichael from *Life*; Peter Solomon from the *Times*—saw that a nerve had been touched, at the very least. And from that night on, the word went forth. It was just a joke in the immediate Saigon circle, but it spread the way truly inspired gossip does—and it expanded to fit Lincoln Rathburn's presence, which was rather imposing even in his midtwenties. He was a solid six feet with thick, straight, straw-colored hair and light blue eyes— in those days, he affected McGeorge Bundy glasses, with very unflattering flesh-colored rims, the eyewear of choice for the foreign policy elite—and he had a shockingly handsome, easily caricatured chin, with a deep cleft. That he was almost always in the company of a stunning woman (back then, and ever since) didn't hurt the Madame Nhu rumor, which came to include several of the Soong sisters. The story had taken on a life of its own, Charlie suspected, because of a need among people who barely knew Linc, and didn't like him, to render his apparent perfection imperfect.

Linc remembered exactly where and when the rumor had started, and who had started it—but he had never used that against his friend, which was his way of using it, his way of letting Charlie know that it was something he had done, however inadvertently, that was so hurtful to Linc's reputation that he couldn't bear to burden their friendship with it. Charlie played along with the conceit, usually. It was a measure of his desperation that he raised it now. He wasn't proud about that. He supposed that he owed Linc some honesty.

"This wasn't too bright, coming here," he said. Linc was silent; masterfully so. "I just had to get out of there, out of Washington . . . before Lynn filled up my social calendar. Condemned to eternal social contrition." Linc still hadn't said anything. "But what happened in Colorado was so absurd—so much a perfect comeuppance for making a fool of myself in the campaign. I mean, the worst possible fantasy. Stanton thinks I was asking for it, traveling without an aide. . . ."

"You talked to Stanton?" Linc asked, always ravenous for the latest—and curious now, to see if a rapprochement could be effected between the Martin and Stanton camps. Charlie assumed that Rathburn had been testing the Stanton waters, to see if some kind of foreign policy advisory position might be worked out for himself. And, no doubt, he'd been spending a good deal of phone time doing postmortems with reporters about the Martin campaign. Somehow Linc managed to be a helpless gossip and remain a deathless friend, a balancing act of breathtaking complexity.

"We talked. He was all yak-butter and horseshit." Charlie said. "It was nothing to write home about. You know, I still think I could've beat the sucker, if I'd ever gotten him one on one."

"Charlie, we've known each other for nearly thirty years, and during that time you have done two astonishingly self-destructive things," Linc said, in a tone of voice he might have used to introduce the senator as the after-dinner speaker at a banquet. "First, you had yourself transferred out from MACV to the snake-eaters—at the very moment you'd come to the conclusion that the war was not only unwinnable, but also wrong—"

"Well, I was pissed—"

"And second, you decided to run for president well before your time, when you had nothing to say, when you were unprepared, and then you stayed in long after it became obvious that—"

"What about my marriage?" Charlie tried to short-circuit the lecture.

"That was private."

"Going to the boonies was a private decision."

"That affected your public career—"

"Yeah, it made me a political commodity."

"And that's why you did it? Oh, come on, Charlie—you're fifty-what, don't you think it's time to get serious?"

"*You're* fifty-what," Charlie said. "I'm forty-nine."

"I could understand your decision, back in '65," Linc continued, "it was a cockeyed sort of honorable." Interesting that Rathburn would acknowledge that now, Charlie thought: the decision had been made after

Linc had been rotated back to Washington. They'd never really discussed it. "And classic you: only you would protest the war by going to war."

Back in Saigon, Linc had sensed that Charlie might eventually ask for a transfer to the front lines; he could feel the guilt and tension whenever they went out into the field together. They would drive down Highway 4 through the cane fields to My Tho, to the Seminary, where the U.S. Army advisers were based in the Delta, and check out the war. Charlie was friendly with Colonel Tom Charles Kelly, the American adviser attached to the ARVN forces in the area. T.C. was a perpetually infuriated redneck—he hated the Communists, and he hated the Vietnamese troops under his command for not wanting to fight the Communists, and he hated the American higher-ups in Saigon for not wanting to take the war by the throat and wrestle it to the ground.

Tom Charles showed them the war. He took them out on helicopter patrols with skittish ARVN troops; he showed them, by day, villes the Viet Cong controlled at night. And he was the one who'd christened them: "Well, if it ain't the Lords of the Delta," he'd proclaimed as Linc and Charlie pulled into the Seminary one day—the two of them brilliantly symmetrical, light and dark, diplomat and soldier, tall, clean and in khakis, defiant of the dust and sweat that came with the territory. They were the most fabulously American Americans imaginable. "We are so fucking honored by your presence."

In other circumstances, Charlie and Linc probably would have been rivals—and they were, at first, suspicious of each other—but they didn't have the luxury of competition in Saigon. They soon found that they could confide in each other about the impending disaster, the brutal reality that so few of their superiors were willing to face, which was an immense relief to both of them. It meant they weren't going dinky-dau: a fairly major issue since it was clear, to both, that T.C. was sliding off the charts, furious with the fates, talking too much to the press—he eventually was court-martialed for shooting a Vietnamese colonel who tried to withdraw his troops in the midst of a battle.

At times, Gideon Reese—chief of the embassy's political section—and Mike Coleman, Gid's assistant, would join the conversation; certain reliable journalists were allowed into the inner circle as well. But the innermost circle was Charlie and Linc.

Linc did most of the talking, of course. He was a walking library of military history and American diplomacy; he knew every detail of the French war; he had read Sun Tzu, long before that became popular, and understood Asian military strategy. He was one of those people who was somewhat older than he looked, which worked to his disadvantage among the higher-ups who didn't know him: he seemed a perpetual acolyte. He had a wife and children back home—a marriage going nowhere, he confided—and a striking, upper-class Vietnamese girlfriend in Saigon; Charlie had a marriage back home, too, also going nowhere. That was another thing they had in common.

For Charlie, the daily conversations with Linc balanced the ceaseless meetings where Lieutenant Martin had to sit against the wall, watching the pompous fools—including his pompous fool—at the main table, and not say a word because he was just a junior G-2 and no one ever asked his opinion. Junior intelligence officers weren't supposed to be intelligent; they were merely supposed to be officers.

For Linc, Charlie was a ticket to military authenticity—he couldn't hope to have guys like T. C. Kelly talk to *him* with any candor about the war. He was amazed and honored by Charlie's friendship: most military hotshots disdained the striped-pants boys. But Martin treated everyone the same. Even diplomats. It was an odd, democratic tic he had.

"Charlie," Linc said, less dismissively now—remembering who Charlie was, who Charlie had been, and trying to steer their phone conversation in a more affectionate direction. "You went to war because you were angry about the war. What pissed you off enough to run for president?"

"Oh, I don't know," Charlie said, laughing at Linc's formulation. "They all seemed like such dopes. It was beginning to seem so dopey."

"What?" Linc asked. "Politics?"

"No." Not politics. He loved politics—at least, the craft that Patsy Dunn and Clarice Martin had taught him: a cross between Petunia pragmatism and Mother Martin's morality. There was an elegance to good politics. It was celestial navigation—indirect, subtle, measuring your path by flickering lights, calibrating moving targets. It was all about finding the most artful way to frustrate your enemies, to achieve what you wanted. But the game had been mechanized and denatured by the marketers; it had grown ugly and stale. "Linc, you ever been to a focus group?"

"No."

"Bunch of average folks in a room," Charlie said. "It seems okay, almost natural. They're drinking coffee. They're eating cookies. Chatting about politics. You run things by them. Not you, a guy who you hire: *you* stand behind a two-way mirror and watch. You don't talk to the folks; they are talked to on your behalf. That's how you find out what works, what they want to hear—not just positions, but words. You find out which words are effective and which aren't. And then, you go out and use the good ones. Remarkable, huh?"

Linc didn't particularly think so. Everyone knew about focus groups.

"It's the exact opposite of leadership," Charlie said.

"No it isn't," Linc said. "It's just a tool."

"It's fucking *cheating*," Charlie said, furious. Linc realized that for Charlie Martin, running for president had been John Henry against the steam drill, starring Jack Stanton as the steam drill. The things that had always worked for Charlie—the spontaneity and informality, the casual courage, the willingness to think aloud and sometimes get angry—were disadvantages in a modern campaign. Anachronisms, perhaps.

"Linc, this focus group stuff is fucking dangerous. How can you trust someone to lead when they can't trust themselves to say the right thing?"

"Depends on the person," Linc said, not wanting to get into an argument about the efficacy of political marketing methods. He had hoped Charlie would eventually pause, reflect and adapt, but he was beginning to suspect that might never happen. Anyway, there was other business to discuss.

"You know, you're an asshole calling me this time of night, figuring I'd be awake," Charlie said, not too interested in ragging Linc about politics, either. "What is it, midafternoon there?"

"Coming up on four in the morning," Linc said. "I'm in Singapore."

"No kidding. Watching *Harum Scarum*?"

"Sumo wrestling on *Prime Sports*," he said. "But I flipped around. I knew it was there."

"What are you doing in Singapore? Bidness?"

"Yes, and also . . . Actually, I was going to do a bit of work for the government. . . ."

"You're working for the Republicans now?"

"There's some work the Republicans can't do for themselves, not while they're in office—at least, they don't think so, which is ridiculous."

"Enough, Linc. What are you doing?"

"Vietnam," he said. "You been following this Mustafa Al-Bakr situation?"

Charlie hadn't been following anything except Schollwengenalia.

"Vietnam vet, black guy, gets caught by the Vietnamese coming down the Mekong from Cambodia in an outboard. They toss him in jail, the word gets out and the veterans' groups back home are going berserk. What the veterans don't know, what the Vietnamese don't say, is that the boat is filled with all manner of combat matériel—Kalashnikovs, Thompsons, RPG launchers, ammo—and heroin and, you are going to love this, a stash of Rambo tapes, just to really piss them off."

"Cool," Charlie said. "Why don't the Vietnamese just tell the world what they caught him with?"

"For several reasons." Rathburn was now deep into smooth, mellifluous briefing mode. "Mostly, because they don't want to keep him. They don't want anything that looks like a POW situation just as they're angling for diplomatic recognition. They also probably figure that if they announced what he was carrying, no one would believe them."

"So, why was he—"

"Don't know. He won't talk to the Vietnamese. Just gives name, rank and serial number. The spooks think he's either running guns to one of the drug gangs in the area or, more likely, that he's just some madman who wanted to restart the war."

"And what is his name, rank and serial number?"

"Mustafa Al-Bakr. Born Frederick Carter, Paterson, New Jersey—honorable discharge from the Marines, purple heart. No criminal record, except for a couple of possession busts right after he came back. Worked in the shipping department for a catalog company in York, Pennsylvania, until three months ago. Then he disappeared. He's got a common-law wife and a couple of kids. She says she doesn't know why he's in Vietnam, and doesn't care. Just as long as he never comes back."

"Why? Did he smack her around or something?"

"Don't know," Linc said.

"Noncom?"

"A corporal."

"And let me guess," Charlie said. "Since the administration doesn't deal with the Vietnamese officially, they asked you to go in and get him out."

"Well, I *was* going to do that," Linc said, working up to the punch line. "Then I heard that you were out here—and I figured that you'd be a lot better at this sort of mission than me. In fact, even if you hadn't been out here, I would have suggested you for this. . . . Interested?"

"Fuck no."

"Charlie—"

"No."

"A United States senator. A decorated veteran. A fellow Marine. I wouldn't know what to say to the guy. You can *bond* with him," he said, laughing now. "You can tell war stories—"

"Fuck you, Jack."

"And you can make everyone forget about Martha Schollwengen, get a little bit of your good name back, become a hero to the veterans' groups. If you bring him back alive."

"Bring some loony grunt back into the world? No thanks, Linc," Charlie said, but he *was* beginning to think about it.

"Have you been back to Vietnam?" Linc asked, knowing that Charlie hadn't been. "It's still there, the way it was. It's not like Bangkok. You might want to check it out before it becomes like everyplace else."

"It will never be like everyplace else," Charlie said, "for me."

"There's an added bonus," Linc said. "You know who the Vietnamese contact is, the guy we're working through?" He paused a beat. "An old friend of yours, Quoc Van Huong."

"Thua's uncle?" Charlie said. "He worked for AP?"

"And for the VC, as it happened. He mustered out a general."

"Thua's uncle was VC?"

"They don't make that distinction," Linc said. "They now say there never was a Viet Cong. It was all one liberation army—"

And Charlie had been a prime source of information: all the meals and drinks they'd had, bitching about the stupidity of the brass—how many times had Quoc been there, quietly listening? How much had they told him?

"The Frito Bandito," Charlie said.

"Excuse me?"

"You don't remember, Linc?" They had called him the Frito Bandito because he had the miniature Mexican look that some of the Vietnamese men seemed to favor: longish, curly black hair, small round face with cocoa skin and a scraggly black mustache. A deep, residual fear began to rise from Charlie's innards up through his chest: "God, Linc—what did we tell him? You think we got anyone killed?"

"We got a lot of people killed," Linc said softly. "But not because we were talking to him."

"Did you see Thua?" Charlie asked. "You think she knew?"

"Who knows?" he said, too easily.

Clearly, he hadn't seen her or even thought to ask about her. Thua would be in her forties if she was still there, still alive: Other memories of Saigon were beginning to come back now—not the obvious things, the nights on the roof of the Caravelle or in the café at the Continental— but street scenes, the street the AP office was located on, the reporters who lived on Rue Pasteur, and Thua, who had been Rathburn's girl, de- mure and gorgeous, prohibitively proper, the Vietnamese equivalent of a Calvinist.

"Remember your going-away party?" Charlie asked.

"Barely," Rathburn said. "At Brodard's, right?"

"Yeah." Charlie said, wincing at a particular memory of that night.

"Brodard's is still there," Linc said. "The government runs it now. And Givral's as well. So—"

"I'm not going," Charlie said.

"Oh yes, you are," Linc replied, utterly confident. And with good rea- son: they hadn't been friends so long for nothing.

*   *   *

Remarkably, the Vietnamese government provided Charlie with a room at the stolid, stucco Rex Hotel in the center of Saigon, where he had been billeted in 1964. It was another case of traveling an eternity and going nowhere—although the Rex was not quite the same as it had been in his day. It was now air-conditioned and renovated for the Japanese businessmen and German tourists who clumped through; and there was cable—CNN, even there. He was given a better room than he'd had in the old days, as a junior staffer. It faced the small park in front of the hotel, but was close enough to the corner of Le Loi that Charlie could see a good slice of the Music Hall, painted a blinding noonday yellow, and a thinner slice of the Caravelle Hotel, which was where the journal- ists had hung out. Saigon was like a dream, he thought, literally like a dream: as if the Americans, the big Green Machine, had never been there.

He had landed in late morning. A silent, smiling Vietnamese driver wearing a white short-sleeved shirt and gray pants picked him up at Tan Son Nhut—where there were still reinforced concrete revetments near the runways, but most of the old military construction, including the Mil- itary Assistance Command Vietnam (MACV) headquarters, had been torn down. He was breezed through customs, and into an air-condi- tioned official sedan, recently purchased from the Japanese.

They floated slowly through the traffic, which was, if anything, thicker than he remembered—only a few cars, but millions of motorbikes, scattered cyclos, bicycles and carts. The trees were still painted white at the base. And then there were the girls: They paraded on motorbikes, wearing baseball caps or—fabulously, incomprehensibly—straw trilby hats, with long opera gloves to protect their skin from the sun. Not so many in *ao dais* anymore, which was unfortunate: he'd always thought it the perfect garment for an Asian woman, a deeply slit sheath over billowy pants, prim and sexy and exotic. Now they wore T-shirts and blue jeans. He did not take notice of a single male Vietnamese on the ride from the airport to the hotel, only the women—their hair, long and lustrous, or stylishly bobbed, their faces shielded by sunglasses, and sometimes surgical masks; there wasn't much of them to be seen, in truth, but what there was . . . was understated, unspoiled; the juxtaposition of their slight, shy femininity and the jauntiness of their motorbikes was stunning. And that, he realized, was part of what had gotten the Americans into so much trouble: a not very subtle—indeed, a rather virulent—strain of sexual arrogance. They had mythologized the women; underestimated the men. No wonder the Banditos had fought back so tenaciously, so well.

Charlie had been given no instructions by the driver, and he was so overwhelmed by the sights and memories and oddities that he didn't think to ask about ground rules. He wondered if he was allowed to leave his hotel room. No one was guarding the door. He ambled down the hall to the elevators. Up or down? Up, to the Rex roof bar—which was much as he'd remembered it, with the kitschy plaster statues of elephants and such, tropical fish swimming in tanks and birds in cages—and the city rumbling below in the deep heat of early afternoon, beneath the preindustrial luxury of a blue sky; Bangkok's had been a sickly, polluted banana-pulp yellow. He looked south, to where the war had been. They had spent evenings on that roof watching the distant tracers and flashes, an insinuation of percussive impact in the wind.

For the first time in years, Charlie had a craving for a Coca-Cola. But he was too wired and antsy, too curious about the possible limits on his theater of operations to order one at the rooftop bar, which was populated by the inevitable, bleached Aussie-Israeli backpackers, who were busy discussing nature walks through the Delta or buses to Dalat, in the highlands. They were quite oblivious to what those place names conjured to an American of his vintage—and Charlie didn't want to tell them, as he knew he would have to, when they asked, "Ever been to . . . ?" So he went back down to the lobby, and out to the street—and into Vietnam.

There was a crowd of barefoot children in front of the hotel, with postcards and trinkets; they were precisely the same as the kids of his era, pushy and cheery. There were cyclo drivers and motorcycle boys—Charlie shook them all off, glanced over his shoulder to see if there was anyone following him (if there was, he probably wouldn't know—he wasn't trained in that sort of streetcraft), and surprised himself by turning right at the corner of Le Loi, away from the more intense memories located along Tu Do, into the full blast of the city. And quite a blast it was: noise and traffic and heat and smell, the familiar, funky Asian combination of sweat and spice and shit, of exhaust fumes and cooking oil. He walked along the shady side of Le Loi.

There was a row of souvenir shops with goods spilling out into the street. Charlie felt a sudden shock of nausea—the souvenirs were remnants of his defeat, the personal effects of his comrades: dog tags, compasses, field maps and kits, shell casings, utility belts, neatly stacked piles of Zippo lighters; a blithe, matter-of-fact display. He reached out for the dog tags, but couldn't quite bring himself to it—he reached, he realized, with his left hand, as if it were still there—and pulled back, terrified, steadying himself with his right hand on the chilled smoothness of the Zippos. A mamasan guarding the stash said, "No fake. No fake. Real stuff. Cheap."

So that was it. They seemed pretty real. The Zippos were personalized, engraved, with maps of Vietnam on one side and words on the other. The words were sappy or defiant, with few stops in between:

> To Corporal Ronald Dekins
> From Joanne Mokreski
> Love Always
> Marion, Ohio, May 12, 1969.

One said:

> PFC Eugene Lenwood—My Epitaph
> If I Die in a Combat Zone
> Bury me Facedown
> So the World Can
> Kiss My Ass.

Charlie turned away, into the street, into the traffic and froze there, a woman on a red motorbike bearing down on him, just brushing past him, passing him by. The traffic bent and curled to avoid him, as if he were a rock in a stream. It was a curious sensation, half remembered and not unpleasing; he began to move, gingerly, across the street—and through the traffic, which parted effortlessly for him, as it always had. He disappeared into the middle of it, and came out the other side, into the harsh sunshine. He walked diagonally, along Ham Nghi, toward the river, sweating now, pitting out his knit short-sleeved shirt.

He spent the next few hours walking as the shadows lengthened. Up Tu Do, the main restaurant and hangout street, which the French had called Rue Catinat and the Communists now called Dong Khoi, down to the prim, redbrick cathedral—and then right, down Le Duan, where the American embassy stood spectral white in the late afternoon shadows, locked and abandoned, the spookiest place in town. He gazed up at the abrupt, flat helipad on the roof: a perfect monument, the indelible symbol of defeat and disgrace—a result he had predicted, but never expected, in 1965. He stood there for a time until a man approached, a youngish-looking older man, with thick, slicked-back black hair, and harsh, angular cheekbones that seemed far too large for his tiny, hollow face.

"You know this place?" the man asked. Charlie nodded. "I work here, drive for the Americans."

"What do you do now?" Charlie asked.

"My family go to America," he said, not answering. "You help me go there, too?"

"No," Charlie said. "Sorry. I can't."

The man didn't seem surprised or disappointed. "You want girl? You want massage?"

Charlie went back to the hotel, lay down and fell asleep. It was a groggy, inappropriate jet-lag sleep and he awoke, chilled and hungry, around two in the morning. There was no room service, or phone service; there was nothing to do but wait.

By morning, the lack of official attention was beginning to get on his nerves. It seemed a distinctly Asian power trip: were the Vietnamese demonstrating their utter control by leaving him adrift, without a minder? Or had they just forgotten him? He ate breakfast, tried to phone out—to the consular officer in the Bangkok embassy who had handled his papers (in the vain hope that he might know something), to Rathburn, to Donna.

The mechanically polite operator said, "Oh yes. You hang up. I make call." He waited an hour. He wasn't very good at waiting. He called the operator again. She said, "Oh yes. You hang up. I make call." He watched CNN: Stanton had won more primaries. Larry King came on at eight in the morning, real time: it was still the night before back home—and various familiar faces were yapping about what the latest Stanton victories meant. It was torture, watching this.

At about 10:45 A.M., the Vietnamese who had met Charlie at the airport knocked on the door and said, "Okay?"

They drove back out toward the airport through the noonday heat, hung a left down a narrow lane of small restaurants and shops, the restaurants filled with tiny people squatting on miniature plastic stools, slurping *pho* from deep bowls, heads bent over their work with the intense time-conscious focus of pieceworkers in a sweatshop. The lane ended abruptly in an arched entrance to what was obviously the prison. A tall iron gate, painted a very serious gunmetal gray, loomed on the far side of a courtyard. There was a small door cut into the gate, emphasizing its hugeness; the surrounding walls were ten feet high, whitewashed stucco, topped with concertina wire. Inside the walls was a gray stone building of colonial vintage. This had once been a French prison.

The two gatekeepers were wearing fresh, vivid olive uniforms, with fuchsia and gold epaulets. They weren't exactly spit-and-polish. One was overweight; his partner's shirttail was almost hanging out. So these were the enemy? Actually no, they weren't: these were their children—and they obviously weren't cadre; they were prison guards.

The driver showed his ID at the guardhouse, and they pulled into the courtyard. As they passed through the gate, Charlie felt a bit constricted and, he had to admit, frightened. He was in an enemy prison. He was made to wait in a small room—made smaller by a high ceiling, made higher by barred window slits near the top of the wall, slants of light hitting a foot higher than head level, which enhanced the sense of inaccessibility. It was an intelligently planned room, designed by a sadist. There was a blond wood table in the middle of the room—a Soviet import, no doubt—and wooden chairs on either side. Charlie sat and waited, practicing the slow breathing technique he'd learned in recon school: combat repose.

After fifteen minutes, an officer with lighter skin than the guards entered and offered his hand. "Senator Martin," he said. "I am Lieutenant Truong."

Charlie nodded. Truong seemed a bit unsettled; he glanced about the room and sighed. "Senator, the prisoner says he does not wish to see you."

"How do I know that?" But Charlie knew how he knew that: jailers usually can find a way to make prisoners do what they want.

"Senator, this is very embarrassing for us, too," Truong said.

"Can I go to where he is?" Charlie asked.

"I . . ."

"You don't want me to see the conditions in this prison," Charlie said, standing abruptly. "That is outrageous, a violation of the Geneva Convention." Although he was pretty sure it wasn't.

"No, Senator, I assure you," Truong said. "Excuse me for a moment. Allow me to make a phone call."

Another fifteen minutes. Charlie was torn between the stern official outrage that he was trying to affect, and sympathy for the Vietnamese: Mustafa was clearly a handful. Of some sort.

"All right, Senator," Truong said, when he returned. "We can go."

Through yet another set of bars, down a corridor running along a triple-layer cake of cells, the echoey sounds and pungent smells like the elephant cage at the Des Pointe Zoo. Through another set of doors— Charlie had completely lost his sense of direction now—to a guardpost. Truong said something to the guard, who handed him a single key. "We have him in the guard's room," Truong said, "away from other prisoners. We bring in food from hotel, but he refuses it. He wants prison food. . . ."

"Open the door," Charlie said, attempting impatience. "Please."

"Of course," Truong said.

Mustafa Al-Bakr, dark and tall and overweight, was stretched out on a cot. He was wearing jeans, a blue denim shirt and construction boots; Charlie assumed these were the clothes he'd brought with him. The room was less threatening than the first. There was a desk and chair; a locker. The walls were beige, hung with travel posters from Vietnam Airlines. There was a small black-and-white television on a shelf in the corner, a dim picture buzzing with interference, a Mexican soap opera dubbed into Vietnamese.

Charlie pulled the chair from the desk and nodded at Truong, who left them. "You okay?" he asked Mustafa, who stared at the ceiling, arms crooked behind his head—and ignored his visitor ostentatiously.

"Is this where they keep you, or did they just plant you here for my benefit?" Charlie asked.

No answer.

"All right," Charlie said. "I'll just sit here until you say something. I can stay as long as you want to be an asshole, but you don't strike me as the sort of guy who does well with roommates."

Mustafa pulled a long, thin pack of cigarettes from his shirt pocket— Virginia Slims; he lit up with a Zippo, then reached down to the floor with his left hand and retrieved a saucer, which he placed on his stomach. He held the cigarette delicately, incongruously, in his right hand; he seemed to caress the smoke, drawing it in through his nostrils, exhaling perfect rings, still staring directly at the ceiling.

"The Rambo tapes were a brilliant touch," Charlie said.

"I wanted to piss them off," Mustafa replied, in a heavy, resonant smoker's voice.

"And the drugs, and the arsenal?" Charlie asked. "Was that to piss them off, too?"

"Takes a fair amount to get them ticked, it turns out," Mustafa said, with a satisfied smile—but still without looking at Charlie.

"So why'd you want to piss them off?" No response. "Still fighting the war?" Charlie immediately regretted that: it was the sort of thing someone who hadn't fought the war might say. He considered the possibility that he just wasn't very good at hostage negotiation.

"They put me up at the Rex," Charlie said, trying the tactic that always worked in similar situations in the movies: first establish a point of common experience. "It was my BOQ in '64."

"REMF," Mustafa said, meaning: rear echelon motherfucker. "In the rear with the gear," he said.

"For a while," Charlie said. "Then I MOOSEd."

"MOOSEd?"

"Moved Out Of Saigon Expeditiously," he said. "It was a MACV deal when the Vietnamese get nervous about having so many of us in town. Actually, I MOOSEd myself—out to the boonies."

"MOOSEd," he chuckled. "That's good."

"It don't mean nothing," Charlie said, falling back—a little too consciously—into gruntspeak.

"It didn't," Mustafa corrected him, "mean *nothing*. . . . So what's your story: I'm from the government and I'm here to help?"

"Happened to be in the neighborhood, so I decided to drop by."

"I'm not leaving."

"They don't want you here," Charlie said firmly. "I'm here to negotiate your withdrawal."

"Oh really?" he said. "I thought you were the USO."

"So why *did* you insert yourself in an enemy prison?" Charlie was beginning to lose patience. Mustafa had stopped smoking and put the ashtray back on the floor; he stared at the ceiling, hands clasped behind his head. He had not deigned to look at Charlie yet.

"None of your fucking business," Mustafa said. "I belong here."

"In Vietnam or in jail?"

Silence again. The prisoner closed his eyes and yawned.

"You're still here?" Mustafa said, after a moment. He looked at Charlie, finally. "Leave," he said, with perfect, understated drama. Mustafa, it seemed, was something of a thespian. Then, noticing the senator's mangled hand, he said: "How'd you get that, *sir*? Grunts frag you?"

"Enemy grunts," Charlie said.

"There you go. Why, you must have been a hero," Mustafa said, staring at Charlie evenly now.

"No more than most," Charlie said, refusing to acknowledge the sarcasm. "You got a purple heart, too, I hear."

"Big fucking deal."

"How'd you get it?"

"Shrapnel," Mustafa sighed. "It wasn't the most interesting thing that happened to me here. It was just something they gave me a medal for. I bet you got a shitload of medals. You look the type."

"What *was* the most interesting thing that happened to you here?"

"You get the medals for killing lots of enemy? Did you *get some?*" Mustafa asked, using the old grunt term of art.

"I did—kill some. Of them." Charlie noticed that Mustafa didn't call them gooks or slopes.

"How?"

"How did any of us do it?" Charlie said. "We did it, didn't we?"

"It didn't mean nothing," the prisoner said disdainfully. "Right?"

"Why are you here?" Charlie asked again, but less officially—he really was curious now. "What's this about?"

"I belong here," Mustafa said, again. "That's what it's about. Now get lost." He rolled onto his side, turned his back.

"Corporal," Charlie said, "the Vietnamese want you to come out with me. They're willing to forget about the guns and drugs, and the Rambo tapes. They don't want you here."

Silence.

"Let me lay it out for you," Charlie said. "The veterans' groups think you're a POW. The Vietnamese are desperate for diplomatic recognition and they will do anything to make the American Legion and the VFW forgive and forget. I don't know how you feel about it, but I think it's time we let them off the hook. That's not going to happen as long as you're here. You're a complication. A bone in the throat."

Silence. Truong was back now. He'd obviously been plugged into the conversation somehow. "Do you want more time?" he asked.

"Yes," Charlie said.

"No," Mustafa said. "Get Colonel Martin the fuck out of here before I do something stupid and hurt someone."

*   *   *

The driver met Charlie at dusk to visit, finally, with Quoc. It was a lovely time of day in Saigon, soft light and a mild breeze off the river, the afternoon heat broken. "Let's open the windows, turn off the air-conditioning," Charlie suggested. "I want to feel the night."

"The night smelly," the driver said, making a face. Charlie sat back, suitably chastened. He was still stymied by Mustafa. He'd tried to call out from the Rex—to Linc, to Donna, to the Bangkok embassy—desperate for advice. Weren't there people who did this sort of thing for a living? He felt incompetent, foolish. The presidential campaign—another festival of foolishness that he'd managed to forget in the wonder of Vietnam—came rushing back. He considered the possibility that he was becoming habituated to failure. How did a person walk along the street, look in colleagues' eyes, or in the mirror, having been judged a perpetual loser? It was unimaginable.

Quoc's house was not far from downtown. It was situated on a narrow side street near the Circle Sportif, the old colonial tennis club. There was a whitewashed cement wall, and a wide wrought-iron gate, painted baby blue, that opened into a driveway filled with bikes and a red Toyota sedan. The house was an unimposing, boxy rectangle—it looked high enough to carry two stories, but there was only one. There was a small dirt yard with several banana trees and assorted palms in the front.

An ancient, petite mamasan answered the door and did not introduce herself. She ushered Charlie into a large, high-ceilinged room that seemed to serve as living room, dining room and kitchen. The dining room table was in the rear right corner, surrounded by bookshelves. There was a parlor area—a couch, two chairs, a wooden plank coffee table—in the front. There were electric lights, but they seemed dim; there was a ceiling fan, but it was not on. A UNESCO calendar and faded rural prints were scattered about the walls, which were painted a washed-out gray-green. The room seemed a relic of the late sixties, recently re-opened after several decades of nonuse.

Quoc entered from the rear. Charlie barely recognized him. His mustache was gone, his scraggly Bandito hair slicked back, the flesh on his face wrinkly and slack, but his dark eyes were as coy and quiet as ever. He was wearing a white shirt with thin blue pinstripes, the sleeves rolled up, the top two buttons undone. The skin on his chest seemed a waxy gray-green, like the walls of the room. He carried a package of Rothman cigarettes and a gold lighter in his left hand; he extended his right to his visitor. "Senator Martin. Charlie," he said. "So good to see you."

"Mr. Quoc," Charlie said, with the hint of a bow. "Or should I call you General Quoc?"

"Oh," he laughed, a tiny laugh. "They just called me a general after the war—in order to annoy the Americans, I think. Are you annoyed?"

"A little," Charlie admitted. "But I would have been annoyed anyway. At myself. For not knowing. For anything I said that helped you."

"You have very little to be annoyed about," he said, sitting down, putting his feet—he was wearing Nikes and white athletic socks—up on the coffee table. "You didn't reveal very much. There wasn't much to be revealed. My work was defensive, to save lives—"

"I'll bet," Charlie said. "The restaurant bombing—at the floating restaurant, was that you?"

"No," Quoc replied. "I knew nothing of that, or any of the other acts of sabotage. It would have been dangerous for me to know, or for those cadre to know about me. I had a happy job. I watched over your journalists, and your diplomats, and reported back what you knew and what you were feeling. You knew nothing. You were feeling depressed."

"We were geniuses," Charlie said.

Quoc lit a cigarette. "You don't smoke, of course," he said. "My doctor says I should not. I am not feeling very well these days. My health has not been good since reeducation camp."

"Reeducation camp? Why?"

He smiled. "I spent too much time around Americans. My superiors are very cautious. They do not like to take chances. I never gave them good information, they think. But as I said, there was no information. You didn't know anything."

"And were you reeducated?"

He snorted, derisively. The mamasan, a tiny woman with skeptical eyes, barefoot, wearing gray cotton pajamas, came in with tea—and Fritos. "A little joke," he said. "This is Madame Quoc."

Charlie stood. She waved him back down, scowled and left. Quoc poured tea, offered the Fritos with a smile.

"We were fools," Charlie said. "You must think we're real jerks. First, the war. Now we're back looking for skeletons. You must love us."

"No, no," he said. "Quite the contrary. Vietnamese have a great deal of respect for the Americans."

"Why?"

"You build good roads."

Charlie laughed.

"I'm serious," he said. "You did amazing things here. The bridges, the buildings, the runways that appeared overnight. Our people talk about the things we did—the tunnels, the networks of resistance, the devotion. But you were devoted, too. We learned a lot about how to work from you. More in ten years from you, than in a hundred years from the French. We have great affection for you Americans."

"Sure you do," Charlie said.

"You have good qualities."

"We build good roads."

"And you're not Chinese. That is an excellent quality," Quoc said, coughing. He covered his mouth, turned his head, paused a moment and then added, "And you're not Japanese, which is also very good."

It was dark outside now; the light inside was grainy and weak. Quoc decided to get down to business. "So, Senator, this drug-dealing hero who is now enjoying our hospitality," he said. "Will you be able to 'liberate' him?"

"I don't know," Charlie replied. "If he was only a drug dealer, there wouldn't be a problem. He'd want to be liberated. But I don't think he was very interested in dealing drugs."

"Neither do I," Quoc said.

"Why didn't you just hustle him out of the country? Or dispose of him quietly. There must be ways."

"We were fortunate that none of our people who captured him took action," Quoc said, and then, seeing the senator smile, he added, "No, really—we were quite lucky there wasn't an . . . accident. There are sensitivities involved here, and not just among your veterans' groups. And there was—is—always the possibility that Mr. Mustafa is one of your operatives, a little test for us. A test of our civility, our willingness to cooperate."

"If so, you passed," Charlie said.

"Quite so," Quoc said. "Now, can you handle this for us?"

"I'm not sure." Charlie shrugged and shook his head.

Madame Quoc was back, with *pho*. She put out bowls for the two of them on the dining room table, and retreated to the kitchen. The smell—garlic and lemongrass and cinnamon—blended naturally with the faint tropical mildew of the room. Quoc immediately attacked the soup, slurping noodles noisily, unself-consciously; he looked up at his guest, saw him delicately pincing bits of beef and sprouts with his chopsticks. Charlie decided to ease Quoc's hostly concern about the quality of the meal by diving in.

"So," Quoc asked, when they were done. "Will you talk to him again?"

"Sure, but—he didn't seem very interested in talking to me." Actually, there had been one thing Mustafa seemed interested in talking about, which Charlie had avoided. "Why don't you tell him I'm coming back, and I've decided to answer his question."

"Which question?"

"You'll find out when you transcribe the tapes."

Their business was finished. Quoc leaned back in his chair.

"Have you heard from . . . ?" They both started, simultaneously.

"Thua," Charlie finished. They might have laughed at the coincidence, but they were both shocked—at least, Charlie was. And confused, too: Why did Quoc think *he* would have heard from her?

"She's in America. In Houston," Quoc said. "I would have thought—"

"I didn't know," Charlie said. "I don't think Rathburn knows, either."

"Ahh, Rathburn," Quoc said, with a smile. "You really *don't* know, do you?" He called out something in Vietnamese. Madame Quoc shuffled back in, with a photograph. A family picture. There was Thua, looking rather matronly, but still beautiful in a white, sleeveless dress, standing between two men on a terrace. There was a Caucasian man on her right—dark suit, balding, glasses, solid but unspectacular, his left arm was around her back. The man on her left was a boy, a teenager; their son, no doubt—with a splash of dark Asian hair, but with a casual, decidedly American look to him.

"Who's the guy?" Charlie asked.

"Dr. Richard Rosenbaum," Quoc said. "Thua is Mrs. Richard Rosenbaum of Houston, Texas."

Charlie suppressed a smile. But then he noticed that Quoc, and Madame Quoc, were staring intently at him. "It's an old photograph," Quoc said. Charlie nodded. Madame said something in Vietnamese to her husband. "A wedding photograph," Quoc added. "From 1982."

A wedding photograph. "So the boy is not their son?" Charlie asked.

The Quocs exchanged a glance, and more Vietnamese. "No," Quoc said.

Charlie looked more closely at the boy. There was something about his look. It emanated from his eyes, his eyebrows, his *left* eyebrow; it was an insouciance—a performer's look, he was performing for the camera in a way Thua and Dr. Rosenbaum weren't. And then, from a distance of time, from deep in his childhood, Charlie heard the words that went along with that look. It was Buzz, saying, "Thank you. Thanks a bunch, folks. You want to hear another?"

Charlie disappeared. He felt himself falling into the photograph, then back to the night of Linc's Saigon going-away party, a raucous and liquid evening at Brodard's. Everyone had gone with Linc to the airport; he remembered the humidity and jet fuel hanging dense in the air, a numbing fog. He had taken Thua home. She was fairly well blasted, as was he, and, well—this was one time when she hadn't been entirely dignified. The next afternoon, he went to her house and apologized, wondering if the apology would be the start of something nice for them—but she had collected herself, was a very proper Thua again. The night before hadn't happened. And then, very soon, Charlie was gone, too.

"The boy is my grandnephew." Quoc moved behind Charlie, and put a hand on his shoulder. "And your son."

"Whoa," Charlie said—another familiar sound from his past: the sound he'd made flying through the air, after being blown back by the toe-popper on that paddy dike. *Whoooooa . . .*

*   *   *

"You asked how I killed them," Charlie said quietly, staring at Mustafa Al-Bakr. "And I didn't answer you directly. I killed them with guns and grenades, mostly. But once, on a mission into the north, I killed with my hands, and with a k-bar knife. I didn't feel anything. We were trained to not feel. It was a precise, mechanical operation. We called ourselves surgeons of death. That was the style. We were very proud of that. We didn't leave aces of spades on the bodies, like some of the other recon teams—that would have been inefficient, a waste of time and effort. We didn't even take ears."

"You look like shit," Mustafa said. They were sitting across from each other in the visiting room with the high slit windows. "You look like you're back in Vietnam."

"Rough night," Charlie said. There had been several other photographs, though none recent. The boy—his name was Cao Van Rosenbaum—was a guitar player. Thua, ever proud, had gone to Hong Kong during her pregnancy; she had gotten to America, somehow, from there. Quoc did not know why she hadn't contacted Charlie, or whether she had told the boy who his father was. And, of course, Charlie was the father—there could be no doubt of paternity. Actually, it was grandpaternity that was most clearly established. This was Buzz's grandson. He would be twenty-seven or so now. Charlie was curious, and appalled: his son, and Thua's? A bizarre combination. Too weird to contemplate. Too monumental to ignore.

"Reliving it?" Mustafa asked.

"What?"

"Killing them."

Oh, that.

Charlie didn't think much about that. The Vietnamese were warriors; the Americans were warriors. But he figured it wouldn't do any harm to let Mustafa get the impression that he was reliving the war—it seemed the sort of strategy a hostage crisis negotiator might use. He nodded quietly.

"Why were you there, in the north?" Mustafa asked.

"Three of our guys got themselves caught up there. They were being held prisoner, in a corral, in a ville," Charlie said. "We went in to take them out before they were moved to Hanoi."

"But you said you had a grunt company," he said.

"That wasn't until later, after I left force recon," Charlie replied. "I punched three tickets here. I did MACV in Saigon as a staff assistant in recon intelligence and planning. Then I went out with the snake-eaters, then I transferred back to the grunts." Actually, the transfer had been more complicated than that: a mutual recognition, by Charlie and the recon boys, that he didn't belong there. He could eat snakes, but he suffered from indigestion. So much had happened in Vietnam.

Mustafa was watching Charlie carefully, and Charlie stared back at him. Mustafa's long, thin face was thoughtful. His eyes were quiet. He held himself well. Charlie wasn't sure where to take it from there. "Why did you change your name?" he asked. "Are you religious?"

Mustafa chuckled. "Job security," he said. "You come on Muslim, the boss ain't gonna mess with you. You get treated real nice. They don't want the brothers with the bow ties picketing the front gate. So I have dual citizenship: I'm Mustafa to white folks, Fred to my friends."

"So, you want to tell me what this is all about?" Charlie asked. "Did you kill anyone?"

He laughed. "Of course I did. But this ain't about killin'. . . . The ones you killed, you think about them?"

"Sometimes," Charlie said. "More about the guys we brought out."

"Why?"

"Because they were all fucked-up," he said. "You don't want to know."

"All fucked-up," Mustafa repeated. "That's what we used to say. Say the words and see the pictures. You ever think we'd see things like that?"

"They trained the shit out of us in recon school. They trained us to eat glass," Charlie agreed. "They couldn't train us for the things we'd see."

But they weren't getting anywhere. "So if it's not about killing—" Charlie asked.

"It's about murder," he said. "I killed, and that was what it was. A job, not an adventure. I also murdered . . . I murdered a girl."

Charlie let it hang there. Mustafa was either going to tell the story, or he wasn't. He lit a cigarette, staring at Charlie as he did. He curled the smoke in through his nose, puffed out a perfect ring. Charlie remembered doing that, back in the boonies; Mustafa made him want to smoke again.

"There was no reason for it," Mustafa said evenly. "I just did it. I don't know how old she was, you never knew with them, but she was—I think of her as a teenager, just ripe, high little tits." He stopped.

"You raped her?" Charlie asked.

"No. That would have made *sense*," he said. "There would have been something human to it. This was cold. See, we're in a ville, just hanging, y'know? Waiting for the next thing to do. It wasn't a bad day. Just another day. Nothing heavy going down; I wasn't freaked or fucked-up or anything. I see this girl, walking along the road. She's got on that cone hat, white shirt, black pajamas. Typical girl; nothin' special. And I just dinged her. *BAP*. One shot, very precise. In the middle of the chest. No reason. No feeling. To this day. Nothing."

"You didn't think she was . . ."

"Oh, come on," he said. "There were evil villes, you know that, right? And there were friendly ones. And there were villes that just were there. I had no fucking reason on earth to shoot that girl. It was just target practice. The blood spread out like a bull's-eye on her chest. There must have been commotion, screaming, something after I did it. But I don't remember that. It was just *BAP*. Single shot. No excuses."

Charlie had heard a lot of stories. But never one like this: the most gratuitous atrocity imaginable. "And your squad leader, your lieutenant," he asked. "They didn't bring action on it?"

"We were depleted. They needed me. They hated my ass, but I did my killing work like a bastard. Lieutenant Randazzo said, 'Fred, you are one cold, sick fuck.' He got that right."

"You must feel something," Charlie said. "You're here."

"Uh-huh," he said. "There must be something. I'm looking for it. Like the man said, it don't mean *nothing*. There should be hell to pay. But there ain't. I can't shed a tear for the girl."

"That's hell, too," Charlie said, lapsing into therapeutic bullshit mode. It did seem the easiest way to go. "You ever try talking about this before? Go to a vet center or something?" Charlie had fought to fund the vet centers; he'd sponsored the bill. But now the words came out of his mouth stupid.

"Vet center. Right," Mustafa snorted. "Overweight white boys talkin' about how they can't get it up, or how they can't stop gettin' it up, or about their nightmares, or bitchin' about how America don't appreciate them," he said. "All of them so busy *feeling* shit. I ain't felt anything at all since that day. Nightmares? I don't even dream. Figure that one out, Chuck."

"But you are here." Again, Charlie thought he sounded stupid, formal.

"You commit murder, you do the time," he said. "It's the least I can do."

"You're not giving *them* any satisfaction," Charlie said. "You're not repaying any debt. They won. They don't care about making us pay anymore. You're only making it tough on them."

"Yeah, I know," he said. "Fucked-up world when you can't even get yourself busted for committing murder without causing all sorts of shit."

"So why don't you let them off the hook?"

"And then what?"

"Come back with me."

"And then what?"

"You go on like before," Charlie said. "Maybe it's God's way of making you pay."

"That's cold," he said.

"You want sympathy?" Charlie said. "I don't have any. You killed a girl. A lot of us did fucked-up ugly things, but most of the guys I knew didn't."

"Fuck you."

"Fuck *you*," Charlie replied, an involuntary reflex—but there it was. "Target practice! You say you want to pay, but what you really want is someone to say it's okay. Well, it ain't me, babe." He stood up, stared at Mustafa, who had drawn back from the table, shocked by the explosion. "Far as I'm concerned, you can stay here and rot. I could give a flying fuck. Guard! Truong!"

There were, Charlie realized, other options. He could tell the veterans' groups why the Vietnamese had busted this guy. He would have a certain amount of credibility. Truong and two guards appeared.

"No, wait," Mustafa said, quietly now. "This ain't no good."

Charlie motioned to Truong with his hand.

"I need to think about this," Mustafa said. "I need a plan."

Charlie's was about to tell him just how long he could sit there thinking, but his temper—which came and went—had gone. "That's your business," Charlie said. Then he thought of something: "My mother once told me a story about Gandhi—I'm not sure it's true, but it probably should be: A man once came to Gandhi and said, 'I've killed a child. Is there anything I can do to save myself?' And Gandhi said, 'Save a child.' "

"Phew," Mustafa said. "That's deep. . . . Your mother told you that?"

"Not only that, she lived it," Charlie said. He didn't add: to a fault. "Yeah?"

"She did community stuff, ran an antipoverty agency," Charlie said.

"You think I should do something like that?" Mustafa said.

"I don't know," Charlie said. "It's your life."

"That's cold," Mustafa said. "Hey, when you brought those other guys out, did they feel they owed you something?"

"One died on the way," Charlie said. "Another killed himself back home. I've had enough respect for the third to steer clear of him."

"Maybe you owed *them* something," Mustafa said.

"Fuck you, Fred," he said. "In or out, it's your call."

5

_____

Several hours after Mustafa agreed to be liberated, the phone in Charlie Martin's hotel room finally started working—incoming calls only. The first was from Lanny Scott. "Hey, guy!" Lanny said. "That little barbecue joint over past Tu Do still open? Did you _get some?_"

With his grand, portentous voice, Lanny had never been very good at gruntspeak, which was all irony and asperity, a tonal Asian language. In the old days, they had ragged Lanny mercilessly: he was too young, too gung-ho to be real; but he'd achieved lordly status one afternoon on the Perfume River, when he'd abandoned his camera crew and nearly gotten himself killed saving a Marine caught in an L-shaped ambush.

"How'd you find me, Scottie?" Charlie asked.

"Rathburn told me you were back there, up to no good," Lanny said. "He promised I could get to you before anyone else did."

"Get to me? Why? I'm not gonna do that Schollwengen thing."

There was a pause. "Charles, that's ancient history. You're Rambo, _dude!_" Scott said, with a laugh. "You liberated a prisoner of war."

Good news traveled as fast as bad news, it seemed; all news traveled too fast. "Lanny, it was more complicated than that," Charlie said.

"No doubt," Lanny said. "Was he running drugs?"

"How we talking, Lanny?"

"Over a beer." Meaning, off the record.

"It was a war-related thing," Martin said. "He wanted the Vietnamese to bust him."

"No kidding!" Lanny said, beginning to work Charlie. "Great story. You want to tell it?"

"No." Charlie cringed at the thought of a dog-and-pony show with Fred. Then again, if Lanny was right—and this was about to become a

big deal—the show would, undoubtedly, go on. "Well, maybe," he relented. "Gotta ask the POW." He sensed that Fred, who seemed quite
good at drawing attention to himself, would not be averse to publicity.

"Look, Charlie, I don't like to ask a personal favor," Lanny was actually
pleading. "But our new magazine show is in trouble. They want me to
help out, do some pieces. No question, you can get *60 Minutes* or anything you want—but it would mean a lot to me if you gave us first crack
at the story, if it's okay with this Mustafa guy."

He could get *60 Minutes* or anything he wanted? What a country.
Lanny took his silent amazement for calculation. "Look, I know you'll
probably want to think about this," he said.

"No," Charlie said. "If Mustafa says it's okay, we'll do it."

"Really?" he said. "Thanks, man. Hey, too bad you didn't pull this off
a couple of months ago." Lanny assayed a modified Marlon Brando: "You
coulda been a contender. You coulda gone all the way."

Lanny Scott was right. "Everyone" wanted *The Martin and Mustafa
Show*. Charlie was torn: he still didn't quite trust Mustafa, but the re-
demptive publicity would be an excellent career move after his presidential washout. He called Donna from Tokyo and had her schedule a
modest, limited Rambo tour: twenty-four hours in New York. Lanny Scott
got first crack, interviewing them for *Real People Live!*, the semiprurient
network news magazine show.

As it happened, Fred was a master of sound-bitery. He was mournful,
contrite for the cameras. Sensing something resembling a main chance,
he admitted that he'd probably been suffering from posttraumatic stress
disorder—a fabulously facile turnabout: Fred, who'd claimed an inability to feel anything a week earlier, was now emoting on cue.

And he dressed himself well. For their various television appearances,
Mustafa wore a black suit and a creamy collarless silk shirt buttoned all
the way to the neck; a cool dude, no doubt about it. "I just snapped," he
told Lanny. "I had been living with the . . . the horror, subconsciously, I
guess, Mr. Scott. I felt the need to pay for some things I did over there. I
wanted the Vietnamese to put me in prison."

"What things?"

"It doesn't matter now," Mustafa said sadly, shaking his head, feeling
The Horror for a national audience. "But I realized—Senator Martin
helped me realize—that the way to make amends is here at home. The

senator has gotten me a job driving a truck, picking up clothing and fur-niture for Goodwill Industries."

"Well, Senator." Lanny Scott turned to Charlie, who was having trou-ble keeping a straight face: had Fred taken media training in the past forty-eight hours? But then, Charlie had seen this phenomenon before, a standard-issue civilian transformed by the cameras, actually made more coherent than in real life. Community activists were often like that, and the metamorphosis was always slightly creepy. Being good on television was a synthetic "skill." His ex-wife, Johanna, had been that way: shock-ingly eloquent when the cameras came around. And his mother, too? Not quite. But almost.

The senator resolved to steer clear of Fred as soon as—as soon as they were finished being linked forever in the public mind. "Senator, you and I have known each other for how long?" Scott was saying. "More than thirty years? You've had to live with the war, too. At times, it seems to have influenced *your* behavior. . . ."

"Not so much, Lanny," Charlie chirped, and moved on, before Scott could nab him in a Schollwengen moment. "We've got to remember the war was a long time ago. We've got to put it in the past, where it belongs. In this case, I had the very strong impression that the Vietnamese were doing everything they could to be cooperative in the release of Mr. Al-Bakr. I think they're ready to let bygones be bygones, too." There, Char-lie thought: the sort of dull, solid response political consultants love.

"Now, this wasn't the first time you rescued a fellow soldier from Viet-nam, was it, Senator?" Lanny's perfect hair—it even mussed well, Char-lie had learned in landing zones a long time ago—was blindingly silver in the klieg lights.

"No, Lanny, but the other time was long ago—a different world."

"You won a silver star for your efforts—"

"*Received* a silver star, Lanny," Charlie said. "My recon team did. And in a tragic situation like that, given the sacrifices that were made, it proba-bly isn't appropriate to talk about *winning* anything. Most of the guys who really deserved the silver star never made it back."

There hadn't been many moments in the presidential campaign when he'd hit his marks so cleanly, so well. He was proud of himself, but feel-ing a bit soiled, too: saying *anything* in public about a medal was bad form.

"Senator," Lanny Scott said, with a sly grin, fully understanding what Charlie had just done, "there is talk now about you winning a place on the Stanton ticket, given this recent act of heroism on your part, plus your war record—and his lack of one."

"I don't know about that, Lanny." Charlie wondered if there really had been talk or if Lanny was just trying to create some news by saying so. The act of bringing back Fred, he suddenly realized, was far more impressive to civilians than winning a primary: it gave the appearance of real-life accomplishment (heroism, even: Lanny had called it his "latest act of heroism"). "And as I said, it's about time we put that war behind us."

Lanny, who had indeed just started the Charlie Martin for Vice President bandwagon, quietly admired the senator's equable response—and decided to have some fun, pushing the question. "Have you spoken with Governor Stanton?"

"The governor and I chat from time to time." Charlie remembered their last conversation: about the size of the Schollwengen breasts, and the loneliness of the three S's. He was dizzy with the velocity of his recovery.

"Is the vice presidency one of the things you talk about?" Lanny pressed, encouraged by the absence of a flat "no" from Charlie, and wondering if he was actually onto something.

Lanny was, but it wasn't what he thought: The immediate challenge—Charlie was surprised, and disappointed, and amazed, to find himself thinking this way—was how to respond to the question in a way Jack Stanton would find unobjectionable, perhaps even pleasing. "I'd be flattered if Governor Stanton were to seek my advice about the many fine potential candidates for vice president in our party, but from what I've seen of his political ability, and his sense of judgment, I have no doubt at all that he'll come up with the best possible person for the job."

The mechanical mouthing of banalities—phrases like "many fine potential candidates"—had always annoyed Charlie, bored him; it seemed cowardly and fake. That sort of blather was what normal people hated about politics. He had campaigned against it, implicitly, in the presidential primaries. And lost.

"Would you be available for the job?" Scott was surprised and disappointed to see Charlie Martin, of all people—the coolest guy in Saigon, the person Lanny had looked to as the tacit arbiter of acceptable behavior in wartime—sucking up to Jack Stanton. Charlie sensed the disappointment, and also something of a dare in the question: Lanny wanted something clever. He was hoping Charlie would be as outwardly casual about the possibility of the vice presidency as he'd once been about going into combat.

"I wouldn't kick it out of bed," Martin replied, taking up Scott's challenge. Lanny's first thought was: good old Charlie. But this was not Saigon. Which Charlie realized a beat ahead of Lanny, who watched, disappointed, as the senator scuffled to cover his tracks: "Look, I'm sure there are a lot of terrific candidates for the job out there, and Jack Stanton will choose someone eminently qualified." (Belatedly, Lanny understood: the "I wouldn't kick it out of bed" sound bite would find its way into every televised roundup of potential running mates.)

Charlie had just taken a WTF on national television.

Mustafa, meanwhile, had been lost in the shuffle, relegated to second fiddle in *The Charlie Martin Show.* He was stunned to see that his liberator was not just a senator, but a certified Big Deal: a possible vice president, and a significant career opportunity. In addition to the Goodwill gig, he would have to find a way to make himself useful. But that wouldn't be hard: white people needed black people, especially white politicians.

Charlie glanced at Fred and wondered how he would transition back to driving a Goodwill truck after the public love-bombing that had been visited upon them. That night they did *Larry King Live,* and he found Fred nuzzling with a chubby but not unalluring middle-aged stagehand after the show. "See you later, Brother Chuck," he said, assaying ghetto-speak. "What we got tomorrow, *Good Morning America?*"

*　＊　＊　＊*

"I will not let you spend another day in the world of men without someone handling you," Donna said, on the phone from Washington, after *Good Morning America.* "You thought about the 'I wouldn't kick it out of bed' line on Lanny Scott," she said. "I *saw* you thinking. It was premeditated. And, of course, it's gonna be 'Quote of the Day' today in *Hotline.*"

"I owed Lanny for not pressing Schollwengen," he replied.

"The fact that you think a 1960s fratboy line is a good sound bite qualifies you for the public relations intensive care unit."

"Okay, I screwed up. It happens," he admitted. "But Jack Stanton isn't going to put me on his ticket. He'd have to be nuts."

"Right, he would have to be nuts," Donna agreed.

"So, all right. You got some press secretary possibles lined up for me?"

"Three," she said.

"How did I know there would be three?" he said. "Any of them great-looking?"

"No."

"Good."

"You have appointments with all of them tomorrow morning," she said. "And the majority leader wants to see you in the afternoon. A woodshedding session, perhaps?"

"I suppose," Charlie said. "And we've got Fred set up with Goodwill in Anacostia, right?"

"Fred's pumpkin turns into a pickup next Monday. Let's hope he can handle it," Donna replied.

Charlie did not look forward to the return to business as usual—actually, slower than usual: election years were deadly on the Hill. And job interviews, especially for a job so intimate as press secretary, were hard work. You want to be charming. You don't want them to be nervous. But you also want to get some sense of how they'll react under pressure. It's a complicated thing, and without a handbook: there must be thousands of books about how to interview for a job, precious few on how to avoid hiring disastrous jerks to work for you. But his travails were made easier by a new set of home-state paintings, which he discovered when he settled in behind the big desk the following morning. One was a hilarious primitive: the world's most mournful-looking cow, staring straight at him in midchaw, straw sticking out the corners of its mouth. It was by Hilda Madison of Croft County. He'd send her a note.

All three of Donna's candidates for press secretary had rabbis. Brad Farley was Oskar's candidate; Heidi Bromberg came via the Senate majority leader's office; Hilton Devereaux had been recommended by Charlie's old press secretary, Jim Drake.

Brad Farley came first, and seemed straighter than most arrows. An Oskar Special, son of a gimp, of course: Lieutenant James Farley, left leg lost at the knee, Philadelphia Naval Hospital, 1967. Brad was Navy ROTC, out of Vanderbilt. Put in his four years of service, then two more working corporate clients at Hill, Holliday. No thank you, *sir*, when the senator offered him coffee or a soda. Blue button-down oxford shirt, red tie; blue suit; blue eyes; brush cut. His first move was to pull a yellow legal pad from his attaché case. With a list of Ideas: Senator Martin was now "positioned" to specialize in the normalization of relations with Vietnam. Not bad. "Of course, your positioning depends on your goals," Brad added crisply, and listed some possibilities: vice president? Cabinet slot if Stanton wins? Veteran affairs, maybe? "Perhaps you should think about campaigning for some of the Democrats running for Senate this year, especially those with war record and dove problems." Another good idea. But the kid was so damn serious, so unloose. For a good press secretary, Charlie Martin believed, the appearance of looseness was all.

"Nice to meet you, Brad," Charlie said. "Regards to your dad."

Next.

Heidi Bromberg. Nurse Blazer look; glasses, sallow skin, slightest hint of a mustache, few distinguishing sexual characteristics, nothing that seemed likely to tempt a lonely senator, though nothing off-putting either. Except her personality. "Could I have a diet Coke?" she asked straight out, and then proceeded to grill her prospective boss.

"What were you thinking, traveling alone in Colorado? A schmucky-putz number if I ever saw one," she said.

Schmucky-putz? "I don't know, I—"

"Look, you *need* to know in the future. If you don't know, you're gonna keep screwing up," Heidi Bromberg said. "You want me to do this for you, you need to make a commitment. I can stop these catastrophes. But you've got to want me, and you've got to be ready to get your act together. I've got other offers. Spielberg's looking for a Washington rep."

"Well, I—"

"And who in God's name put together your booking strategy for the Mustafa business? Lanny Scott, okay. But I would have tried for Baba Wawa on Friday night over Lanny on a Tuesday. Larry King, no-brainer. But what was that Vietnamese cuisine talk on *Good Morning America?* You're a United States senator, not a chef. And how safe is this Mustafa anyway? What if he blows up a housing project? You want to be that close to him?"

"A lot of times," Charlie explained, "I operate on my gut—"

She snorted. "Yeah, like I hadn't noticed," she said. "Like everyone in Washington hadn't noticed. Look, here's what they say about you: good-looking. Smart. Charming. Great résumé. Flakier than Kellogg's. Donna said you were ready to get real. My question is, how real you ready to get?"

"Not that real," he said.

"That's what I was afraid of," she said, gathered her stuff and left.

And so, Hilton Devereaux. He was tall, lanky, loose-jointed, with a high forehead and calm eyes under rimless glasses. "Would you like something to drink?" Charlie asked. "Coffee or a Coke?"

"Do you have decaf cappuccino?" he asked, with a warm, soft southern accent. Then he laughed. "Only kidding. I spent a year as a waiter on Venice Beach—my California period. Everyone who grows up in Mississippi wants to end up in California or New York, y'know. Anyway, that was the line of the year: 'Do you have decaf cappuccino?' As it happened, the place I was working didn't for the first couple of months. We were seriously behind the café curve."

"Did you like it out there?" Charlie was intrigued. "Why'd you leave?"

"It's one thing to be a waiter waiting for your big break as an actor or a screenwriter," he said. "It's quite another to be waiting for a slot to open in the mailroom at Creative Artists—and wait, and wait for it, and not get the call. Pretty pathetic. I thought I'd make a pretty good agent. I had a high concept: a nongreasy guy in a greasorama job."

"Like flacking for a senator?"

Hilton Devereaux smiled. A pleasant smile. Good teeth. "I like reporters, sort of," he said. "They're more fun than decaf cappuccino addicts. You'll see on the résumé, I worked several ballot initiatives out there. Green stuff, mostly. I started doing some press. Turned out I had an aptitude for soothing the savage beast. Drake suggested I come East, there was a spot at the D-triple-C." Charlie winced: the Democratic Congressional Campaign Committee. "But that's turned out to be megaboring," Hilton continued calmly. "I announce fund-raising totals, and where the chairman is headed next. I tout candidates whom I don't know and who have no chance. I'm not too good at lying. Not serious lies, at least—about breaking the law, or anything like that—or stupid lies, about losers who don't have a chance. On the other hand: useful, nontoxic half-truths, I can do."

"How would you have handled the Schollwengen deal?"

"Tell me about it," he said.

Charlie did.

"Can I say something insulting?" Hilton asked.

"Be my guest."

"You did a dumb guy thing," he said. "You had film of that cowboy decking you. He was in deep shit. I would have sent the world's most serious lawyer out there, very quietly, and told Schollwengen that we were going to bring criminal assault charges and a civil suit against him if he didn't get his daughter to admit, in a written statement, that she had panicked slightly—that she was such a Charlie Martin fan, that she was so excited by the prospect of driving you around, that she sort of lost it and, in retrospect, misinterpreted what was an innocent gesture on your part." He stopped, shrugged. "That sort of thing. At least, I'd try that for starters."

"Ducky sent you?" Charlie asked.

"Uh-huh."

"How come he didn't hire you?" he asked. "He's got a big operation over there."

"He wanted to," Devereaux said quietly, evenly. "But Larkin didn't." He saw that Charlie was about to ask Why the fuck not? and added, "Larkin doesn't hire homosexuals for high-profile positions."

"I do," Charlie said. "You're hired."

"Not so fast," Hilton Devereaux said, although he did like the senator's spontaneity. "I'm also poz. Nobody knows that, but I can't guarantee it won't get out."

"Poz?" But Charlie knew: HIV-positive. "How did—"

"You really want to know?" Devereaux smiled. "I didn't think so," he said. "Anyway, it's a tough call for you. At least, it should be. Not that I'm too sick to do the job. I take more pills than God ever knew existed, and I'm feeling just fine—but if my immune system starts rusting out, or whatever, I promise I'll let you know. If you hire me, I'll owe you that— for sure. But the part that I'm worried about is this: your state happens to be located in America, smack in the middle of it last time I checked. I'm not sure how a Mississippi queen plays in Des Pointe."

"One thing about people from my state," the senator said, glancing over at Hilda Madison's cow. "They're okay. We've got some assholes, of course. But most folks will take you for who you are, not what you . . . do. And if they don't, they're probably not gonna vote for me anyway."

"Yeah, Ducky said you didn't do well with the asshole demographic," Devereaux said.

"I can be one myself sometimes," Charlie said.

"Yeah, he said that, too."

"Consider yourself hired."

"Thanks," he said, standing. They shook hands. Good solid grip (amazing how even a broad-minded fellow like Charlie Martin clung to stereotypes). "Can I give you an opening piece of advice?" Hilton asked. Charlie nodded. "Six months running for president, Schollwengen, Vietnam—you *look* okay, but I'll bet you're whipped. Have you given any thought to a vacation?"

Charlie laughed. He loved the guy. "I tried that one already. Didn't take," he said. "What are you doing this afternoon?"

"Having my eyebrows waxed," he said. "Just kidding . . . testing your limits. I've got no plans. Anything you want me to do?"

"I'm going over to see Donny O'Brien at three-thirty. Maybe you should come, too," Charlie said. "Introduce you to the great man. Then you can go have your eyebrows waxed."

"Not in this lifetime," Hilton said.

*   *   *

As Senate majority leader, Donald Jeremiah Joseph O'Brien of Massachusetts lived somewhat better than his peers. He had a palatial suite of offices in the Capitol itself, on the second floor, just outside the Senate chamber. But he was uncomfortable in opulence, too big and clumsy for it, out of place in all the beautifully appointed rooms but one—a small side office, deep in the heart of the suite, in which he conducted most of his business. When he held court there, he fit himself into the room as if it were a sock, filling it snugly, completely.

But Donny was equally at home on the floor of the Senate. He was the Baryshnikov of the Well. From the galleries, he always seemed the center of the action—and, of course, he was easy to spot, with his famous white hair, bulbous nose and scarlet complexion. He was especially adept at the political equivalent of close-order drill: he invaded your space, leaned on you, took your elbow, steering you (literally, sometimes) in the direction he wanted you to go. Every move was graceful.

As it happened, Senator O'Brien was in neither of his usual lairs that day, but in his outer office—one hand on the elbow of a sleek-looking business type, the other mussing the caramel-colored hair of a small boy. His aide, Dov Mandelbaum, stood off in a corner; a photographer was front and center, trying to arrange the inevitable constituent photo. It was a large oval room, painted sky blue, with gold drapes and seascapes—but Donny made it seem small; he banged into the coffee table, trying to position himself between the businessman and the kid; the photographer pushed back a wing chair, trying to figure out how to get the oversized senator, the midsized businessman and the little boy into the frame.

"Hey-ho, Senator Martin," Donny said, reaching past the photographer to shake Charlie's hand.

"Good to see you, Senator," he replied. "I'd like to introduce you to my new communications director, Hilton Devereaux."

O'Brien kicked the photographer's gear bag trying to get at Hilton. "Oop. Little tight in here," he said. "Good to meet you . . . Hilton. Say something to me."

"It's a pleasure to meet you, sir."

"Hmmm," Don O'Brien said. "Not Louisiana, despite the French name. Something close: Mississippi?"

"You got it," Hilton said. "Tougoulala."

"Hilton Devereaux from Tougoulala, Mississippi," O'Brien said, chuckling and shaking his head. "Isn't that grand! Charlie. Isn't this just an amazing country? Oh. By the way, Charlie, say hello to Michael Price of the First New England Bank—one of our great financial institutions—and his son, Michael, Jr. . . . and we'll just record this moment for posterity," he said, arranging the photograph, steering Price, Sr., into place, flashing a quick smile, then working the Prices toward the door. "Mike, give my love to Doris—and oh, one other thing." He stopped abruptly, feigning an afterthought near the door. "You have a teller, Marie O'Connell, in your Brighton branch. You've had her there sixteen years, I think. Niece of Liam O'Connell, who works in my Boston office."

Donny paused a moment, as if he expected the sleek Mr. Price to say: *Oh sure, Marie! Grand gal! Splendid!* But the banker, who'd obviously not spent much time in the presence of political genius, said nothing and had no idea what was coming next. Nor did Charlie. But, knowing Donny, he sensed it would be glorious. "Well, Mike," O'Brien continued. "I'm sure this is a mistake, but Liam tells me that Marie is about to be laid off—something about your needing fewer tellers because of those new bank machines."

"Well, we are restructuring—" Price halted. Gathered himself. Started again. "But I'm sure, with sixteen years' experience, we'll be able to find a place for Ms. . . . ."

"O'Connell. Marie O'Connell," Donny said patiently. "That's very good, because Liam said your company's policy was to lay off your most senior—and most expensive—people out in the branches. And I told him that I was certain that couldn't be the case because you'd find yourself facing a *wickid pissah* of an age discrimination suit. Oop," Don said, turning to the boy. "Excuse my old donkey mouth, son. . . .

"And in Marie's case," he continued, "she's so well known in Brighton from knocking on doors for me—well." O'Brien chuckled. "You'd probably lose half your business out there, if word ever got around that you'd put her out to pasture. In fact, if you *do* manage to find a 'place' for Marie, it'd probably be wise to find it right in that Brighton branch. She walks to work; she doesn't like to drive."

Price looked as if he'd recently died. O'Brien had never stopped smiling, never changed his tone of voice and now he slapped the banker on the back. "So okay, Mike. Great to see you."

"And I'll be sure to take care of that," Price volunteered.

"I'm sure you will. Now," the senator said, turning away. "We have Senator Mahhh-tin. And you, Mr. Hilton Devereaux of Tougoulala: can I get you something to drink, or a telephone to play with, or is there something else you'd like to do while the senator is visiting me?"

"No, thank you, sir," Hilton said, glancing at Charlie.

O'Brien clamped Charlie's right elbow and funneled him toward his private office. Hilton, clearly uninvited, stayed behind. "And you, Senator, can I get you a Harp, or a coffee? Is there some beverage you wouldn't 'kick out of bed' this afternoon?" Charlie winced and shook his head no. "Dov, could you round me up some tea?" he asked, sidling in behind his desk, staring over Charlie's head at the portrait of his deceased wife, Fiona, on the back wall. "How'd you like that guy, Fee?" he said to the painting. "Wanting to fire Liam's niece. Bloodless Brahman bastard."

"He never knew what hit him," Charlie congratulated O'Brien.

"He knew all too well," O'Brien replied. "I hit him."

"I'll say," Charlie said, not stroking. He liked Don O'Brien.

"High praise from a fellow who knows how to roll with a punch," O'Brien said, getting down to business. "You've had an *adventurous* season of politics, Senator Martin."

O'Brien stared at Charlie, measuring his contrition in advance: it was a shame, the majority leader thought, that the boy was Scots-Irish and not a purebred. If his blood were as Black Irish as his looks, he might have been a better pol—although O'Brien had been as surprised as anyone by Martin's presidential flameout. He'd have to spend some time in the penalty box now, despite the Vietnam exploit—and Don saw that Senator Martin understood that. The kid was easier than most of the preening, thick-skulled turkeys of the Senate: he knew nuances, he could follow a political conversation. It was an odd thing, Don O'Brien thought: when Charlie Martin screwed up it was as if he were *choosing* to screw up.

"Mahh-ty," O'Brien said, using his own affectionate and rather grating nickname for the senator. "I'm not a very adventurous man. I don't like excitement. My theory has always been that God placed me on this earth to make sure that assholes like Mike Price didn't take sweet little ladies like Marie O'Connell to the cleaners. You do that sort of work quietly. If you're going to beat the Brahmans, you have to seem as tight-assed as they do."

Mandelbaum came in with a cup of tea. O'Brien squeezed the tea bag with a spoon and flipped it neatly into a wastebasket. He leaned forward, elbow patches on his desk, teacup tiny in his two big, freckled hands. "Let me put a frame on it for you, Senator," he said. "You gotta give Stanton credit. He's got The Luck—he's got it in ways I don't think I've ever seen it before. But you've still got to figure that a governor from some state it takes two planes to get to isn't going to have much of a chance against the president of the United States. Furthermore, he's careless, and that could cause *us* a world of hurt come November—we may have to start thinking about protecting our majority here. . . . You know, Senator, sometimes I miss the House. You were there. Remember how it was?"

"The endless campaign," Charlie said. "Wall-to-wall constituent service." He saw where O'Brien was headed.

"Right," O'Brien said, seeing that Charlie saw. "Everyone was always running for reelection, and everyone was always conscious that 434 other guys and gals were in the same boat. You get to the Senate and you forget that. If you're not up for reelection, you stop thinking about those who are—you figure you can go off, run for president even if you're not prepared, make the party seem foolish—"

"I didn't—"

"Charlie, the point is, we may lose our majority if Stanton keeps stepping on his dick. You think he'll survive the fall campaign without some other hairdresser falling out of bed? What d'ya think we can do about that?"

He seemed to want an answer. Charlie had none.

"We can make sure we don't reinforce the hippie peacenik image of the party that he's projecting. We can try and control ourselves when we're alone in cars with campaign workers. We can try not to be so flippant when we're asked whether we want to be the vice president of the United States. Am I communicating successfully with you here?"

"Loud and clear," Charlie said. "I'm sorry."

"People up here like you, Charles. They like you a lot," Donny said. "You've got something most other people your generation don't: you've seen how wicked serious politics can get. You've seen the consequences."

"That's why I'm here," Charlie said.

"Then maybe you should act like it." O'Brien paused a moment, assessing the impact of his assault. The kid didn't give away much. You could murder him and he wouldn't let you know it, unless he wanted to. "So now I'll bet you're thinking: how do I get back in the Big Donkey's good graces? Let me tell you. Dov, tell him."

Charlie turned to face Mandelbaum, who was sitting on the couch behind him. "Stanton's going to call you," he said. "You're on the short list for veep."

"Get out of here," Charlie said.

"Not on the *very* short list," O'Brien edited. "We're hearing Larkin. Maybe Pete Downs, who was a governor—pal of Stanton's—before he came up here. But Stanton wants you in the mix—"

"Because of Vietnam," Charlie said.

"Of course, but so what?" O'Brien said. "It puts you in the game. You might even go in there and charm his pants off."

"Sure I will. He just loves me, after the campaign."

"He's smart. Smarter than you, probably," O'Brien said.

"Thanks," Charlie replied, wondering if O'Brien actually believed that, fearing that he did.

"Then don't act proud. It makes you dumb. When you go in there, I want you to offer to do anything you can to help his campaign, and I want you to mean it," O'Brien said. "I want him to *owe* you. If he actually wins—God help us—I'll need all the leverage I can get. You help him, he needs you. He needs you, you help me."

"And that's all?" Charlie asked.

"In politics, little things are everything," Don said, which was true in the sort of small-room politics he played. "You might also tell him I'd be interested in discussing how we might coordinate the fall campaign."

O'Brien stood. He walked Charlie toward the door. "Oh," he said.

"And one other thing. If you want to hire a Mississippi poofter to be your flack, that's your business. But if he gets caught porking a page in the men's room, it becomes my business, and your colleagues' embarrassment. I'm sure you'll make sure he knows that." Donny smiled, enveloped Charlie's hand. "God bless, Senator Martin."

6

———

Don O'Brien was right about the phone call from Stanton. It came in late June. And he was also right about it taking two planes to get to Mammoth Falls, Jack Stanton's capital city: you could only get there from Washington via Chicago, Nashville, St. Louis or Dallas.

Or you could get there via Houston.

Charlie had spent several months trying not to think about what was waiting for him in Houston. He'd told only one person about it—Rathburn, and that had been an exceedingly strange experience. They'd had a late dinner in New York, at "21," during the Mustafa Victory Tour. Linc was in a celebratory mood: instead of his usual diet Coke, he ordered a glass of Chablis. His Mustafa strategy had resuscitated Charlie's career. And he was in no mood to talk about anything so real as what Charlie was about to lay on him—he was going on, in the musty, steaks-and-chops darkness of the Grill Room, about how Gid Reese was screwing up Stanton's foreign policy operation, and about how stupid he thought the ancient hack foreign affairs columnist for the *Times* was. And—

"Linc," Charlie said. "I've got to tell you something. A weird thing happened back there in Vietnam. . . ."

Rathburn looked up from his steak tartare, which he'd been delicately apportioning onto thin crackers, lined perfectly across the plate in front of him. He didn't look all that different from the old days: his hair was still thick straw, his face was craggier, perhaps—he had aged well. He dressed precisely, an earnest Hoosier effort to emulate New York social clubwear. Tonight he was less formal than usual, a forest green tie, a brown tweed sportscoat with a white pocket square whose tips resembled a schooner's sails. Charlie wondered how, and where, one learned to make a handkerchief do that.

"I had dinner with Quoc," he began, "and at the end he showed me a photo of Thua, who is now living in Houston, married to a doctor named Rosenbaum. . . ."

Linc hooted. "Perfect! Sometimes people get just exactly what they deserve in life. . . ."

"There's a child," Charlie said. "Quoc showed me the photo. And it's clearly not Rosenbaum's kid. It's—"

"Mine?" Rathburn was now fully engaged.

"No," Charlie paused. "Mine."

Linc uncoiled himself slowly, setting down his utensils—he grunted, or perhaps coughed—picking up his napkin, his lips quivering . . . with, what? Anger? No, he was laughing. "Yours?" he said. *"Yours?"*

"It happened the night you left Saigon," Charlie said warily. "We were both pretty drunk."

"Thua was drunk? That was a first." Rathburn said. There was curiosity, but no real heat there. Charlie was relieved, but also not relieved: there was still some explaining to do.

"I went to see her the next day, and it was as if it never happened."

"I'll bet!" Rathburn said. "That girl was the most uptight . . . hey, did she let you take her clothes off?"

"Huh?" Charlie couldn't remember. Well . . . actually, yes: she had.

"Ours was not the most romantic of liaisons," Linc said, reading Charlie's affirmative nonaffirmation. "In fact, it was pretty half-assed. We both, neither of us, felt right—I still had Abigail and the kids back home. . . ."

"The point is, Linc," Charlie said, "I have a kid."

"Amazing!" Linc was laughing again. "Thua got herself knocked up? She's about the last person—what was I saying about people getting just what they deserve? I was wrong! This is the last thing I'd . . . So, have you talked to her?"

"No."

"Yeah, right," Linc said. "I wouldn't want to face that, either."

"You don't think there are political implications?" Charlie asked, pretty sure that wasn't what Linc meant.

"Are you kidding? A child born nearly thirty years ago, in a wartime situation? Whom you were never told about? Not even Phyllis Schlafly would begrudge you that," Linc said. "No, I was just thinking: maybe this is one of those things you leave well enough alone. If she'd told the kid, he probably would have tried to find you by now. But that's your call."

And so, permission to avoid responsibility was officially granted. But

Charlie couldn't quite let it go at that. His initial curiosity about Cao Van Rosenbaum curled into a furtive worry. Obviously, Thua hadn't wanted him to know. She must have had her reasons. It might be best to respect that. But his responsibility was no longer to Thua; it was to the kid—now that Charlie knew he existed, it would be dishonorable not to make himself known. And he remembered the look, the insouciant eyebrow.

So, in late June, he called Thua.

"Hello, Thua," he said. "It's Charlie Martin."

"So you know," she said. Just like that.

"I had dinner with your uncle Quoc in Vietnam."

"He thinks his birth father was killed in the war," she said. "The boy."

"That's nice," Charlie said, then relented. "I guess it was less confusing that way." But it still felt awfully cold.

"Richard's been a good father," she said. "He adopted the boy."

"I'm sure he has," Charlie said, and didn't know what to say next. "So—"

"So you want to see him," Thua said.

"I think so. I don't want to cause any trouble," he replied, allowing her access to his mixed feelings, trying to seem reasonable. "What is Cao like? You think he wants to see me?"

"He's not Cao anymore. Cao Van became Calvin. Everyone calls him that, anyway." There was some exasperation in her voice; Calvin was not a source of unmitigated pride.

"He plays the guitar?" he asked.

"And little else," she admitted. "From what I can gather."

"From what you can gather?"

"He's twenty-seven years old, Charlie. He doesn't live here anymore."

Twenty-seven. Charlie had known that, but he'd thought of the kid as a teenager—the picture Quoc had shown him. "Is he in school, or working, or something?" he asked.

She laughed. "Half the Vietnamese kids his age in Houston are in medical school," she said. "The other half are getting MBAs. Cal took some courses at Harris County Community College, then dropped out. He's got his band. He works in a record store, in a mall, down by Clear Lake."

"Where does he live?"

"Down there," she said, with disdain. "On the other side of town."

"You don't sound too happy about it."

"Do you know Houston at all?" she asked.

"No," Charlie said. "The other side of town isn't so good?"

"Look, you want his address? I'll give it to you. I guess I owe you both that," she said. Charlie was trying to picture what she must look like now, extrapolating from the old photos Quoc had showed him; she sounded different from the Thua he remembered, the timbre of her voice was different. She almost sounded American.

"Do you think it's a good idea?" he asked. "Getting in touch with him?"

"I don't know," she said, stubbornly refusing him a final exit strategy: if he was going to inconvenience her, raise a lot of dead memories, by calling, then she would return the inconvenience.

"Thua—"

"I'm not *that* Thua anymore," she said, as if she'd been following his thinking.

"You're—"

"Fine," she said. "I've got a good life." But not a great one, it seemed. "I did what I had to do, for me and the boy, and for Richard," she said. "Calvin is—he's—actually, I don't *remember* you well enough to know if he's like you. He certainly isn't like me. He's not a bad person, but he's not like me."

"I remember *you*," he said.

"You remember the way I looked."

She gave Charlie a phone number and an address. He tried the number; no one answered, and there was no phone machine. But he decided to take a flier and stop there anyway on his way to Mammoth Falls. The impulse was in the same emotional neighborhood as a WTF, but different; he was being propelled by something resembling a sense of responsibility—and by the slightest twinge of compassion, since the conversation with Thua. He'd read about how the children of American servicemen had been treated as outcasts in Vietnam. This boy was a stranger to his mother. He looked like Buzz. Charlie would search for him on Saturday.

He was scheduled to be at a Sunday photo op in Mammoth Falls. There had been elaborate negotiations between his people—the two D's, Donna and Devereaux—and Stanton's cast of thousands. No big airport ceremony. Stanton would greet the senator at his mansion; they'd do the photo then—Charlie would come out alone, afterward; Stanton didn't want to be cornered into answering questions. "*You* get to grin like an idiot and say it was a good meeting," said Hilton Devereaux, whom Charlie had christened D-2, much to his dismay. (Donna was now D-1, much to hers.)

"*You* get to come with me," Charlie said. Actually, he'd been thinking about that. He knew he wanted D-2 in Mammoth Falls, but did he want him in Houston? No. Despite Schollwengen, there were some things a person—even a person who happened to be on the medium-short list for vice president—had to do on his own. He'd meet D-2 at the airport in Mammoth Falls on Sunday, which was good on another count: Hilton could prevaricate wonderful things about Stanton to whatever press happened to be hanging around, waiting to greet Senator Martin's plane.

"You want to tell me why you're going to Houston?" Devereaux asked.

"No." But Charlie told him.

*   *   *

Charlie rented a white Taurus at Houston International. He spent the drive thinking about all the things he would tell Calvin, and ask him. He'd brought pictures of the grandparents; he'd thought about what sort of offer he might make—the Rosenbaums had, no doubt, offered him money for college. But why an offer? The moral equivalent of paying a fine for his mixed feelings? . . . What if the kid wanted to live with him? No. They were both too old for that; it would be too weird. What if Calvin didn't want to have anything to do with his father? That would be easier, in a way.

Driving south from the airport, Charlie found himself back in the Great American Anywhere. But it was a GAA slightly askew: as he approached Calvin's address, he noticed Vietnamese language signs in some of the strip mall stores. Nguyen Minh Cleaners next to Radio Shack next to Rite Aid next to Little Cholon Chinese-Vietnamese Restaurant. The area was a sort of denatured, Americanized Vietnam—what might have happened back there, if the Green Machine had won the war. The sky was basic Bangkok banana pulp, the air furnace hot and soggy like Southeast Asia, a thin petroleum reek wafting north from the refineries on Galveston Bay. Thua was right: it was the other side of town. It was nearly the other side of the world.

Charlie was so caught up in his thoughts, he almost missed Calvin's apartment complex—which was one of those awful, fake neo-mansard shingled, two-story brick things that had sprouted in the seventies: Gal-Bay Villas. It looked okay from the road, but when he pulled closer it was, clearly, a slum. Toward the far end of the parking lot he saw a bunch of kids lounging about, leaning on cars, listening to loud rap music and drinking from quart bottles sequestered in paper bags; they were, he realized—with utter horror—*Amerasian* kids. They were wearing the unisex uniforms of disaffected youth in the nineties: baseball hats turned around, garish, ventilated team jerseys—football, basketball and hockey—baggy shorts and enormous, complicated sneakers that looked like something developed by the space program. Was Calvin one of them?

There were several young black women with stupendous sculptured hairdos, and babies in strollers; they stood chatting on the landing of the foyer to the boy's apartment. They gave Charlie the evil eye as he pushed past: he was social services, a cop of some sort, obviously. He regretted showing up there in uniform, blue suit and tie. How silly he'd been: he'd decided to wear a Nicole Miller music tie—electric guitars, saxophones and drumsticks on a black field—rather than a serious political stripe as a way of making a connection with the boy. But to these folks, a tie was a tie—the only people who wore ties were those who could cause them trouble.

Charlie took off his jacket, flipped it over his shoulder Kennedy-style and rang the buzzer. No answer. He rang again. A sleepy voice: "Who is it?"

Good question. That's how well prepared he was: not at all.

"Who is it?"

"Ahh, a friend of your mother's." Charlie was buzzed in and walked up the stairs, his knees spongy.

Calvin had the door open a crack, and was standing just behind it; Charlie saw Buzz's eyebrow. He was big for a Vietnamese, just about six feet—almost as tall as Charlie.

"So: a-friend-of-my-mother's," Calvin said. He didn't have Buzz's voice, or Charlie's; it was deeper.

"Well, it's a little more complicated than that," Charlie said. Calvin didn't budge the door. "I used to be a friend of your mother's, in Vietnam. I—"

"You look familiar."

"You ever watch the news?"

"No," he said, with a smile and a shrug, and opened the door, and there he was: a tank top T-shirt and jockey shorts, his skin pale, his hairless legs solid, long and awkward in their nakedness—although he didn't seem very self-conscious about his near nudity; a slight stale whiff of sleep oozing off him. All of a sudden, Calvin was a little too real. "You're on the news?" he asked.

"Sometimes," Charlie said, and extended a hand. "I'm a United States senator. Charlie Martin. You're just getting up?"

"What time is it?"

"About two."

"Sounds about right." Pure Buzz. Calvin's familiarity—this boy was literally *familiar,* Charlie mused—cut against the strangeness of the situation. He had never experienced this particular cocktail of emotions before: pride, curiosity, diffidence, terror.

The apartment wasn't as bad as it might have been. There were a few dishes in the sink, but no clothes on the floor. There was a red Stratocaster and amp sitting in a corner; there was a small Sony sound system and a television; there were posters—Reggae Sunsplash, Red Hot Chili Peppers and a third:

I
N
INTERRACE
INTEREST
R
O
IN YOUR FACE
K

Charlie found the poster beguiling, and reassuring. It acknowledged him, in a way—the INTERRACE part. It played with words. It was ironic. Calvin saw Charlie staring at it. "It's my mantra," he said.

"What does it mean?" Charlie asked, making conversation.

"What it says," he said, but not edgily. "A girl I know did it." He sat down on the bed. There was a chrome and gray Formica breakfast table near the kitchenette. Charlie pulled out a chair and sat on it. The room was air-conditioned, but not overly so. It was not an uncomfortable room. The senator reconnoitered himself: he was seriously, but not totally, freaked out. And it was now his move.

"What sort of music do you play?" he delayed.

"Basic Loud." Calvin said. "New Wave Ska Funk, or something."

Charlie sat there, semistumped, staring at the poster: INTERRACE, IN-TEREST . . .

"Look," he said, after what seemed a pregnant pause. "I've seen this scene played a hundred times in the movies, and I can't figure out a new or clever way to do it, and I know your mother told you one thing—and that probably made sense to her, and I don't want to shock you—I mean, this has certainly been a shock for me. I just found out about it from your granduncle Quoc in Vietnam. . . ."

Charlie was losing steam. The kid was figuring it out. He was calm, but not slow. "Calvin," he said, "I'm your father."

The kid didn't show much emotion of any sort. His head kicked back slightly, from the force of the revelation. But Charlie couldn't tell if he was pleased or pissed or perplexed.

"You just found out about it?" he asked. Charlie nodded. "You mean, she never told you?" Charlie shook his head. "That must have been some kind of mind fuck . . . I mean, how *well* did you know her?"

Charlie could see what he was thinking. "Pretty well—as a friend. She was my best friend's girl—and it's: no. It wasn't like that. He was leaving Saigon. She was angry. We were drunk."

"I was born," he said, neatly falling into the rhythm, a lyricist's timing. "Not quite a *love* child. . . . That figures, given Mom."

"Don't be too tough on her," Charlie said. "She hasn't had an easy life. . . . She was one of the most respected women in Saigon. She had real dignity. And then her world fell apart."

"Yeah, she married Dick," Calvin said.

"He's that bad?"

"No."

"You know," Charlie said, searching for a hook, " 'Not quite a love child . . .' isn't a bad lyric."

Not bad at all, Charlie Martin thought: the kid caught his drift.

" 'I got a right to be wild,' " Calvin tried. Grimaced. "Gotta be something better than that."

"Put your pants on," Charlie said. "If you're not going to work or something, I'll buy you breakfast and we'll think about it."

So the deal was: on first impression, confusion. Charlie liked his son—sort of. Or maybe he was just trying very hard to like him. The kid was a stranger, and also not: there was, palpably, more than a little Buzz there. In the car, Charlie told Calvin about his visit to Saigon, his dinner with

Uncle Quoc. Calvin didn't seem particularly interested, and Charlie asked him why he wasn't.

"I know too many people who look like me," Calvin said quietly, "who got treated like shit over there. Because they looked like me. The ones who never spent any time in Vietnam are curious about what it's like. But the ones who remember what it was like don't buy the rice paddy nostalgia bit. I trust their judgment, even though I don't remember the place at all."

"Are you treated okay here?" Charlie asked, hazarding a glance at his son. He remembered stories about redneck fishermen furious with Vietnamese refugee shrimpers on the Gulf.

"Oh sure," Calvin replied, looking straight ahead. "But then, my father wasn't black. You want to see fucked-up and pissed, you should hook up with some of those folks."

They went to a Denny's. Calvin had a Grand Slam breakfast. Charlie had an iced tea. "You don't seem like a senator," Cal said.

"I'll take that as a compliment," Charlie said, then proceeded to answer the question implicit in his son's statement: what being a senator was like. "It's like being a musician, only harder—I mean, different." He didn't want to sound condescending. Being a father was a minefield. "Being a musician isn't easy, Lord knows. But politics is similar: You're out there performing. A lot of time the performance is boring and phony, but if you don't do it right, you're in trouble."

"Like playing the hokey-pokey at a sweet sixteen?"

"Exactly! Although there are rewards. You do get to help people sometimes. And the other thing is, once in a while something serious happens. I knew a lot of guys who died because of decisions people made, or didn't make, back in Washington. I lose track of that sometimes—it's not something you really want to remember, y'know? What happened back there . . ." Charlie paused, thinking: but *Calvin* happened back there. And also: boy, do I sound like a self-righteous jerk.

"How come you get the music stuff?" the kid asked, uninterested in the politics or the self-justification.

"Your grandfather's a musician," Charlie said proudly, playing his hole card.

Calvin dropped his fork, sat back in his seat. "A father—*my* father—I used to think about that a lot. But a grandfather, wow."

"You come equipped with one of those, too." Charlie pulled out a picture of Buzz on a bandstand, back in the fifties. "Pretty neat guy, in his way. I always used to think he looked like Dennis the Menace's father—in the cartoon, not the television show. You remind me of him, a little. Actually, more than a little."

"Really?" he asked, whiffing on the Dennis the Menace reference. "How about a grandmother?"

"She's dead now." Charlie gave Cal a picture of Buzz and Clarice together, the day she was sworn in as mayor. Buzz looked bewildered; Clarice, in charge. "She was something else altogether—not at all like your grandfather. She was the daughter of a county judge. She became a politician, the mayor of Des Pointe—which is where we're all from. But that was sort of an accident: her real vocation was chief do-good lady on the poor side of town."

"And my grandfather? What kind of musician?"

"Local bandleader. Played a lot of hokey-pokey. Played the accordion, although now he tells me he's moved on to an electric keyboard. He still plays some gigs."

"And he's how old?"

"Seventy-three."

"Cool. How'd he make a living?"

"Gigs. Lessons. Mom was the one who kept us afloat," Charlie said. "And you?"

"I work in a record store," he said. "Mom thinks I'm a real fuck-up."

"And what do you think?"

"That I'm not quite . . . Hey, how about this: Not quite a love child / not quite born to be wild. Workin' for the man / workin' for a while. Hard to make it giggin' / when you got no style. . . ."

"That's ballsy," Charlie said, laughing. "A self-deprecating rock lyric. But not bad. Not bad at all. But . . . is that what you think of yourself? No style?"

"Sometimes," he said. He took out a pen and began to scribble the words on his place mat. Charlie watched and thought: The kid's a musician, and therefore oblique. Musicians were essentially feline—maybe that's why Dizzy and Bird and the old be-boppers called themselves "cats." It was useless to ask a musician basic questions like "Do you have a girlfriend?" or "What are you going to do for a living, now that the drummer's overdosed and the lead singer's become a shoe salesman?" The direct approach was mortally unhip. Charlie understood he'd have to work at Calvin the same way he did Buzz—on an angle, low-key, cool—

and be satisfied whenever the kid chose to purr or rub up against him. This was good news, in a way: Calvin wouldn't be demanding. Charlie wasn't sure he was ready for too many fatherly demands.

"You want to hear my band sometime?" Calvin asked.

"Sure," Charlie said, with less enthusiasm than he'd hoped to convey. "What are you called? Where do you play?"

"Wherever we can get paid," Calvin said, retreating. He seemed embarrassed. "We're called the Semi-nuked Gook Troopers."

It wasn't the sort of name that would get you a lot of sweet sixteen parties. "If I come to see you play," Charlie asked. "Will you come to see me play sometime?"

"Washington? Whew," he said.

"It's not so bad," Charlie said.

"You got a wife, kids?"

"No," Charlie said, smiling, trying to charm the kid. "You appear to be my only immediate family, Cal."

Calvin didn't buy the charm. "Why's that?"

"Boy, is *that* a long story." But it wasn't really that long. Bad luck. Limited options. Incredible selfishness. Charlie couldn't explain it to himself, much less to Calvin, and he couldn't stick around to hear the kid play a Sunday afternoon gig at the Clear Lake Boys and Girls Club picnic. "I've got to go to Mammoth Falls," he explained. "To see Jack Stanton."

"That's grim." Calvin said. "Almost as grim as a Sunday afternoon gig."

"You don't like Stanton?"

"I was thinking about Mammoth Falls." Cal shrugged. "Stanton's the guy who's running for president?"

"Yeah," Charlie said. "I did, too, for a while."

"Cool."

"What do you think of him? Stanton?"

"He's okay, I guess." Charlie could tell the kid didn't have a clue.

When Charlie dropped Calvin off, back at the apartment, they shook hands. He was going to put his left *thing* on Calvin's shoulder, but the kid noticed it coming, and Charlie didn't want to discomfort him. He hesitated, awkwardly—and then he worried that Calvin thought he was pulling back from him.

"Tough to play the guitar with that," Calvin said.

"Unless you're a lefty," Charlie said, with spurious cheer. "I played the drums when I was a kid, so I haven't missed it much. Hope this hasn't been too weird for you, meeting me?"

"Not *too* weird?" Calvin laughed.

"It's okay? We'll do it again?" But the thought of exactly when and how another meeting might take place boggled Charlie.

"Sure," Calvin said perfunctorily. Charlie saw that the boy was picking up on his uncertainty. "We'll do that. If it's not too weird for you."

"No way," Charlie said, letting go, hugging him—not a sappy hug, a guy hug. "Absolutely," he added, hoping that he sounded as if he meant it. "We'll do it soon."

7

There are a number of qualities that are essential for a successful vice president, most of which aren't easily found in the sort of people—ambitious politicians, that is—usually asked to do the job. Patience and humility are important; the very best vice presidents have a flare for obscurity. Public displays of intelligence must be tasteful and understated. Spontaneity is to be avoided at all costs. And, most important: in private discourse with the president, one must be able to fawn with a maximum of enthusiasm and a minimum of irony. Charlie Martin was not very good at any of these, and Jack Stanton knew it—and Hilton Devereaux saw it, and he winced privately at his boss's determined but futile efforts to demonstrate fealty to his party's nominee for the presidency that June Sunday in Mammoth Falls.

"Hey, Jack, congratulations," the senator said, unfurling himself from the rear of the Ford Bronco that Stanton had sent to retrieve them. A laconic, Sunday-duty flock of camera folks and reporters gathered behind a yellow nylon cord, off the oval driveway in front of the governor's mansion. Susan Stanton stood on the far side of her husband, still dressed for church in a dark pants suit and a scarf. "Hi, Susan." Charlie waved.

"Good to see you, Senator," Stanton said, greeting him with a warm smile and a comfortable, slow-motion handshake. He was dressed less formally than his wife: a jacket and slacks, a teal button-down shirt open at the collar. He put his left hand on Charlie's elbow—and, with Donny O'Brien facility, assembled the three of them symmetrically, facing the cameras. Smile. Smile. Click, click, click. "When are you going to announce your choice, Governor?" a reporter asked.

"In good time," Stanton said. He had changed, Charlie thought, grown quieter, moved slower—in public, at least, the appearance of thoughtfulness was what passed for gravitas. The presence of a dozen Secret Service guys didn't hurt, either. Charlie had left the presidential campaign in its retail phase, the candidates still working small crowds, face-to-face. This was different, bigger now and more serious. The return to center stage caught him off-guard. He'd spent most of the plane ride from Houston thinking about Calvin—their distant and yet emotionally exhausting meeting. He was disappointed by his own ambivalent reaction to the boy. He wondered if he should call Thua and try to learn more about the kid. And then he thought: I may know as much as she does. I can tell her about Buzz.

He'd prepared himself for the Stanton meeting, too, but it was an afterthought, and he'd prepared for the old Jack—the preanointed one.

"Is it gonna be Senator Martin?"

Stanton smiled grandly.

"Has he asked you, Senator Martin?"

Charlie smiled, not quite so grandly.

"A few months ago, you said Jack Stanton was damaged goods," an ambitious reporter asked. "You think he can win in the fall?"

"Absolutely," Charlie said, but not quite from the heart. He'd stumbled over the very same word with Calvin, the day before.

And that was about it for his vice presidential campaign.

The press didn't notice the equivocation; Charlie seemed stone confident on the evening news that night. But Stanton, who had an otherworldly ability to read the microscopic striations of nuances, understood that it wasn't an unequivocal "absolutely" and never would be. Charlie felt the chill breeze from the nominee. And Hilton Devereaux read the body language.

Hilton had never experienced Jack Stanton firsthand before. He was struck by how large the man was, and how needy: he needed absolute "absolutely's." He was surrounded by bustling little absolutophiles. He was yelling at one, as they moved inside: "Perry, you've gotta make the numbers work. You can't fuck with this. Call Walt Wheeler up in Boston. Call Bill Robinson. I want this out, and done right, before the convention."

"But, Governor—" poor Perry persisted. "The tax cut is killing the numbers—"

Stanton stopped. Glared at Perry, who was sweaty with satchels and files and computer printouts. "Wheeler said it would work," Stanton said. "He's got a Nobel goddamned prize in economics."

"His numbers," Perry gulped, "are off."

Stanton rolled his eyes. "You're telling me—"

"We have to cut the tax cut," Perry said.

"Henry!" Stanton called. They were moving down a hall, through a kitchen, into what seemed to be a family room. There were three televisions in the room; they were all on—a basketball game, golf and CNN.

Henry Burton appeared. What a good-looking guy, Hilton thought as he dispatched himself to a chair off in a corner, away from the action. Burton was neat, calm, small and mocha-colored: the young Julian Bond, a human decaf cappuccino, wearing a pumpkin-colored knit shirt and perfectly faded Levis. "Hi, Senator," he said to Martin, friendly and confident.

"Henry, can you supervise Perry on the numbers?"

Burton nodded, steered Perry off, away. There were other aides, other people dashing about. Hilton tried to imagine himself one of them: Jack Stanton seemed both more accessible and more remote than Charlie Martin. No sense of humor, for starters. A distinctly southern, and rather feminine, combination: charming but unironic. And now Stanton sat down, suddenly entranced by the sports on the television, ignoring his guest. Hilton was struck by the rudeness of it; Stanton's charm was electronic—he could turn it on and off.

"How was Vietnam, Charlie?" Susan asked, filling empty space. "Was it tough going back there?"

Everything she said had some distance, a formality to it. She doffed her suit jacket and had on a canary-yellow silk blouse; dark slacks, black velvet headband.

"It was—" Charlie started. "Quite something."

Hilton was finding that after several months he could think along with his boss: a serious answer would have meant a serious conversation, which would have been far too personal for this sort of situation. For Charlie Martin, seriousness was *serious*; it wasn't an act you put on for political reasons—informality was the act you put on for political purposes. This wasn't, Hilton thought, going very well: the boss had prepared himself for an actual meeting, a discussion of the vice presidency. Not a *really* real discussion. But the sort of canned earnestness that passes for candor when politicians attempt to communicate with each other privately. This wasn't even close to that, and Charlie hadn't prepped himself for irrelevance.

"It's amazing you were able to bring that man out," Susan said, as if the conversation were taking place on television. "The administration was just sitting around—Jack, wasn't it terrific that Charlie was able to—"

Charlie was a bit distracted. Hilton saw him floundering. Would he tell her that he'd been working indirectly at the behest of the Republican president—their enemy to the death now? Stanton seemed distracted, too: listening to the conversation, sort of, but very deep into the games he was watching. "How'd you get in there?" Stanton asked, not quite looking over at Charlie.

"Lincoln Rathburn called me," he said. "I think the administration had called him. They want to normalize relations, but they can't—"

"Yeah, the vets' groups," Stanton said. "It's a bitch. And if the Republicans can't, I sure as hell can't, and I believe we probably should, don't you?" Stanton suddenly looked directly, and rather desperately, at Charlie, hoping for reinforcement, wanting to hear him say that his nonservice in Vietnam didn't matter.

"Absolutely," Charlie said.

"Absolutely," Hilton thought, was not a very good word for an honest politician—too many syllables out there to be equivocal with. He would advise the boss to try "sure" next time. "You know, Jack," Charlie continued, with significantly more squish than was his norm, "even in the toughest moments of the campaign, when the press wanted me to take you out on this—"

"Yeah, I know," Stanton retreated, slightly miffed, not having received the absolution he'd been hoping for. "God, look at Mickelson clear that bunker!—and yeah, I appreciate that, Charlie."

Charlie was trying to grovel, and Stanton was back to watching golf. Hilton was infuriated; Charlie, nonplussed. Even Susan seemed a wee bit disgusted with her husband. "The Republicans won't be as kind as Charlie," she said to him. Then, to Martin: "How would you deal with them when they come after Jack on the war?"

"I'd be happy to help, any way I can," Charlie said, too quickly. Hilton had the feeling that even though Stanton was making a visible effort not to pay attention, he was reading every tea leaf, aware that Charlie was attempting the limited, qualified suck-up route, and thinking less of him for that. Sucking up is an art; it has to be effortless, seamless—anything less than totally convincing is a disaster. Hilton knew his boss didn't have the chops. In a way, he was happy about that.

"It might not be a bad idea," Charlie tried again, "for you to have some

Vietnam guys—surrogates—organized and ready to support you if and when they come after you."

Stanton seemed to ignore the offer of help. Burton was back, whispering in his ear. "Tell them three minutes, Henry," Jack said.

Charlie glanced over at Hilton, who rolled his eyes.

"Rathburn's working with the administration?" Stanton asked.

"No. But they know he knows the area, and he's discreet," Charlie said. "They didn't want their fingerprints on it, but they wanted Mustafa out."

"And what about Rathburn?" Stanton asked. "What do you think of him?"

"He's the most talented diplomat in our party," Charlie said.

"I hear he's something of a self-promoter," Susan said.

Well, yeah. But so what? Charlie assumed Gideon Reese had been filling Stanton's brain with this stuff—subtly, as Gideon always would. He decided to try some counterspin. "You know, Jack, we all knew each other back then—me and Gid and Linc and Sly Parkinson—back in Saigon," he said, then thought: should I be calling him Jack? Hilton saw the hesitation and thought: how un-Martin. The boss couldn't quite get himself untracked in Stanton's presence.

"And we all felt pretty much the same about the war—pretty much like you, ultimately. And Gid did his rebellion in public, which was fine. I didn't begrudge his resignation in protest, or the speech he made at the Washington Monument. But Linc kept plugging away from the inside, always working to end the war. You can nitpick why he did what he did, but—" Charlie was struck by a belated insight: Gid, who was so much more publicly austere than Linc, had had a far more extravagant reaction to the war, resigning in protest from the foreign service, going to teach at Georgetown, starting AAW (Academics Against the War); Linc's response had been more juridical, staying in the State Department, lawyering the codicils of the Paris Peace Accords even after the Nixon election.

"Anyway, Linc." Charlie tried to remember what he'd been saying, but was interrupted by another thought: Gid and Stanton were linked by the need to overcome anti-Vietnam activities that both now considered embarrassing. "Linc has this thing about loyalty. And loyalty's a quality, I hear, that presidents value."

"I understand Rathburn's very loyal," Susan said, "to you."

Burton was back; he and the Stantons communicated with a glance. Jack stood up, getting ready to end it. "Well, it's really good of you to come by," he said, as if Charlie had just made a trip around the corner.

"I appreciate your coming here and offering your support like this. It's important to put our past disagreements behind us."

"Jack," Charlie said, taking one last run at it—for Donny O'Brien's sake. "I really do think you can win this thing, and you should. I want to do what I can to help."

Stanton nodded. He didn't believe a word of it. "Thanks, Charlie, I may have Richard Jemmons call you about organizing the vets."

Without pushing, he was herding Charlie and Hilton toward the door—as if they were on a moving walkway at the airport. "Oh, Jack," Charlie said, pushing back against the tide. "Don O'Brien wanted me to say hello for him, and he says that it might be a good idea if we start thinking about how we're going to coordinate the presidential and congressional campaigns in the—"

"Tell him to have Dov Mandelbaum call Richard," Stanton said, stopping at the door. "Great to see you, Charlie."

Outside, there was a barrage of clicks and lights and questions. "Did he offer you the vice presidency, Senator? Senator! Hey, Charlie, over here. . . ."

Charlie smiled, waved, did the hokey-pokey and turned himself around, and got into the car with Devereaux.

"Jeez," he said.

"I wonder what his *next* meeting was," Hilton said.

"He's a busy man," Charlie said. "There are vice presidents to pick, golf to watch, hairdressers to boink. . . ."

"I thought you did Rathburn a good turn."

"Susan caught me up on that."

"She's sharp," he said. "Sharper than him, I think."

"Not in a million years," Charlie replied. "So, who does he pick? Who's the veep?"

"Someone for whom adulation is not an effort," he said.

"No flies on you, D-2."

"Senator, I appreciate the compliment," Devereaux said. "But if you call me D-2 one more time, I will surely scream—"

"What should I call you?"

"Hilton sufficed for my parents."

"You never had a nickname?"

"Some of the kids in high school used to call me 'faggot,' " he said. "I always thought nicknames were kind of butch."

"How about 'Butch'?"

Too much rectitude roils the soul. Charlie had been a good soldier, a good boy, and Every Good Boy Does Fine—but rectitudinous boys wind up with spiritual arthritis. He was getting bored with himself. He'd been so good. After Mammoth Falls, he went back to Des Pointe, gave an extended interview to Bob Hamblin of the *Register-World,* offering Mustafa details that no one else had and making up some "color" about the meeting with Stanton. Then he reacted with great public enthusiasm when Stanton picked Senator Thomas Atkinson III of Missouri to be his vice presidential nominee. Atkinson was someone he'd often voted with, but never befriended. He seemed eminently vice presidential.

In truth, Charlie didn't care very much about the presidential campaign anymore (although he was quietly pleased that desperate Democrats around the country had begun asking him to make campaign appearances). He spent his time working the home turf, tending to business. A small but irksome part of that business was accepting the fact that Mustafa just wasn't going away. When he wasn't driving the Goodwill truck, he was hanging around Charlie's office: not a bother, exactly—he tried to make himself useful, and too often succeeded—but a complication. He did dry-cleaning runs, food shopping for Donna, stray messenger work. "Moose's weird," she told the boss, "but dependable."

Still, Mustafa existed at the periphery of the senator's radar screen; as did the other enduring consequence of his Vietnam trip—Calvin. Charlie called his son regularly. The calls were uniformly awkward. He found himself pushing the kid to come visit, come on the road with him. The harder he pushed, the more reluctant Cal seemed, as if he knew Charlie couldn't figure out anything else to talk about. But Charlie kept trying—not a full-court press, but frequently enough to convince himself that he was making the effort. He bought a Red Hot Chili Peppers CD (Calvin had said they were his favorite band); he listened to it several times and found himself depressed when several of the songs stuck in his mind, like gum on a shoe.

All of which is to say that he was ready to kick back and enjoy himself at the Democratic convention in New York.

There are plenty of ways not to have fun at a Democratic convention. You can take part in panel discussions about the need for campaign finance reform, you can give speeches to special-interest groups obsessed with abortion rights and voter registration. You can have labor skates bend your ear about the perils of free trade, over soggy cheese puffs and jug wine. Charlie was scheduled to do his share of that stuff. But he also had been invited to frolic on the wilder shores of Democratic social life, the places where married senators from, say, North Dakota, are never seen. On the Sunday night before the convention, he attended a reception that *Rolling Stone* magazine and GreenPAC, a Hollywood enviro-rock-and-roll lobbying group, were having in an Upper East Side art gallery.

Charlie was swarmed when he walked in. He was, in this entertainment industry-cum-cause-junkie crowd, something of a celebrity. He stood near the door, shaking hands while scoping the room, not quite fixing on the people he was shaking with, smiling a lot, laughing a notch too easily, acting like a politician. The place was jammed, there was just too much to take in—the exposed-brick walls were dotted with minimalist modern art that seemed much less engaging than the prairie portraits in his office—but something across the room immediately caught his eye. It was a woman's back, a perfect one. She was wearing a lavender sundress with straps somewhat thicker than fettuccine and a kind of shoelace latticework starting just below her shoulder blades, plunging downward, not too deep, but deep enough, in a perfect V. She had terrific shoulders and thin arms, and a sheen of thick onyx—Asian—hair. Then she was gone, lost in the crush. He extricated himself and began to work his way in that direction, searching for lavender, a controlled primordial lunge, smiling and shaking hands all the way. He saw her again, halfway across—she was talking to a blond, surfer-staffer sort of guy, a younger guy. A bit closer, Martin saw her profile—fabulous, dark eyebrows, pale skin.

And then she looked directly at him and said, "Oh! *Hi!*"

She was younger than her body. Somewhere in her twenties. But she was great-looking and heading his way. "Senator Martin?" she said. He nodded and smiled senatorially. "Hi. Hello," she said, extending a hand. "I'm Elizabeth Makrides. I think you knew my father." She took his disappointment—her *father?*—for incomprehension, but she was right: Charlie did know her father. "Harry Makrides," she said. "He was in Saigon with Reuters."

Yes, he was. But Harry Makrides was goggle-eyed and slouchy with Brillo hair, and looked a lot older than he probably was. How could he possibly be the father of—

"Oh sure," Charlie said. "Great guy. Older than me, I think—just leaving town when I arrived. How's he doing?"

She sobered, looked down. Long lashes; Harry had given her a narrower, more angular face than most Asians. What a knockout. "He died a few months ago," she said. "Heart attack."

"I'm so sorry," he said, having no trouble with the projection of sadness: life can be so cruel.

"You were in Vietnam recently?" She looked at him very directly now, dark eyes shiny and intent. "I've never been. I'd give anything to go. What was it like?"

"Lovely," Charlie said, distracted by the memory of how astute Calvin had been on the subject of Vietnamericans and the home country: of course she'd never been. "Back to what it was, what it's always been, despite us and the Chinese and everybody, ever since the dragon flew south."

"My mother always said that," she said, squeezing his arm, "about the dragon."

"That's when it all began, right?" The legend was that a dragon had flown south to marry a fairy princess and create the Vietnamese people.

"It's where the toughness comes from—from the dragon," she said.

"The way I always heard the story," he said, "it was a gentle dragon."

"But it was still a dragon," she replied. Then, with a twinkle: "My dad always said you were a very cool guy."

"He did?" Charlie had barely known the man.

"No," she said, with a smile—and with intent, he thought. "Not really. But I always thought you were kind of cool, when I saw you on TV."

What could he say to that? "Are you in town for the convention?" he asked. "Are you an elected official?"

She laughed, lots and lots of very white teeth.

"A delegate? A dedicated party worker? A lobbyist? A—"

"A journalist," she said.

"Uh-oh," he said. "I want you to know," he whispered, "this whole conversation is on background." She laughed again, nice and easy. He realized he might be headed for serious trouble. But, WTF. "What kind of journalist are you?"

"I'm a consumer reporter—for Channel 5 here," she said.

"What a coincidence," he said. "*I've* been consumed by reporters." Someone knocked into her, knocking her into him; he supported her with his right arm, which somehow found its way around her waist, which was tiny. She was a feather.

"What did you say?" She tilted her head up, her lips brushing his ear.

"Reporters have had me for lunch."

A tap on his shoulder. Rathburn. Rathburn smiling, glancing at the girl. "Senator," he said, making it three syllables filled with mock portent.

"Hey, Linc." Charlie had known Rathburn was going to show up. "This is Elizabeth Makrides. . . ."

"Harry's daughter?" Linc said. How did he always know everything?

Linc was with a date, but she didn't seem his usual sort: older, not as flashy. But not unattractive. He didn't introduce her immediately; he was consoling Elizabeth on the death of her father. Charlie was watching this, a bit too intently, still transfixed by the stunning young woman who seemed to be making a move on him. So Rathburn's date introduced herself. "Arabella Palmerston," she said, extending her hand and looking Charlie straight in the eye. She was tall—and interesting-looking, curly blond hair the color of old brass, like Milky Flancik's cornet; her voice was a cornet voice, too—deeper than a trumpet, mellow but sharp.

"Arabella?" he said.

"Family name. I come from a long-named family. Call me Nell," she said. "And you're Charlie Martin, of course. I've been waiting to meet you: Rathburn says you're not boring. That would be nice. So far, all his friends have been incredibly busy saving the world. Foreign policy this, economic policy that."

"You want to talk about Most Favored Nation status?" Charlie asked, thinking: she's right, Rathburn did tend to hang with a deadly serious, banker, lawyer, former-diplomat crowd.

"Italy," she said.

"Italy?" She had a long, thin nose with a slight bump in the middle and an aristocratic upturn at the tip—an intermediate ski slope; her eyes were blue-green-gray, oceanic, calm and sad and smart.

"My most favored nation," she said. "And Florence is my most favored city. What are you doing here?" she asked, glancing over at Elizabeth, who was listening intently—or seemed to be—as Rathburn regaled her with stories of her father. "Day care?"

"That's cruel," Charlie said. All of her features were interesting—quite wonderful, in fact—but they didn't exactly fit together, or maybe they did in an unexpected way. She was dressed in a gray linen shift with a boatneck, cut perfectly to follow the line of her collarbones; she had small pearl earrings and no other jewelry, except a gold signet ring on her left pinky. Charlie found himself staring at her stupidly; he couldn't decide if she was plain or extraordinary. So odd for Rathburn to be with someone like this: he usually trafficked in straight-ahead beautiful women. This one was a winding road. "What are you doing with Linc?" he asked, or maybe blurted.

"Defrosting him," she said. "It's tough going."

Charlie laughed. "He's the only man I ever met who never had an armpit stain in the tropics," he said.

"What's that?" Linc turned toward them. Elizabeth moved to Charlie's side quietly, curled her arm inside his left elbow, her index finger on his wrist, resting lightly on the scar tissue, causing the hair on his arm to rise.

"Senator Martin was remarking on what a cool customer you are," Nell said, with a mischievous smile.

"Nell's teaching me how to be fashionable," Rathburn said, putting an arm around her waist—which, Charlie noticed, was more of a waist than Elizabeth's, but not bad for a grown-up.

"The truth is," he said, "we were discussing Most Favored Nation status."

Rathburn looked hopeful.

"Nell said, 'Italy.' "

"God only knows what she would have come up with," Linc said, "if you'd mentioned arms control."

But Charlie knew: Nell had spotted Elizabeth's arm in his, her fingers tickling his wrist. She looked there, then up at him. They seemed to have fallen into a very intense unspoken conversation.

"I've seen you on TV," Nell said then, to Elizabeth. "You're very lively." She glanced at Charlie again: he sensed that she wanted to say "perky," but had restrained herself. He was surprised, and pleased, to be thinking along with her.

"They like lively," Elizabeth said. "They like me to call myself Betsy. The anchor guy pronounces it 'Bitsy.' They want their Asian women reporters bite-sized. It's part of the job. It feels foolish sometimes, like when you're talking about *E. coli* outbreaks. But I guess everyone has something that's awful about their work. What do you do?"

"I'm a designer," Nell said. "Swimwear."

"Cool," Elizabeth said. "For what company?"

"I have my own," Nell said. "It's small."

"Have I heard of it?"

"Probably not." Nell shrugged, but she had done another interesting thing—she seemed to have completely forgotten about Linc and Charlie, and was focusing all her attention on Elizabeth. Women in Washington didn't do that very often—at least, not in the senatorial circles he was used to. (On second thought, maybe they did and their men were too self-entranced to notice.) "It's called *Mer*Maid," she said, with a very authentic French lilt on the "mer."

Elizabeth laughed. She got the pun. Charlie was heartened. "Sounds pretty high-end," she said. "How many seasons do you do?"

"Two," Nell replied. "We just showed 'Cruise.' Now I'm making the rounds, trying to get orders."

"You don't have a sales staff, an agent or something?"

Linc rolled his eyes, but Charlie was fascinated. How refreshing: a conversation that was not even tangentially related to politics. He considered easing Linc's pain and gossiping a little—there was plenty to talk about. But he was enmeshed in the swimsuit business. He wanted to know all about sales. He could gossip with Linc anytime; they gossiped constantly.

"Oh, sure, I have sales reps," Nell was saying. "But I still have to go out, keep up the personal relationships I've built over the years. The customers expect it. . . . What kind of suits do you wear?"

"Well, I really am a swimmer," Elizabeth said, with a perfect pause for effect. "So I don't shop for suits."

"Of course not." Nell laughed and predicted: "You go conservative, Speedo sort of stuff—one piece, solid color, something you can actually swim in without falling out of it."

"You got it," Elizabeth said. "Sorry."

"No problem," Nell said, and sounded as if she meant it. "It's amazing how much of the market is designed for just sitting around the pool—Lycra lingerie. . . . But I do have a few real swimsuits, too—I've been getting into prints, designing my own."

"That's great," Elizabeth said. "Like what sort of thing?"

There was a rustle in the room, strong enough that Nell looked up, away from Elizabeth, to see what was going on. It was Stanton coming in. He was shaking hands on the far side of the room, moving toward a makeshift podium with Jann Wenner, the *Rolling Stone* publisher—who was beaming—and they were accompanied by an attractive woman with startling red hair, the star of a television series Charlie had never seen and the spokesperson for GreenPAC. The crowd noticed the movement and began to applaud, first tepidly, then more enthusiastically. Charlie applauded, too, in his proudly abridged fashion, slapping the back of his left hand, what was left of it, into his right palm.

Nell leaned over and whispered in his ear, "I've always wondered about the sound of one and a half hands clapping."

He pulled back, startled. No one had ever said anything quite so bold to him before—but she was smiling, enjoying her double entendre: she had been referring to his relationship with Stanton, too. He smiled back at her, desperately trying to rearrange his face after the shock, and then he began to laugh. She grinned, mostly with her eyes—they were, he thought, the color of the North Atlantic. The woman seemed to have taken his measure. She'd known that he'd be titillated, not offended; she'd known precisely what the traffic would bear.

And another thing: as she leaned in, he caught a whiff of her perfume. He didn't like perfume much; it seemed a vestige of less forthright times, a diversionary tactic—harsh and garish and sticky sweet. But Nell's perfume blended with and augmented whatever it was that came out of her pores. It was subtle, narcotic, adult and entrancing. He found himself trying to figure out a strategy to lean over, whisper some clever reply to her and smell it some more. But he had no clever reply; she had aced him.

Stanton's speech that night wasn't memorable: campaign blah-blah, and mercifully brief. He looked presidential. When it was over, Linc put his arm around Nell—she draped her arm, casually, on his shoulder—and said, "We're going over to the *Vanity Fair* party, you guys want to come along?"

Elizabeth skidded a nail along Charlie's wrist; he felt a shiver down his spine. "No thanks," he said. "One celebrity party a night is about it for me."

Nell smiled; she caught, or perhaps sensed, Elizabeth's move. They shook hands. "Next time," she said to Charlie, "arms control."

"We could focus," he said, "on biochemical weapons."

Charlie and Elizabeth grabbed an immediate cab. She gave an address, turned her head back toward him and there they were, kissing. It seemed an entirely natural act; gropeless, easy. She was lovely. But Charlie found that he was thinking about Arabella Palmerston.

*   *   *

"So, who is she?" Charlie asked Linc as they sat in the nether reaches of Madison Square Garden several days later, watching Senator Bob Draboskie of Delaware, a former professional football player, fumble the keynote address at the Democratic convention. The floor roiled with delegates doing everything but listening; Draboskie was a mediocre piano player in a very chatty cocktail lounge, lost in the disrespectful din. Charlie had momentarily escaped the clutches of his home-state delegation; he could see them down below, on the jammed convention floor, brandishing cornstalks and pig placards. He admired their enthusiasm.

"Who is who?" Linc asked.

"Your date the other night—Nell," he said. "She isn't your usual type."

"My usual type, that's nice," Linc said. "What does that mean?"

"Beautiful. Brilliant. In need of career counseling," Charlie replied. Linc was, at times, the world's most exclusive finishing school. "This one has been around."

"I'll tell her you said that," he replied.

"You know what I mean," Charlie said. "She's an adult. And sharp."

"Isn't she extraordinary?" Linc asked. Casually. Rhetorically. "She's a Darbyshire."

"What's that? Anything like a Black Angus?"

"You remember the family," Linc said, ignoring Charlie's contrived farmboy act. "Distant royals, five children, very eccentric. They all wrote memoirs. One was the aviatrix who crash-landed near Kiev and married the Ukrainian mechanic who fixed her plane, one converted to Islam and attended Queen Elizabeth's coronation in a black chador; one was the writer—Jane Palmerston—and there were several brothers, less notable: the one who didn't die of syphilis, Harry, married an American, a Coxley. You know the Coxley family, right? Faulknerian southerners?" Charlie didn't. "Randall Coxley. Coxley Power?" Distantly. "His daughter, Susannah, was a great beauty; they were spectacularly alcoholic together, Harry and Susannah—Arabella is their daughter."

Charlie wanted to know more about who she was, and how serious Linc was about her, but these were not the sort of things guys talked about with guys. The ground rules were precise, if implicit: they could praise the looks or smarts of each other's latest triumph; they could tease each other—tastefully, vaguely—about sexual escapades. They could gossip about other friends' women. But serious discussion of real-time romantic situations, especially difficulties, were off-limits, unless a relationship was in the process of being terminated. Women were either "extraordinary" or they were nonexistent, or they were gone.

Rathburn had successfully avoided marriage since his first one—to a very wealthy Bostonian named Abigail Porter, slightly older than he—failed in the early seventies. Gideon Reese had introduced Linc to Abigail. She'd been a childhood friend of Gid's sister; the Porters owned

property next to the Reeses at Bar Harbor. Abigail was a very serious
botanist; Linc was a Hoosier, trying to pass for proper. Gid had been
stonily perturbed with Rathburn for stepping out on Abigail in Saigon: it
was wartime, flings were allowed. But he was furious at Linc, later, for
never quite making it all the way home to Abigail after the war.

Gideon Reese had always been prohibitively Presbyterian: even his
anti-Vietnam rebellion had been a dry, moralizing, New England aboli-
tionist sort of fury. His fierce reaction to the divorce had seemed, to Linc,
an object lesson of a perverse sort: if you involved yourself in a friend's
romantic business too deeply, the friendship might suffer. But Rathburn
also was convinced that Reese's pinched righteousness about the marriage had its roots in other resentments.

Linc had been determined to remain loyal after Gid defenestrated
himself from the upper reaches of the State Department—the sixth
floor, assistant secretary level—in 1968, landing with a thud at Georgetown University and in the antiwar movement. They even became closer
for a time: Linc was Gid's lifeline to respectability, to the world he had rejected and that now considered him a pariah; as long as Linc treated him
with the same respect as ever, Gid could believe there might be a way
back to government service when the insanity subsided.

But Linc's devotion was grating, too. He was a bit too conscious of the
ennobling power of an inconvenient friendship. Of course, Reese would
have come to resent Rathburn even if the friendship hadn't come with a
price: Gid detested dependency as a matter of principle; he despised his
own neediness. He had always stood apart, and above, even on those rare
evenings when he agreed to carouse with Linc and Charlie in Saigon. He
was never quite able to achieve informality. He never finished a beer.

And so the friendship had an excuse to shatter when Linc finally
bailed on his marriage, and then on his diplomatic career, in the early
seventies, moving to New York and private law practice. Charlie was in
Des Pointe during the Great Linc-Gid Dissolution (which, in Linc's
mind, was more devastating—certainly more unexpected—than the divorce), and he felt a renewed surge of interest from Rathburn. Suddenly,
there was an urgency to Linc's calls; their friendship, perfunctory for several years, resumed Vietnam intensity. Charlie was arriving in Washington, a freshly minted congressman, just as Linc was leaving; Linc was
discovering the world of postmarital delights just as Charlie was beginning to look for an escape hatch from Johanna. The daily phone calls
began. For Linc, a compulsive observer of the events of the moment,

Martin replaced Reese as prime interlocutor. For Charlie, still a political neophyte, Rathburn became an unofficial adviser and a portal to the world of fancy women.

"So, what did you think of her?" Linc asked now, which worried Charlie: he wasn't sure why Linc was suddenly *re*asking something so . . . personal.

"Of who?"

"Of Nell, of course," Linc said, then—happily—proceeded before Charlie could answer. "She's impossible. She thinks all my friends are jerks."

"All your friends *are* jerks," Charlie said.

"Except you," he said. "She said you were a babe."

"A *babe?*" Charlie laughed.

"You seemed to get on with her, too." Linc was staring at him intently now, assessing.

"She's fun," he said, "for a Darbyshire."

"Hey, by the way: don't tell me you played hide the salami with Harry Makrides's daughter. . . ."

"Jealous?"

"Curious," Linc said. "And appalled."

Charlie shrugged, smiled, patted Linc on the back.

"Anyway, about Nell—" Linc began again.

"Hey, I've been meaning to tell you," Charlie interrupted, initiating diversionary action. "I sat down with Bramlette to talk about Vietnam. About normalization." Bartle Bramlette, a middle-aged southerner who bore a passing resemblance to Spanish moss, was the chair of the Armed Services Committee.

"A suicide mission if there ever was one," Linc said, easily distracted, as always, by policy.

"Yeah, he said, 'Tell it to the vets.' "

"You think Bart is looking for a job?" Rathburn asked. "If Stanton wins?"

"Of course he is. Maybe secretary of state," Charlie said, flexing an eyebrow, torturing Linc—who hoped for the job himself, but knew that Gid would prevent him from ever getting it. "He thinks of himself as more than an aircraft-carrier-enabler these days. He's a statesman. . . ."

"Yeah, sure he is. If he had half a brain, he'd listen to you about Vietnam," Linc said. "He could provide cover for Stanton, coming from Alabama, Mr. Military and all. Good thing he's too proud for that. He won't give Stanton an inch, and then he'll be pissed that Jack never calls. And he'll be even more pissed when Parkinson becomes secretary of defense. Got to give Sly credit for latching on to Stanton like that—he saw his chance and he took it."

"You talked to Slick lately?" Charlie asked. "He's all over me."

"All the time. Before he runs a defense idea past Stanton, he tests it on me. Barney Rubin has got him taking TV lessons." Barney was Sly's Donna, with degrees in history from Harvard and physics from MIT. Linc paused; Draboskie droned on about the shame of the cities. "Charlie," he said, "there are times that I think I may ask her to marry me . . . and times I think—"

"Who?" Charlie asked, disgusted with himself for stepping on the second half of Linc's sentence, the important part, the caveat—astonished that Linc had returned the conversation to "private" business and even more astonished that Linc was contemplating marriage. "What?"

"Nell," he said. "You're right. She is different. She's been through a lot. Her first husband has AIDS. She's a good mother, her business is like an extended family. We don't have very much in common, but she has this quality—I just can't explain it . . . She's *unusual*," he said, making it sound wildly exotic. "Don't you think?"

"As I said, not your usual type."

"Yeah, but you meant *my* usual type. You've now changed the emphasis to suggest how unusual she is," Linc replied, and Charlie was struck, as ever, by the precision of Rathburn's auditory powers: the mark of a good diplomat.

"And so?" Charlie asked.

"And so, I don't know," Linc said, and then asked again. "So what did you think of her?"

"Can you *believe* Draboskie?" Charlie said. "Going on about the Japanese?"

WASHINGTON

———

8

————

Lynn Thurston lived in an understated but perfect white brick center-hall colonial on a very good street in Cleveland Park. She'd won the house and the custody of her two children, now college age, in the divorce settlement; her husband had won his legal secretary, and a new life in Laguna Beach. The settlement had been enough to allow Lynn to work part-time at a not-for-profit group, lobbying for more government funding of the arts. She spent her spare time fund-raising for the feminist wing of the Democratic party, which was how she'd met Charlie Martin.

There were political posters in the foyer, and pictures throughout the house of Lynn with the disastrous Democratic candidates of the past thirty years—her hemlines went up and down, her hairstyle changed a bit, but the hair color was always frosted ash-blond and the facial expression was ever-pleasant. The house was a bit cramped for spectacles, but fine for the midsized dinner parties at which she excelled. As a Washington hostess, Lynn was the equivalent of a small, vaguely prestigious liberal arts college—Vassar, perhaps. An invitation to her table was welcomed by the city's elite, if not quite prized.

In late October, Lynn decided to have a small Friday night party to celebrate Charlie's return to the city, after his season of campaigning in ten states for six hopeless Senate hopefuls, four good possibilities and for one very probable president of the United States, all of whom had Vietnam problems. She hadn't thought of inviting Lincoln Rathburn down for the party—New Yorkers were assumed Martians in Washington society—but when Charlie mentioned Lynn's plan, Linc immediately asked if he might be included, too (and, of course, he was). Linc was hoping to make several low-key appearances in Washington to jiggle the zeitgeist, insinuate his availability in the coming Stanton senior foreign policy advisery sweepstakes and cast subtle aspersions on the other contenders. He would bring Nell with him, which was a surprise: Charlie hadn't seen her, and Linc hadn't spoken of her, since the Democratic convention, although Charlie had found himself paying attention on the campaign trail to women with clever, Nell-ish looks, searching them out—the way Buzz zoned in on sweet-stemmed girls in chiffon dresses—courting them with his eyes. This was more a diversion than an obsession; he hadn't actively pursued a Nell surrogate—but she had opened a new area of possibilities, a different sort of woman to ogle and fantasize about.

When Nell and Linc arrived, Charlie was enmeshed in politichat with Holly McGuire, the widow of an esteemed political columnist, and Holly's new beau, William Fairchild, an ancient, slightly crumbling pillar of the Washington legal establishment. Charlie heard Lynn greeting Linc in the foyer; actually, he heard Linc's voice and he glanced over Holly's shoulder toward the doorway, causing Holly to swivel, too—an involuntary social reflex—and William Fairchild to follow her lead.

Lincoln Rathburn was sufficiently handsome that heads still turned when he entered a room, and his arrival was more noticed than Nell's by everyone except Charlie: She looked different; her thick blond hair was up, back, caught by a butterfly clasp atop her head. She was wearing an olive khaki suit over a burgundy silk shell. The suit had a slightly military feel to it; the jacket was Eisenhower length, fitted, with buttoned cuffs; the skirt was floor-length—the ensemble seemed off, a notch too dramatic, amidst the demure cocktail dresses of D.C.

She saw Charlie across the room and smiled. After a round of handshakes and introductions choreographed by Lynn, Nell drifted from Linc's side to Charlie's. "Okay, Senator, you're my life raft," she whispered, with a desperation that seemed, perhaps, a bit put on. "This is my first Washington dinner party. What do I do?"

"You nod your head appreciatively whenever Linc says something that seems pithy," he said, inhaling, hoping she was wearing that same perfume. She was. "If you want to make a splash, you can denounce welfare reform or something."

"What about drinking?" she asked. "Does one, in Washington?"

"Red or white?" he said. "Allow me."

"Brown," she said. "Jack Daniel's."

"Oh, dear!" he said, furrowing his brow, reaching for Nell-ish irony.

"Women who drink Jack Daniel's in Washington—and they are mostly of a certain age—tend to stoke up privately, before the party."

"How *fascinating*," Nell replied extravagantly. "How-*ev*-er . . . if I did want one, if I asked for one—would I be in deep shit? Does your Lynn keep any in stock?"

"I'll see," he said, titillated by the offhanded profanity, although the mention of "his" Lynn brought him back to the world, Lynn's world, of which the guest list was a pretty fair generic sampler: his-and-her journalists, a prominent black lobbyist, a senator and an ambassador. Sly Parkinson, looking suddenly svelte, was the star attraction—a bona fide Stanton "insider." His wife, Maggie, borne along on Sly's surge, was more of a presence than usual, too, in a slightly too-tiny black dress.

When Charlie returned with Nell's drink, she was off in a corner with Maggie Parkinson, talking . . . pottery?

"The good stuff!" Maggie said, eyeing Nell's bourbon. "If only I had the courage!"

"If I had the courage," Nell said, "I wouldn't need it."

If I had courage, Charlie thought, I'd do something more than flirt with her. "Sly's looking good," he said to Maggie. "A testament to the power of carrots?"

"He's been working so hard for this," she said, eyes glistening. She'd been working hard, too. She'd lost weight, or gained breast, or something. Her hair was permed and frosted, her face powdered; she looked neither oppressed nor faded—her usual states of disarray—but not quite fresh, either; a bit frazzled, perhaps. "He lives on the NordicTrack," she whispered.

"He'll be a great secretary, Maggie," Charlie assured her.

"I know," she said. "And a grating spouse."

They sat down to Lynn's perfect table, the silver and crystal shimmering, a puddle-of-yellow-roses centerpiece, a baby-everything menu—pygmy lamb chops and a dribble of field rice and eensy-weensy string beans. The table talk was suitably and equally minuscule. Charlie noted that most of the women left food on their plates, even though they'd been presented with tiny portions—a dainty tribal ritual of recent vintage. He had lascivious thoughts about the massive, unsubtle steaks and center-cut pork chops back home. These Washington people were grease-deprived.

There comes a moment in some good dinner parties, but in every bad one, when the conversation becomes general. This inevitably occurs when one of the duller men decides he's patronized the adjacent women long enough, makes eye contact with one of the other men at the table (a man he hopes to flatter or impress) and asks a question about Topic A in town. That night, the moment came when Nick Davis of *U.S. News & World Report,* a frequent sitter on the more obnoxious news-chat shows, asked Charlie Martin who he thought would be the secretary of state in a Stanton administration.

The room stopped. Linc interrupted his dissertation about the prescient columns Robert McGuire—Holly's late husband—had written about nuclear proliferation. Sly Parkinson glanced away from his conversation with the Swedish ambassador, checking to see if Martin had heard anything new.

"Richard Nixon," Charlie said.

Sly returned to his Swede, but Linc stayed tuned. It was show time for him now.

"Oh, come on," Nick said. He was postmaturely blond, the sort of person who looked younger than his age on television; up close, his face sagged under the weight of years of feigned comprehension.

"What do you mean, 'Oh, come on'?" Charlie asked. "Nixon knows an awful lot about foreign policy."

"Sly . . . Mr. Almost-Secretary-Designate, who do *you* think Gid Reese wants?" Nick asked. "Gid's set for national security adviser, right? He can't be secretary of state because of his antiwar history."

"I'm sure the Stanton people are too busy to even think about this stuff yet," Parkinson said in the bored, dismissive manner used by people who actually knew things—a clever ruse on Sly's part: Gid wasn't confiding in him or Charlie; and he certainly wasn't talking to Linc.

"Oh, come on," Nick said.

"Nick, why don't you tell us who it's going to be," Linc patronized. "You probably know a lot more than any of the rest of us."

"Well, I'm told that Gid is thinking about an academic, rather than the usual New York lawyer—maybe someone like Richard Lampton, up at Harvard. He was an 'under' in the Carter administration."

"Gid, huh?" Charlie scoffed. This numbnuts calling Gid *Gid* was intolerable: Reese wasn't even in office and he'd already become a first name, like "Henry" or "Zbig." "Who says that's what Gid wants?"

"Oh, you know," Nick said lightly. "The Great Mentioner."

The projectile spewing of Washington patter was giving Charlie a

headache. He wondered if he'd always been so impatient with these people, or perhaps—was he trying to see them as Nell might? But when he
broke his discipline and glanced over at her, she seemed very serious, her
head tilted back thoughtfully. He realized that Lynn—seated directly opposite Charlie at the other head of the table, her usual near-connubial
placement—had caught him watching Nell. But Lynn was more concerned with Charlie's impatient tone, and she was giving him a look,
communicating a quiver of concern—a vertical wrinkle, tracing up from
the bridge of her perfectly straight and utterly exquisite nose.

"You must know Lampton, Linc," Nick said. "From Carter days."

"Rick wrote a wonderful book about the Aguinaldo Insurrection after
the Spanish-American war," Linc proposed, damning with faint praise.

A palette of microscopic sorbets for dessert, with syrup dribbled ar-
tistically around the edge of the plate. Lynn then delicately tinkled her
glass with a butter knife. "Rather than play the same old Washington
name game," she said, "I thought it might be nice to spend a few minutes talking about the foreign policy challenges the next president will
face."

Charlie made an effort not to wince. He nodded back across the table
at Lynn. If there was a moment in life he truly loathed, it was the post-
sorbet debate initiated by hostly glass-tinkling. There were two possible
roles to play: one could be a holder-forth, or a wry questioner. Journalists and academics tended to be holders-forth; people with actual power
usually sat back and punctured the pontificators with wry questions.
Linc, who had the soul of a journalist and the breadth of a historian,
could be counted on to hold forth with brilliance and aplomb, but he
wouldn't go first. Nick Davis, Charlie guessed, would break the ice—and
he would talk about the Balkans. Charlie decided to wait for an appropriate moment to break off, go to the bathroom, get out of there, and
then return in time to ask a wry question.

"The biggest problem is that Stanton has just about guaranteed that
he's going to take action in Bosnia," Nick said, on cue. "And that is
bound to be a disaster . . ."

"Actually," Linc said, "I was in Brussels a few weeks ago, talking to Jim
Jerome at NATO and . . ."

Charlie made his move, wending his way toward the bathroom via the
kitchen, where he said hello to the Irish couple who always did Lynn's
catering. When he came out from the bathroom, he headed toward the
den—he would give ESPN a quick try, see if he could catch a play or two

of the Saturday night football game. And there was Nell, staring at a photo of Lynn with Michael Dukakis.

"She's quite beautiful," she said, wearily seductive, turning to Charlie. "But she's too old for you."

"She's five years younger than me."

"And twenty years older than the last one I saw you with," she said. "Why can't you pick on someone your own age?"

"You weren't interested in the Balkans?"

"Mairzy Doats and Serbs eat Croats," she said, draping an arm on Charlie's shoulder. Was she, he wondered, a little looped?

"It's Cro-ats." He smiled, allowing her arm to rest where it was. "One must be correct about such things in these precincts."

"You, Senator," she replied, "are real trouble."

She moved to kiss him, opening her mouth slightly—a hint of bourbon in the breeze—but diverted to the safety of his cheek at the very last moment. "But," she added, "I've had enough trouble for one life."

"I'm trouble?" he said, having come very close to doing something treacherous with his best friend's girl, deeply regretting that he hadn't. *"You* are trouble. . . . And what about Linc?"

"He's blond. I want the blond guy for a change," she said. She *was* a little looped. "The solid, straight-ahead blond guy. Blond on blond."

"You make him sound boring," Charlie said. "I can assure you: he's not."

"He's not dangerous," she said. "You are."

"I don't know about that. Endangered, maybe. An endangered species. . . ." What was he saying? She was making him feel drunk, too. "We'd better go back in," he said.

Rathburn was holding forth on the sins of Rebecca West, stylish Serbophile. It was time for Charlie's wry question. "Do you think, Linc," he said, "Stanton's hard line on Bosnia is more or less credible than his hard line on China?"

"More, I'd hope," he answered seriously . . . and went on to a discussion of Most Favored Nation trading status for China.

Charlie glanced over at Nell—not too abruptly, he hoped. She was looking at him, with an arched eyebrow and a wry smile. "Italy," she said, moving her lips silently.

Later, as they were saying good-bye to the last guests, Lynn leaned into him at the door and rubbed his ribs. She always smelled profoundly clean, as if her skin emitted talc rather than perspiration. "Charlie," she said, giving him her calmest look. "Is something going on? You seemed edgy tonight."

"Oh, just been a while since I've been to one of these—hard to take all these know-nothings who know everything. And seeing Linc so desperate—"

"He's not so desperate and they're not so bad," she said correctly. There were worse. He kissed her softly on the lips, ran his right thumb along her left eyebrow, which was straight and full, darker than her ash-blond hair. She really wasn't so bad, either: but she was not, even remotely, dangerous.

"Election night," he said, "you want to go to the Brits' with me?"

"It should have been *your* election night, Charlie."

"No, it shouldn't," he said. "But you're sweet."

*   *   *

Charlie spent most of the next few months in Des Pointe. The holiday season was time for all good politicians to stay close to home. The Senate was in recess, awaiting the arrival of the nation's first Democratic president in more than a decade. For Charlie, the charitable holidays—Thanksgiving and Christmas—had always meant a particularly intense period of good works and nostalgia, carrying on his mother's traditions at the East Side Community Center. He and Buzz and Edsy spent both holidays at the center: Charlie and Edsy serving meals, Buzz dressed as Santa Claus, distributing gifts and leading sing-alongs. He was out most nights between Thanksgiving and Christmas, attending holiday parties around the state and giving after-dinner speeches. He drifted into a Buzz-like schedule, musician time: staying up late at night after he came home, digesting his chicken and peas, watching old movies on cable.

He had gotten hooked on the Muffler Man ads, which he'd catch, alone in his room, after the late news most nights. There *were* a fair number of people who needed muffling. Lee Butler's choices were pretty astute: a baby crying in the row behind you at the movies, a fern bar waiter going on about the specials. Occasionally, he'd throw in a public figure: Saddam Hussein, Stanton, Louis Farrakhan, Yeltsin. The ads weren't exactly high-tech. Butler used audiotape and a series of still black-and-white photographs; the cuts from photo to photo were jerky, obvious, humorous—and the last photo would be doctored crudely: the victim would have a red scarf covering his mouth, and the audiotape suddenly muffled. There was an edge of populist menace to it. Butler offered a 20-per-cent discount on mufflers for American cars. But his tag line, delivered with a smile and wink—and that very professional voice—was nice: "Too bad everything isn't as easy to muffle as a car. . . ."

The week before Christmas that year, Butler took the funny ads off and ran an old one, of his grandfather wearing a Santa Claus cap in-stead of his usual straw boater, saying "Dat's a fun-ny noise" in smudgy kinescoped black and white. "We've been part of your life for half a cen-tury," Lee Butler said, surrounded by a smiling, blond generic wife and blithely perfect preteenage children in a living room that might well have been a set. "And you've been a part of ours. And here's a wish for the holiday season: may all the funny noises in your life be the sounds of laughter." And then, with a full orchestral version of "O Come All Ye Faithful," a slow-motion montage of people laughing—old people, young people, families—and the words "Season's Greetings from Butler Muffler."

Charlie actually found himself choked up the first time he saw the ad. He'd asked Calvin to join the family for the holidays and been turned down. Cal's excuse was gigs, which was credible. The holidays were peak season for musicians. But Charlie wondered what he'd have to do to make a connection with the kid. The impasse nagged at him: he knew the initiative had to be his; he understood—and almost admired—Calvin's caution. And he was disappointed in himself, disappointed that his paternity remained more official than emotional.

Buzz hadn't seemed too excited about the news of a grandson, either, when Charlie had told him about his trip to Houston. The old man's lack of interest was both aggravating and unthreatening: Buzz's laissez-faire patriarchy was, like Clarice's legacy, a very mixed blessing. He and Char-lie were easy with each other—Buzz had been impossible to rebel against (and so had Clarice, in her way: her good works were too admirable for even an adolescent to scorn).

Charlie found himself raising the Calvin question again, over brunch in the knotty-pine kitchen nook with the old man and Edsy, on the Fri-day after Thanksgiving. "You could have used Cal last night," he said, as Edsy fried up some cholesterol. "The Buzzards are sounding a little thin these days."

"Harlan's dragging bad." Buzz sighed, ignoring the mention of his grandson.

"You know, I'm really pissed the kid wouldn't come up for the holidays," Charlie pressed. Edsy looked up from the skillet. "I offered him a plane ticket."

"Well, he'll come in his own good time," Buzz said.

"Maybe you should go down there," Edsy suggested, then thought again. "Well, I guess it's tough, given all our good works this time of year. . . ." She paused, glanced at Charlie: Clarice was a burden for Edsy, too.

"Tryin' to think if I know any Oriental musicians," Buzz mused, nudged to some sort of response. "Not sure they have the chops for it, like the blacks and Latins. Too tight to swing. Too much treble in their music; not enough bass."

"Too bad I didn't have a quasi-Cuban kid," Charlie said.

"Brazilian wouldn't have been bad," Buzz said. He was very much into the lambada that winter. "Charles, how about this? The lambada, 'Blame It on the Bossa Nova' and 'Begin the Beguine'?"

" 'Begin the Beguine' doesn't fit," Charlie said, curtly, hoping that Buzz would notice his pique. But of course he didn't.

Phone. Linc. Hong Kong. "You awake?" Linc said. "That's a good sign. But why aren't you out collecting Toys for Tots? Isn't it that time of year?"

"It's Linc," Charlie announced.

"Ask him about the medley," Buzz said.

Charlie rolled his eyes, but complied. "Okay, Rathburn: The lambada, 'Blame It on the Bossa Nova' and blank . . ."

" 'Mambo Italiano,' " Linc said. "Rosie Clooney."

" 'Mambo Italiano'?" Charlie asked Buzz.

"A little thick," Buzz said. "Too Tin Pan Alley."

"I've got another one," Rathburn said. "It's on the tip of my tongue."

"That's where it always is with medleys. Where are you, the Mandarin? What's on the tube? How's Nell?"

"A *Name of the Game* with Tony Franciosa," he said. "Nell's swell— wouldn't meet me in Hawaii. Christmas play or something. You hear about Rich Lampton?"

"No. What?"

"He's it. Secretary of state."

"That's a shocker," Charlie said.

"Gid's fondest dream," Linc sighed. "A cipher secretary."

"Lampton's tolerable," Charlie said. "I mean, aside from Kissinger, how many dynamic sec-states have we had?"

"I kind of hoped that Stanton would do something interesting," he said.

Poor Linc: the first friendly administration since Carter, and he was in danger of being shut out of it. And it was all Charlie's fault—if Linc hadn't been so loyal a friend, he might have outflanked Gid in the Stanton camp, or outfoxed him.

"They'll come to you when they're in trouble," Charlie said. "They'll have to."

"Charlie," Linc said. "I've been talking to Sly. He wants me over at the Pentagon with him as an 'under' for Policy."

"Oh, God, Linc. Wrong side of the river." And, Charlie thought, a real recipe for trouble: State and Defense were natural enemies. Sly's strengths were theoretical and strategic. He'd lean on Linc for help in fighting the inevitable indoor battles with the State Department and the White House—and Linc would be only too happy to match wits with Gid Reese. "What does Barney Rubin say?"

"Barney's okay with it," Linc said. "He's gonna have his hands full inside the building. You know how the brass feel about Sly."

They hated him. He was a pointy-head. And he'd been pushing them to do something uncomfortable: think about what the military should look like in a world without a cold war. "Good thing he's lost all that weight," Charlie said. "Brass'd be merciless with a porky sec-def."

"They'll be merciless anyway. Sly's no warrior," Linc said. "He's never fired a weapon in anger."

"He's never done *anything* in anger, come to think of it." Charlie laughed. "You ever seen Slick angry?"

"Hungry," Linc said. "Horny."

"Poor Maggie," Charlie said. "Linc, I don't know about this—you across the river. Has Sly cleared it with Gid?"

"You think Gid'll fight it?"

"Of course not," Charlie said. "But he *will* find a way to tank it—and even if he doesn't, you really want to spend the next four to eight carrying water for the brass, finding ways to sabotage State?"

"What makes you think I'll do that?" Linc said. "I'm not out to ruin Gid."

Charlie laughed.

"Really," Linc said angrily.

"It's structural, Linc. It's part of the job. The Pentagon *exists* to come up with arguments for not doing the things that the dips over at State want to do," Charlie said. "I shouldn't even have to say that. You have it coded in your DNA. You're a dip. You love all the things the brass hates.

You love to 'intervene.' Forget about Gid. You're just not gonna spend the next four to eight working against the things you actually believe. I don't see it."

"At the Copa . . . Copacabana, the hottest spot north of Havana . . ." Linc crooned, badly. "Music and fashion were always the passion at the Copa—or was it music and passion were always the fashion? Anyway, that's your medley. Tell Buzz."

He was absolutely right. And Buzz thought so, too. "Use the Copa song to frame it—like the lambada and 'Bossa Nova' are dances they'd do at the Copa," he said. "Need a better drummer, though. Some bells and whistles, Mardi Gras stuff. Nice if I had the players to bring it off."

For Buzz, the medley game was getting all too hypothetical.

* * *

Charlie returned to Washington for New Year's Eve, and another tradition: accompanying Lynn to the annual party at the Georgetown home of Ben Bradlee and Sally Quinn. It was more work than revel, a floating press conference even though lawyers usually outnumbered the journalists in the room. This year, at the dawn of the Stanton era, he spent the evening in acute discomfort, not-gossiping with the Posties who filled the tomato-soup-colored living room, desperate to know if the senator had a line on who was going to be undersecretary of this and assistant secretary of that.

Sly Parkinson—now a prized catch as a guest—arrived late, Maggie in tow. He enveloped Charlie and planted a magisterial kiss on his forehead. "The fun begins," Sly said, calm—for once—and confident.

"Happy New Year, Mr. Secretary-Designate," Charlie said, returning the hug. "How's the Bugs Bunny diet going?"

Sly reached into his pocket, smiled sheepishly and pulled out a carrot. "It's a wonder my hair hasn't turned orange."

"Well, it's been worth the effort. You almost look fit. Mags, you look great, too."

"An actual vacation will do it every time," Maggie said, who was tanned and, as at Lynn's, wearing a very revealing, but floor-length, black silk dress. "I'm sure you missed the boy's constant calling these past few weeks."

In fact, Charlie had been amazed that, rather than tear into his new post, Sly had slipped off to the Caribbean with Maggie: a sign of sanity, perhaps.

"Yeah, well, I'm all vacationed out now," Sly said. "And ready for action. How about you?"

"His vacations are no vacation," Lynn interjected, slipping an arm around Charlie's waist, beneath his jacket, running her nails in the small of his back. "He's the Salvation Army of Des Pointe. I'd love to get him away sometime."

"Maybe the four of us," Maggie said. "The big guy gets an airplane with the job. Maybe we could go inspect a hot spot."

"My sort of hot spots, dear," Sly said, pausing for effect—and smoother than Charlie could ever remember seeing him, "are not your sort of hot spots."

And so Charlie was a bit surprised when Sly called him in early January and said, "I need to talk to you. ASAP. We got problems."

An hour later, Parkinson bounded into Charlie's office, sweaty and disheveled as ever, as if the New Year's Sly had been an apparition. They sat in armchairs, facing the marble fireplace—normally the chairs were turned away from the hearth, toward Charlie's old leather couch, but it was a cold winter day and there was a nice blaze going.

"Charlie, this sucks," Sly wailed, lurching right to the heart of his lament. "A hundred tons of bullshit is standing between me and the good stuff. I'm never going to be able to get my force reevaluation into Stanton's budget this year. Jack just doesn't want to make the fight. He's scared of the brass. And he figures he's going to have enough trouble raising taxes, he doesn't want to piss off the military porkers. Truth is, Jack loves all the jobs these obsolete weapons platforms generate. Look at this."

He handed Charlie several sheets of legal paper, a wish list of weapons to be cut or combined. He kept up a steady stream of jabber as Charlie was scanning. "I did another rejigger. See, you give the Air Force the new fighter, and the Navy the helicopter. Eliminates duplication twice! Saves zillions! I mean, is that so unreasonable? And you know what? No dice. They don't even want to talk about it. Not till next fiscal year. I mean, what's the point of having me as secretary, if I can't shape the force?"

"So, you know what?" Charlie said. "You're Mr. Maneuver Strategy. What happens when a force meets resistance? You search out the enemy's weak point. Put your assets there. And then, when you begin to succeed, you reinforce success. You taught me that. Right?"

"Right, but look at this," Parkinson said, pushing his glasses up his nose, handing Charlie some typed pages, with graphs. "A rough cut on a new war-fighting strategy. Did it over Christmas. Check out what I did with the Navy—"

"Sly! I'm sure it's fucking brilliant, but you're not listening."

"Okay, okay." Parkinson sighed. "It's just *frustrating* how few people care about doing it right."

"You thought winning was going to change that?"

"Yeah, I guess winning just means they fight us harder," Sly agreed, with a laugh. "So how do we fight them harder?"

"You don't get frontal," Charlie said. "You take the rear. Learn the building from the inside out"—insiders called the Pentagon "the building" and the State Department "the department"—"charm the brass a little. Do some traveling. Use that plane—but make sure you pay Maggie's way. Then figure out the best way to bust their chops next year. . . ."

"Yeah, well," Sly said, with a sigh. "It's the sort of scenario that makes the Doctrine of Overwhelming Force seem pretty attractive. No wonder the brass like it so much: Ka-POW. Ka-BOOM. So long, suckers! . . . Jesus, Charles." He paused, thinking, jiggling his leg. "I wish politics was as easy as doctrine. I'm gonna need your help with the committee. You know how Bramlette's always been. He hates my guts. Talk about maneuver: he's got the building laced with his people—a fair number of them in uniform. He's gonna be looking for ways to fuck me up."

"He's there, Sly," Charlie said. "An immovable force. You're going to have to finesse him."

"Finesse him? Give me a break." Parkinson was up, overheated, pacing. "He's trying to kill me! He's at it already. He's got lists of people he wants in place. Undersecretaries. Assistant secretaries. *His* people. He and Gid are in this together, trying to fuck me. Gid's got lists, too. He says Stanton wants diversity—but that's just a cover. What it is is Gid and Bramlette are squeezing my ass from two different directions. Two different lists. And, guess what: none of the people on their lists are on my list."

"What does Linc say?"

Sly stopped, grabbed his armchair, slid it over directly in front of Charlie and plopped down in it. "Charlie, Bramlette doesn't want Linc. He doesn't want him anywhere near the joint."

"What did you expect?" Charlie said, thinking about how much Sly needed someone with Linc's talents to steer him through the swamps. "Sly, you do have some leverage here. You're gonna be Mr. Secretary."

"Charlie," Sly said, leaning forward, putting his hands on Charlie's knees, his face close in, a faint, sour sweatiness filling the space between them. "Charlie, these people are so fucking insidious. There's other stuff going on. As for Linc, Gid says they have other plans for him."

"What, Siberia?"

"Close," Sly said, up again, pacing. "Ambassador to Russia, I hear."

"You're kidding, right?" Charlie shook his head and laughed. When it came to his rivalry with Lincoln Rathburn, Gideon Reese could be hilariously unsubtle.

"Look, Charlie, I gotta get going—I gotta fly down to Mammoth, see Stanton. There's—you don't want to know."

"What?"

"It's bullshit!" Sly exploded, then quickly calmed himself. "Standard confirmation bullshit. I can handle it. But help me with this. Look, I know my weaknesses. That's why I wanted Linc. Do me a favor: think of anyone else who could do war-game political strategy for me?"

"I'll think about it." Charlie stood and put an arm around Parkinson, walking him to the door. "But, Sly, listen: you've gotta cool it. You're gonna have a coronary. You've got to roll with it. So they work you over a little now, but once you're in the building, you're there—you'll know more than they do, you'll figure out how to fuck them back, get the good stuff done. Remember how impossible base closings seemed at first? Remember the day you punched the hole in the wall of Frenchy Pierce's office? But who figured out the answer, the independent commission? You did, Slick."

"Charlie," he said, not listening. "You gotta help me."

In addition to his other talents, Hilton Devereaux had a master's degree in gossip. He was religious about *MacNeil/Lehrer* and *Crossfire*, of course, but he'd also keep track of *Entertainment Tonight* and *Hard Copy*— and he was wired to the informal press secretaries' trashline on the Hill. Charlie was perpetually amazed by Hilton's storehouse of delights. And so, after Sly left, Charlie called him into the office and asked if there was anything in the wind about the secretary of defense–designate.

"Like what?" Hilton had never entertained such a request from the boss before. "Must have been a fun meeting in there."

"Like anything," Charlie said. "I don't know. You know how it works: guy gets nominated, all sorts of vermin start crawling out—Sly's had marital stuff, and who knows what else. Anyway, we should try to keep track of the garbage, be an early warning system, stay out in front of the story. Anything happens, people are going to be asking my opinion. Right?"

But it was Lincoln Rathburn, another world-class information receptacle, who provided the goods on Sly Parkinson, the morning after the secretary-designate's histrionic visit to Charlie's office.

"Remember that two-week trip to the Caribbean Sly took last month?" Linc asked. "He went to a very interesting island: Walnut Hill Hospital."

"What?" Charlie felt sandbagged. So *that* was why Parkinson had been so exercised in his office. "For what?"

Rosemary popped her head in. "Your father's on the phone."

"Tell him I'll call him back."

"For phentermine," Linc was saying. "Apparently it's a knockout diet pill . . ."

Rosemary popped her head back in. "Your dad asked you to call him as soon as you can."

That didn't sound like Buzz. Charlie wondered if something was wrong. He realized that Rathburn had been talking as he'd been thinking. Now Linc was saying "So he starts in on downers to limit the effects of the diet pills—and soon he's hooked on both, and he's got to kick them both."

"Wait a minute, Linc," he said. "Back up."

"Back up?"

"Sorry. Grand Central Station here," Charlie said. "Okay if I put Hilton on the other line? He should hear this, too." He motioned to Devereaux, who picked up the phone over by the leather couch. "So, Linc, start from the beginning."

"Okay. The *Times* called me today. They have a story working—breaking tomorrow, probably—that Sly checked himself into Walnut Hill last month because he was popping diet pills like Tic Tacs. There's a rumor he was doing downers, too, to counteract the other stuff."

"There's a rumor?" Charlie said.

Donna appeared now, slapping a Post-it on the desk: *O'Brien—Ugt. Mtg. in $^1/_2$ Hr. His office.*

"Well, who knows what they have," Linc went on. "I'm surprised they haven't called you."

"Hilton, have they called?" Charlie asked. "The *Times*?"

"I'll go check the list."

"Linc, Sly was over here yesterday. That's why I was trying to get you last night," Charlie said.

"Did he tell you that Gid screwed me?"

"Yeah," Charlie said, restraining himself: Linc's employment saga was a sideshow. "But he was slightly more concerned about Gid and Bramlette screwing him. I figured it was classic Sly. He panics at the sight of a brick wall, then he figures out how to knock it down. But this is bigger, more public than he's used to—"

Rosemary ducked her head in. "Mike Coleman for you, from Mammoth Falls."

"Hey, Linc," Charlie said. "Mike Coleman's on the other line—three guesses why, I imagine."

"Okay. Call me tonight. And Nell wants to know, the Midwest Ball is formal, right?"

"Nell's coming down?"

"Of course," Linc said. "She's never been to an inauguration. So?"

"So, what?" Charlie noticed Hilton noticing his reaction to the Nell news.

"Is it formal?"

"How the fuck should I know?" Charlie said. "I'm a Democrat. I think I wore a leisure suit to Carter's inauguration."

He punched in Mike Coleman. "Charlie, you hearing this shit?"

"What shit?"

"The *Times.*"

"Rumors," Charlie said. "What do they have?"

"They got a tip, disgruntled staffer or something—Barney Rubin says he knows the woman—who claims Sly was popping diet pills, and so out of it that he had to check himself into Walnut Hill last month. The admissions records confirm it."

"And what does Sly say?"

"He says it was a heart thing." Mike sighed. "Atrial fibrillation."

"And what do the doctors say?"

"They haven't yet."

"So what's your play?"

"We're shrugging it off, officially," Mike said. "But, Charlie, why the fuck couldn't he have told us?"

"You know Sly," Charlie said, meaning: how the hell should I know?

"Charlie, what's it look like on the committee?" Mike asked. "We got any trouble?"

"Funny you should mention that," Charlie said. "Sly seems to think Gid and Bart Bramlette are double-teaming him."

"Look, we made a mistake. We assumed the whole world knew we were going to name Sly," Mike said. "So we didn't make the usual pre-announce call-around. A major fuck-up. Bramlette calls Gid, furious because he wasn't consulted on the nomination—so now he wants to be consulted on everything. Every fucking assistant secretary. And he doesn't want Linc—"

"And I'm sure Gid's really upset about that," Charlie said.

"Stow it, Charlie," Mike said angrily. "I think it'd probably be wise if you and I stayed clear of the Linc and Gid situation, huh?"

"I think it'd be a lot wiser if you guys didn't play bullshit games with Bart Bramlette against your own fucking secretary of defense," Charlie shouted, losing it a little. "You're playing with fire, Mike. The last thing Stanton wants to do is lose control of the Pentagon."

"I don't think there's much chance of that," Mike said calmly. "Although there might be, if Rathburn were there."

"Bullshit," Charlie said, although he knew Mike had a point.

"Charlie—could you do me one tiny fucking favor?" Mike asked. "Could you see past Linc and keep an eye on Bramlette for us? You're right. He's trouble. We're gonna need you to be our guy on the committee. Sly's gonna need you."

"Fuck you," Charlie said, letting Coleman off the hook. "When you coming north?"

"Weekend," Mike said. "Charlie, this whole operation is whacked."

"That good, huh? Tell me."

"Sometime when we can drown it."

"See ya, Mike."

Rosemary now. "You want to talk to Mustafa?"

"Jesus Lord." The office was suddenly humming; crises—and big deals, like inaugurations—cranked things up: public life as pinball. He caromed about, slamming targets, bouncing off bumpers, flippers flapping, lights flashing, bells and whistles: *bingbingbingbingbing*. "Is Moose here?"

"You kidding?" Rosemary rolled her eyes. "Where else would he be?"

Mustafa had tried to stop the senator in the outer office several times in the past few days, but Charlie had blown past him and he was feeling guilty. "Okay, send him in."

Mustafa ambled in, looking neat and workerly: white shirt, sleeves rolled; dark slacks. "Hey, Fred. Whassup, you okay? I've only got a minute."

"What you doin' this Sunday, boss?" Mustafa stretched out, he almost seemed to be lying down, in the chair across the desk from Charlie.

"Not sure."

"I was hopin' you could be around. I'm having my Ceremony of Rebirth—and since you're the guy who started it all . . ."

"Ceremony of Rebirth?"

"My baptism, Chuck," he said. "I've come to know the Lord."

Charlie bit his tongue, tried to think of something to say—

"I'm *feeling* again," Mustafa said, rising up in his chair, placing his hands flat on the desk. "I'm saved. You gotta come. You're the only family I got, man. DonnaMendoza's coming," he said, running her name together rhythmically.

"I don't know. We'll see."

"How 'bout Wednesday night?" Mustafa said. "Reverend Ronny could probably do it then, too."

"We've got an inauguration Wednesday. . . ."

"Yeah, that reminds me: You think you could score me twenty or so tickets for some of the kids from the church?"

"Only twenty?" Charlie smiled.

"Be super for them, seeing the President and all—"

Devereaux and Rosemary at the door.

"Hold on, Fred," Charlie said.

"Billy Bergstein, from the *Times*, called fifteen minutes ago," Hilton said, popping his head back in. B.B. was their lead Defense Department guy.

"You know what to do," Charlie said.

"No *kidding*," Hilton said. It was what journalists—the good ones—always did when they were pumping you, feign surprise and intense interest in whatever you were saying: "No *kidding*!" or "Really!" or whatever else might make you spill more than you wanted to. Devereaux would reverse the process, and find out what the *Times* had.

Donna popped in: "Frank Mix on the phone."

"Bingbingbing," Charlie said. "Fred?"

"Yo."

"I gotta take this. Donna, see if you can score Moose some inaugural tickets," Charlie said.

Frank Mix was the Republican boss, the Senate minority leader. South Dakota. World War II vet. Lost an eye (and one of his testicles, it was said) at the Bulge. Talked like that—diamond-sharp sentence fragments.

"Chuck," he said. "Whatchagotabout Sly?"

"Garbage. Same garbage you're hearing."

"He got some food thing, or what?"

"Frank, what if he did?"

"Charlie, it's not me. Dickie Ganther's giggling his ass off. Says Bramlette wants to torpedo Parkinson."

"What a jerkoff," Charlie said, thinking: *bingbingbingbingbing*. Ganther was the lead Republican on Armed Services.

"Chuck," Mix said slowly. "You know, I could trade for any of your guys, it'd be you."

This was just about prolixity for Frank Mix. Something bad was up.

"Thanks, Frank," Charlie said. "You, too. I don't know about some of those other Wiffle balls you've got, though."

"Trouble is, Bart Bramlette's not alone," Mix said. "Th' wing nuts are restless. They want Sly's scalp."

"That's great," Charlie said sarcastically. "For dieting too seriously?"

"Pills are pills. Anyway, it's not about Sly," he said. "It's about Stanton."

Of course, it would be: hurt Stanton right away, put him on the defensive, don't let him get a head of steam for his first hundred days.

"So you're telling me you're bailing on Sly?"

"Didn't say that," Mix said. "But if you see this thing going down, give me a heads-up. If I do back him, don't want any surprises."

"Frank, he's not going down," Charlie said reflexively, a stab of doubt undermining the force of the defense.

"Hope not," Mix replied, understanding the unstated caveat. "Sorta think he's on the right track with that force reevaluation stuff. Anything that ticks off the brass can't be too bad."

Devereaux was back. Donna came in. "The majority leader wants to know where you are—he was expecting you a half hour ago," she said.

"I'm on my way," he said. "Donna, I need to talk to Sly, soon as I'm out of O'Brien's. He's down in Mammoth Falls with Stanton. If you can't find Sly, get me Maggie." Then, to Devereaux: "Let's walk instead of taking the subway. I need some fresh air."

"Senator, it's freezing out," Hilton said.

"Come on, Hilton, don't be such a sis—" Charlie stopped abruptly, turned crimson.

"You're such a *liberal*," Hilton said.

———

"Mr. Tougoulala," Don O'Brien said, greeting Hilton instead of Charlie. "I think your senator and I are going to want a private discussion here."

"Don, I'd like Hilton to sit in—he's got a good head for this stuff," Charlie said. O'Brien eyed him quickly—okay, you son of a bitch: I'm not gonna fight you on it, but you're starting this conversation with an IOU.

"All right, then," O'Brien said. "Would you care for a beverage, Mr. Devereaux? Senator?" They both shook him off. "Good, I'll get right to it: Bramlette, that horse's ass, wants a closed session of the Armed Services Committee to deal with Mr. Parkinson's weight-loss strategies. The good news is, I finally rated a phone call from the next leader of the Free World. Called me at midnight. At home. He wanted my 'input.' Listening between the lines, I gleaned that he wanted me to stuff Bartle."

"And?" Charlie asked.

"I informed him that the Republicans would probably want all this out in an *open* session. But I wanted your thoughts before we move on it, one way or another. Sly's your guy, no?" Don said, pleased with the rhyme. "Dov, call Senator Bramlette's office. Ask him to come over now. . . . Charlie, what do we know about this?"

"Not much," he said.

"That's helpful," O'Brien said. "We do know that Porky's lost a lot of weight."

"We do know that," Charlie said. "Maggie said he was addicted to NordicTrack. And I know he was eating a lot of . . . carrots."

O'Brien snorted.

"Yeah, I know," Charlie said, feeling like a mortal idiot. "He was pretty jumpy in my office last night. But Sly's always been a little hyper."

"An excellent quality in a secretary of defense," O'Brien said. "This is what your generation is offering us in the way of leadership?" Charlie didn't know what to say. "I'm going to get Mike Coleman on the squawker when we're all assembled here, and sit all over him, find out what the White House actually knows. Can you believe that Brahman dipstick Gideon Reese refused to participate? He won't do conference calls. We have to live with this nonsense for the next eight years?" He looked at Charlie, to see if he thought it was going to be eight years. Charlie wasn't sure. "What's your assessment of the Committee politics?" O'Brien asked.

"Bart wants to run DOD from his office," Charlie said. "So he'll be all over Sly—humiliate him, but not wipe him out, I'd guess."

"Look, Senator," O'Brien said, with a perfunctory smile, "I'm in your corner on this one. I know Parkinson's strengths. But he's not the most polished boyo to come down the pike—and a House guy, to boot. Anyway he's your guy now, Chas. You're steering the nomination, far as I'm concerned. And best of luck: you're steering through heavy traffic."

Charlie was mulling this mixed blessing when Bartle Bramlette arrived, elegant in a double-breasted blue blazer with brass buttons and a bold, strawberry-checked shirt, a sky-blue tie, cuffless gray slacks and black Gucci loafers—he looked as if he were dressed for cocktails on a lesser cruise line. The senator from Alabama was a truly unattractive human being: bald, liver-spotted forehead and hands, uneven lower teeth visible when he spoke, a grinding, phlegmy voice made barely tolerable by his slow, 'Bama drawl. He was accompanied by Laura Meadows, tall, plain, prematurely graying, earth-tone clothes—the chief of the Armed Services Committee staff. Laura's height reinforced Bart's lack of; it was always a surprise how short he was—he played larger, especially on TV. "Senator," Bramlette greeted Charlie warily, then turned to O'Brien: "This smells of swamp gas, Don. They don't consult. And they didn't vet this guy properly. It just won't do."

"You call a 'closed' session and it'll communicate that the United States Senate is worried about—"

"Pills are pills," Bramlette interrupted. It was becoming a refrain. "And what Ahhm proposing is a compromise, Mr. Majority Leader. Ahh've heard you understand the concept. The press and the more ex-*ci*-ta-ble Republicans want all this in the open. We can handle the personal business along with the usual security issues in closed session, then open it up for the policy."

"Bart," Charlie said, "we don't know what 'all this' is yet."

"We know damn well what 'all this' is," Bramlette purred. "Sly's not cut out to be the secretary of defense. He's got a lot of fancy theories. He can take them on up to Harvard and be a star. Down hee-yah, however . . ." Bramlette paused for effect. "Well, he's slovenly, undisciplined, self-indulgent. I don't see how the military can respect a—"

"The military fucking better," Charlie interrupted. "Any member of the brass who can't find a way to respect the secretary of defense should get his butt cashiered. I'd much rather have Sly"—he stared directly at Bramlette and hit him where it hurt—"than someone who never served in the military and mythologizes those who do in order to make up for his own deficiencies."

"Boys, boys, boys," O'Brien said, chuckling.

"The point is," Bramlette said to O'Brien, turning angrily away from Charlie, "if Mr. Parkinson is popping pills, I want Stanton to know we are displeased—and we'd request that he pull this puppy back before it pisses all over us."

Happily, a secretary came in with the news that Mike Coleman was on the phone. "Well, Bartle," O'Brien said. "Maybe now we'll be able to find out what 'all this' is and assemble a strategy to keep ourselves unpissed upon. Michael, you there . . . ?" Donny shouted at the phone, regarding it skeptically, as if it were an immigrant taxi driver in an unfamiliar city.

"Yup," Mike said. "Good afternoon, Senator."

"Now, Mike, I have Senators Bramlette and Martin here, and members of our staffs. I want you to know there's a fair amount of concern here. We all know and respect Congressman Parkinson, but there is concern. We want to support the President, but we won't be able to do that well unless we have every last bit of information available."

"We understand that, sir, and we're grateful for your support," Mike said.

"So what do we know?" Bramlette asked. "What's Parkinson's *story?*"

"Hello, Senator Bramlette. Good to hear your voice again," Mike said. Bart emitted a skeptical snort. "The President-elect, Gideon Reese and I just got out of a meeting with Congressman Parkinson, who was kind enough to fly down here last night."

"And?" Bramlette pushed.

"It was a very good meeting," Mike said. "Congressman Parkinson told the President-elect that he'd had some trouble with prescription diet pills. Apparently, they were causing an irregular heartbeat. Because of his history of cardiovascular troubles, he checked himself into Walnut Hill, and had the problem taken care of."

"Mike, you saying he was hooked on the diet pills?" O'Brien asked.

"Not quite, Senator," Mike said. "He was in a preaddictive phase."

"What kind of therapeutic crapola is *that?*" Bramlette asked, laughing derisively. Charlie winced and wondered: given Sly's history of heart problems, what sort of doctor would prescribe diet pills in the first place?

"He wanted help with alternative dieting strategies," Coleman said. "He was afraid that if he suddenly stopped the pills, there would be a bounce-back effect."

"Mike, it would seem to me," Don O'Brien said, all caramel, "if you have to go to a hospital to stop using a medication, you've got a problem."

"I don't know," Coleman said. "The President-elect thought it was very admirable that Congressman Parkinson took these precautions."

Bramlette shifted disgustedly in his chair.

"Look, we're not talking about heroin," Mike said. "We're talking about diet pills. Sly sensed they were having an impact on his heart. He wanted to figure out a way to stay in shape. He—"

"Who prescribed them?" Bramlette asked. "What kind of horse's ass prescribes diet pills to a man with a heart condition?"

"Sly's doctor was an old family friend," Coleman said calmly. "Sly apparently talked him into it. And by the way, he's got a clean bill of health from his cardiologist."

"Well, that's just great," Bramlette said biliously.

"Look, Bart, let's bottom-line it," Coleman said calmly. "Worst case scenario: he's beginning to feel a dependence on these pills. He has the good sense to realize his own frailties and goes to get help before the medication gets the upper hand. You want to deny him the chance to serve because he acted responsibly?"

"Why was the jackass taking the diet pills in the first place?" Bramlette asked.

"They were part of a carefully supervised regimen of exercise, plus a low-fat, high-fiber diet," Coleman said evenly. "He wanted to be in fighting trim if this assignment materialized. You knew that, right, Charlie?"

"All except for the pills," Martin said.

"So, Bart," Coleman continued, "you think there'll be much sentiment for denying Sly this post because he was a little too enthusiastic getting into shape for it?"

"Is that what *The New York Times* is going to say?" Bramlette asked.

"Who knows what the *Times* will say?" Mike replied. "But that's what Sly told them. And let me tell you what the President-elect would like: Congressman Parkinson has agreed to address these problems in his opening statement in open hearing when you meet to confirm him. We don't want a closed session. If we had one, there'd be leaks and rumors. People might assume that something's really wrong with the guy. That would be counterproductive, if not unfair."

Interesting: Stanton had outthought both Bramlette and the Republicans. He was giving the wing nuts what they wanted, an open hearing, daring them to do the embarrassing demolition work in public, gambling that the American people would sympathize with a secretary of defense who'd Had a Problem and Dealt with It. Charlie was lost in admiration until Hilton tapped his shoulder and handed him a yellow sheet of paper with a single word on it: "Downers?"

"Mike," Charlie started, then realized he'd better raise the question later, privately, with Sly.

"What, Charlie?"

"You're going to make sure that all of this is laid out square?" Charlie saw that O'Brien had noticed his reticence.

"Sure," Mike said. "You fellas have anything else you wanted to ask?"

"The question is, Mr. Coleman," Bramlette drawled, "you are sure that the vetting is now complete?"

The answer was: not entirely. But Mike wasn't going to say that. He simply expressed his confidence in Sly, expressed his confidence that the Senate Democrats would support the nomination and left the unstated message that it would be really smarmy for them to stab their first president in twelve years in the back before he even took the oath of office.

Donna couldn't find Sly. He was in midair, apparently—and perhaps appropriately—on his way back from Mammoth Falls. In late afternoon, though, she did manage to locate Margaret Parkinson. Charlie took the call, sitting on his leather couch, legs up on the coffee table, working through a stack of go/no go public appearance memos from Donna and Mary Proctor, swigging a Diet Pepsi. "Mags?" he asked. "You okay?"

"Fabulous. You know what happened today? I get a call from a *Post* Metro reporter working a profile—our life in Rockville and so on—and she's got this hot tip: Sly 'abused' our daughter." Maggie began to laugh. "You know what the 'abuse' was? It's Parkinson family legend! Sly always had to have candy around, saltwater taffy. He was ad— hooked on the stuff. Anyway, Becca once found his stash and ate an entire box. He wanted to kill her . . . you know how impatient he is and you know where he lives, Charlie: in his brain, doing his calculations. The precision of the F-16 versus the tonnage delivery of the F-14. That's all that matters."

"Whooaa, Maggie," Charlie said. It was dark in the office; most everyone had gone home. "Slow down. Are you saying that Sly did something—hit Rebecca, or something—he shouldn't have?"

"Of course he hit her," Maggie said, exasperated. "I mean, if you ever had a kid, Charlie, you'd think this was hilarious. . . . I mean, *this* is the stuff of headlines? Jesus, belting her wasn't even the worst thing he ever did as a father. At least," she laughed, "he was paying attention to her for a minute or two. The truth is, Mr. Secretary didn't know that she existed. I couldn't get him to a school play or a soccer game. With Mikey, either—one year, he agreed to coach Little League, assistant coach of course, and he didn't make it to a single game. Sly's a lousy father, Charlie. My kids are orphans. That's the real scandal."

"Maggie, uhh, no—forget it."

"What?"

"No, I was just wondering," Charlie said. "Why'd you guys get back together?"

"You really want to know?" she asked bitterly.

"Sure," Charlie said. "Unless you don't want to tell me."

"No, it's just—how long have we known each other? Twenty years?" Maggie said. "And you've never really asked me a personal question before. It's always been 'How's the kids?'—and then you don't even listen when I tell you. Just like him. But now, all of a sudden you're curious—is it because you care about us, or because you don't want to be embarrassed?"

"C'mon, Mags, Sly's a friend."

"Bullshit, Charlie. Far as I know, Sly has no friends. He has longtime acquaintances, like you. It passes for friendship. Isn't that what you Lordly guys do? Pretend to have friends, because admitting you don't have any would be socially unacceptable? I mean, you're never lonely. You always have your fabulous selves to keep you company."

"C'mon, Maggie," he said.

"Boy, it's a good thing you weren't into marriage." Maggie was careening, furious. "You saved untold numbers of women serious pain."

"Thanks a lot," Charlie said.

"It's not that you're not nice guys," Maggie continued, unstoppable. "Sylvester's a nice guy. Smarter than God. And unlike Sylvie, you and Linc are even sort of charming—but jeez, the sun rises and falls on you guys, and on you alone. It's not even that you're selfish, although you surely are: it's that you're oblivious."

"Well, I'm not sure that—"

"All right, Charlie, I'm venting." Maggie sighed, relenting finally. "But the Big Guy took off for Mammoth Falls last night without even telling me he wasn't coming home. Calls me from there at midnight. That sort of thing can make you crazy. It's innocent. It's always been innocent. He's innocent. It was also just totally innocent that glorious day he came in and announced, 'Look, Mags, I've got this other woman—and I'm leaving.' Just like that. I'm devastated. I'm in tears and he looks at me and says, 'Well, for chrissakes, this isn't easy for me either.' He wants *my* sympathy."

"Nice," Charlie said, not wanting to hear more.

"Well, you *said* you wanted to know," Maggie scolded. "We were apart for eighteen months. I read every one of the books about women who pick the wrong men, women who get trapped, women who hate themselves. I did emotional abuse workshops. The whole thing. I worked superhard after he left to get my act together. I lived at the gym, got a face-lift, a boob job. I'm ready to go out—and then, right then, he comes back. Now he's teary. Now he's all alone. I tell him to get lost, and I'm feeling really proud of myself. But he's back, with flowers. Every day. At school." Charlie remembered, vaguely: Maggie was something like a high school guidance counselor. She had a life, too. "Relentless. That's another thing about you guys: you don't know how to take no for an answer. You always get what you want. What are my sorry workshops against his stupid will? But you know what? It's been okay. A miracle of miracles. The world's oldest adolescent becomes a para-grownup. We've been having fun together this past year. We're playing tennis. We go to movies. We're in a book club—nineteenth-century novels. And now, every damn thing we ever . . ."

She trailed off.

"Maggie," he asked, "what about the diet pills?"

"It was nothing," she said.

"How'd he get the prescription?" Charlie asked.

"He didn't," she said. "I got it for him."

"Do the Stanton folks know that?"

"No. We papered it over. Doc's an old family friend, retired now. He was pissed at me, but he doesn't give a shit about lying. . . . Gimme a break, Charlie," Maggie said, calmer now, sensing his concern. "Sly was getting himself together—he really has, you know. Gotten his act together. He knows secretary of defense is serious business. He wants to look like Patton. So he tries the pills, starts fluttering, goes to Walnut, drops the pills."

"Did he use downers to take the edge off?"

"Define downers."

"What do you mean?"

"Is Valium a downer? Is booze?"

"I guess the question, Mags, is whether he was hooked."

Maggie laughed. "Oh, come on, Charlie. He's hooked on *everything*. Saltwater taffy. Carrots. NordicTrack. Efficient weapons platforms. He's hooked on life."

* * *

At home that night, riding his Exercycle, trying to decompress after Maggie finished downloading on him, Charlie watched the news shows on television—Parkinson's problems weren't news yet, but there was another drug controversy brewing, a firestorm over the musicians who'd be performing at the inaugural events: some had not only used drugs but written songs—twenty-five years earlier—celebrating drug use. Various righteous sorts were pummeling the Stanton administration over this.

"You know, this whole fucking country needs shut-up therapy," Charlie said, when Linc phoned in that evening from Sun Valley. "You wonder how the Sly story is going to play in this atmosphere. I've got to admit: I'm worried. And pissed at Sly. Taking the pills was really dumb. Not telling us about Walnut Hill, game-planning this, was even dumber. And, Linc, weren't you just in New York?"

"You think diet pills disqualifies him?" Rathburn said derisively.

"It doesn't make a difference what I think," Charlie said. "You know the argument: recklessness, poor judgment."

Linc laughed. "About his own life, no question," he said. "But in matters of military force architecture, can you think of anyone less reckless, anyone with better judgment?"

"One of the things you hire a secretary of defense to manage is his own fucking life," Charlie said. "So he doesn't ruin ours."

"Well, there are two theories about this—about where you put a visionary in a bureaucratic structure," Linc said, beginning a lecture. "You can put him at the top and surround him with a strong staff, who actually run the place—or you can tuck him away in an office somewhere, pick and choose his least upsetting, and probably least innovative, ideas and—"

"Linc, I gotta go," Charlie interrupted. He had drifted into a rumination about the management of his own life: he had forgotten his father's phone call in the fury of the day. Talk about oblivious. Buzz with an important message?

"It must be something big." Linc laughed. "I thought I was being pretty brilliant."

"You're always brilliant," Charlie said. "You ever get bored with that?"

He called Buzz immediately.

"Sorry, Pop, for not getting back sooner. You okay?"

"Free and breezy, just wanted to thank you for the late Christmas gift."

"The Christmas gift?" he asked, thoroughly relieved to hear Buzz sounding same-old, same-old.

"Grandkid. Showed up on my doorstep yesterday," he said. "Middle of that blue howler—dumped two feet, canceled my Elks gig. Weird name, Rosenbaum. You should work on him, get it changed: I can see the Calvin Martin Quartet . . . the Cal Martin trio."

"So what's the deal, Pop?" Charlie was startled, but there was another, more intense reaction beneath the shock: he was pleased, and curious. Cal and Buzz had found each other. He wanted to be there, to see them together. "How long is he there for?"

"Didn't say," Buzz replied. "But he's cool. We've been jamming a little."

"Any good?"

"Not bad. And he's been doing the shopping for Edsy."

"Is he there?" Charlie asked, desperately curious about Cal's reaction to Buzz. "Can I speak to him?"

"No, he's out somewhere—Edsy says he went to the theater," Buzz said. He still pronounced it the-ya-ter. "Brought his own car, Japanese thing."

"Well, ask him to call me," Charlie said. "Hey, what's the muffler guy doing this week?" He wondered if Sly had become a story back home yet. Muffler Man, not the *Register-World*, was now his gauge for that.

"Big news is Muffler Man's got himself a radio show now, on KDES," Buzz said. "Noon hour. Takes phone calls from the folks. DP office didn't tell you about that yet?"

"Haven't checked in with DP," Charlie said. "Been kinda crazy up here."

"Hey, Chas . . ."

"Yeah?"

"He's okay," Buzz said. "The kid."

9

———

There is no moment in political life quite so benign as an inauguration. All is forgiven, for a day or two. And, in the transitional eupho-
ria, Sylvester Parkinson's diet crimes seemed eminently forgivable. The
New York Times exegesis of Sly's Walnut Hill stay had been huge, but im-
penetrable—in the *Times*'s manner, stuffed with qualifications and
smudgy ink. Sly had not allowed himself to be interviewed for the article—it was standard operating procedure, preconfirmation, to lie low—
but he'd issued a statement, in which he'd admitted to being a bit too
enthusiastic in his dieting strategies. The Stanton spinners produced
some very good surrogates on the Friday night talk shows, and they dis-
missed the problem derisively; the fact that Letterman and Leno had fun
with the story—the carrots (Letterman wondered if Sly was preparing a
defense strategy against Elmer Fudd) were as prominent as the pills—
didn't hurt, either.

By the Sunday morning shows, Sly was a footnote. His "scandal"
seemed a passing squall. The big news was Stanton's proposed budget—
which included tax increases, and not the slightest hint of the tax cut
he'd been promising when he'd whipped Charlie Martin in the primaries. Henry Burton was on *Meet the Press*, very smooth and very young;
the vice president provided midmorning nap time on Brinkley.

On the evening of Jack Stanton's inauguration, Lanny Scott gave a
dinner for the Lords in a private dining room at the Mayflower Hotel.
Everyone looked crisp and stately, blindingly formal in black tie and ball
gowns—even Sly, whose shawl collar tented up behind his neck and
whose left cuff was linked with a paper clip. "Fancy haberdashery," Charlie said, when Sly's contraption was revealed as he reached for an oyster
fork to demolish his appetizer.

"Lost my cuff link," he said sheepishly. He was sitting one over from Charlie—Delia Scott, Lanny's wife, was between them—toward the middle of a long oval table.

"You're going to need a valet, you want to survive the Pentagon," Charlie said, only half kidding. "Generals are neatness freaks," he explained to Delia Scott. "You're wearing scuffed shoes, and they won't take you seriously."

"No kidding!" Parkinson agreed. "I was meeting with Art Lance"—the chairman of the joint chiefs—"and he asks my cholesterol level. Can you imagine? I'm proud I'm nudging two hundred after all this . . . stuff. Then he tells me his: one sixty-five."

"You can bet that every colonel in the building keeps track of his." Charlie touched Delia on the arm and added, "And the more ambitious ones probably know what the competition's is, too. It's a warrior culture, beneath all the planning and purchasing. They go one-on-one on everything."

"Sounds like my health club," she said.

"You work out at Lord of the Flies?" Sly asked, and Delia laughed. She had chestnut hair and freckles, and an entirely sweet disposition. Lanny and Delia were high school sweethearts, out from Charlie's neck of the woods. They had come from nowhere, all the way to the pinnacle—and they still managed to communicate a slight, quite healthy sense of skepticism and amazement about it all.

Charlie looked around the table, dividing the Lords and their ladies according to province. Gid Reese sat at the far end of the table, pinched and precise, ever the reluctant reveler. He was from Boston, extremely so; Mike Coleman, New York, quietly so. The world of Washington was no big deal to them; it was, in many ways, less daunting than their hometowns. Linc was Indiana, and still powerfully moved by the grandeur of the nation's capital; Sly was from New Jersey—but he lived in the space between his ears and was oblivious to Potomac seductions. Lynn sat between Mike and Gid, the picture of demure Pacific Northwest beauty, listening intently to Gid—gathering information, a role that she performed with grace and diligence; she lived for such moments, she still felt privileged—as Charlie did—to be part of such a gathering. . . . And then there was Nell, interrupting Charlie's train of thought, sitting between Gid and Lanny Scott, diagonally across from Charlie: she was wearing a subtle, metallic brown ball gown, with a neckline that plunged in a narrow V and did not reveal much except for her neck, which was bare and long. She was talking to Lanny, working her hands as if she were mixing something; they moved together in clever little flurries. Lanny was laughing, chatting back, more animated than his usual puffed, magisterial anchorliness. Charlie wanted desperately to know what they were talking about.

"Did you like the speech?" asked Anne Reese, who was sitting to his left.

"It was okay," he said absently—Nell was wearing an odd two-color satin shawl, which slipped off her right shoulder as she was gesturing; it was a regal shoulder, slim and square. He had missed saying hello to her during cocktails because he'd been to a home-state Democratic party reception and had arrived just as dinner was served.

"You were up on the stage with the celebrities," Anne tried again. Charlie realized that this was business: Anne was Gid. She was austere, hawklike, dark hair parted severely in the middle and pulled back tight; a navy blue satin dress with a high collar, long tight sleeves ending in little lacy frills at her wrists. She would have been perfect in period costume at Sturbridge Village. She taught poetry at Wellesley.

"Damn cold out there," he said. He'd sat next to Bart Nilson, the Senator from Wisconsin who'd been a fellow loser in the presidential primaries—and they'd been struck by the moment: Jack Stanton taking the oath of office. "But Jack looked just right," he said to Anne. "He looked like a president. I was sitting next to Bart Nilson, and we were reminiscing about New Hampshire—thinking about Jack back then, and now: the duckling becomes a swan. I think he'll be fine," he added diplomatically.

And indeed, Charlie found that he truly wished Stanton the best. He'd asked Nilson if he could imagine himself standing there, taking the oath. "Only when I'm fooling myself, shaving in the morning," Bart said. "You always think you can make the decisions better than the guy in the office, right? But it's funny, you never imagine yourself standing out here, with your hand on the Bible. That's a level of . . . of history most of us can't handle. . . . And you?"

Good question. A year earlier, Charlie had thought he'd had the answer—but he'd been wrong, monumentally so. And now, he simply could not imagine himself standing there—at least, not without making some changes in the way he went about his life. Most of all, he could not imagine himself standing up there alone.

Stanton had Susan, who glowed that day; no matter how strained their marriage, there was a ballast to it, a solidity that kept them afloat in the roughest times. And ballast had turned out to be crucial in the gusty upper atmospheres of presidential politics. But, sitting on the inaugural podium, Charlie wasn't really thinking about politics: he was sick to death of his own solitude. The realization was a jolt, a physically painful thing. His chest ached, the way his absent fingers sometimes did; he was chestless. The loneliness, reinforced by the frigid blasts of wind sweeping down from the northwest, shook him; and the chill had lingered. He looked over now toward Nell, who felt him staring; she glanced his way. He nodded, smiled and turned.

"Are you going to live here?" he asked Anne Reese.

"Oh, I don't know," she said exasperated: he'd touched a nerve. "Part of the time, I guess. You know Gid. He'll sleep on the office couch two out of every five nights anyway, so what's the point?"

"And you're teaching?" he asked. "Or are you one of those professors who just hang out and act smart?"

"Well, it's not a very heavy load," she admitted. "But I do have a Yeats seminar. Do you like poetry?"

"I'd like to like poetry," he said.

She laughed and said, "Gid really appreciated your help in putting out the fire on Sly's nomination."

"It wasn't much of a fire and I wasn't much help," he said. "I'm getting pretty aggravated by all these scandals, Anne. . . . It's as if a fast-moving, low-grade stomach virus has settled in over the city. You're flat on your back for twenty-four hours and then it disappears. Everyone catches it sooner or later."

"Illness as metaphor," Anne Reese scoffed.

"Better than sports," Charlie replied.

"Just barely. And if you must indulge, you should be more precise: these scandals are more debilitating than a stomach flu. They leaves lesions. One never totally recovers." She paused, stared across the room at her husband. Gid had aged significantly since Saigon. His youthful softness had wizened, his features were now as tight and spare as his personality. He'd lost most of his hair, his perfectly ovoid head an imposing dome now, his rimless glasses punctuating the ancient, clerkish quality of his presence. Anne was right: Gid had the look of a man who had suffered a debilitating illness and just barely recuperated. "It's been a long road back for Gid," Anne said now. "And his virus is still there, dormant. You wait, Charlie—they'll use it against him yet. He'll have to be so tough. Do you know how exhausting toughness is?"

At that moment, Lanny Scott clinked his glass and stood up. "Twenty-seven years ago, we were kids together in Saigon. Now, I look around the table and I see the secretary of defense–designate, the national security adviser, a United States senator . . . and"—he suddenly remembered Linc, who smiled, betraying nothing—"various other dignitaries. A more modest member of a more modest group might say, Who'd have thought it? Who would have imagined this back then, back in Saigon? But looking around the table and remembering what you—what we—were like, I can only say: what took you so long?" Laughter. "This is going to be hard for me," Lanny continued. "I've known you all so long, and I don't want to compromise my journalistic integrity. *But* . . . now that it's you guys in charge of the world, I can only say: I'm scared to death." Applause and laughter. "But I toast you anyway, and I thank you, in advance and as always, for any and all services rendered—to me. Seriously, gentlemen, congratulations on this new day."

Lanny sat down, and Linc stood. "I'm not scared to death," he said softly, quite seriously. "I'm very proud. This is what we dreamed—and, sometimes schemed—about for nearly thirty years. And no, I'm not scared. Because I also remember what we were like back there, even what you were like, Lanny. I remember how clearly we saw what was happening to Vietnam, how hard we worked to change the result, how anguished we were by our inability to do so. I know we carry those lessons with us—*lessons*, not scars, as some would have it. Lessons that will inform the way we conduct diplomacy and, God forbid, military action, in the years to come. I hope you act wisely, I know you will act honorably. I salute you."

There was a gasp, a burst of applause. Anne Reese had tears in her eyes. No one seemed to know what to say to Linc—he was, arguably, the most qualified person at the table, mentor to them all, and he was out in the cold. That thought, punctuated by an embarrassed silence, seemed to occur to everyone at the table simultaneously. It was up to Gid to respond; the entire table seemed to turn his way. He shook his head, "I can't compete with the master—"

"Right, Gid," Lanny Scott said, trying to lighten what had become a grave and emotional room. "You can only be inspirational when you've got a quarter of a million antiwar kids screaming for you at the Washington Monument."

Gid let that slip. Charlie was always surprised by Reese's height: taller than expected, his size diminished by his slightness, the academic stoop of his shoulders. Gid's manner had always been distant and diffident, but now his withered physical presence rendered him a wisp of a shadow, as if every calorie he consumed was immediately metabolized into strategic analysis. "Linc is right," Gid said, his voice thin and taut as piano wire. "This is the work we were meant to do. And, Linc, I hope you'll join us in doing it. The President wants you to join us . . . and Spaso House is not too shabby, now is it?" So, Charlie thought, they really were trying to send Linc off to Russia. It seemed crude, indiscreet and vaguely insulting to mention that now. An unusually careless lapse, which Gid seemed to realize belatedly. "But that's a discussion for another time . . ."

A door opened. Barney Rubin came up behind Sly Parkinson, whispered in his ear. Sly betrayed nothing but said, "Excuse me," and disappeared. Maggie Parkinson, seated between Lanny and Linc, shot a quick glance of concern at Charlie—what's this all about? Charlie shrugged, uncertain.

"For now," Gid continued, pretending to be oblivious to the distraction, but rushing to a conclusion, "I'd like to toast all of you, and all we've seen and done together, and all we'll do—and I would like to also raise a glass to the President of the United States."

They stood for that—Maggie staring at Sly's still-empty place—and raised their glasses, and said, "The President of the United States." And, solid citizens that they suddenly were, they truly meant it.

Linc and Nell traveled with Lynn and Charlie to the Midwest Ball, which was to be held at the Air and Space Museum; Lynn had valet-parked her Audi, and drove. Charlie rode shotgun. Nell was directly behind him; he couldn't see her. He could see Rathburn, though, blond hair haloed in the Connecticut Avenue headlights—and Linc was in a less high-minded mood than he'd been at dinner. "What do you think was going on there?" he asked Charlie. "Trouble? Gid seemed even more his desiccated, jejune self than usual."

"Lynn," Charlie asked, "this Audi come with a dictionary?"

Parkinson hadn't returned to the room. An aide had finally come for Maggie, and whisked her out. Gid's beeper had gone off; he and Mike Coleman left, too. Dessert had been left on the table.

"Anything international and I would have been beeped," Linc said. "It's got to be—God, I hope it isn't—another Sly story."

Charlie pulled out his cell phone and dialed Hilton. No answer. He'd given D-2 the night off, so he decided not to page him. He tried Donna at home. She said there'd been nothing on the news; she hadn't heard anything. Linc checked his voice mail; nothing.

"I thought it was a very moving evening," Lynn said, filling dead air.

"Until it moved elsewhere," Charlie said, but that was thoughtless, dismissive of Lynn. He reached over with his right hand and put it over hers on the wheel. "But you're right, hon. You gave a great toast, Linc. . . . Hey, Nell, that's a major Rathburn talent—he sure can do serious. Can't tell a joke to save his life, but he gives great profundity."

"So what's Gideon Reese's problem?" Nell asked. "He strikes me as the sort of man who could use a blood transfusion and a laxative."

Lynn inhaled, Charlie cracked up.

"I don't know about that," Linc said, laughing. "Gid's not big on sentiment. And he was sitting on some new information, tonight. He was suffering. You could see that, Charles—right?"

"Dunno," Charlie said. "Lynnsie, you were pumping him. He divulge anything?"

"Well, he said he was pretty tired," Lynn reported. "But exhilarated. He watched part of the parade with Stanton, and he told me that all the stories about the President not caring about foreign policy were just nonsense. I asked which areas Stanton was particularly interested in."

"Good for you." Charlie gave Lynn's elbow a squeeze and then regretted the gesture: it seemed patronizing.

"Russia and China," Linc predicted dismissively.

"He had a lot of wonderful things to say about you, Linc. Seriously. He did." Lynn paused skillfully. "I didn't know your relationship was *that* bad."

There was a burst of laughter in the car. "Touché," Linc acknowledged.

"Still," Charlie sighed, "I wonder what the hell is up."

Happily, there was valet parking at the Air and Space Museum. They walked in, two by two. Lynn was wearing a good Democratic cloth coat— royal blue, with black velvet collar and cuffs—over her ball gown, which was a robin's-egg blue—and had a kind of Jane Austen look, a high waist marked by a big bow just below her breasts. Her hair was up, and curled in frosted ringlets; it was clear she'd spent a fair amount of energy working at this. They stood together in the cloakroom line: Lynn was a good soldier when it came to chatting up Midwest Ball types, Senator Martin's monied constituents, but he was sure she would have preferred one of the more prestigious parties—and Linc, too, no doubt, especially now: the Parkinson story, if there was one, would be percolating elsewhere. This was bound to be a gossipy night, and they were consigned to the Fly-over Ball.

"Senator Martin." A big fellow with a crew cut nailed him. "Jack Carter, Hollowell Feeds. Great to see you."

Hollowell Feeds: five thousand dollars from CornPAC for the presidential campaign; $37,000 in bundled contributions from the executive suite.

"Just *great* to see you, Jack. You should have called, given me some warning," the senator said. "You're in town from . . ."

"Minne—"

"—apolis. Right," he said.

"And this is my wife, Marianne." Dark hair, sharp blue eyes, diamonds and more diamonds, and breasts. "And you probably know Brendan Lofton—from our Washington office."

"Of course. Hey, Bren." Charlie had worked, for years, at preventing Brendan Lofton from getting too close to him. He had won and lost at this: he usually spared himself the humiliation of being personally greased and slathered—he rarely let Lofton into his inner sanctum—but he almost always wound up voting the way Hollowell Feeds wanted; it coincided with the needs of Charlie's constituents (although not, perhaps, with the long-term best interests of anyone but the Hollowell executive suite).

"So, you think Stanton's gonna murder us?" Carter asked, with a level of subtlety appropriate to a midwestern feed baron.

"It's too early to tell," Martin said senatorially. "But it's clear there'll be some sort of tax increase in there." Nell had come up; she was watching this intently, Linc-less.

"So long as it's fair," Jack Carter said, wrapping a very strong arm around Charlie's shoulder, squeezing hard and whispering, "Don't want them messing too much with ag—"

"Right," Charlie grunted, expelling air from the force of the squeeze. "We'll make sure it's fair."

Nell was wearing an amber teardrop necklace and earrings; since it was chilly in the concrete and glass museum, she had kept her wrap, which was startling—brown velvet, more chocolaty than her dress, on one side; a very light turquoise on the other. And again, Charlie was having trouble assimilating all the different parts of her. Her beauty seemed complicated, a collection of nuances and subtleties—from some angles, she was striking; from others, ordinary. Jack Carter was looking straight past her, toward Ames McMahon of Nebraska, who sat on the Senate ag committee. But Charlie couldn't stop looking at her. Her outfit seemed just right, effortless, as if she'd not worked very hard at getting herself ready for this. She had a nice, full lower lip; her mouth was slightly open, her head tilted rakishly. Her eyes were sharp, ironic. Charlie was discomforted by them; without saying a word, she made him feel transparent. He didn't want her to know the disconcerting impact she had on him. But he was certain that she knew.

"Senator, howwww-dee." A white-haired man with black-rimmed glasses, wearing a pig pin on his left lapel, and a cow pin on his right. "Ben Thompson, from the Payute City—"

"Stockyards," Charlie said. Five thousand dollars, StockPAC; $23,000 from the stockyards executives. "Haven't seen you since Rodeo Days."

"Good memory, Senator." Not really, Ben. A little below average for a politician. "And you remember my wife, S—"

"—arah, of course." Nell was smiling at this. Charlie gave her a nod. Linc had come back from the men's room, or wherever, and was talking to Lynn. "And how's your daughter?"

"Nancy?"

"The twirler? Right?" With the great figure.

"Oh, that's Joanne," Ben Thompson said. "She's off to Mason." The state college of agriculture. "Nancy's in vet school there, too."

"I was just up there," Charlie said. "The biogenetics lab is pretty darn impressive," he added, home-state-style. "We got them some nice money in the higher-ed title of last year's ag bill."

"Shows. Mason's about three times as big as it was when I was there," Thompson said. "Hey, you been listening to the Muffler Kid?" It was interesting: home-state folks always assumed you were home all the time, and also in Washington all the time.

"I've seen the ads," Charlie said. "Pretty funny."

"The radio show's what everyone's talking about," Thompson said. "Just started. Sarah won't miss a day. Honey, what's he doin' you said was so funny?"

"The adventures of Slime Porkington," Sarah said. She had permed gray hair and butterfly glasses, and a canary satin gown that amply demonstrated the degree to which she had been doing her patriotic duty on the local barbecue circuit; she was wearing pig and cow pins, and a stalk-of-corn pin as well. "He's the guy who's up for secretary of—something."

"Defense?" Charlie offered.

"Yeah, right. The pill popper."

"I think he kicked the habit," Charlie said.

"He did?" Sarah seemed surprised. "The Butler Muffler fellow had this skit, with Porky hopped up, bouncing off of walls, launching atom bombs on McDonald's. 'Die, you commie cheesegurgers! Die!' Then he had another one. . . . It's a hoot."

"I'll bet," Charlie said. Finally, they'd reached the head of the cloakroom line. "Well, great seeing you, Sarah. Ben."

"You'll be there for Rodeo Days this year?" Ben asked.

"Wouldn't miss it," Charlie said, and made a mental note to have Mary Proctor in his Des Pointe office assign someone to listen to the show every day. Better still, he'd call Pat Dunn—who, no doubt, hadn't missed a minute of Muffler Kid.

They walked in the general direction of the party, toward loud, blarey music echoing off the glass and concrete—a big band, in tuxedos, on a podium with a presidential seal hanging behind it; they were playing excruciating covers of Rolling Stones songs. Charlie had Lynn's arm, she was wearing long velvet opera gloves—like the girls on the motorbikes in Saigon; she was smiling and nodding at the people who smiled and nodded at him.

Nell came up beside them. "So this is what you *do*," she said to Charlie. "I don't think I've ever seen a politician working up close before."

"Just another day at the office," he said, and felt idiotic having said it. Lynn glanced sharply at him, then at Nell; she noted the nervous chemistry between them—high school chemistry—and considered remarking on it, but she couldn't think of anything to say that wouldn't seem heavy-handed.

"Senator!" Jim Waterfield, from Waterfield Tractors. Five thousand dollars from TracPAC, plus $86,000 personal, a maxed-out contribution from every member of his extended corporate family. He was trailed by Elaine Engstrom, the state Democratic party chair and her husband, Arne, usually described in the *Register-World* as a prominent Des Pointe lawyer (actually, he was one of the more powerful state lobbyists—Waterfield Tractors was a client, natch).

"Hey, Lainey," Charlie said, hugging her. "I'm sorry I couldn't stay for dinner tonight. We've got everything set for tomorrow, right?" A lunch meeting with all the home-state honchos, letting them vent on legislative priorities. Donny O'Brien had given Charlie one of his conference rooms in the Capitol, and promised he'd do a "surprise" drop-in. They'd like that.

"Charlie." Jim Waterfield again. "We've gotta have a sit-down about trade. I've got this China deal cooking—and Stanton's acting like the Chinese are Hitler."

"I'm with you on this one, Jim. You know that," Charlie said. "And I'll bet you anything the anti-China stuff was just campaign talk from Stanton."

"Maybe. But you and I should sit down and talk strategy. Can I have my girl call your girl?"

"Of course, Jim." Charlie suppressed a wince. "Have you met Lincoln Rathburn? He knows an awful lot about China. Linc, this is Jim Waterfield. . . ."

"Waterfield Tractor, of course," Linc said. "You really thinking of putting up that assembly plant in Wuhan?" He actually seemed interested. And Lynn had gotten caught up by Amy Rogers, the wife of CBS White House correspondent Sam Rogers—who'd gotten caught up by a horde of midwestern autograph hounds; Amy was a lawyer with House and Case, she did serious ag lobbying, which was why she'd dragged Sam to the Midwest Ball, and she also was one of Washington's leading freelance gossips. And she was all over Lynn, who seemed relieved to find a familiar face.

Which left Nell standing there. "You want to dance?" she asked. "Or should I have my girl call your girl?"

"My girl leaves my dancing to me," Charlie said. The band was now massacring the Beatles, but slow ones: "I Will" . . .

"Tough day at the office, I figured you needed a coffee break," she said. She was easy in his arms; her cornet-brass hair brushed his cheek; it wasn't soft hair, but thick and rough—a vital presence. Her wrap had slipped down around her elbows and Charlie had a good look at her neck and shoulders, which were pale and creamy and elegant; there were tiny, occasional, provocatively placed beauty marks on her neck; the muscles in her upper arms were clearly defined—and he caught a whiff of her perfume again, the same subtle, intoxicating scent as before.

"Not so tough a day," he said. "You should've seen those birds when their passive loss provisions went down in '86."

"Passive loss provisions." She played with the words, rolled them around in her mouth. "How thoughtful—one should always provide for passive losses."

"I always sort of liked the term." Charlie acknowledged the wordplay, and reached to keep up his end of the deal. "So much warmer than . . . accelerated depreciation."

"The story of my life," she said. "Accelerated depreciation." Her gray-green eyes could be so sad when she worked them that way.

"In your case"—he paused melodramatically—"I wouldn't say the depreciation was anything more than minimal."

"Minimal!" she said. "A gentleman never acknowledges depreciation, however minimal."

"See, now: I've suffered a passive loss of your esteem."

"I'd say, it was a pretty active loss—"

"But you're right, *providing* for passive losses sounds as if it might be an act of kindness, a sort of solace," he said, working to keep the riff going. She made him feel light on his feet. "How many times in my life I've said the wrong thing—or, more accurately, not said the right thing—and suffered a passive loss that needed providing for."

"The senator from Dorkland?" she said. "I doubt it."

Charlie pulled back. "What color is that dress?" Which gave him a chance to check her out frontally.

"Let's see how good you are," she said, knowing he was looking, inviting him to look. "What color do you think it is?"

"Sort of an red-orangey-brown with a metal backbone," he said, playing with her. "Wait a minute. In the Crayola forty-eight colors, when we were kids—it was like, what? Copper." She shook her head no. "Bronze!" he said.

"In honor of the Bronze Age," she said. "When metal weapons were introduced, and barbarism institutionalized."

"You see parallels in the Age of Stanton?"

"Don't you?"

"Not really," he admitted, hoping that he hadn't missed some obvious reference—hoping not to seem too slow for her.

"Me neither." She laughed. She pulled him in closer and whispered, "Charlie, should Linc go to Russia?"

"No," he said. She squeezed his arm, thrilled that he'd be an ally; it was very depressing. "Linc should keep doing what he's doing," he said. "Travel around, chat up people like that tractor guy, Waterfield, and wait for Stanton to come to him. He will, too. When there's trouble."

"You're a good friend," she said, bestowing a painfully chaste kiss on his cheek. "So what is it about Gid and Linc? Weren't they friends once, too?"

"Yeah, they were," he said. "But they kept bumping into each other. They both wanted the same seat at the table."

"They couldn't work it out?" she asked. "Take turns? They're diplomats. Isn't that what diplomats are supposed to do? Work things out?"

He didn't know what to say. How to explain the tangle of loyalty and resentment in twenty-five words or less? Talk about passive losses.

"Boys," she scoffed. "So have you talked to Linc about Russia?"

"Sure." Not really.

"Veddy big . . . Russia," she said. When he didn't respond immediately, she grimaced, pulling back her chin and wrinkling her brow: "That was a reference, Dorkland: Noël Coward, *Private Lives*." Again, Charlie had no comeback: he desperately wanted to amuse her. They were quiet for a moment, moving together easily; he found himself growing aroused, to his profound embarrassment.

"Noël Coward," he said, pulling back abruptly. "A contemporary of the Marx Brothers."

"Hail Freedonia," she said. "Do you ever get to New York, aside from political conventions?"

"Sometimes, why?"

"Linc needs friends," she said. "Especially when he comes over to my house and is surrounded by my friends, none of whom is very well versed on East Timor."

"I wouldn't expect you to have timorous friends," he said, kicking himself as he said it: he was trying too hard, way too hard.

"But you must come over for dinner sometime," she said.

"With your kids?"

She laughed. "No, not the infernal tykes. I wouldn't dream of inflicting SpaghettiOs and Niblets on you."

"What are they like?" he asked, suddenly quite curious because they were *her* children.

"What are they like?" She was tickled by the intensity of his interest. It was the sort of question that men rarely asked; Linc never had. "They're . . . Have you got a year?" The music was over. They started toward Linc and Lynn, but Nell stopped abruptly halfway. "You know, I never noticed kids before I had them. Never went 'kitchy-koo' when confronted with a baby. Never sighed and said 'Ohhhh, how darrrrling.' I thought I had zero maternal instincts. Boy, was I wrong about that—they're . . ." Her eyes filled unaccountably with tears. "They're my liberation from the family curse. . . . They're *normal.* Well, sort of . . ."

"You know," he began, "maybe you could help me. I have a—"

"Charlie!" Lynn said, moving out on the dance floor to get him. "You're not going to believe . . . Amy Rogers was just telling us that the *Post* has a story tomorrow that one of Sly's former staffers says he once pinned her up against the wall and tried to kiss her."

"And there may be others," Linc added, joining them.

"Shit," Charlie said, distressed by both the information and the interruption. "This has got to be nonsense. I mean, why now?"

"It sounded pretty serious," Lynn said, eyeing Charlie carefully. "Amy said the woman was on the record, with corroborating witnesses."

"Did Amy say whether this woman had filed a sexual harassment suit?" he asked impatiently.

"I don't—" Lynn started.

"How much you wanna bet she didn't?" he said. "Funny how these things just pop out of nowhere at the most interesting times."

"But—"

"But look what happened to *me*, dammit," he said. Charlie's eyes had gone icy, murderously cold—Nell was shocked by the change. A few heads turned; Lynn seemed stricken.

"What happened to you was isolated and clearly questionable," Linc said, reaching out to calm him down, and then stepping back into analytical mode. "This is a lot more difficult—and it's going to be hard now, with the pills and everything else, for Stanton not to pull the plug."

"Aw c'mon, Linc," he said.

"Well, you wonder why Sly didn't tell us," Linc said.

"Maybe," Charlie said, "because it never fucking *happened.*"

"Charlie—" Lynn started.

"It's a public humiliation!" Charlie was almost shouting; he'd just lost it. "Jesus, we've known Sly how long?" But had they known him? Of course they had. As well as you could, which was why Charlie was beginning to lose steam—because the story about the disgruntled staffer sounded right. Because his flash of anger had been, at bottom, about the trouble Sly was going to cause *him*. The chances were, this wouldn't be clear-cut. These things never were. There would be Sly's story, and hers, Madam X's. There would be witnesses—but not eyewitnesses; indirect ones, friends who'd been told. Maybe. Or maybe not. It was going to be a mess, and Charlie was locked in: Sly's lead defender. "Look, I'm sorry," he said, cooling down. "It's just that everyone in town—all the gossip junkies . . . I mean, talk about an addiction—all the assholes are getting a buzz off Sly's bad fortune right now. He's raw meat; he's carrion. They're feasting. Another banquet for assholes. It just turns my stomach."

"Charlie—" Linc tried.

"Maybe we should go," Lynn said, scalded by the outburst.

"Absolutely," he said. "Let's go." He remembered Nell, and was suddenly embarrassed. He looked to see if she was appalled by him. But no, there was only concern in her gray-green eyes, and a fretful network of wrinkles above her eyebrows, which were raised—the inside tips were raised (how did she do that?)—empathetically: she had seen right past the anger to whatever it was, the loneliness and disgust, festering below that.

10

———

"Good morning," said Donna Mendoza, "and boy do you look like shit."

"Umm," Charlie Martin replied. His eyes were blurry, bloodshot; his hair, still wet from the shower; his collar was open, he was holding a limp red-and-blue-striped tie in his hand.

"Pretty wild night of inaugural partying, huh?" She assumed he'd been dragooned into the Parkinson crisis.

"Yeah, right. At the Marriott in Rockville."

A nearly all-night Sly session. Mike Coleman presided; Charlie and Linc, plus Barney Rubin of Sly's staff and the secretary-designate himself, had been present. They'd had trouble finding a place to meet. The White House was too obvious; Sly's modest split-level ranch was surrounded by press; all the hotels in the district were filled with inaugural revelers—but Rubin had been able to book a suite near Sly's home in the suburbs. They gathered at one-thirty A.M. and stayed until four. Mike led the interrogation, quietly, patiently, never losing his temper, but never letting Parkinson off the hook—although, in the end, nothing of significance had been learned: only a flat denial from Sly, who contended that Jessica Mahon, the woman who had leveled the groping charge, was a little nuts and had carried a grudge against him. She'd been the source for the diet pill story as well, so it did have the look of a vendetta. But neither Charlie nor Linc was convinced that was all there was to it, and the concerned parties had left the meeting exhausted and dreading the next day's battles.

"Remember how the evening began?" Linc mused as Charlie drove him back to the Mayflower in the predawn darkness. "The dinner. The toasts—the sort of evening I'd always imagined for us, though you've got to admit, sitting in Saigon in 1964, you wouldn't have predicted that Sly would be the first of us to reach cabinet rank. Although I guess Gid is up there, too."

"You remember how he used to treat the girls in Saigon?" Charlie asked.

"Slick? You don't believe him about Jessica Mahon?" Linc asked, then answered himself. "Yeah, I don't either."

"I just have this real specific image in my mind," Charlie said. "Sly, with his hand on some poor Vietnamese B-girl's breast, his tongue in her ear, on—what was that street behind Tu Do?"

"Poor Vietnamese B-girl?" Rathbun laughed. "Charlie, you remember some of the things you used to do—and who you used to do them with?"

"Fair enough," Charlie almost conceded. "But you know exactly what I'm saying about Sly."

"It was wartime. We were kids," Linc said. "Sly was a kid."

"He's still a kid," Charlie said, and then added, "Tell you the truth, I'm worried about this, Linc. You think we'd be giving Sly the benefit of the doubt if he weren't a friend—if he were, say, a Republican? We'd be laughing our asses off."

"Oh, come on," Linc said, yawning. "They don't make Republicans as sloppy as Slick." He laughed. "Maybe we should start giving them the benefit of the doubt."

Charlie dropped Linc off at the Mayflower at five, and drove home by way of the downtown monuments. Jefferson and Lincoln seemed frigid and alone, uninviting in their marble cells. He parked his car near the mall and walked the path down to the Vietnam memorial, a dark slash, darker than the darkness, amidst the skeletons of trees. He went to the place he always went, and traced the name of Richard Marcelino—Richie Radio—with the index finger of his left hand. "Hey, brother," he said. "There you go."

"Hey, brother." A nearby echo, a filthy hand extended from a pile of rags. "Spare a grunt some change?"

"Name. Rank. Unit?"

"Howard. Corporal James. Delta Company, Marines, one-three."

"What year?"

" '70–'71."

"Bad year, I hear."

"Weren't many good ones," Corporal Howard said.

Charlie gave him a twenty, and went home.

———

"So, D, you have any skinny on this Mahon?" Charlie asked, sinking into the leather couch the next morning, "Were there rumors about Parkinson? I know it's over on the House side, but—you have any friends over there?"

"I can work my wires," Donna said. "You want some coffee? I'll actually get you some myself, you look so awful."

"Wait . . . Donna, what do you think? What's your gut? You've seen Sly in action. You have an intuition here?" Charlie flipped on CNN: talking heads were talking—journalists; no one serious. Sly now rated his own cable news crisis title, The Parkinson Nomination, and portentous theme music when the commercial breaks came; it was a sign the story had moved into the red zone. Donna stood near the television, checking it out.

"I don't know," she said, careful to avoid a personal judgment—her gut was that Parkinson was a jerk, but if being a jerk were a disqualifier for public service, Washington would be severely depopulated. "Maybe Marvin knows some of the Armed Services Committee folks on the House side. The *Post* story was sourced through personal staff."

Donna had, of course, devoured the *Post* story in true Washington fashion, examining every nuance, figuring out the sources of the blind quotes, spotting the seed corn the reporter was dropping, sensing where it was headed. She knew the story looked worse than the reality might have been; it wasn't ironclad. Jessica Mahon claimed the congressman had come up from behind a year earlier, grabbed her breasts and licked her neck; she'd wriggled away and he didn't pursue her. She'd remained on staff; she'd brought no complaint against him. The inaugural-night gossip had been wrong: there were no corroborating witnesses. There was a blind quote, from "a House staff member familiar with the Parkinson office" to the effect that "he had a reputation for squeezing where he oughtn't." But there were no sources from the Armed Services Committee, where Parkinson had many of his closest advisers and expended most of his energy. This had the look of a one-shot grope. If that.

Charlie buzzed his top legislative assistant, Marvin Tam, who waddled into the inner sanctum, the Pillsbury Doughboy grown old: he was almost entirely round, with stray thin straggles of graying hair stretched across his prodigious dome; he had thick glasses, a broad nose and full lips, and, even in the dead of winter, insisted on wearing polyester short-sleeved shirts, blue or white, the top button unbuttoned, his tie loosened just below. "Glad you buzzed, boss," he said. "I need to brief you on the caucuses. We got rogue Russkie units splitting off, plundering—major-league chaos. And I would guess Chechnya is—"

"We'll schedule that, Tammy," Charlie said, though he felt a bit guilty that he hadn't been keeping up with committee business. "Right now, we've got really serious stuff to talk about: you ever hear any gossip about Sly Parkinson from the folks on the House side?"

"His folks, or the lifers?" Marvin asked. "And do you mean intellectually—or sexually?"

"Intellectually," the senator said, staring at the ceiling, imploring the heavens. "C'mon, Tammy, you know what I mean."

He sat down in an armchair facing the boss; Donna sat in the other.

"Sexually, I didn't hear much," Tam said. But he'd sat down, which meant there was something.

"You ever talk with Beth Willets?" Donna asked.

"About theater nukes, all the time," he said. "About sex, no."

Donna gave Charlie a look: Marvin Tam was a refugee from the Planet of the Wonks.

"What do you mean, you didn't hear *much*, Marvin?" Charlie finally asked. "Did you hear anything?"

"Just that Sly was a little inconsistent," he said. "He'd drift off at times; he'd go ballistic, others—"

"Everyone knows he has a temper," Charlie said dismissively.

"I suppose," Marvin said. "But let's put it this way: I wasn't surprised by the *Times* story last week—the word was, Sly was in a mega-jumpy phase, bouncing off walls, taking happy pills."

"And sex?"

Marvin shrugged. Rosemary came in. "Majority leader for you, Senator."

"Okay," Charlie said, reaching for the phone on the end table next to the couch. "Thanks, Marvin. You hear anything, let me know. Hello, Don?"

"It's Dov," said Dov. "I'll put him on."

"Charles," Don O'Brien said. "Dov, stay on. Charles, what can you tell me about your friend Mr. Parkinson's latest?"

CNN was flashing a photograph of Jessica Mahon—she had black-framed glasses, a bland academic look. Charlie tried to do a Stanton scan: check out her shoulders. But they told him nothing.

"They've got a picture of her on CNN right now," Charlie said.

"I know," O'Brien said. "Dov says the word is she has great legs. This isn't good, Charles, is it? We have a critical mass problem, don't we?"

"A critical mass of rumors," Charlie said stubbornly. He had no choice but to stand with his man. "We had Sly on the griddle most of the night. Apparently, this Jessica Mahon was the source for the *Times* story last week. That didn't blow Sly out of the water, so she upped the ante. Apparently, she's got some sort of bug up her ass."

"Do we know that for a fact?" O'Brien asked. "Of course not. Senator Bramlette is a pig in shit over this. You'll be hearing from him in a few minutes. He wants a private, informal committee session with someone from 1600 this afternoon. I don't think that's unreasonable, but maybe we can limit it to a few senators from each side, players, not suits, and hold it in a safe place."

"There aren't any safe places anymore, Don," Charlie said. "One angry woman can cause all this?"

"Life is sad," O'Brien said.

*   *   *

The Senate Armed Services Committee is not an institution particularly well equipped to deal with scandal. It is a hardware store. Its members are consumers of weapons systems, purveyors of defense contracts, dispensers of jobs. In the old days, a slot on the committee had been a ticket to serious good times: defense industry lobbyists were one-stop vacation shopping centers—they proferred hunting lodges, private jets to golf and ski vacations and female companionship. The post-Watergate reforms had ended all that, but Armed Services remained a fabulous place from which to raise campaign funds and build a record of achievement (in other words, to steer defense contracts homeward). Most of the committee members were stone weapons junkies, although there were also a significant number of former warriors, like Charlie Martin, and a smattering of defense intellectuals—Sly Parkinson had been the prototype—more concerned with strategy and the fusty, nonprocurement aspects of military life, like "readiness." Ever since Vietnam, there had also been a smattering of antidefense intellectuals, liberals who'd then be quickly seduced by the reality of defense spending: the Pentagon was, in fact, Franklin Roosevelt's truest legacy, the last New Deal–style jobs and public works program.

A confirmation fight over a prospective secretary of defense was an unwelcome diversion. The members of the committee knew they had to deal with scandal on a fairly regular basis—there was just too much money sloshing around for everyone to stay sober, to say nothing of the sexual temptations of a coeducational fighting force; warriors were hormonal, it came with the territory (and a statistically significant sliver of them were hormonal in nontraditional ways, a lifestyle that Jack Stanton had promised to defend—and a problem most members of the committee did not want to face). The truth was, scandal was bad for business: the committee members were happiest when they were able to quietly operate the hardware store.

But the members chosen for the afternoon meeting were not displeased by the sudden possibility that they might be able to jettison Parkinson—a technician likely to question their hardware—and land themselves a more congenial sec-def. They arrived promptly, a shocking sign of senatorial interest, at the committee's private conference room in the Russell Building, a sanctum lined with curiously unaffecting color photos of fabulously lethal weapons systems. Both party leaders, Don O'Brien and Frank Mix, were present—sitting at the far end of a long, rectangular table, which filled most of the room. Bartle Bramlette sat at the head; Dickie Ganther, the senior minority member, on his immediate right. There were no assigned seats, but three Republicans flanked Ganther down the right side of the table, and four Democrats sat opposite. Charlie chose a seat in the middle of the Democrat row. Mike Coleman, the White House's emissary, sat between O'Brien and Mix, facing Bramlette directly, but far away—the geography of the meeting awkward from the start.

"I had a conversation with the President this morning," Bartle Bramlette said, opening abruptly. "I advised him to withdraw this nomination. He asked if I was speaking for the committee. I said I suspected the members weren't pleased by the news reports. I also asked him to send a representative to answer any questions you might have; he sent Mr. Coleman. So that's where we are. What say you, gentlemen?"

"Gentlemen?" noted Francesca Warren, the junior senator from California, a Democrat, and a newcomer to the committee. Charlie was surprised Bramlette had included her. "Senator Bramlette, you are truly museum quality. Mr. Coleman, can you tell us where the administration stands on this nomination now?"

"Where we always have," Mike said. "Behind it."

"How far behind it?" asked Mike Rotello of Florida, a spend-less (except for defense) and don't-bother-me Republican.

"Way behind it," said Darrell Billups of North Carolina, a sandy-haired former professional baseball player, the last remaining tobacco chewer in the Senate—he carried a small tin can with him for committee meetings and expectorated therein with startling aplomb and perfect accuracy. "No matter what's true, you boys actually think Sly can represent the United States of America with any dignity after all this?"

"Senator, I'm sure you are an expert on dignity," said Senator Ted Panepopoulos of New Jersey, a stuffed shirt who was forced—by home-state coincidence—to stand as Sly's formal sponsor for his nomination hearing, "but Congressman Parkinson's credentials are impeccable. He has written the textbook on military strategy in the next century. He has—"

"Excuse me, gentlemen," Francesca Warren broke in. "Mr. Coleman is our guest. Let's hear what he has to say before we start nattering. Could you tell us why the administration is so intent on this?"

"Senator Panepopoulos said it," Mike said. "There's no one better qualified. And yes, Sly's been subjected to some grief over the past week—but we're convinced it'll pass."

"Mr. Coleman," Bramlette asked, with absurd formality, "how do we know we're not going to get some new story every day for the next week?"

"Because of the nature of what we've had so far," Coleman replied crisply—but not very convincingly, Charlie thought. "Jessica Mahon was the primary source to the *Times* for the medication story—and now she's resurfaced, as the primary source for the *Post*'s sexual harassment story. You think one woman should have it in her power to destroy the career of one of our most distinguished—"

"Yes, if she's right," Francesca Warren interrupted, cutting to the chase. "And I think she may be right."

"And how on earth would you know?" Charlie asked.

"I talked to her," Francesca said, craning her head around Panepopoulos, a pillar of self-absorbed stolidity between them. "You talk about distinguished: Jessica Mahon has a Ph.D. in environmental planning from Columbia, she loved Parkinson's interest in tidewater and pine barrens preservation. She was devoted to him. I'd say she has a fair amount of credibility. And she's got the names of some others, who aren't willing to come forward, but they will privately—"

"And did she tell you about her two marriages, about how family court gave custody of her little boy to the father because of her instability, and did she tell you about the rest of her psychiatric history?" Mike Coleman jumped in, hard as Charlie had ever seen him, a bit too hard. He sensed Mike wasn't thrilled with the assignment: this was dreadful, obnoxious work.

"You did *oppo* on her?" Senator Warren lashed back. "The campaign's over, Mr. Coleman. Don't you think it's about time we shut down the war room?"

The Republicans were watching this, just about giddy. It confirmed everything they'd always believed about what happened when Democrats came to power.

"Senator," Mike Coleman said evenly, "we didn't have to do oppo. James Mahon, who is a surgeon at Cornell Medical Center, came to us. He told us that his former wife is manic-depressive."

"That doesn't mean she made this up," Senator Warren shot back.

"Enough, enough!" said Bramlette, with a slight smile. "This is unseemly."

"Why is it always that when a woman is victimized," Francesca Warren interrupted, "she's a hysteric, one way or another? You gentlemen—not all, but some of you—have been using your female staff as party dolls for—"

"Quite enough," Bramlette said.

"Prove it!" Darrell Billups shouted, pounding the table. "If the senator from NOW is going to make wild accusations, she'd better back it up."

"Perhaps we could call the North Carolina highway patrol to come in and testify"—Francesca Warren was calm, smiling—"about the prayer meeting you were having with that waitress in the backseat of your Lincoln on—"

"ENOUGH!" Bramlette gaveled his hand down on the table with a splat.

"All I'm saying," Francesca Warren continued, in control, "is that the public and press demand we take this seriously . . . just as you did, Mr. Chairman, when you agreed to my request to be involved in any discussions of this matter."

"Nobody said we wouldn't, Fran," Bramlette said. "I think we should probably have a closed hearing and call Ms. Mahon."

"Why close it?" Darrell Billups said. "Public has a right to see the government in all its glory."

Mike Coleman rolled his eyes. And Charlie had a chilling thought: he looked down the row of Democrats—Francesca, Teddy Panepopoulos, ancient Hank Barnes of Washington State, who'd not said a word yet—and he realized that if it ever came to a public hearing, he'd be the designated hitter. He'd have to take Jessica Mahon apart.

"That's right, Darrell—plenty of 'glory' here to go around," Charlie said. "I don't know if Jessica Mahon is telling the truth or not. But I do know two things. One is that a random grope may be obnoxious behavior, but being obnoxious doesn't disqualify you from being a good secretary of defense. The other is, and I know this from personal experience: the press will do what it wants, but if we start giving unlimited credibility to the she-saids in he-said, she-said situations, every last one of us is vulnerable. Even you, Francesca—some boy toy says you patted his fanny, I'll be happy to take your side. If the world's going to judge us guilty until proven innocent, the least we can do for one another is try to assume the best until shown otherwise. It's just outrageous that everything Sly Parkinson's worked for can be taken out—like that." He snapped his fingers, the sound crackling through the small room. "It means every one of us can be snuffed on a whim. I'd be standing with Sly, even if I hadn't known him for thirty years."

Even if it meant becoming the lord high executioner of Jessica Mahon at a public hearing? Charlie thought: WTF.

"And therefore, what?" Francesca Warren said. "Therefore we let boys be boys, cover this up—"

"No," Don O'Brien suddenly said, causing every head to swivel south. "What we do is act like senators." He paused, and smiled. "We give it a day or two. We wait. It's Thursday. We have a hearing scheduled for next Wednesday. If Senator Billups, or Senator Warren, wants to have Ms. Mahon testify, I suppose we're going to have no choice." He turned to Mike Coleman. "And if the administration feels so strongly about this nomination that it is willing to endure the spectacle, more power to them. What do you think, Frank?"

Frank Mix shrugged. "Seems 'bout right. And you, Mr. Chairman?"

Bartle Bramlette was beginning to understand that a Grand Guignol might be in the offing, placing him squarely in the national spotlight. "Fine with me," he said.

"Wait a minute," Dickie Ganther said. These were the first words spoken by the ranking Republican on the committee, which was very much unlike him. "I'd like to say something to Senator Martin: Charlie, I have great sympathy for your position, even though I don't have much love for Sly Parkinson." He glanced at Francesca Warren. "Any stray lady screwball can deep-six any one of us. And I wonder, how'd this Jessica Mahon dress for work? How short her skirts, how tight her blouses—some of these girls, y'know, are just looking for it. . . ."

"Senator!" Francesca Warren.

"Senator." Dickie Ganther smiled. "That's just my Stonehenge-cowboy way of getting around to agreeing with you. Couldn't do that without pissin' you off a little first. Wouldn't seem right. See, folks, the junior senator from California does have a point. We live in a different world now. Situations just go . . . bloooey." Charlie realized that Dickie Ganther might be worried about just such a situation himself; it was why he wasn't jumping all over Sly. "We have to be careful, do this right. Public expects it. We don't want pig slop splashing all over the rest of us here, do we?"

"Perhaps we should convene this group again Monday," Bramlette agreed. "See how we're feeling after the weekend."

"Not Monday," Darrell Billups said. "I got folks to poke."

They all had folks to poke back home. Charlie had the Crescent Lake ice fishing festival; he had a Lutheran pancake breakfast in Salzburg; a Super Bowl party at the Des Pointe YMCA. Most important, there was the prospect of Calvin and Buzz, together, on Oak Street.

"Okay, Tuesday breakfast?" Bramlette asked.

There were grumbles, but it was agreed.

Frank Mix called Charlie afterward. "You notice?"

"What?"

"No unit discipline. On either side."

"How'd you like to assault a tree line with a platoon of senators?" Charlie asked.

"Wind up in Arlington," Mix said. "Most of 'em with back wounds."

"Not Francesca Warren," Charlie said. "Gotta admire that about her."

"Or something," Mix said. "Charlie, you gonna keep an eye on Sly for us? Check in on him?"

"I suppose. Why?"

"Someone damn well better. And, after all, he's your boy."

"Thanks a bunch, Frank."

Francesca Warren called, too. "Charlie, you've been good on our issues. I don't want you to step in it on this one."

Our issues? "My mom used to say that stepping in it was good luck, Francesca," he said.

"I've got two other women who say Sly groped them," she said. "In one case, 'grope' might be a little mild. A court might call it rape."

"How come we haven't heard from them publicly?"

"Oh, come on, Charlie. You know how this works. If you were them, would you want to get yourself bombed and strafed by the White House and the press? Not much fun, is it?" That was true enough. "Look, you don't have to take my word for it," she said. "You can talk to them, too. I can arrange it. If you'll agree to keep it strictly confidential."

"I don't know," he said.

"You do know," she replied. "You just don't want to *really* know."

"Let me think about it." he said, in a way that indicated he had no intention of thinking about it. "It must be nice to go home to California for the weekend, instead of the frozen Midwest."

"Right, Charlie. The red-eye back to D.C. Monday night is especially wonderful," Francesca said impatiently. "And then there are my constituents. In California, Senator, I am considered a moderate."

"I've *never* been considered a moderate," he said, flirting a little. Francesca Warren was divorced, and not bad-looking: dark hair pulled back, dark eyes, the northern California anorexic jogger look. What would it be like to date a senator? A lot of foreplay, probably; a fair amount of manipulation. They could inspire each other.

"You've never been considered a wuss, either," she said. Flirting back? Or just manipulating? Hard to tell. "You should look this one in the eye, Charlie."

* * *

Often, at the end of a day, Charlie would drop by Donna's cubicle, sit across the desk from her and catch up—postmortems, planning, idle chatter; sometimes they'd watch the six-thirty news together. Donna had a row of dusty, pathetic plants on the windowsill and pictures of her kids up on the wall, as well as a scattering of pictures of herself with various politicians, including Charlie's favorite photo of the two of them: sitting next to each other on the leather couch in his office, feet up, shoes off, heads back and laughing—perfectly symmetrical.

Late that afternoon, Charlie wandered in and found Donna and Mustafa, heads bowed together in prayer—a startling sight, as if he'd caught them in flagrante. "Hey," he began, and stopped abruptly. "I—"

"Do you want to join us in a silent devotion?" Mustafa asked. He was sitting in the senator's usual spot, across the desk from Donna. "It won't take but a minute."

"Praying on company time, Donnzo?" Charlie asked. This seemed prohibitively weird. He knew Donna was a churchgoer, but there was something ostentatious about being religious in the middle of a workday.

Donna stared back at him evenly. "There's no harm in it. And Moose was a savior today. This place was nuts with all the Parkinson business. The interns were up to their eyeballs. Mustafa went over to Dirksen, got everyone lunch. He walked the mail over to the back office, walked the mail report back."

"The devotion's just a way of taking a breath, boss," Mustafa said. "A spiritual coffee break. Me and Donnz were just giving thanks for the Lord's help in getting us through a busy day."

All right. But why did that seem so creepy?

Mustafa saw the skepticism and made ready to leave. "You gonna need me tomorrow?" he asked Donna.

"Things'll probably slow down—Friday and all," she said.

"And you are gonna do the sewing project, right?" Mustafa asked, stopping in the doorway.

"Do I have a choice?" Donna smiled. "Only kidding . . . I'll do it. I'll do it."

"Do what?" Charlie asked when Mustafa left.

"Sewing class for preteen girls at the church," she said. "He's pretty persistent."

"I don't know," he said, taking Mustafa's still-warm leather seat.

"I know you don't know," she replied.

"And you know?"

"The scene at the church was pretty damn moving. Mustafa stood in front of the congregation and told them how you had convinced him that the only way to save himself was by saving others. You're the hero of the piece. And, from what I can tell—and from what the minister told me—Moose has been spending every spare moment with the children there, especially the teenage boys. He runs a study hall for them most evenings. So why do you have your prune face on?"

"The speed and totality of the conversion," Charlie responded, without hesitation. "He doesn't feel anything for twenty years—not for his wife, his children—and then, all of a sudden, he's Empathy Central?"

Donna shrugged. "I thought we were supposed to give the benefit of the doubt to do-gooders, even those who are mortal smoothies and have nicotine stains all over their fingers. If your life is empty and you find something to fill it, it can fill up pretty quickly."

"Okay, okay," Charlie said guiltily. "But don't you go too righteous on me, huh? Keep the snake handling and speaking in tongues out of the office." He smiled; she didn't. He began their usual end-of-day wrap-up. "So, are we cool for the weekend? Any interesting Parkinson gossip?"

"Yes. No. Amazing how fast the word got around about Mahon—that she was the same one who leaked the diet pills. Those folks at the White House don't mess around."

"Think it's fizzling?" Charlie asked, relieved that Donna could switch back to business so readily.

"Hope so, for your sake," Donna said, then abruptly switched back to Mustafa. "And, *chico*, keep an open mind on Moose. I haven't seen him take a false step yet—and he's taken an awful lot of true ones."

Back in his office, packing up, Charlie decided to call Lynn. "Hi," he said, as if he hadn't made a fool of himself at the Inaugural Ball.

"Hello," she replied, a little chilly.

"Whatcha doin'?"

"Home alone."

"Can I come over," he asked, "and apologize for acting like a jerk last night?"

"You *were* a jerk," she said. "But you were right, too. This Jessica Mahon doesn't look like anything to write home about."

"Yeah, well," he said. "Still. I was a jerk."

"All I've got for food is girl things," she said.

"Yogurt, arugula and water lily sprouts?"

"Close . . . I suppose you want me to call Domino's?"

"I'll roust around the kitchen, see what I can find. You've got brandy?"

"Of course."

"Then I'll be right over."

They sat in the den, on a couch covered in what seemed to be Middle Eastern rug material, their food—cheese, crackers, assorted hors d'oeuvres—before them on the coffee table. They watched the feminist sexual harassment panel discussing Parkinson on *MacNeil/Lehrer,* the evening pyrotechnics on *Crossfire,* some *Equal Time* on CNBC, Larry King. It was all pretty grisly.

And a funny thing happened. Charlie made the first move, nibbling Lynn's ear after a stiff Courvoisier; she inhaled and put a hand on his cheek. He moved his hand, his left hand, onto her thigh and she fell open for him. Pretty soon, Charlie had her skirt up and was rolling her panties and panty hose off. He slipped down to the floor on his knees, spreading her legs, the right leg up the side of the couch, the left leg down toward the floor, and he was moving his lips down her right thigh, and his right hand up her left leg; moving slowly, quite remarkably slowly, but with an ardor, and a curiosity, that took him by surprise. It wasn't that they hadn't already ventured into all the various possibilities—but those moments had mostly come earlier, and they had settled into a fairly standard routine. They had never, so far as he could remember, made love anywhere but in her bedroom before.

But there he was, absolutely enjoying what he was doing; his face buried in her—and she was, or seemed to be, quite excited. She made a noise Charlie hadn't heard before, a full-throated sigh. And then, as she grew more agitated, she tried to pull him up on top of her. *"Okay,"* she said.

He'd been hoping for something more transcendent than "Okay." He'd been hoping for something like "Take me! Take me!" He'd read that once in a Max Shulman comedy. The woman had said, "Take me." The guy had said, "Where?" Still, he'd always thought it would be an incredibly sexy thing to say in the right circumstances, and if Lynn had said it then, his life might have turned a different corner—it seemed, on some level, that she was close to saying something wild and unprogrammed—but she didn't, and Charlie, wanting to show her a place he hadn't taken her before, persisted in his big cat licking and lapping. Indeed, he upped the ante, sneaking his right thumb inside her, just below where his tongue was working, and his pinky just below that, around back, and she began to shake—her legs shuddered—and she let out the most satisfying "OHHHH" imaginable.

They lay there for a few minutes, watching Larry King. Finally, Lynn asked, "Why did you do that?"

"Didn't you like it?"

"Yes, of course. But what about you?"

"I loved it," he said. She began a move toward his zipper, but he stopped her. "There's no quid pro quo," Charlie said, not that he wasn't aching. But a nonspontaneous Lynn Thurston assault on his tree line would have had the precise opposite effect on him that his performance had had on her. He'd make do with an imaginary rendezvous back home later on.

"You're a strange fellow, Charlie Martin," she said, tousling his hair. He pulled away, stood, moved to go. "You're *leaving*?" she asked, wounded.

"It's the weekend; I got the early flight to D.P. As Darrell Billups said in solemn colloquy today, 'I got folks to poke.' " He took her by the shoulders. "I'm sorry I blew up in public last night. I really am." He kissed her cheek. "We'll go out, have a date, see a movie or something, next week."

"Charlie," she asked hesitantly, teasing out his name.

"What?"

"What do you think of Linc's friend?"

He didn't want to be too coy and ask which friend . . . but why were people always asking him what he thought of Nell? Was it that obvious?

"Different," he said, wondering if Lynn had deduced a connection between his ardor of the evening and something she'd picked up the night before. "Why do you ask? What do you think of her?"

"Oh, I don't know," Lynn said. "I'm not much for those wry, aristocratic types."

"Me neither," Charlie said, heading toward the door. "But Linc seems pretty happy with her."

*　*　*

Two nights later in the Oak Street den, after several days of marathon folk-poking across the state, Charlie Martin found himself slightly overwhelmed by the sight of a perfectly matched set: his father and son, noodling together like a couple of old sidemen.

"Hey, Cal!" Charlie gave his son a hug when he came in. "It's so great that you're here!"

"I don't know. This seemed a more comfortable way to—well, you know—get to know the family," Calvin said, sitting back down on the floor, stretching out his legs, idly picking at his guitar. He spoke coolly, laconically, without making eye contact—was this his natural tone or was he already imitating his grandfather?

"You would have loved the music at the inauguration," Charlie said.

"You mean, all those druggies?" The controversy over drug-using musicians was one political story that Calvin could follow on MTV. "What a bunch of assholes—"

Charlie was in complete agreement with Cal, but sensed this was an assault on him—on his world, at the very least.

"Calvin's not a Brie and freezy fellah," Buzz said, and Charlie wondered: was the old man consciously siding with his grandson in this subtle struggle, or was he just riffing?

Buzz had brought the synthesizer down from the bedroom. His thick fingers fluttered over the keys, finding chords to back his grandson's bluesy wanderings. It was a form of intimacy that didn't need words; occasionally, they'd glance at each other, raise an eyebrow, as if to say—not bad, interesting idea, cool move.

"So, Charles," Buzz said, "you ever hear this Steely Dan?"

"Sure, Pop. Why?"

"Kid turned me on to them," Buzz said, nodding at Calvin, who picked the signature Steely Dan riff from "Reeling in the Years." Buzz nodded, with pleasure, at his grandson's facility. "They do, like, Modernaires harmonies with jazzy licks and a rock beat . . . and dig this, Chas, we came up with a new one: A 'Ruby' medley . . . Start off with the old harmonica song 'Ruby, It's You.' Then the Rolling Stones, 'Ruby Tuesday,' and then—right, kid?—Steely Dan's cover of Dion's 'Ruby, Ruby, When Will You Be Mine?' Pretty spiffy, huh?"

"Mega-spiffy," Calvin said. "But it wasn't Steely Dan's cover. It was Donald Fagen's after he went solo."

"My one problem with the kid," Buzz said, "is he don't want to live here. Gettin' himself a pad over Lapham Bridge."

"I don't want to hang out here, listenin' to you and Edsy rattling the bedposts," Cal said, crumpling a Bud can. "Make me horny."

"Mind your mouth, *dude*," Edsy said. She was looking not bad at all, in a tight V-necked sweater and jeans; Charlie was always surprised, and impressed, by her ability to get away with dressing young.

"Okay, Grandma," Calvin said affectionately. He made eye contact with *her*, Charlie noticed.

"Why Lapham?" Charlie asked, wincing as the words came out: he was the squarest, most literal Martin in the room. "Not too far," Calvin said. "Got a deal—same as Houston, apartment near the mall with the record store where I'm gigging."

There were all sorts of fatherly impulses stirring: why not try something a little more ambitious than the record store, why not go back to school, why not live *here*? But Charlie, in his maiden moment of paternal restraint, decided he'd have to build some chits before he could start ragging the kid. In truth, he was happy to just sit there and listen to his father and son go on; he'd been running his mouth, massaging the civilians, for two days. It hadn't been bad, but this was better. It was past one now, prime time for musicians. He gave them center stage—and happily allowed himself to be an audience, for a change.

From a distance, that weekend, Washington had seemed . . . distant. He had checked in with Sly, who said he'd heard rumblings that Mahon was backing down. He invited Charlie to his home for dinner on Monday "to celebrate."

"You don't think it's a little early for that?"

"Not from what I hear," Sly said mischievously. "You'll come? I'm working on my opening statement for the hearings. Need you to take a look. If we get bored with that, there's great college hoops on the tube."

"Okay, Slick. I'll be there."

The Parkinson story did seem to be in remission again. It was off the front pages of the *Times* and *Post*, which Hilton faxed to him. There would be a story below the fold on the front page in the next day's—Sunday's—*Register-World*, but that would have a local angle: MARTIN BACKS FRIEND.

Charlie had given Bob Hamblin a Saturday interview as they skidded down the back roads from Crescent Lake to Lewis in the green Chrysler minivan the senator used back home (Chrysler had an assembly plant in Singer Rapids; Ford had one in Port Sallesby—but with about 850 fewer jobs than Chrysler). Mary Proctor, Charlie's Des Pointe staff director, was traveling with them; and Barry Powter—a college kid with improbably vivid red hair—was driving. It was a raw day, windy and gray; the sky seemed reluctant to do anything drastic, although there were occasional, hard, bristly flurries. Charlie performed his usual home-state ceremonies: picking up the local Democratic county chair wherever they went—and leaving him in Mary's good hands, in the backseat, chatting about who was up to run for sheriff. They visited the cops and firemen in each town large enough to have a police station or firehouse, had coffee with local newspaper editors, shook hands in every café along the way.

Hamblin followed behind, in his Chevy Blazer; then they moved the reporter into the van for the stretch between Nebble Forks and Lewis. Charlie drove the minivan that leg, giving Hamblin a little bit of color for his story (while Barry drove Hamblin's car). Thus, the inevitable: "The senator was behind the wheel, negotiating the slick roads of Coatulla

County, while answering questions about the latest Washington im-
broglio." Charlie didn't give him much more than solid, unequivocal
support for Parkinson. Off the record, he asked Bob, "Folks talking
about it much out here?"

"A little. Compared to Byron Harper? Not much," he said. Harper was
the brilliant freshman point guard for the state university basketball
team; he was headed for the pros—perhaps as soon as the end of the season. "You hear, Muffler Man is starting a campaign: Keep Byron at State.
Buy him a Caddy."

"Young Muff keeps himself busy," Charlie said with mild derision.

"He's got a lot of folks listening," Bob said. "Pretty clever. You think
he's got ambitions?"

"Undoubtedly."

"You think he'll run for governor?"

"Oh, you mean *political* ambitions? Jeez Louise. Not if he's smart,"
Charlie said, playing dumb. "What say you, Proctor?"

"Stranger things have happened." Mary was wearing a wine crewneck
over a navy-blue turtleneck, a long gray tweed skirt and lace-up boots; she
looked very much the middle-aged wife of a high school principal, which
she was, but she did come equipped with a mouth. "*You* ran, and won."

"Is he a Democrat or a Republican?" Charlie asked.

"He calls himself a Depublican," Proctor said. She'd been doing her
homework, listening every day. What they didn't tell Hamblin was that
the Muffler Man wanted to interview Charlie about the Parkinson situation for Monday's show; they hadn't quite decided to go or not yet. They
were planning to talk it over in a conference call with Devereaux.

"Maybe Muffles'll come after me," Charlie said. "Run for my seat."

"Yeah," Hamblin snorted. "Sure."

There are politicians who love working the home state; there are a
great many more who see it as the political equivalent of paying the bills.
Charlie had never minded it all that much. He did it the way most men
his age mowed the lawn, or washed the car. It wasn't particularly exciting
or challenging, but there was a certain satisfaction in doing it well.

He kept computer files—they'd been three-by-five cards when he'd
started out—on every politically significant person in every city, town and
hamlet. He knew all the names. He knew what they cared about. He
could talk the local history of water and sewer money with any mayor or
alderman; he could talk EPA, and Title I, and Section 8—every grant
he'd gotten, every penny of it. He could talk regulatory procedure, talk

it stiff, talk it till the cows came home. He hadn't known that politics would entail all this busywork when he started out, nudged into the fray by Dunn—with a not-so-subtle push from Johanna as well.

Johanna Lecoutre Martin had thought politics was all about making speeches for the kids and against the corporate interests. She was disconcerted by the fact that noncombatants, normal people who were neither oppressed nor oppressors, were involved, too—people who wanted to have their hands shaken and their babies kissed, people who needed to know that their senator was every bit as obsessed as they were about the prospects for the state university's historically brilliant wrestling team. She was amazed by how immune the folks were to serious discussions about "issues" like guaranteed employment and a living wage; she'd been equally amazed that Charlie didn't try very hard to educate the public on things that, she was certain, they needed to hear—like the need for higher gasoline taxes. Within a year of his election to the Congress, she left him over a vote he'd given Oskar on capital gains taxes. It was an almost mythic moment: they were watching *60 Minutes*, a chasm separating them on the love seat. And he'd said it to provoke her, "I'm gonna do something this week you're gonna hate. I'm voting with the GOPs on capital gains."

She'd stood, stared at him. She looked, at that moment, quite beautifully severe; she was wearing shorts, and had the most graceful legs, thigh to toe, he'd ever seen, the most perfect and delicate little feet. He wanted to tell her that. But he knew it would be the worst possible thing he could say. The best possible thing he could say was "Just kidding!" The second best was "Look, the economy's stalled. We need to create jobs. Maybe this'll juice things a little." He tried the latter, but it didn't go over very well.

"You are a fucking disgrace," she said.

"You know, you have really terrific little feet," he replied, with a cruel smile, thinking: WTF.

And that was that. Johanna stormed out; Charlie made not the slightest effort to stop her. When asked what happened to his first marriage, he would say that his was the only divorce in history precipitated by a vote on the capital gains tax.

Not that anyone else in the state seemed to care about how he voted on capital gains, or much else for that matter. They liked him, assumed he voted the right way on ag and trusted his judgment on all the rest. The folks would ask, dutifully, about things going on in Washington—

mostly because they seemed to consider it a civic responsibility of some sort. He was a walking social studies test. "Hey, Senator, you guys ever gonna balance the budget?" But they didn't really expect Congress to balance the budget. And they rarely asked about the embarrassing stuff. There hadn't been any questions that weekend about Sly Parkinson.

Charlie had agreed to do the Brinkley show—Gid Reese actually called and asked him to—on Sunday morning from Des Pointe. It proved painless. Meanwhile, on *Meet the Press*, Frank Mix was saying that he didn't anticipate much of a battle over the Parkinson nomination. "Least it seems that way. Never can tell, though. May have some unpaid parking tickets, or something. Tough to confirm him, if he jaywalked or whatever."

After Brinkley, he called Devereaux: "Anything happening?"

"Well, the *Post*'ll report tomorrow that Jessica Mahon's been hospitalized with nervous exhaustion. You talked to Parkinson?"

So that's why Sly had been so celebratory on the phone. "Do we know where she is?" Charlie asked. "Mahon?"

"I can check. Why?" But Hilton heard the concern in Charlie's voice.

"Casualties are always a bummer, Hilton," he said, disgusted. The very word "hospital" could still summon specific, humiliating memories. Did the Stanton folks have to be so vehement, and public, about destroying the poor woman's credibility? They had orchestrated the husband's side of the story as if it were D day. "Catch you later."

Charlie had been standing with Pat Dunn in the frozen, glary parking lot of KFAS, the local ABC affiliate, as he talked to Hilton on his cellular. He continued to stand there now, holding the frigid phone, lost in space, stopped dead by the odd intensity of his reaction to the news about Jessica Mahon, wondering about the distance between the civil indifference the folks had been giving him all weekend and the apocalyptic warfare in Washington. Hadn't there been a time when the stakes were *only* victory or defeat? Now the losers ended up in jail or mental hospitals, exposed and humiliated.

"You coming?" Dunnsie had gone ahead, slipping and squinting across the parking lot. Pat minded the cold more than in the past, and often found himself envying the farmers who managed to get south for the deep freeze. He tried to hustle Charlie into the van now. "You want to go down the Flats? Get some food?" he asked. "We could hit Holy Name on the way."

"Naww, let's go home. How much time we have?"

"Depends on how many Super Bowl parties you want to do," Pat said. Charlie slid into the front seat, next to Barry Powter, leaned back, closed his eyes. "What's up, Senator?" Pat asked. "You're pensive. That's dangerous."

"Great night last night, watching Buzz and Cal together," Charlie said. "You close to your grandkids, Dunnsie?"

" 'Course I am, Charles." Charlie had had his picture taken with all four Dunn grandchildren, had sent flags flown over the capitol to both daughters—but he'd done it on autopilot. He'd never expressed the slightest interest in Pat's family life before. And Dunnsie was beginning to pick up other strange vibrations: the day before, at the Lutheran pancake breakfast in Leeton, he'd watched several of the moms getting on Charlie: "Senator, when are you going to get married and settle down?" This was nothing new. Ever since Clarice died, ever since Johanna had split, every mature woman in the state had been auditioning for the role of Charlie's mom or wife. But now, for the first time, Pat noticed a certain discomfort in the senator—not directly, of course; Charlie responded with the usual killer smile and hug. And yet, it was almost as if the boy had finally begun to hear the part of the Mom Chorus that he'd always ignored, the subtext of concern: these people thought it was wrong that he hadn't remarried. His solitude nagged at them. They voted for him *despite* it.

Pat stared at the senator. "What?" Charlie asked.

"Just thinking about you having a kid, all of a sudden," he lied.

"Yeah, it's sort of like an immaculate conception," Charlie said. "Ever since Schollwengen, Dunnsie—things keep happening to me, without quite happening to *me*."

* * *

On Monday morning, Charlie came downstairs early and found Edsy puttering around the kitchen—neither Buzz nor Calvin had roused themselves yet. He sat down, scanned the *R-W*, nursed some weak midwestern coffee in the breakfast nook.

"Cal's a good kid, Charlie," she said. "He's done a wonder for Buzz."

"Thanks, wish I could say I had something to do with it." Once again, he felt irrelevant and was almost envious: Calvin had finally found the family he needed—his grandparents.

"Makes no difference," Edsy said. "You didn't know. Anyway, he's here now and it's good all around."

"Edsy, it's official," Charlie said abruptly. "I'm in the market. Now that I've got a son, I'm looking to fill out my portfolio: I need a spouse."

" 'Bout time," Edwina said, not exactly believing him. "You want some toast or something?"

"No, thanks. I don't know . . . I've been feeling it lately. The last year, suddenly, life seems to be coming at me from a different direction. You know what I mean?"

"No," Edsy said. "I just take it a day at a time, and don't sweat the small stuff."

"Can't argue with that," Charlie said, a bit surprised by how easily he'd fallen into a conversation about personal things with Edsy. "But it's not easy to get hooked up with someone when you're my age and a senator. The field is limited. You've got widows, divorcées, spinsters and teenagers."

"They're all just girls," Edsy said. "You're a good-looking guy with a fancy job. There shouldn't be any problem."

"No, there shouldn't be," he said, trying to remember if this sort of intimacy had ever been possible with his mother. "But there is."

"How about Nancy Brunelle? Alma Brunelle's daughter?"

"Her husband's divorced or deceased?" he asked.

"Deceased. But so what? She's a history teacher at D.P. South. Good-looking. Lots of fun, too. Always a good sign when you can remember the way someone laughs. I can, with her. You remember her at all?"

Vaguely. And not bad, as advertised; but local—somehow he felt he'd progressed beyond local. And if there was a laugh he couldn't forget, it was Nell's. "Hey, Edsy," he said, suddenly. "Did you and Buzz—"

She looked at him. "What?"

"Did Milky ever know about you and Buzz?"

"About me and Buzz what?" She put her hands on her hips, purposefully opaque. Charlie wondered if he'd have the courage to ask what he really wanted to ask: how do you snake your best friend's girl?

"Well, was there always a thing—a chemistry between you and Buzz? Even before?"

"A chemistry?" Edsy scoffed. "I flunked chemistry." She realized she was answering his question by avoiding it. "Did I sense that Buzzy was looking at me a certain way? Of course. You always know that."

"And you felt the same way about him?" She nodded slowly. "How did you let him know that?" Charlie asked.

"I tried not to. I talked about Milky this and Milky that."

"But?"

"But none of your business," she said, looking at Charlie as if to say: why now? And then, having asked herself the question, she knew. "There are some things in life, son, you just can't *think* your way through. Even if you really want to. 'Chemistry' is one. If it's real."

"And how do you know if it's real?"

Edsy tilted her head as if to say: you can't be *that* thick. But then, Charlie was Clarice's son, too. And Clarice didn't have a clue about chemistry.

"I can invite Nancy Brunelle over to dinner," Edsy said, changing the subject with absolute authority.

"I'll think about it."

"Don't," she said. "If you've got to think about it, it ain't gonna happen."

11

———

"S o, Senator Martin," said Leland Butler, riffing a bit, playing at broadcast pomposity. "An honor, indeed. Have you recovered from your Super Bowl hangover yet?"

The Muffler Man show. Monday noon. By phone, from Charlie's Des Pointe office in the Federal Building downtown, a place Charlie had never spent much time in or given much attention to. It was the sort of place that conservatives imagined when they thought about government: soulless, styleless, enormous.

"I've learned not to expect too much from the Super Bowl, Lee," he began. Charlie wasn't going to call him Muffler Man. Hilton had said: stay informal but show respect, call him Lee or Mr. Butler, keep a safe senatorial distance—which was one reason to do the interview by phone. "Big news this weekend, far as I'm concerned, was Byron's performance on Saturday night against the Illini," Charlie added. Political sports chat: disgraceful, but a petty misdemeanor in a world of fans.

"You were a two-sport guy at State, weren't you?"

"I was an athletic cliché," Charlie said. "A good-field-no-hit shortstop, a step-too-slow halfback. Nowhere near Byron's level."

"Think you can pass a bill to make him stay?" Muffler Man asked.

"I've proposed a Byron Harper Empowerment Zone," Charlie said. "Special tax incentives for point guards operating at the state university. But I don't know how many votes I can get for it."

It was going well.

"How many votes you getting for Slime Porkington?"

Well, maybe not so well. "I expect we'll confirm Congressman Parkinson," Charlie said, hitching up his pants, getting formal. "Easily," he added.

"Why on earth?" Muffler Man asked, with a chuckle—as if this were the dumbest idea in recorded history.

"Because he knows his stuff," Charlie replied, midwestern.

"Apparently, he knows his staff, too."

Muffler Man was fast. Charlie decided to get slow and made a mental note: no more phoners with this guy. He needed to see Butler, sense his moves. He tried to imagine the blond, smooth baby face. "Congressman Parkinson," he began, "has been one of our leading defense experts. He took a hard line, consistently, with the Soviets. He supported the placement of Pershing missiles—"

"Yada-la-dee-dah," Muffler Man interrupted. "He supported the Panama Canal Treaty, like you did. He supports the United Nations, like you do, Senator. He's a member of the Trilateral Commission—"

"Aw, c'mon, Lee. Don't tell me you're into that paranoid conspiracy stuff." Charlie had been startled by the interruption, the raw disrespect of it. He'd never been treated with anything but adulation on the local airwaves. What's more, the guy was spouting dangerous, deeply harebrained things. But Charlie had now taken the bait. He had been warned not to do that.

"You think it's paranoid to worry about these big corporations exporting American jobs overseas?" the Muffler Man replied with a snort, happy—thrilled, in fact—that the senator was playing ball, "You think it's paranoid to worry about exporting American sovereignty to international organizations? About supporting tinhorn dictators who are puppets of the international bankers? I know you fellows in Washington feel differently, but a lot of folks back here don't like their money going to pay for all these international bureaucrats—and they aren't so sure they want Slime Porkington stripping the national defense with his fancy ideas."

"Lee," Charlie said, working to keep cool, "I've just spent the weekend traveling around the state, talking to folks—like I do most weekends. And you know what? Not a single question or comment about the Parkinson appointment—"

"That's because they're embarrassed," the Muffler Man shot back. "Mrs. Mom at the Methodist bake sale isn't gonna ask you, how can you vote for some pill-popping slurpie who gropes his staff. She's gonna be polite. She's gonna ask about the budget deficit. Or the weather. Am I right or what?"

He was right and he was wrong. He was also outrageously crude. Charlie understood that this sort of blowhard populism might come off as re-freshing to the folks. Or some of the folks. But he had no idea how to re-spond to it. Real life was just too complicated to communicate on this jerk's radio show. "I don't know, Lee," he said, kicking himself for hesi-tating a nanosecond too long, for sounding even the slightest bit uncer-tain. "Most folks around here will tell you the truth about what they're feeling—and they'll tell it to you unmuffled."

"Then how come you guys twist it all around in Washington?" Muffler Man said. He pronounced it Warshington.

"We do some good things, too," Charlie said, retreating to the safety of boilerplate. "You should go visit a vet center sometime—or the new biogenetics lab up at Mason, which we got funded last year. It's easy to be cynical."

"It's easy to be cynical when you guys insist on making some pervert the secretary of defense," Butler said nonchalantly. Just another show.

"If you're going to make charges like that, you need some solid evi-dence to back it up," Charlie said, as calmly as he could, amazed that But-ler wasn't backing down, amazed by the disdain in the man's voice.

"The liberal *New York Times* says he's a druggie, that's good enough for me," Muffler Man said, shutting the senator down. "Well, it's been good talking to you, Senator Martin . . . and I'm sure you guys in Warshington will keep on *groping* for answers. . . ."

Charlie was shaking when he put down the phone. Mary Proctor rushed in. "Asshole," she said.

"Me or him?" the Senator asked.

"You had to do the show," she said, reprising their earlier conversa-tions on the subject. "If you hadn't, he'd have made a campaign out of you ducking it."

"Yeah, but I should have been better prepared," Charlie said. "I should have had Devereaux around this weekend, working this."

"You and Hilton spent an hour on the phone. You've got to let that boy have a life. Anyway, you did fine," Mary said, wrinkling her brow into four absolutely perfect parallel creases. She didn't think the boss had been mauled, but she was dismayed that the public ugliness infecting other, edgier parts of the nation was now seeping into the Midwest—Mary's sensibility tracked perfectly with that of National Public Radio: her vehement, open-minded liberalism was militantly polite. She found it odd to think that Lee Butler represented the future; impossible to think that Charlie Martin represented the past. "Butler scored some

points, but you did, too. The one thing I'd suggest is you work on not letting him get under your skin. Next time—"

"Next time?"

But of course there would be a next time.

*   *   *

Sly and Maggie Parkinson lived in a comfortable, low-slung ranch
house on a quiet street in a profoundly middle-class neighborhood in
Rockville, Maryland; indeed, they lived as most Americans lived, which
was rare for a politician. It was an arrangement that made manifest one
of Sly's strong points as a human being and public figure—he was a fairly
flagrant nonmillionaire. His defense expertise and connections would
have landed him on Easy Street without breaking a sweat had he not
been so scrupulous when it came to dealing with the military-industrial
complex, a rare bit of discipline on Sly's part.

When Charlie Martin arrived for dinner that Monday evening, the
rooms in the front of the Parkinson house were dark, although there was
a light on in the hallway. He rang the bell and, after a minute, Sly came
to the door in his stocking feet, disheveled, wearing a wrinkled white
shirt and old chinos, which seemed in danger of falling off his slimmed
torso. "Hey, Chas," he said, enveloping him in a bearhug that quickly
spun out into rapid, percussive back-patting—a distracted, impersonal
greeting, despite the physical intensity of it. "We did it!" Parkinson said,
clapping his hands together, then raising his fists in triumph. "Great,
huh?"

Sly turned and padded along the sky-blue hall carpeting, assuming
Charlie would follow him to the den, where there were shelves of books,
and plastic models of ships and aircraft—the sort of things little boys put
together with glue—and a wall of family photographs. In the center, was
an old, hilariously domestic picture of Sly and Maggie and their children
on the Jersey shore. "Great roundball in a few minutes," Sly said, standing in front of the couch, facing the television. "ACC—Carolina against
Duke. We're just . . . Great night for a celebration, huh? We're over the
hump. Just great. I told you this was all gonna blow away. Just crazy stuff.
Baloney bullshit."

Sly seemed to be jumping out of his skin. His eyes were darting, his
hands flying about, gesturing, pushing his glasses up his nose, scratching
behind his ear.

"Sly—"

"Sit down, sit down, Charlie. Some Fresca? Diet Coke?" Then, with a giggle, "How about some fucking carrots? We've got a ton of them! See, didn't I tell you about Jessica Mahon? Nuthouse Central. Crazy b—"

There was a thump and a crash from the kitchen and Parkinson darted a nervous glance toward the door. "Shit. She's—I . . . I just . . . I forgot to tell her I invited you over . . . I better go help . . . Y'know?"

Charlie stood alone in the room, thinking: uh-oh. He heard another crash from the kitchen and Maggie shouting, "Out!" and he debated whether he should stay where he was or go to the kitchen and say hello. He stayed: the Parkinsons had a right to a private predinner cataclysm. He sat down and tried to watch the basketball, which was just beginning in an awkward, tentative fashion as some big games do, the players nervous, the crowd too hyper, screaming way too loud.

He had expected Sly to rejoin him in the den, but he didn't. Ten minutes passed. Neither Duke nor Carolina could gather much steam, the defenses tenacious, lots of fouls and turnovers, the ball bouncing off stone hands and vagabond legs. Ten more minutes, and Sly still hadn't returned; Maggie hadn't come in to say hello, either. Charlie stood, waited through a commercial break. When the game resumed, there was an immediate foul. He decided to see what was up.

Maggie was in the kitchen, standing over the stainless-steel sink and staring out the window, wearing an oversized navy flannel shirt—one of Sly's, no doubt—and blue jeans.

"Hey, Mags!" Charlie said, and she seemed to start.

She turned toward him, narrowed her eyes and said, "Oh . . . Hello."

Charlie crossed the room to give her a kiss, but Maggie seemed to pull back slightly. "Veal chops," she said, pushing past him to the oven. "Think they're done now. Why don't you go sit down?"

He passed through the louvered door into the dining room, which was small and spare—a blond Danish modern table and sideboard, lime-green wall-to-wall carpeting, a modest chandelier, several innocuous, starving-artist-level seascapes on white Sheetrock walls. Sly was already seated at the head of the table—but he was a markedly different Sly, quiet, staring idly at his place setting. He jerked his head up when Charlie entered the room and smiled. "Sit down, friend. . . ."

Maggie was just behind Charlie with a platter of very large veal chops sprinkled with rosemary, oozing juice, and a bowl of boiled potatoes. She sat at the far end of the table across from her husband. Charlie was placed midway between them, facing the kitchen door. "Here," she said, passing Charlie the chops. "Start."

Charlie looked at Maggie, who was placing a lone potato on her plate, and reaching for the string beans. "Maggie?" he asked, passing Sly the chops.

"Would you like some wine?" she responded, finally looking directly at him, her brow furrowed, her eyes bleary. She'd been crying.

"No . . . thanks." Charlie said. He passed the potatoes to Sly, who tried to slide a few from the bowl to his plate and missed, one landing with a splat on the table and the other in Sly's lap. "Whoops," he said, looking at Charlie—from a distance: Mars, perhaps. Drugged, it seemed.

"Okay," Charlie said. "Would you guys mind telling me what's going on here?"

"What's going on? What's going . . . *on*?" Maggie said acidly, putting down her fork. "We're celebrating! Mr. Secretary is off the hook!"

"Maggie, don't," Sly said, resting his head back, as if he couldn't hold it up.

"Don't what?" Charlie asked.

"Don't tell you about Jane Berger and Molly Giovane—both of them former staffers. Actually, no: Molly's still hanging in there," Maggie said, staring directly at Charlie, ignoring her husband. "Don't tell you about Barbara Faulk and Judy Hershkowitz and Etheline Jones—and who knows how many others. Etheline sounds like an automotive additive, doesn't it? I'm not sure about the last three. I didn't talk to them. I did talk to Jane Berger. She pushed him away. But Molly—she went along, shall we say, *very* reluctantly. Apparently, she suffered an involuntary loss of her virginity in the Cannon Building. Jane took care of her, afterward. She said the girl couldn't stop crying for a week."

" 'Snot true," Sly said, wagging his head.

Maggie ignored him. "Charlie, why don't you ask me how I found these women?"

Charlie nodded. He glanced over at Sly, whose eyes were closed, head resting back again. Maggie, reading his concern, asked her husband, "Hey, Parkinson, how many did you take?"

Sly whispered, "Four."

"Jesus," she said. "Why don't you go lie down on the couch?"

Sly stood, smiled at Charlie, patted his shoulder as he walked past and said, "I'm gonna go take a little nap."

When he'd gone, Charlie asked, "Pills?"

"Lately," Maggie said, "he's been feeling very optimistic about his capacity for Valium."

A pill-popping slurpie who gropes his staff.

"So how did you find these women?" Charlie asked Maggie, his throat dry and constricted.

"I went to visit Jessica Mahon," she said. "In the hospital. She told me about the others. She was telling the truth about Sylvester, of course. We all knew that, didn't we? Poor fucked-up girl. But not a liar. . . . Not much of a looker, either." Maggie made a face. "But proximity is destiny with the Big Guy, it seems."

"And the others?" Charlie asked. "Why haven't they—"

"Come forward?" Maggie shook her head, disgusted with him. "You guys. Well, Jane Berger—she's working for leadership now, for Larkin, and she didn't want to cause a stir. You make an accusation like this, you're tainted forever. But she told me. Kind of lit up her life, the fact that I called. She'd been wanting to vent for a long time. I had to promise that we'd keep it among us girls. And Molly—well, Molly's still working for Sly, if you can believe it. So I didn't have the guts to call her. Charlie." She smiled. "What's the matter? You seem to have lost your appetite."

"Maggie, what are we going to do?" His voice felt tiny, foreign to him.

"About what?"

"About the—" Nomination, he started to say. Then felt ridiculous.

"You guys," Maggie said again. "You and your stupid government." She stood. "Who cares about your goddamn public service? Why don't you ask me the big question, the really tough one?"

"About . . . what?" Charlie asked, rising with her, moving toward her.

"About me, you dunce," she said quietly, turning her back, moving away from him, toward the door. "What on earth am I still doing here?"

She left him standing there. He let himself out.

Tuesday morning, members of the Senate Armed Services Committee reconvened in Bartle Bramlette's office in the Hart Building. The outer office was filled with Alabama memorabilia—photos of the Gulf Coast; the statehouse; Bear Bryant and the Crimson Tide. And another eruption of photos inside, Bartle Bramlette smiling, uneven lower teeth visible, with just about every world leader imaginable, and some quite unimaginable. The senators sat on couches and chairs; Bart behind his big desk.

No O'Brien or Mix this time. No Mike Coleman. Just the eight of them: four Democrats, three Republicans, and the chairman. Laura Meadows, the staff director, took notes. "Any thoughts?" Bramlette asked. "Any conversion experiences?"

No one said anything, at first. Then Dickie Ganther: "The dipstick weathered the weekend. I think he's in the clear."

Francesca Warren: "In the clear, because the White House destroyed Jessica Mahon. I still think this is a bad idea, a farce."

Darrell Billups: "Much as I hate to agree with the gentle-lady, I agree with the gentle-lady."

"Laura," Bramlette asked, "what's the Mahon situation? Will she testify?"

"It appears not, sir," Meadows said. "She'll file a statement, but won't testify."

"Do we accept the statement if she isn't willing to be questioned?" Ted Panepopoulos asked. "Doesn't seem right. What's the procedure?"

No one seemed to know. Charlie shifted in his chair. It had been a difficult night; he'd called Mike Coleman and told him about the scene at the Parkinsons'. Mike had whistled and said, "*Shit.*" He'd asked a series of questions about the women and the extent of Sly's drug use. Mike then asked Charlie what he thought should be done next. Charlie had said he wasn't sure, but they both knew: the plug had to be pulled. Sly's nomination was history. He was stunned, exhausted . . . and embarrassed. He couldn't stop thinking about Lee Butler—what fun he'd have with this. He asked Mike what he thought. Mike pretended not to know either. "I've got to say, Charlie, it doesn't look too good. I'm gonna have to call around, see what Gid and the President think."

Mike asked Charlie not to tell the other senators what he'd seen, to stay mum and let Stanton take the initiative. "I'll call you first thing, let you know what's happening," Mike had said, but he hadn't called. Charlie assumed they were busy moving their next candidate into place.

And now Bramlette was asking, "Any other gropees, or recovered memory victims, or diet quacks Sly Parkinson might have employed who wish to enlighten the public? Minority have any witnesses?"

"No," Ganther said.

"Okay, then we'll go ahead tomorrow." Bartlette sighed. Charlie was dizzied by the disparity between what he knew and what they didn't.

"Wait a minute," Francesca Warren said. "Senator Martin has been staring at the floor, at the walls and at the fireplace. He hasn't said a word, which isn't like him. If memory serves, he was Mr. Parkinson's strongest defender last Friday. Is your silence to be taken as assent, or something more complicated, Senator?"

An argument against women in politics, Charlie thought: they read body language. The men had been oblivious to his turmoil. And now what? He looked up at Francesca Warren, a small smile playing on her rather nice mouth; she knew she had him. "Senator, have you something to say?"

"Not really." Meek as a mouse.

"Interesting. Charlie," she pressed, "if we were voting Sly Parkinson up or down right now, how would you vote?"

Charlie had figured that Jack Stanton was going to save him from ever having to confront that one. But now, here it was—anything less than wholehearted support would send a huge signal to his colleagues. And, before he knew it, the signal had been sent. He had delayed his response a beat too long. He hadn't vehemently and immediately said "Aye." Every senator in the room was staring at him. They were not dummies: the jig was up.

"I'd have to say no," Charlie said, looking at Francesca, then down at the floor. "I will, with the most profound possible regret, vote no."

"Yeeeee-haaaa!" said Darrell Billups. "We got us a ball game." Charlie wanted to slug him.

Bramlette actually licked his lips. Charlie was aligned with everyone he despised.

"Charlie, what the f—" Ted Panepopoulos said.

"I have reasons to doubt Sly's fitness for the job," Charlie said. "I'd prefer not to discuss them."

Would anyone press him on that? No way. They were senators.

"Well, Mr. Chairman?" Ganther asked. "Where do we take it from here?"

"We proceed as planned," Bramlette said, "although I assume Senator Martin will inform the administration of his change of heart. Or have you done that already, Charlie?"

It was, Charlie believed, the first time the son of a bitch had called him by his first name.

"You're right, Mr. Chairman," he said, not wanting to divulge his conversations with Mike Coleman. "I'll do that."

He was the first to leave; it was the right thing to do—the others would need the space to gossip behind him. But Francesca Warren caught up as he traversed the echoey passages from Hart through Dirksen toward Russell. She slid her arm in his, a more than collegial gesture, and said, "That can't have been easy, Senator."

"It wasn't because I saw the wisdom of your views," he said snappishly.

"Of course not," she replied with mock sobriety, reacting more graciously than he imagined she might.

"But you did give me pause," he allowed. "You made me think twice."

She stopped, turned, looked him in the eye. "Charlie, there are people who do things up here for the worst possible reasons. You are not one of them. I think it's safe to say that everyone in that room—maybe even Darrell Billups—understood your motivation was honor, not politics. I don't know what your reasons are, but my assumption is you did it for the country . . . and I'd like to buy you dinner sometime."

"You making a pass at me?" he said, giving her a look.

"Yes," she said. "It's scary as hell, but face it, Senator." She smiled, "Honor is a very alluring quality in a guy."

He laughed. "I've never been propositioned by a senator before."

"It's an invitation," she said. "Not a proposition."

"And I accept, with pleasure," he said. "But now I really must go back to my office and slit my wrists."

And, kaboom.

It was like the footage he'd seen of atomic bomb blasts, a blinding detonation, then a deep, rolling percussive blowback, then the blowback gets bigger and more powerful than you could have imagined, then mushroom cloud, smoke and cinders.

"What *happened*?" Donna asked, when he slithered back into the office. "You have phone calls from Don O'Brien, Frank Mix, Mike Coleman, Gid Reese, Maggie Parkinson—and from the President himself."

"Well, let's start with the President," Charlie said, "and we'll work our way down. Also, you and Hilton—and, dammit, I will call you D-1 and D-2, if I want to—you should be in my office as we work this. All Ds on deck."

"What's *this*?" Donna asked. The boss looked weary, drained.

"I've changed my mind," he said. "I'm voting against Sly."

"Jesus, God." Donna whistled.

He sat down behind his desk. He stared directly at Hilda Madison's cow, which seemed to be mocking him, masticating merrily. He bent paper clips.

Donna went out and then came back in. The intervening silence had been mesmerizing. "President's gone into a series of meetings. Gid asked if you could come down to 1600 at eleven-thirty," she said. "I assume you can."

"Donna, I think the cow is a keeper," he said. "Let's see if Hilda Madison will sell it to us. . . . Helll-o, Hilton," who saluted as he came through the door, sleeves rolled, gray wide-wale corduroys, brown suede Hush Puppies.

"I'm sorry about Mr. Muffler," Hilton said. "I should have prepped you better."

"It's not your fault," Charlie said. "He was quicker than I expected. Now we know."

"Do we have a subsequent crisis," D-2 asked, slowly picking up the vibes in the room, "or are we still unmuffling ourselves?"

"He's voting against Parkinson," Donna said.

Hilton whistled, too. "Do we know his reasons?" he asked Donna, as if the boss weren't there. She shrugged. They both turned to Charlie. He smiled and shrugged.

Rosemary: Frank Mix was on the phone. "Must've been more than parking tickets," Mix said, referring to his *Meet the Press* sound bite, which had made all the newspapers on Monday.

"Yup."

"Coulda told me, before I made a fool of myself on TV."

"Didn't find out till last night," Charlie said. "Had a fascinating dinner with the Parkinsons."

"I don't want to know the details, do I?" he said, then before Charlie could answer: "You tell Stanton's folks?"

"Coleman, last night," he said. "I'm going over there in a bit."

"A great day for the yahoos," Mix said. "Too bad. . . . Damn, I hate that the wingers will be laughing and farting over this."

"Frank," Charlie asked, "has it always been this brutal, or am I going soft?"

"It's always been brutal," he said. "But now—you guys, your generation, did some sorry stuff, drugs and all. Makin' us pay for it. Y'get the feeling that it's a big game hunt, and we're the game. We're all gonna be stuffed and mounted before it's over. The jungle'll be left to pygmies and hyenas."

"That's a happy thought, Senator," he said.

"They call me Mr. Sunshine."

He flipped on CNN: nothing there yet. A nutty thought: maybe this hadn't really happened.

"Boss," D-2 said. "Have you thought about press strategy on this one?"

"No," Charlie replied. "Like what?" But he knew like what.

"Sir." The senator liked it when Hilton called him sir, but he only seemed to do it when he was invading Charlie's privacy. He was sitting on the leather couch, long legs stretched on the coffee table, Hush Puppies crossed. "Would you mind telling me why you've changed your mind?"

"All right, Hilton," he said. "I went over to the Parkinsons' house last night, and realized that Sly wasn't—right for the job. But no way I say that publicly."

"What do you mean, 'right'?"

"Just what I said." Charlie looked at Hilton directly; he seemed not to blink, but it wasn't a hard or angry stare. It was simply resolute.

"Great," Hilton said. "And you won't even let me say that you changed your mind after a meeting with Parkinson?"

"No," he said.

"You realize how dangerous it is to say nothing?"

"Yes," he said stubbornly. "But discretion is the better part of valor."

"Ohhh. Valor," Hilton said, nodding his head. "Coo-ol. We'll just let the press decide, on their own, why you did it."

"All right, smart-ass," Charlie said. "Earn your money. Work up some sort of statement, spin something—and you can't use 'health considerations' or any euphemisms. You can think about it on the way to the White House. We have an appointment."

"With the Big Guy?"

Charlie shrugged. "With someone."

It was the first time Hilton Devereaux had ever visited the West Wing of the White House—the business wing, the site of the Oval Office—but, after the thrill of driving through the southwest gate and having the front door opened by a superstudly Marine guard, the experience proved something of a disappointment. The place seemed impermanent, like a stage set, a belated add-on to the mansion—a feeling of plywood floors, low ceilings, thin walls, narrow corridors, office cubicles. There was none of the grandeur of the congressional office buildings. It was sort of like Tokyo: minimal aesthetics, phenomenal real estate value. The politics of West Wing real estate was one of the early, cutthroat battles in any new administration—second-tier advisers to the president would rather have a broom closet under the same roof as the boss than a palatial, high-ceiling suite of rooms in the Old Executive Office Building, just an alley away.

Charlie and Hilton sat in the west foyer, reading newspapers; Hilton looked up each time someone passed through, hoping to spot one of the young, new celebrities of the Stanton administration—at one point, he saw Henry Burton cross the lobby, talking with Perry Steinwicz, the rumpled young economics adviser Hilton had seen in Mammoth Falls. Charlie, by contrast, was fixed on a single thought as he pretended to read a long article in the *Post* about family planning on the subcontinent: why was this meeting happening? He'd been wondering about that ever since he'd agreed to come to 1600. There were all sorts of possibilities: perhaps Stanton wanted a more detailed accounting of the scene at Sly's, or consultation on his next selection—was it possible that Senator Charles Martin might, perhaps, be their next choice for secretary of defense?

Eventually, Mike Coleman came to retrieve them. He smiled at Charlie, but said nothing and moved them through a door, and then another, into the Roosevelt Room—which was dark, windowless, with a long, highly polished mahogany table, Federal-era breakfronts with various historic but oddly unengaging collectibles. A large portrait of Theodore Roosevelt, in Rough Rider garb, on one wall; Cousin Franklin on the other; several Remington sculptures scattered through the room.

Gid came in. He materialized through the door opposite the one Charlie and Hilton had entered. He was all in gray: charcoal-gray suit, gray patterned tie, gray demeanor. "Senator," he said, "have a seat. Thanks for coming."

Reese, who seemed to Hilton far older than Charlie Martin, opened a file and began to study it, without saying anything. Charlie glanced over at Hilton, who had taken a seat against the wall. "Well," Gid said, looking up from the file, "you've been keeping yourself busy."

Well, Charlie thought, I guess they're not going to ask me to be the next secretary of defense.

"Is this another of your grand acts, Charles?" Gid asked. "Like transferring back to the grunts—or running for president?"

"Gid—" Charlie was stunned. "What are you talking about?"

"Keelhauling our nomination," Gid continued.

"Gid, are you saying that—"

"I'm not saying anything," Reese said. "I'm just curious about your motivations here."

"My motivations? Did you talk to Mike? Did you talk to Maggie? Jesus, Gid." Charlie stopped, gathered himself and quietly said, "You would have made the same judgment if you'd visited the Parkinsons last night. And it was an investigation *you* should have made—no, I take some responsibility, too—we *all* should have made before Sly and Maggie were put through this."

"And now you've done the investigating for us. How did you come to be snooping around their house last night? Maggie says you weren't invited, and you didn't call in advance. . . ."

Maggie?

"Sly invited me over for dinner. *Maggie* was the one who did the investigating," Charlie insisted. "She was the one who talked to Jessica Mahon, and to the other women."

"That was a private matter and will remain so," Gid said, with equal firmness. "I don't think we should interpose ourselves in the Parkinsons' marriage. If you had a marriage, Senator, I don't think it would be appropriate for us to interpose ourselves in yours, either."

"A private matter? He raped a staffer!" Charlie slammed his fist on the table, but calmed quickly. He had to think his way through this: they couldn't possibly be going ahead with the nomination. What was Gid up to? "And what about the pills?"

"What pills?"

"Sly was whacked on Valium." Hilton inhaled. So that was it.

"Sly said he was exhausted by this ordeal," Gid said. "He took a nap."

"He was bouncing off the walls when I walked in, then he disappeared and when he reappeared he was a zombie," Charlie said. "He took four pills. He told Maggie that." Hilton watched Reese, who was flipping through another file, careful not to look up, careful not to betray any emotions. Charlie seemed to be pleading now. "Gid, you know Sly is a friend—one of . . . *us.* You know how—"

"I know how you and Rathburn would manipulate him back in Saigon, get him drunk in order to find out what was going on back in Washington. It must have been disappointing to learn that this administration would not allow you and Rathburn to do something similar with Sly at the Pentagon."

"You think that's what this is about?" Charlie was amazed; disgusted.

"What, then?" Reese said, looking up. "Your sudden discovery that Sly is an unfaithful husband?"

"An unfaithful husband?" A horrifying possibility occurred to Charlie: he wasn't going to have to go public with what he'd seen, was he? "You can't be serious, Gid."

"You're the one who has trouble being serious, Senator," Reese said disdainfully.

"Oh, fuck you, Gid."

"No, fuck Jack Stanton," Gideon said with quiet vehemence. "That's what you're doing. Two birds with one stone. Jack Stanton and me. Don't get mad about running a total embarrassment of a presidential campaign last year. Get even."

"Jesus, Gid," Charlie said. "Think about what you're saying. I've known Sly for thirty years. I'm one of maybe eight people in town who actually understands his military theories, and supports them. I'm way out on a limb, I was his strongest supporter. Why can't you just acknowledge that I saw something very disturbing last night?"

"You saw a troubled marriage," Gid said.

"You're actually going ahead with this?" He looked around for Mike Coleman, who hadn't come back.

"You think *you* have veto power over the President of the United States?" Gid hissed. "That's cheeky."

"Sly was in trouble when you had my support," Charlie said. "Now—"

"It's true that this certainly isn't helping us any," Reese acknowledged. "O'Brien'll still support the nomination, but he said he's far more concerned about other legislative priorities—in other words, he'll stick for a price."

"Do you have a second choice?" Charlie asked.

"If I did," Gid said, rising, "I surely wouldn't tell you. And I hesitate even to communicate the wishes of the President to you, but he said to tell you that as far as he was concerned, Linc would make a splendid undersecretary for policy at the Pentagon."

"Gid," Charlie said slowly, "do you actually believe that's what this is all about?"

"Me?" Gid laughed. "No, Charlie. I know you. You're the guy who transferred to the boonies because it was more honorable for you to kill people than to have other people do it for you."

Burton back, whispering. Hilton watched Charlie watching the byplay, and he could tell that his boss would have happily killed either one of them at that moment. Gid whispered something to Burton, who shrugged.

"Will you follow me, Senator?" Burton said.

Charlie and Hilton followed Burton through the door into a hallway saturated with Secret Service officers. The wall opposite them was convex: the outside of the Oval Office?

It was. Burton opened the door, but before they could enter, Jack Stanton came out, huge in the hallway—"Charlie," he said. "I'd invite you in, but I've got to rush. . . . Susan has an event, then we're off to a town meeting in Dayton." The President nodded at Hilton, acknowledging his presence, threw an arm around Charlie's shoulder, walked him toward the lobby door. "Charlie, I know Sly's a good friend of yours, and how upsetting it must have been last night—but boy, are marriages weird! You've sort of lucked out in that regard. And I really need your help on this one." He had stopped near the door, was staring directly into Charlie's eyes. "Really. We surround Sly with the right folks, like Linc, for example. We'll keep him in line and get the benefit of all that brainpower. Right?" He squeezed Charlie's shoulder. "Think about it. Promise me that, okay? This ain't so far gone that you can't walk it back. Nothing public yet. Think about it. It's what Sly and Maggie, what *all* your friends, want."

He slapped Charlie on the back then and was gone, and suddenly there was more breathing space in the narrow hallway.

*   *   *

"Can I ask you something?" Hilton began, midafternoon, sitting in the wing chair. The boss was flopped on the couch.

"If you promise the question is followed by a full report on the progress you've made in formulating a successful press strategy," Charlie replied.

Hilton snorted. "Senator. You sensed early on there was something funky about this nomination, didn't you? You asked me to keep an eye out for rumors—why didn't you just oppose it from the start?"

"Because Sly was my fucking friend, you nimrod," Charlie said, sitting up, furious—but not at him, Hilton realized. "Can you believe those assholes think it's about Linc? Can you believe that greaseball Stanton, trying to bribe me into turning around? What do they think I am? Some cheap . . ."

And then he realized what the intricate choreography at the White House had been about. He was amazed by the cynicism.

"You know they'll use the Rathburn thing now, right?" Hilton said, arriving at the same place as Charlie. "Not publicly, of course. But they'll get it out. They'll need an explanation."

"And when the reporters call and ask if I discussed the Rathburn appointment with the President, I'll have to be evasive—which will confirm the story: Martin turns on Parkinson because he can't land job for friend." Gid's maneuver—if, indeed, it was Gid's—wouldn't change the bottom line: Sly would still be gone. But it would spread the blame, hurt Charlie, hurt Linc—not much in the real world, but in Washington the reasons for his defection would be the most delicious of dinner-table chatter. He'd have to call Linc, fast.

"You'll need an explanation, too," Hilton said.

"About *what*?" Charlie snapped, instantly regretting his anger.

"About why you're changing your mind, if you don't want to talk about what you saw last night."

"No I don't."

"Well, here's a possibility. Not an explanation: a diversion," Hilton said. "I've checked with minority staff. Sly owns some Tech-Range Targeting stock. In 1990, Armed Services switched contracts on shoulder-held missiles from Armstrong to Tech-Range."

"So?" Charlie asked. "It must be in a blind trust."

"Yes, but there were some curious transactions on the part of the trustee, just before the committee acted. The trustee, one Robert Boulware of Philly, started buying Tech-Range, both inside the blind trust and in his own accounts. Minority couldn't get it past coincidence. Boulware and Parkinson denied they'd discussed the deal. There was no way to prove it."

"So your 'plan' is that to avoid embarrassing Sly personally, we embarrass him financially—on the basis of coincidental stock trading, which he didn't even control himself? Embarrass him in the one area—money honesty—where he's been a complete fucking saint? Great choice, Hilton." It was the first time he'd ever gotten angry at Devereaux, who was momentarily startled by how cold Charlie could get. But he said nothing, and the moment passed, and he quietly began to explain his strategy.

"It's just a tiny misdirection," Hilton said, "to save you and Sly some face. Your statement remains 'no comment.' But I, in my insidious off-the-record way, work to have the following clause added to the story—without any fingerprints on it, especially yours: 'But committee sources said that Chairman Parkinson's financial records had turned up some questionable stock transactions.' My deal with Billy Bergstein over at the *Times* will be, I'll tell you this, if you promise it didn't come from Charlie Martin. And then, if we're lucky, Billy will call minority staff and they will confirm the possibility of such a story. The press will charge off in that direction, another front in the Parkinson investigation will be opened—a blind alley."

"Still, Sly will be seen as a crook rather than a creep," Charlie said.

"It's a nuance," Hilton said. "The big story is going to be Stanton pulls the plug, gets Sly to remove his name—but we're playing for face, here. And if the White House wants to spread the word that you screwed them for personal reasons, we can counteract that by putting more reasons out there . . . and save you the embarrassment of ever having to deal with what happened last night."

Charlie wasn't sure about that. He wasn't even sure that the results of Maggie's investigation shouldn't be public—although, on second thought, that was probably up to the women involved. Most of all, he wasn't sure he wanted to be part of this . . . game. This wasn't what he'd signed on for.

"Oh, by the way," Hilton added. "The word is, the White House has Abner Walker in the bull pen."

"Abner *Walker*? That sleazeball pissmeyer?" A real smoothie: a human merry-go-round, in and out of the defense industry and the Pentagon omnivorously, without regard to party or philosophy; the only constant was that he'd keep the military toy store open for business.

And that was another terrible thing: not only was Sly Parkinson about to be humiliated—at Charlie's instigation—but any chance to enact the reforms that Charlie and Sly had been talking about since Vietnam was going out the window with him.

"Well, you've got about five minutes. Everyone's on to the story. I'm going to have to start returning calls," Hilton said. "Otherwise, the administration gets to tell the world that you did this out of pique, because your best friend wasn't going to be Sly Parkinson's puppet master."

"This stinks," Charlie said.

"To high heaven," D-2 agreed. "You got another strategy?"

*   *   *

Linc's assistant ran him to ground in Basel, where he was drinking port and smoking Cuban cigars with the finance minister of Indonesia.

"It's Senator Charles Martin, from the States," Linc told the minister. "He's a friend of your friend Oskar Millar, and a very important foreign policy player in his own right."

"Oh, cut the crap, Linc. He knows you're wired," Charlie said. "Stanton just tried to bribe me with a job for you in return for not selling out Sly."

"Well, I'm in the midst of a very important meeting right now, Senator," Linc said, in a tone of voice that was almost plausible. "I'll have to get back to you on that."

It took him fifteen minutes. "God, I couldn't get rid of that guy," he said. "Has it hit CNN yet?"

"We've got *Inside Politics* coming on—"

"In about ten minutes," Linc said. "Did I hear you right? Selling out Sly? What the hell's going on?"

Charlie told him about the Parkinson dinner, the meetings in Bramlette's office and at the White House. "Stanton almost had me turned around. He's good."

"No kidding." Linc sighed. "Well, you did the right thing. It was obviously a trap."

"That occurred to me, too," Charlie said. "Get me to take the bait, then yank the nomination anyway—and say that I scuttled it because of you."

"Hey, Charles. Guess what? They'll say that anyway. Gid's gonna use this to fuck me," he said. "He'll make me sweat on Russia."

"You want to go to Russia?"

"I want to be *asked*," he said.

"He asked you the other night, in front of Lanny Scott and half the known world."

"Charlie, Charlie." Linc sighed. "There are so many things he can do. He can float other names. He can float my name and then have people start rumors against me."

"But that would only make them look more inept," Charlie said. "You're being paranoid."

"You're being naïve," Linc shot back.

"Hey, hold on . . . *Inside Politics* is coming on," Charlie said. D-1 and D-2 were gathered in the office. They stared at the screen. And there, over Bernard Shaw's left shoulder, was a picture of Sylvester Parkinson's face—and a picture of Charlie Martin. The senator reported the salient phrases to Linc: "Stunning setback for White House . . . CNN has learned that a key Democrat has changed his mind. . . . Now, they're going to reports." The report from Capitol Hill was a review of the past few weeks—and the possibility of financial irregularities. Hilton had made his move at the speed of light. Then over to Wolf Blitzer, at the White House: the administration was shaken by this turn, infuriated with Martin. "The word I have is that they are actively considering other possibilities, Bernie—"

Bernie had two ways to go: why does the White House think Martin turned? Or, who are the other possibilities for secretary of defense? He chose the latter. Good man. Hilton sighed.

Now Shaw turned to symmetrical talking heads—Randall Potoskin, from *The New Republic,* and Leslie Burns of *Time.* Potoskin was the sort who tried to seem erudite on television, but usually came across as heavily sedated. He seemed to devour hours of airtime. Blah-blah-blah about the different stages in a confirmation scandal. And more blah-blah about the role of the media.

Bernie, to Leslie Burns, a tiny woman who appeared to be perpetually embarrassed by the inanities of talking-head-dom: "Leslie, do you have any information as to why Senator Martin turned against the nomination?"

"Well, there's no love lost between Charlie Martin and the President," she chirped, gamely assaying insiderhood. Hilton tried to remember if he'd ever talked to the woman; he hadn't. He looked over at the boss, who shrugged. "Stanton whiffed on Martin for vice president last summer. That couldn't have been fun. So, you know: don't get mad, get even. And he's gotten even in the most effective way imaginable, lying low, then turning against Stanton's nominee at the most devastating moment, turning this into a real embarrassment for the President."

Is there a name for an emotional state in which you are totally infuriated and totally relieved? She'd made Charlie seem petty—but hadn't mentioned how odd it was that the senator would turn on a man he'd known for thirty years. Thank God for cynicism. Thank God for the press.

"Charlie," Linc was saying, "what are you going to say?"

"I'm not going to betray Sly."

"Screw him, but not betray him," Linc said. "That's real honor."

"So you want me to go out and say, 'He abuses pills and his wife told me he raped a staffer.' " He looked at Donna and Hilton staring at him. "Just so people don't think I did this for you?"

"I didn't say that," Linc said coolly. "Anyway, Gid'll get the knife in my back somehow. But you do understand what the worst part of this is?"

"Okay, Linc." Charlie had had it with the Rathburn Encyclopedia of Everything. "What's the worst part?"

"Gid gets a two-fer," he said. "He's probably been looking for a way to scuttle Sly ever since the diet pills. You made it easy for him. Not only that, he gets to smear me in the process."

"It's no wonder you and Gid used to be such great friends," Charlie said. "You have so much in common: You both think it's about you."

"Donna," Charlie said, when he got off the phone, "didn't you mention something a while back about what a wonderful vacation spot Tahiti is?"

"Senator," she said, "can I interject something here?"

"Be my guest."

"You've acted honorably," she said. He waited for what came next. Nothing did.

"So?"

"So act like you've acted honorably," Donna said, "instead of slouching around like a criminal."

"A lot of good that's going to do me," he said. "Honor without profit."

Donna came around to where he was sitting, behind the big desk, and did an odd thing—a first, actually: she planted a motherly kiss on his forehead. "Not without profit around here," she said. "It's nice to work for someone worth working for."

The Parkinson nomination was withdrawn the next morning. The White House issued a statement from Sly, thanking the President for his support, and adding, "A successful national defense demands a secretary of defense less controversial than I, apparently, have become."

Within twenty-four hours, the White House named Abner Walker, the president of Seres Technologies and former secretary of the Air Force, their next attempt at secretary of defense. He was easily confirmed a month later.

There was fallout. David Farraday, the most respected op-ed columnist at *The New York Times,* was given the "inside" scoop. It was a two-fer for Farraday, too. He got to be high-minded and mash the White House for abandoning Sly Parkinson's defense policies—and he did something nice for a new source in the White House. The column didn't quite make sense, but it was very stirring—a defense of Sly against the financial impropriety and Jessica Mahon charges, and against an overzealous press. Briefly, lower down in the piece, there was some juicy speculation that Sly had been the victim of a longtime rivalry between Gideon Reese and Lincoln Rathburn. "The accumulation of scurrilous charges," a White House official said, "made it possible for Charlie Martin to get payback when it became clear that Stanton wasn't going to go along with a prominent Pentagon position for Martin's Machiavellian pal."

But Hilton Devereaux struck back. He had lunch with Nathaniel Sarris, a *Washington Post* columnist—less senior than Farraday, but respected—and a column soon appeared, titled "Something Happened," in which the musical question was asked, Why would Charlie Martin be Sly Parkinson's strongest defender one week and take him down the next? "None of us really knows why Charlie changed his mind," a senator was quoted as saying. "He seemed truly saddened by it. We all knew Parkinson was a friend of his. Everyone in the room believed he'd acted out of honor, not politics."

Thank you, Francesca Warren.

Back home, Lee Butler took full credit for Charlie Martin's change of heart about Sly Parkinson. He began calling the senator Shifty Charlie Martin. And in Charlie's honor, he offered free transmission fluid to the first one hundred customers who came in seeking new mufflers.

NEW YORK

12

———

That spring, Linc began to confide more about his difficulties with Nell; given the rules of Lordly friendship, Charlie figured the romance was almost over. The subject was broached gingerly, infrequently, and almost always as a bothersome subplot of the grander drama, the quest to get the Rathburnian diplomatic future squared away. The eternal Gid-Linc fandango had reversed itself: now Gid was the insider, and Linc desperate to prove that he was not some sort of pariah. It was embarrassing for a diplomat of his abilities to be excluded from the new team; he needed Russia.

Nell didn't. She didn't understand the intensity of Linc's need; she didn't scour the morning papers each day, looking for signs that Gid was preparing an ambush; she had little sympathy for Linc's seriousness, which, under strain, tended to become ponderous. Linc was frustrated and tormented by this, and hurt: if Nell really cared about him, she would understand that this was one of those nuanced, absolutely crucial moments. She would tolerate his occasional impatience with her cleverness; she wouldn't tease him quite so much. His career—his real career, not the lawyering and rainmaking—was at stake.

Finally, over dinner at La Colline in late April, as Charlie kept the ambassador-designate company on the night before his confirmation hearings, Rathburn seemed to explode with frustration. "Half the time, I get the feeling she's mocking me," Linc said. "Everything is so damn coy. She doesn't take anything I do seriously."

"Sure she does," Charlie said, remembering Nell with her head tilted back, listening hard—a proud, proprietary listening, it seemed—as Linc explained something over dinner at Lynn's house. The memory was vivid, indelible; it was one of the ways Charlie always pictured Nell.

"She's been angry ever since I told her that I was going to Russia," Linc admitted. "She said that if I really loved her, I wouldn't go. What nonsense! I asked her to *marry* me! And she laughed. She said she might come over, try it out, see if she liked it. Can you imagine? An ambassador living in sin?"

"There is a tradition," Charlie said, preoccupied by the sudden rush of news: Linc had popped the question. Nell had said no. Wow.

"Franklin and Jefferson?" Linc laughed, oblivious to Charlie's efforts to restrain his curiosity. "Two hundred years ago."

"You could probably find more recent examples." And, Charlie thought: if you really were desperate for her, you'd find a way.

"That's not the point. She doesn't *really* want to come over," Linc said glumly. "She wants me to be someone different. Look, even if I weren't going to Russia, this thing would be in trouble. . . . By the way, she wanted me to invite you to a party she's throwing—a good-bye party for me, at her place on May eighth. It's no big deal. You don't have to come."

"I'll be there," Charlie said, hoping not to seem too eager—and failing miserably.

* * *

Arabella Palmerston lived in a loft on the Lower West Side of Manhattan, just north of the more fashionable downtown sectors. Her building had a dull, industrial authenticity; there was a heavy steel door and a serious alarm bell of a buzzer downstairs—like the period-change bell at West Des Pointe High School, Charlie thought—and then a slow-moving freight elevator. When the lift lurched to a stop at Nell's floor—it was remarkable that an elevator could move so slowly and still lurch when it stopped—an elderly Hispanic woman with a tray of champagne greeted Charlie at the door and pointed him past a startling expanse of polished blond wood floor and white walls to a long, broad terrace that overlooked the Hudson River. The sun was setting in a rolling splash of pink and purple over New Jersey; a soft breeze off the river hinted summer. Charlie was thrilled, breathing deeply, feeling free—the awful Parkinson winter was finally, palpably, over.

He saw Linc standing alone near the parapet, looking forlorn. Charlie made his way over, scanning the other guests, none of whom he recognized. They seemed an exotic lot. "Well, I'm sorry about this," Rathburn immediately apologized.

"About what?" Charlie asked. "This is fabulous."

"She invited none of my friends, except you." He took Charlie by the elbow and maneuvered him into whisper range. They stood shoulder to shoulder facing the river, with their backs to the rest of the party; it seemed rude. "I don't know what's going on," Linc confided. "She said it was a going-away party for me. But these aren't people I know, except for the members of her family—her brother, her cousins and so forth. And she knows I don't have much patience for them. Utter nincompoops."

Charlie felt an arm slide through his, felt lips on his cheek and smelled the familiar perfume. "Hello, stranger," Nell said, and he wondered how much of their conversation she'd overheard. "Let me introduce you to everyone."

She laced her fingers through his—she had taken his right hand—and leaned her head on his shoulder. "Along the way," she said, ignoring Linc, "we could discuss arms control."

He was speechless, guilty and swept away—off into the party. They moved effortlessly from group to group on the terrace; Nell seemed able to orchestrate every conversation, making graceful, unobtrusive introductions and then moving along to the next group. "You will not be expected to remember names or PAC contributions, or promise to attend any festivals," she whispered at one point, her lips accidentally brushing his ear. "No feed barons here. This is a night off, Senator."

No feed barons, indeed. Not many nincompoops, either. Charlie didn't want to seem too interested in these people, out of loyalty to Linc, but—there was a storklike woman writer-in-residence at Princeton; a gay investment banker who specialized in Central America, and his architect lover; a woman with a long gray braided ponytail who owned an antique bookstore; there was Nell's older brother, Ted, who was a goateed, rail-thin furniture-maker who lived in Brooklyn—and there was Nell's ex-husband, Lucius Belligio, a serene, strikingly handsome homosexual, who was of some exotic West Indian-Italian-Creole provenance. The dress was colorful and skewed, ranging from ball gowns to denim, with not many stops in between. Indeed, Martin and Rathburn were the only men present wearing business suits and ties (Nell was done up fairly traditionally, too—a sleeveless black silk cocktail dress; but she was barefoot). Charlie felt as if he were in one of those 1930s screwball comedies where everyone was clever. There hadn't been many evenings like this in Des Pointe, or in Washington, for that matter.

Having swept him through the crowd, Nell clapped her hands and announced, "Hey, everyone, dinner!" and then she escorted Charlie inside to a long wrought-iron and glass table, which ran horizontally next to the row of French doors that opened onto the terrace. She seated him immediately to her left. As she went off to seat the others, he checked out the room: there was an odd, distended Manhattan loft spaciousness to it, with vast acreage between the various venues—the stainless steel kitchen *way* over there, the living room *way* in the opposite direction. The French doors and terrace seemed to define the place: Nell had made her home a patio. The living room was wicker and rattan, arranged on an enormous jade Chinese deco rug. Severe isosceles Chinese flags, of rich and unexpected colors like coral and turquoise, were draped from each of the supporting pillars, which were of thin, fluted iron; the flags gave the place a jaunty but regal informality.

"Senator, what are you reading these days?" the woman seated to Charlie's left asked, interrupting his reverie. She was very dramatically done up with a black lacquered pageboy haircut, scarlet nails and lipstick and an extremely low-cut vermillion ball gown.

What was he *reading* these days? "History, mostly," he said. And he did try to keep a book or two going. "Actually, I'm reading this terrific book about Germany at the beginning of World War One, called *Rites of Spring.*"

"By whom?"

He couldn't remember the author's name. It was not an easy one. "Ahhhh . . ." He realized he was blushing. "It's a fellow who teaches up in Canada." And then—phew!—he remembered: "Modris Eksteins. By the way, I can't remember your name either. . . ."

"Gwyneth Coxley, one of the dreadful cousins." She had a wonderfully alto Carolina drawl. "Do you think World War One was romantic, or the opposite of romantic?"

"The opposite of," Charlie said as a vivid, unexpected flash of battle— the heat, the stench—collapsed his chest. He shook his head abruptly, reflexively, to clear his mind.

"What?" Gwyneth asked and then answered herself, "Oh, of course: memories. I'm sorry."

"The poets were good," Charlie recovered. "In Flanders fields, the poppies blow/Between the crosses, row on row. . . ."

"Memorial Day," Gwyneth said. "They recited that every year in our little town when I was a girl."

"And what are you reading?"

"Anaïs Nin." Charlie wasn't quite sure who or what Anaïs Nin was—he guessed European, artsy, nineteenth century or early twentieth. "An American in Paris in the twenties," Gwyneth bailed him out. "A lot of orgifying—that was a reaction to World War One as well. Are you interested in sensuality, Senator?"

"I divide my time," Charlie replied, "between sensuality and nuclear proliferation."

"Very good!" Gwyneth said, delighted that he could play. "I always thought nuclear proliferation was very sensual, myself. All those missiles."

"Gwyn loves missiles," said Cousin Grigorii Urgovich—the son, Charlie later learned, of Aunt Mush (Michelle) and Uncle Yuri (the Ukrainian mechanic who had fixed Mush's plane when it crashed near Kiev in 1934). Grigorii, now well into his fifties and looking splendidly Brit in houndstooth, his hair gray and sweeping, his eyebrows pitch-black, was a wine importer. "She's a sculptrix," Grigorii explained. "Tell the senator what you sculpt."

"Things," Gwyn admitted reluctantly.

"Men's things," Gregorii said.

Charlie looked over toward Rathburn, who was down the other end of the table, geographically and emotionally; Linc shot him an angry look, annoyed that Charlie seemed to be enjoying himself.

"I'm surprised, Senator," Grigorii, clearly the family blowhard, went on, "Gwyn hasn't asked you to sit for her."

"Senator," Gwyn responded, glaring at Grigorii, "don't you agree that Slavic men are swine? And anyway, Grigo, I believe Cousin Nell has dibsies on the senator." Gwyn whispered to Charlie, "I think our Arabella is sending your friend Mr. Rathburn a message. This is not a going-away party. It's a sending-away party."

Charlie turned to Nell, who put her hand on his knee and squeezed it. "Did I introduce you to Lucius?" she asked. Lucius was sitting directly across from him, on Nell's left. Charlie started shaking his head no, then nodded yes, preoccupied by the worry that he might be some part of the message that Nell was sending Linc. "Lucius is my business partner," she explained, "and a real pal . . . sometimes men and women can be pals. Lu, what do you think of Senator Martin's pal potential?"

"I think," Lucius said, smiling evenly—he had a quiet, elegant manner—"he must have something going for him."

"What does that say for Mr. Ambassador?" Gwyn asked, tweaking Nell. "He's way down the other end of the table."

"He's symmetrical," Nell said.

"Perfectly," Gwyn laughed. "Look at him. Blond hair and blue eyes. Blue shirt and yellow tie."

And in agony. Linc was in agony. Charlie was sympathetic, but agog: Linc was symmetrical. His eyes and shirt did match, as did his straw-blond hair and pale tie; his clothing seemed a perfect, self-referential reflection. What a remarkable thing to notice.

"I think I'm going to go home," Linc said as soon as an exit was plausible, as the main course remnants were removed from the table. He stood, placed his napkin on the table. "I have a lot of work. Charlie, where are you staying?"

"Oh! Linc! But you mustn't," Nell said. "I haven't made my toast. I haven't served my special Linc-related dessert. Excuse me, excuse me," she said, hugging Lucius, kissing his forehead. She pushed back from the table, but the chair caught, tipped back and would have fallen over if Charlie hadn't grabbed it. "Oops," she said, standing abruptly. She clasped her hands to her heart, batted her eyes at Charlie, said "My hero," and tousled his hair. "I'll wait on my toast," she said. "But now, kitchenward!"

When Nell stood, so did everyone else. The party moved back onto the terrace. Charlie joined Linc, standing at the parapet, staring out at the river. "She's kissing me off," Linc said. "And you're helping."

"Jesus, Linc, what do you want me to do?"

"Stop looking at her as if—"

"As if, what?"

"As if you were half in love with her yourself."

"What?" Charlie said, too quickly, as Grigorii and Ted joined them.

"So congratulations," Grigorii said to Linc. "You're going to my father's fatherland: . . . Would that make it my grandfatherland? Actually not, I guess: the Ukraine is a separate country now. My uncle-land, perhaps?" Linc smiled politely. Charlie drifted off, upset by Linc's bitterness, needing to clear his head—he wondered if he was slightly tipsy, or perhaps it was just the company. He wandered back into the loft. There was a broad staircase near the entrance, with stairs up and down. He went halfway down and saw several rows of design tables, each with a mannequin, in semishadow, illuminated only by a distant fluorescent; bolts and swatches of dramatically hued Lycra leaned in a long, open closet on the far wall. A row of bathing suits drooped, pretumescently, on a rack nearby. Hanging above the rack, a poster of a Picasso-inspired mermaid—the company logo: MerMaid. Charlie had forgotten about that part of Nell, the business part, but now he remembered her conversation with Elizabeth Makrides at the convention party, and he felt a stab of nostalgia for the unencumbered, fresh, first-time experience of meeting her. And curious: this was an uncomfortable evening, but still—he'd invested ten months in stray fantasizing about Nell Palmerston, and this would probably be the last chance he'd ever have to investigate her life. He turned and went back up the stairs, up a flight to the bedroom floor, on a recon mission. He wanted to see her bedroom.

There was a wide white corridor, lined with family photographs— some ancient, some recent: her parents, grandparents, children. Her children: where on earth were *they*? There was a picture of the two of them on a weathered porch with dunes in the background: the girl, older and more Caucasian-looking, with blondish hair and straight features and Nell's smart, sad eyes; the boy was darker, with dark eyes and Lucius's soft, curly black hair—he was staring at the camera, his sister was more oblique, bored or just innately uncooperative.

Down the hall, he saw a striking photo of Nell—young, in Paris perhaps, flirting with the camera, very close-up, wearing the sort of felt pillbox hat that Charlie dimly remembered his mother wearing, with a fishnet veil. The hat was a joke, and yet alluring—and in her eyes, through the veil, a very Nell-like look, the perennial hint of . . . what? It was as if she had just found out something embarrassing about you. Or perhaps, she had just caught you in the act of surreptitiously being yourself. He wanted to linger, to study this—but he didn't want to be discovered staring, especially not by her, and so he moved down the hall toward what appeared to be a family room. And there, among a jumble of giant pillows, dimly lit by an amber table lamp on a polished maple steamer trunk in a corner, sat Lucius with Nell's children—his children, too, of course—watching *Ren and Stimpy* on a big-screen television.

"Hello," Lucius said, muting the television, which precipitated a struggle over the clicker with his daughter. "*No*, Pims!" he said, holding it aloft; the daughter got up on her knees, grabbing for it. "Don't be impolite."

"But, Lucius," she said, "we're missing."

"It's not that heavily plotted, Pamela," he said. "We can catch up. Senator Martin, this is Pamela. . . . Pimster, this is a friend of Mother's."

"A new boyfriend?" Pamela scowled. Her face, even more Nell's minia-ture than it had seemed in the photo, was too subtle for her body, which was long and stringy and profoundly preteen.

"I don't think so," Lucius said. "There's still Mr. Rathburn."

Pamela stuck out her tongue. "Oh, guck, Lucius. You're way behind. That guy is *so* two months ago."

Lucius gave Charlie a look, and a smile. "And this, under here, is Robin," he said, pointing the clicker at the bundle of curls filling the cav-ity beneath his left arm perfectly, as if the child had been measured for the space. Robin looked up from the television at Charlie, an even, in-telligent look.

"So, you into *Ren and Stimpy*?" Pamela asked Charlie. "Or are you lost, or are you just snooping around? I mean, Lucius, am I supposed to be, like, polite for-*ever*?"

"Forever, Miss Pim," Lucius said gently.

"Guck," said Pamela. "So?" she said, to Charlie.

"Lost," he said.

"Bathroom?" she asked. He nodded.

"Do you have to go bad?" Robin asked, looking up, lapsing into lightly carbonated giggles, then deeper chuckles, self-tickled.

"Real bad," Charlie lied, doubling over, knees together.

Robin laughed harder still.

"So funny I forgot to laugh," Pamela said. "Turn around. Second door on the left. See ya."

Lucius shrugged, unmuted the television. "See ya," Charlie said.

Second door on the left. He didn't have to go, but he went. At a cer-tain point in life, you can always go a little. The bathroom was long, nar-row and industrial: a big duct, painted aquamarine, ran through it. There was a glass-walled steam shower down the end, and lots of chrome—fixtures, pipes, spigots. The walls were blank, except for several carefully placed sketches of the same scene: dunes, reeds, the upper story of a beach house behind. Hers? There was a basket for magazines— *World of Interiors, House & Garden, Vogue;* nothing political—next to the loo.

There was a knock at the door. "You in there?" Nell. Whispering.

He opened the door, and there she was. "Dessert's ready," she said, closing the door behind her. She spotted herself in the mirror, ran a hand through her straggly hair, which teased out, electrified: "Disgrace-ful," she said. "You, on the other hand, have really good hair—and you probably don't even have it streaked or anything. . . . You know, I'm not going with him. That's what this is about."

"Good," he said, and she kissed him. It was a serious, grown-up, no-messing-around kiss and he reciprocated, but he found himself distanced from it, his mind wandering: too fast, this was. His "good" hadn't been *that* enthusiastic. It was intended to convey something like: I think that it's probably for the best that you aren't marrying Linc and going to Russia, because I'm not sure it would have worked out well for you or for my friend Linc . . . and . . . how odd. He was suddenly where he'd wanted to be, where he'd fantasized being, and he wasn't quite there. Maybe it was because he hadn't precipitated the kiss; she had . . . and . . . it was a really terrific kiss. Physically phenomenal; her lips were warm and full and soft, her tongue was careful, emotionally intelligent, her mouth was . . . her arms were around his neck. His neck was burning and, down below, the object of Gwyn's aesthetic interests pushing suddenly through his boxers against his zipper. He was thinking about everything; he was thinking too much.

"I was hoping you'd say something like that," she said, pulling back finally, stumbling a little. But what had he said? "Dizzy," she explained. "You're *good,*" she added. He hadn't thought at all about his part of the kissing. She kissed him again, on the cheek, and took his hand, his right hand, and said, "Okay, dessert."

Linc was outside in the hallway waiting for them. "My darling," he said, an even tone, but his mouth was taut and his eyes cold, "and my pal. Having a meeting?"

"A meeting of the rump caucus," Nell said, snaking her right arm through his left. Now she had them both. Charlie tried to catch Linc's eye, but Linc was looking down, beginning to negotiate the stairs. "All right, fellas!" Nell said, too cheery by half. "Time for my toast . . ."

Downstairs, again. A cheesecake sat in front of Linc's spot at the head of the table. Upon it, the words "bye bye" were written in strawberry syrup script. Grigorii was opening champagne, then pouring it; people were standing about. Nell tinkled her glass with the cake knife. "Let's all take a sip first," she said. "I want to say that Mr. Ambassador Rathburn is going off to Russia to buy me a hat. . . . Make it mink, Linc!" She took another sip of champagne, leaned an elbow on Charlie's shoulder. "And I say to him, Congratulations and *au revoir* . . . and however you say it in Russian."

Linc stood, staring at his cake. A return toast was in order. He lifted the glass slowly, to eye level, sighting it like a rifle. He glanced at Charlie, stared at Nell. *"Na zdorovye . . .* is how it's said in Russian. I will surely miss my unforgettable *mer*maid—and ensemble. To you, Nell," he said, and took a sip. "And mink it shall be."

They were out the door and on the lift very quickly, Charlie tagging along behind Linc, who was silent, staring straight ahead as the elevator creaked back to earth in a rattle of chains and turbine hum.

"I'm sorry . . . about the bathroom," Charlie said.

Linc ignored him.

"Nothing happened, you know."

"Don't," Linc said, "insult my intelligence."

* * *

And for a while it seemed that nothing, indeed, had happened. Linc went to Russia. He and Charlie still talked by phone most days, but no longer about personal things: Charlie had the distinct sense that Linc believed their discussion of his Nell troubles had led, somehow, to the bathroom betrayal. Charlie also had his own doubts about Nell: had she just been using him as part of her sending-away tableau? He realized this was an irrational, adolescent sort of reaction—but then, the entire evening had been a high school sort of situation. And yet the kiss, as he recalled it, had not been at all devious or theatrical; it had been terrific. Still, Charlie didn't hear from Nell afterward, and he didn't call her. He was sorely tempted to call, especially on his very occasional visits to New York. But that would have been a premeditated betrayal of his friend, as opposed to a tipsy indiscretion. A summer slipped by.

Four months later, he didn't even recognize her name. "A Mrs. Belligio from New York called," Rosemary said. "She says she knows you."

"Uh-huh," he said. "What time for Hufsteter?"

"Four," she said. "And Mrs. Belligio? She had your private number."

A New York fund-raiser, perhaps? An internationalist do-gooder? "Call her back," he said. "Find out what it's about."

Bernie Hufsteter, of the United Auto Workers, promised to be a difficult meeting. The UAW would be smart; they knew they wouldn't be able to get Charlie's vote against free trade with Mexico, the current hot topic among the talking heads—his state's farmers and feed companies loved overseas sales—but the union would be looking to leverage that, and get his help with something else. He'd had Marvin Tam check to see what he'd done for them lately: he'd voted for Stanton's budget, he'd even held his nose and pushed the defense contract for the new helicopter the Navy didn't want (but the UAW did, since it provided about eight thousand jobs spread over eighteen states). He wasn't proud of either vote, but they would be ammunition when Bernie asked him for whatever he was going to ask him for.

"She said it was about 'arms control,' " Rosemary said, ducking back in. "Mrs. Belligio."

"Arms control?" A do-gooder.

"It was strange," Rosemary said. "I asked her, 'What, specifically, about arms control?' And she said, 'Oh, I don't know. If that doesn't work, try Most Favored Nation status.' "

"Italy," Charlie said, experiencing an involuntary, adolescent chestly tingle. "You have her number?"

The meeting with Hufsteter didn't go well. The union wanted an advance commitment of support for Stanton's health care plan. "Too soon," Charlie said. "I've got to see what's in it."

Bernie Hufsteter was not your usual labor skate. He was thin, pockmarked, balding, horn-rimmed glasses: the working-class kid who'd been good at school. He had a law degree from a state university in the Midwest, one of those giant education factories that offered high-quality meat-and-potatoes learning. "Senator, you're not with us on trade, which is real important to our members. We don't expect total loyalty. But"—he paused, but not too dramatically—"you have an election coming next year. It may look like a walkover now, but you never know when you're going to need some friends."

"I also have a job to do," Charlie said, "which includes finding out what's in a piece of legislation before I support it."

"Thanks for the civics lesson, Senator," Hufsteter said calmly. "Your evasion will be recorded in The Book of Life."

Could he have handled this better? Most likely. Would it cost him with the UAW? Most likely not. Labor needed all the friends it could get. Still, Charlie was displeased with his inelegance, and Donna—who'd sat in on the meeting, in strict adherence to the rule of three—saw it: "Tired?" she asked. "Distracted?"

"Not tired," he said. "Maybe a little rusty." But mostly distracted. Donna left and he dialed the number, got MerMaid, was put on hold— and was surprised by the constriction in his throat when he heard her voice.

"Mrs. *Belligio?*"

"You remember Lucius." Yes, but he hadn't remembered Lucius's last name. "Anyway, that's my official name," she replied. "I figured that I should be official when calling a senator. How are you, anyway?"

"Fine, and you?"

"Fine." She paused. "Linc said you were coming to town for the UN."

"Linc did?"

"He still checks in," she said. "You know how he is."

"All the world's a local call," he said. "You having second thoughts about going to Russia?"

"Oh, Lord, no," she said, vehemently. "I mean, could you imagine Pamela in Russia? Robin, maybe. But Pamela? 'I mean, like, Moth-errrr, what's there to, like, *do*?' "

But that was about the kids, not about her. "And I," she continued, thinking along with him, "well, MerMaid's in a little trough and I want to stay on top of it and—well, Linc was always more of an interesting concept than a reality, you know what I mean?"

She stopped. He wanted to say something—something clever. About Linc, maybe. The problem was, he wasn't exactly sure what she meant. "Look, you want to come for dinner when you're here?" she asked abruptly, filling the silence.

"I don't know, I've got all these . . . functions," he said.

"Oh, well, of course." She seemed flustered, for once. "Well, anyway . . . if it's no, it's no."

"It's not no," he said, figuring: WTF. "There's a dinner at the UN ambassador's residence on Tuesday. Would you consider coming with me?"

"All Linc's friends will be there," she said. "I haven't been uptown since—"

"I'm one of Linc's friends," he said. She was quiet now. "Well, if it's no—"

"It's not no," she said.

*   *   *

The UN ambassador's residence is a most unlikely piece of government real estate, located high in the Waldorf Towers. Charlie and Nell agreed to meet at the clock in the hotel lobby. Charlie was late; he'd been on the inevitable Middle East Peace Prospects panel, sponsored by a Jewish coalition in a midtown synagogue. He'd been a lesser member of the panel, third fiddle to Yitzhak Rabin and the Israeli UN ambassador, Uri Savir, plus the assistant secretary of state assigned to the

Mideast. Afterward, he'd been buttonholed—not by Rabin or Savir (they didn't have much to say to a mere senator) but by several of the American Jews in the audience who couldn't shove close to Rabin and were too sophisticated to allow themselves to appear "pushy," yet ever intense in their devotion to the cause. Charlie found himself considering their suits, to see what distinguished them from his own, which were five-hundred-dollar D.C. and Des Pointe jobs. He couldn't tell; the effect of money on couture in these precincts was subtle, beyond his ken.

"How can you tell a really expensive suit?" he asked Hilton, who had accompanied him and would be along for dinner, too (a senator was allowed a retainer at such events), as they walked Fifty-fourth Street from Madison to Park, and then down toward the Waldorf. The streets were clogged with limos. The UN put on this show each September, an elaborate and nearly effective reminder of its existence.

"Fabric, fit," Hilton said. "There's a creamy, perfect feel to a good suit. It just hangs right."

"But it's not obvious, right?"

"A cheap suit is obvious," Hilton said.

"Are my suits obvious?"

"No-oh," Hilton said.

"'No-oh'? What's that supposed to mean?"

"It means they're not obvious. They're serviceable."

"'Serviceable.' That sounds like—" But the sight of Nell caught him short. She was standing beneath the clock, looking . . . fabulous: a greenish silk dress, the color of a copper roof exposed for decades to the elements, knee length; dark hose and moderate heels. But it wasn't what she was wearing. It was something more complicated, in her eyes and smile: she was thrilled to see him. The reaction was unequivocal, a rare clarity for her—everything had always been camouflaged and ironic. But the sight of him had caught her short, too. She hadn't had time to prepare, to mask herself; nor had he. They were startled by their mutual delight at seeing each other.

His impulse was to take her in his arms, and he started the move—but stopped. She noticed that, of course. Always that slight hesitation, she thought. If he ever made a fully confident, unencumbered move on her, she'd be lost. But she was semilost as it was, floating in his gaze, which seemed guileless. No, she was more than semilost.

"You look wonderful," he said, squeezing her left arm gently, just below the shoulder, as he kissed her cheek. She moved toward him; a kiss and linger, her hair against his cheek, her perfume insinuating itself, extending tendrils, binding him. And then they looked at each other, pulling back slightly, perfectly in time, his hand still on her arm—and it was done: everything that needed to be said, and without a word. She smiled at him slightly; he nodded, almost imperceptibly, in acknowledgment. His hand slid down her arm, resting briefly at her elbow and then to her wrist and they held hands, still staring at each other, their fingers interlaced.

Hilton thought it was one of the most romantic moments he'd ever witnessed, but who was this woman? The boss had never mentioned her. She had an old-fashioned look and, clearly, she knew how to put herself together: she wasn't straight-line uptown, she was opaque and interesting—there was a mindfulness to her look—the sort of woman Hilton had always thought Charlie Martin deserved, but despaired that he'd never find. They simply didn't exist in Washington or Des Pointe. But New York—perfect. Who *was* she? He gawked at the two of them, which broke the spell. Nell glanced over, saw that Hilton was with Charlie . . . and also saw that he had understood what had just transpired. She felt extremely calm; it was an unexpected, almost narcotic feeling. She extended a hand. "Nell Palmerston," she said.

"Hilton Devereaux," he said.

"Mississippi or Louisiana?" she asked.

"Mississippi," he said. "But you—"

"South Carolina," she explained. "And a bit of Sussex. And you work with Senator Martin?"

"Sometimes against," Hilton said. "Always for. I handle the press."

Hilton saw that Nell was one of those people who would not need an explanation: she knew he was gay and more—she did not mind; indeed, she seemed a bit relieved by it. Whoever she was, she wasn't in politics.

"He a difficult boss?" Nell asked as they glided—effortlessly, on air— toward the elevators.

"A pussycat," Hilton said.

There were other people in the elevator. "Senator." A man greeted Charlie, who nodded. Nell linked her arm through his, and reinforced the move by placing her left hand on his shoulder, attaching herself to him—but lightly. He looked at her, smiled with his eyes. She looked at Hilton, who smiled, too.

There was candlelight upstairs. The ambassador stood just inside the door, greeting all comers. She was extremely tall, a former congresswoman from Montana, the daughter of a prominent mining family, a widow with a hard, weathered western face. "Good evening, Senator," she said.

"Madame Ambassador," Charlie replied with a smile. They knew each other well from their days in the House together. "This is a friend of mine, Nell Palmerston."

"And a good thing, too," she said. "A French speaker. I've deputized her for the evening. The French ambassador. Our dear ally. Oh, Charlie," she added, noting his bemusement, "you think I don't do my homework? It's the diplomatic equivalent of constituent service. Arabella Belligio née Palmerston. MerMaid swimsuits. Friend of Linc Rathburn's. Daughter of Harry Palmerston and Susannah Coxley; cousin of you know who . . . and a delight. We had a terrific chat by phone the other day. In French. Had to be sure the table placement would work. You will entrance him, won't you, dear?"

"Pâté in my hands," Nell said. "I'll 'do pretty' with him."

"Ver-ry good!" the ambassador said, laughing. Charlie was bowled over. For a languorous soul, Nell could be lightning fast. "What was that from?" the ambassador asked. " 'Doing pretty.' I remember reading it a long time ago. It's always been there, somewhere in the back of my mind."

"Trollope," Nell said. "Lady Glencora."

"Trollope?" Charlie said, with a skeptical look at the ambassador—he thought of her as a tough, western populist.

"Teenage acne," the ambassador explained. "Time on my hands. In any case, 'doing pretty' is a great marching order for women diplomats." She turned to Charlie. "An advantage you'll never have."

"Oh, he can 'do pretty,' " Nell said.

"Yes, of course," the ambassador said, smiling, picking up the chemistry. "Of course he can."

At the entrance to the cocktail room, a waiter stood with a tray—white wine, bubbly water, champagne—and Nell reached for the champagne, then thought better of it: she didn't want even the slightest alteration in the way she was feeling.

"No drink?" Charlie asked.

"I'm high on life," she said, squeezing his arm again. He took some bubbly water, and Hilton, a flute of champagne.

"To the two of you," Hilton said. "Or maybe, just to you—Ms. Palmerston. I toast him every payday."

"I should have a glass to raise in response," she said. Charlie handed her his. "To each of us," she said, "fulfilling expectations."

And then they were engulfed by the party. Charlie fell into chatter with *The Washington Post*'s New York correspondent; and Nell, with a series of familiar sorts, starting with Fred Trostman, the chairman of the board of the Council on Foreign Relations, who still associated her with Linc, and who launched a conversation about the upcoming parliamentary elections in Russia, and the chances that communists and neofascists might do well. "Is Linc concerned about the threat?" he asked.

As if she'd know. It was the sort of moment that had appalled her in the past—but now it was peripheral, the main event was taking place down by her right hand, which was wrapped around Charlie Martin's left arm: the ease of it, the utter comfort. Nothing else mattered. "Linc seems to be doing just fine," Nell said, not quite responding. "He's especially happy that the residence has a satellite dish."

Everything, their movements and conversations, seemed choreographed. They'd be together, talking to someone; then separate; then back again. All of it, easily, subtly, in slow motion. At a cocktail party, there are bees and flowers—the bees buzz about, searching for the right conversation; the flowers suffer the bees. Together, Charlie and Nell were a most exquisite bloom, radiating—jointly now, he imagined—a slight, subtle perfume; her perfume.

Then, dinner. Separate tables. At each, a foreign head of state paired with an American official. Charlie sat near the president of Lithuania, a former music teacher—they talked big bands (the Lithuanian had just read a biography of Artie Shaw), to the astonishment of the woman between them, the wife of a prominent American banker. Nell had her Frenchman, a *beau-laid* of the Yves Montand species, but they were a sideshow at the table where Mike Coleman was placed adjacent to the president of Ghana, who proved quite a showman and seemed more interested in catching Nell's eye than in the light policy conversation that usually obtains on such evenings. At one point, Charlie was able to glance over at Nell—she was at 270 degrees, a serious twist over his left shoulder, but not impossible—and caught her feigning extravagant outrage, her hand against her brow, palm out, as the Frenchman laughed. And then, sixth sense, she glanced over at Charlie and smiled, as if to say: whatever is happening between us is still happening, at least for me. Mike Coleman happened to catch this, and gave Charlie a mischievous look.

Charlie was preoccupied: what comes next? Afterward? He was staying at the Sheraton on Seventh Avenue. Entirely utilitarian, but not very romantic—a place for an assignation, not for a transcendent moment. In any case, he couldn't say to her, "Would you like to come to my hotel room?" He would have to offer to take her home. His mind was crowded with questions, details. He was, he realized, nervous.

In the event, everything happened wordlessly. As the dinner ended, she was at his side. They said good night to their hostess, the ambassador, who gave him a knowing, you're-not-just-sitting-in-for-Linc-are-you? look, and a nod of approval. "I am many years past MerMaid," she said to Nell. "But I'll tell my daughter you seem the sort of person who'd make an interesting swimsuit."

Nell curtsied and said, "I'm glad someone like you is here, doing this—very prettily, I must say."

They went down the elevator with Hilton, who was grinning like an idiot. Nell gave him a hug and a kiss, and whispered, "Wish us luck." And then, she and Charlie were out onto Park Avenue, waiting on the cab line . . . when the French ambassador called out, from his car: "Nell! Madame!" He rushed out clumsily. "Where do you go? I have a few blocks only—to the UN Plaza—" He acknowledged Charlie, understood that they were together. "Senator, would you accept a ride in my car? It will take you anywhere. . . ."

"Will there be diplomatic implications?" Charlie asked, with a smile.

"I certainly hope so," the ambassador said.

They sat three across the backseat, Nell in the middle. "Madame Belligio, you are a delight," the ambassador said. "Do you often come to Washington?"

"Only when invited," she said.

"Then the Senator must invite you to accompany him to one of our evenings," the ambassador said. "If he is careless, I will be sure to. But the Senator is not a careless man?"

"Occasionally," Nell said, "he is less than careful."

"Not anymore," Charlie said to her. And then to the ambassador: "We'd be delighted to see you in Washington, as always—"

"It will be arranged," the ambassador said. "And now, I am here at my hotel. And the car is yours. Where will you be going?"

"Tenth Avenue and Seventeenth Street," Nell said.

"SoHo?" the ambassador asked.

"Not quite, but the same general principle," Nell said.

"*Oui,* downtown. *La vie de bohème.* Very exciting, Senator," he said, with a nod to Charlie. "Very."

And then, they were alone in the backseat—and kissing lightly, briefly. She nodded toward the driver, whose eyes were riveted to the rearview mirror. She smiled. They watched the city together. When they reached her address, and he began to ask . . . she took him by the hand and led him from the car. She pulled a prodigious set of keys from her purse, and opened the door to her building. Inside, she pushed the elevator button—there was a grudging click and a hydraulic whir—and she turned to him, and put her arms around his neck and kissed him dreamily. "I'm so glad you're here," she said.

His mind was cluttered with tactics, logistics, objectives, preparations—field command obstructions. He wondered how aggressively to move, whether to kiss her again when she pulled back. (She kissed him again.) And as she was kissing him, and he was beginning to feel aroused, whether to move against her. (She moved into him.) And the logistics of getting their clothes off, and what about birth control—and then, there were the children. And how would he get back uptown in the morning?

Out the elevator. Up the stairs. Down the hall, to the family room, where Lucius sat, watching an old movie. "The dreadful tykes?" she asked.

"Splashdown," he said. "Hello, Senator."

Charlie nodded. A whole new set of questions crowded his brain. Does Lucius live here? And why would that be? Did he and Nell still have . . . Was Nell infected?

And they were in the bedroom. "Does Lucius live here?" he asked.

"Mmm," she said, kissing him, moving to remove his jacket. She was remarkable. She was kissing him, both her hands in his hair. He found the zipper in the back of her dress, and tried to unclasp the tiny thread clasp at the top, but that wasn't so easy with one and a half hands, and she said, "Let me," and she did, and then her bra. There were stretch marks on her breasts, but they were round and . . . just perfect—she took his right hand, which was suddenly cold, and put it there, and shivered, kissing him, reaching down into his pants. And—

"Are you okay?" she asked.

He blushed.

"Is it war-related?"

"Opening night jitters," he said. "I'm sorry."

Their next attempt was, if anything, more embarrassing. A week later. They had talked every day, but there was an underlying tension—at least, on his end. He'd invited her down to Washington, to a dinner at the State Department in honor of Benazir Bhutto, hosted by the Vice President. Nell was much taken by the art and antiques in the public rooms on the seventh floor; Charlie, too nervous to be entirely charming.

In the receiving line after the dinner, Bhutto said, "Nell!"

"Hello, Pinky," Nell said warily. "I was hoping you wouldn't remember me."

"You think I'd ever forget Blake Foley?" Bhutto said. She was tall, and slim, and looked stunning in a lime and gold silk shalwar kameez. She shook Charlie's hand and said wickedly to Nell. "Who'd you steal *him* from?"

"He stole me," Nell replied.

The Vice President, standing next to Bhutto, gave Charlie a smile. "I know Nell, too," Tom Atkinson said, more personable than he'd ever been during their days together in the Senate. "Pinky—Prime Minister Bhutto—and I were at Harvard together. Blake and I played basketball. Nell was . . . what were you doing there again?"

"Art history, for a while," she said. "It was a drive-by."

"It was a heist!" Bhutto said, then turned to Charlie and abruptly changed the subject: "Senator, I know you're skeptical about the F-16s. But I'd love for you to come visit us, meet with our military, and get a better sense of our current difficulties, and"—she paused and smiled at Nell—"if you can bring *her,* so much the better."

Then Bhutto leaned over and whispered something into Nell's ear. They separated, laughing. "I'm sorry," Nell said.

"I'm not," Bhutto replied.

In the car on the way back to his apartment, Charlie asked, "So what was the whispered bit at the end?"

"She said that if I hadn't stolen Blake Foley, she might not have become prime minister of Pakistan." Nell snuggled closer to him, put her hand on his thigh.

"I didn't know you went to Harvard," he said, somewhat daunted, very much a state university graduate from the Midwest.

"I barely knew it myself," she said, hearing his uncertainty. "Admission was a family legacy. It didn't take."

This time, après Bhutto, Charlie erred on the side of aggressiveness.

He kissed her, hard, in the elevator; she staggered backward. He felt fool-ish. It was the first time they'd been clumsy together. They walked into his bland, horizontal apartment and—it was as if he were seeing it for the first time, through her eyes: a hotel room. No one lived there. At least, no one interesting.

She was, again, spectacular. She seemed supremely unnervous. He rushed into her.

"Close," he said, five minutes later, embarrassed. "But no cigar."

"Cigar," she corrected him, "but not close."

He was stung by her honesty. The hydraulics had worked, but there hadn't been much intimacy: he realized that he'd been thinking, worry-ing, about his performance without giving much thought to whom he'd been performing on, or how she was reacting. He looked at her now, and felt foolish, boorish. "We may have to work on this."

She didn't say anything. "How much time do you spend here?" she asked, surveying his bedroom. There were a few photographs of home on the walls—Charlie and Buzz, laughing on the front porch at Oak Street; Charlie and his mom and some of the kids from the East Side Center. There was a television on a metal stand; there was a queen-sized bed, mahogany night tables and straight-up lamps; there was a bureau and a closet with cheap, sliding plywood doors.

"Not much," he said.

"That's good," she said. "If you actually lived here, I'd be worried. . . ."

"I live in my office," he said.

"Depressing."

"Well, you do, too," he said. "Right?"

"Above it," she said. "But yeah, I guess you're right . . . But that's not—I really have a home. You—I mean, is the furniture rented or some-thing?"

"Or something," he said. "I've just never had enough time to think it through. Not like my office."

"Maybe we should try doing it there," she said.

"You have to go back to New York tomorrow?"

"Mmm," she said, yawning. "When can you come again? This week-end?"

"Gotta go home," he said. "Work the folks."

"How often do you do that?"

"Too often," he said. "You want to come?"

"Kids," she said. "Weekends with kids. There's all sorts of chauffeuring."

"And Lucius couldn't do that sometime?" he said. "Or maybe you could bring the kids."

"Seems like a lot of lugging," she said, resting her chin on her hands on his chest, looking up at him.

"For a little loving?"

"Don't get down on yourself, buster," she said.

"Not down," he said. "It's a half-decent lyric: a lot of lugging for a little loving. Got to try it out on Buzz—my dad. I think you'd like Buzz. He's very hep, or was—when it was hip to be hep . . . and he'd like you. Sweet stems, he'd say. And oh, with regard to kids," he added, determined to unpack all his luggage, "there's something I ought to tell you: I . . ."

"Have one," she said. "Yeah, Linc told me."

He was stunned by the thought of Linc and Nell together, talking about him. He was stunned by the thought of Linc and Nell together. And he was mortified by the thought that Nell now had the most immediate sense possible of their relative merits—and that she was seeming distant, disengaged from him.

"So," she said coolly. "You have a habit of poaching Linc's girls?"

"Is that what this is?" he asked.

"No," she admitted.

"The first time wasn't really anything," he said, certain that it was only that—coincidence, not symmetry or, heaven forbid, a pattern. He thought of Linc's other women: a very impressive brigade, but he hadn't been particularly attracted to any of them.

"Tell that to your son," she said. "You sure this isn't about some weird thing you have with Linc?"

He sat up, and so did she. "Positive," he said. "This is about a weird thing I have with you."

"That's a compliment?" she said, trying to steer back to safety, but she was worried. This had taken an odd turn. She had enough experience with men to understand that thoughtful lovemaking came slowly, more often than not, if it came at all—men were so overwrought, so foolish that way. But she had expected more from Charlie; she had expected everything.

"What's a good compliment? What would work?" he asked. "I'm a desperate man."

She shrugged, turned, fluffed her pillow, eluded him.

"You want to watch *Nightline?*" he asked, reaching for the clicker, a nervous, thoughtless, reflexive reaction. It was what Lynn always did after making love: turned on the late news.

"Somehow I get the feeling that's not a question," Nell said. "What is it with you guys in politics? You watch more TV than my kids— Oh, dear." She put her hands on her cheeks and made her mouth an O, like the Munch painting *The Scream.* Linc was on *Nightline.* "A *ménage d'électronique!*"

The topic was Chechnya. There was a Russian foreign ministry official, a Chechen exile from Berlin—and Linc, from Moscow. Speaking very slowly, soberly. Extremely concerned. Internal matter, but it must be re-solved quickly. Anything we can do to help. The Russian rumbled slowly uphill, something about organized criminal elements. The Chechen re-sponded forcefully. Then a commercial break.

Charlie looked over at Nell, who was suddenly asleep or pretending to be, her head under the pillow: not at all interested in Linc? Or perhaps she had had it with *both* of them. He realized that he was feeling very competitive, and that he might be losing the competition. He stared at her back, the exquisite undulations of her body, her long legs, stretched out, tapering perfectly from waist to ankle. He didn't want to blow this.

He clicked off the television, turned off the light, stared into the gloom. He massaged his left hand against his stomach: it was always there, the idiot skin hook, something to think about. Between the hand and the naked, high-wire formality of his work—the possibility of getting caught off-guard, making a wrong step, getting Schollwengened—there didn't seem to be much room left for simply living his life. He tried to re-member the last time sex had been something more than sex. . . . It had happened, he knew the feeling—a lightness in his chest—but it hadn't been since . . . when? He remembered Johanna in a fluttery stare one day, when he was all caught up in the kids at the East Side Community Center—he had seen her smitten, and perhaps he was, too: they became lovers almost immediately after that. Love had been a passing moment of weakness for Johanna, and perhaps for him. He hadn't been in love since.

Normally, the last thing he'd do before bed would be to assess the three-by-five card with his next day's schedule that Donna thoughtfully provided as he pushed out the door—he'd scan it, preparing for the peaks and valleys, the moments where he'd have to concentrate and the meetings where his presence was merely a formality. Now the index card was sitting in his suit-jacket pocket; he hadn't even thought to look at it.

He'd check it out over breakfast. Breakfast: what did he have? What would she want? He thought about his refrigerator. Would she see it as barren as the rest of his apartment? Undoubtedly. Breakfast was coffee and instant oatmeal. She'd want—what? He was boggled by breakfast. He tried to think back to what had happened the morning he'd awakened at her loft a week earlier; but he'd dashed out, embarrassed. Her hair had been morning wild, crinkly, in her face—he did remember that; she was wearing an old seersucker robe. He couldn't wait to see her again in the morning, but was afraid that he was well on the way to losing her. He would take her out to breakfast, to the Jefferson Hotel.

The phone rang. Linc, from Moscow. "You saw it?" he asked.

Nell stirred. "Who is it?" she asked.

"It's Linc," Charlie said.

"Who's there?" Linc asked.

"A friend . . . you think it was wise to go on *Nightline* like that?"

"Coleman asked me to do it," he said. "You don't think I'd be careless enough to . . . a friend, huh?"

"Of course I do," Charlie said. "Anyway, there's always the possibility that they're putting you out there, setting you up—"

"Yes, and there's also the possibility that they don't have anyone else around who can string two coherent sentences together on television," Linc said with mock weariness. "You've seen the secretary of state on the air. And you won't see Gid doing anything public. So . . ."

"You're the fall guy."

"Charlie, there are reasons for everything," he said. "You should come out here. You owe me a visit."

He certainly was right about that.

"I'm going to visit Linc in Moscow," he said abruptly the next morning. "Next week, I think."

"Why?"

"Well, you saw it on TV last night, Chechnya—" he lied, and saw that she was seeing through him. "I also want to tell him about us."

"What about us?"

"That we're seeing each other."

"Why?" she asked coolly.

"It doesn't feel right—"

"It doesn't feel *right?*" she said, disappointed: his precipitous insistence on going all the way to Russia to break this news didn't feel "right." It was premature, at best. It seemed a teenage boy's fantasy of the "honorable" thing to do. And then he actually said it:

"It's the honorable thing to do, if we're going to be seeing each other."

But they weren't quite *seeing* each other yet, at least not with the clarity she had anticipated—the clarity she'd experienced in that first instant at the Waldorf, after not having seen him in four months; the startling . moments of clarity that had been there every other time she'd been with him. She had always sensed—no, she'd always been certain—that Charlie saw her, had *gotten* her, in a way that few other men had. Perhaps she'd been snookered by his politesse—that odd, immediate and yet casual intimacy, the private joke they seemed to share from the very first. Was it just some sort of vaporous political parlor trick, the illusion of an ironic intelligence? No. Not possible. She'd met more than a few politicians now, and none of them was even remotely like Charlie. But this rather silly, melodramatic flight to Russia was cause for concern; she couldn't understand why he was so uncertain about himself, and impatient. She would have liked him to wait until the emotional bond between them was stronger, until he had established some sort of friendship—or level of tolerance—with the children. There were so many things that could go wrong.

She didn't want to tell him that, though. There were some things you couldn't discuss with a man, not even one with Charlie's potential for breaking past the standard masculine physical dumb pride. There were some things you needed to be sure a man could find out on his own. There was also the extremely remote possibility that he knew what he was doing—that this trip was somehow necessary. And on that gossamer string of possibility, she decided to give him the benefit of the doubt.

"Godspeed, Charlie Martin," she said, when he called from the airport a week later, agreeing to meet him in New Orleans two weeks hence, for some sort of political thing he had to attend.

"Everything is going to be . . . fine. Nell, I promise. We'll have a great time in New Orleans. You'll see," he said.

We'll see, she thought.

*   *   *

The gloom at Sheremetyevo Airport was seriously Slavic. The sky was lowering, with occasional fizzes of ashen snowflakes. Most of the lights were off in the terminal, and Charlie wondered if the darkness was due to an energy conservation effort or a shortage of lightbulbs. The customs officers, who'd seemed so stone-faced in the Soviet era, were more human now—the women wore makeup, some of the men had facial hair, a few were listening to rock-and-roll music on tinny transistors. There was a mordant edge to the usual brutish sluggishness: Russia had taken a national WTF, but Charlie wasn't very interested.

He wondered how his talk with Linc would play out. Charlie wasn't sure about the status of Rathburn's feelings toward Nell, the depth of his disappointment when she had refused marriage and Russia. But he was absolutely certain that his recent intimate awkwardness with Nell had its roots in his guilt about Linc.

A junior foreign service officer met Charlie at the gate and deposited him in the VIP lounge while papers were passed, and then whisked him into an embassy car, a black Mercury sedan, for the trip into town. "Here's your schedule, sir," the young diplomat said.

"Factory tours?"

"Those days are over, sir. There are no model factories anymore."

"Thank God," Charlie said. "And you are?"

"William Finneran. From Port Sallesby, sir. A constituent of yours."

"No kidding!" A Rathburn touch. "So how is the ambassador doing?"

"Oh, gosh," Finneran said reverently as they bounced over rutted roads on the way into Moscow, new advertisements—gaudy splashes of capitalist color—impinging on the austere broadness of Leningradsky Prospekt. "He's my fifth ambassador. This is my third country. And it's the difference between black and white and Technicolor. Everything gets attention, everything is thought through. Most ambassadors are reactive; he's proactive."

Charlie masked a wince. He hated that nonword: proactive. It was redundant. But maybe Linc needed something like that, a modifier that expressed something beyond "active"—one that didn't deprecate, like "overactive" or "underemployed."

"And when do we see the great man?"

"Cocktails at Spaso House. He's put together—"

"A little fiesta," Charlie finished. "How many hundreds?"

"Just a few dozen."

"Of course," Charlie said. "And before that, you'll test my jet lag with economic, military and intelligence briefings at the embassy, right?"

Finneran smiled. Early afternoon was the worst for new arrivals in Russia, still predawn back on the East Coast. Charlie had done the calculations on the plane—he and Linc wouldn't get down to business until after dinner, which would be late afternoon back home. That was good: he'd be more awake then, at less of a disadvantage.

Actually, when the time finally did come, Charlie found himself on much firmer ground than he'd expected—thanks to the presence, at dinner, of Marisa Carter of CNN, whom Linc had placed to Charlie's right, the hostess slot. Marisa was black, and considerably more attractive than television good-looking, and considerably smarter than television-smart. She had been a Wilson School fellow at Princeton, a Russian specialist, and she was—quite clearly—ticketed by CNN for a larger future than Moscow correspondent. She also seemed to be ticketed for a fairly significant role in the life of Lincoln Rathburn, though that didn't become clear until after dinner when Marisa lingered after the other guests had left, joining Linc and Charlie in the ambassador's study, which was an exceptionally warm and pleasant room on a bitter Russian evening—the staff had the fireplace prepared and blazing—a north wind pelting the windowpanes with icy snow pricks.

"Did I do the job with Grushkin?" she asked Linc.

"You were brutal." He smiled. "Join us for a brandy?"

"I've got a standup in two hours." She glanced at Charlie, and explained: "They usually want me live for 'World Report.' Six o'clock at home is two A.M. here. Hence—"

She was all business, a human hospital corner: crisp and tucked together perfectly—except for her hair, which was pressed and bobbed, a bit too old-fashioned and churchified for someone her age. She was rail-thin, with high cheekbones and full lips—but her beauty emanated from her intelligence rather than her physical features; there was an effervescent confidence to her, the sense that she didn't miss a trick. She stood in front of the fireplace, in a blue blazer over a white blouse and long gray flannel slacks; Linc slipped into an easy chair and Charlie flopped on the couch, his feet up on the coffee table, facing the fire. He watched Linc watching Marisa until Linc caught him at it; Charlie dropped his eyes, sloshed his brandy around the snifter, then asked her, "What was 'the job' with Grushkin?"

"Tell him the truth about foreign aid. Again. And do it in a way our government officials"—she nodded at Linc—"can't, diplomatically. It is just a-*maz*-ing what these Russian so-called economists don't know about economics. Of course, the ambo over here isn't exactly a whiz on the subject either," she said affectionately, hitching a thumb in Linc's direction.

"He likes more traditional diplomacy, peacemaking, haggling, line-draw-ing, the discussion of cultural exchanges. But you must know that, Senator."

"Come on, Marushka," Linc said, with a decidedly un-Lincolnian soft-ness. "I read the Aslund paper."

"You flunked the quiz," she said with a smile, then turned to Charlie: "And worse—he's an idealist. He thinks we can actually reform these folks past the Mafia phase."

"We can educate th—"

"You don't need to educate people about economic self-interest," she said, cutting Linc off, continuing to focus on Charlie. "It's hardwired. Senator, what we're doing here is dumb—giving them money for stock market regulatory commissions and suchlike, as if they won't be com-pletely corrupted within eighteen minutes. Your average Yuri thinks we're giving foreign aid directly to the Mob, and he's got a point. It'll take them a generation or two to get past the Mafia phase, just as it did for us. If they're lucky, the *muzhiki* throwing their weight around now will be the Vanderbilts and Rockefellers of the twenty-first century."

"She wants us to fund social services," Linc said dismissively, but smil-ing, with obvious admiration. "As if we can provide a social safety net for a couple of hundred million—"

"It's PR," Marisa said, interrupting him again: this was an argument they'd had before. She sat down next to Charlie, addressing her remarks to him—but with the real focus on Linc. "It's symbolic. We do some stuff for the veterans of the Great War."

"Vet centers?" Charlie asked.

"Exactly. With food," Marisa said. "Some of them are pretty hungry. Pensions wiped out by inflation. And we do something for the kids. Friendship Camps."

"Band-Aids," Linc said. "Cosmetics."

"We have the smartest, hippest culture in the world. Why do we have to have the very squarest government? Hey, I've gotta go." She stood, shook Charlie's hand, gave Linc a peck on the cheek. "You know, Mr. Ambassador, if you weren't so damn good-looking, you'd have more re-spect for the power of cosmetics."

And she was out the door, before Linc could get up and escort her down to the foyer.

"Whew!" Charlie said.

"Isn't she extraordinary?" Linc asked.

Which is not to say that Charlie's subsequent confession went smoothly. Linc admitted nothing with regard to Marisa Carter. He was clearly smitten, but furtive when it came to divulging details; the relationship was a work in progress, perhaps not yet consummated—and Linc guarded the mystery zealously.

"You're hooked!" Charlie said.

"Am not," Linc replied, playground-style, trying to deflect Charlie's interest in the situation by making fun of it.

"She's great," Charlie said hopefully. "And great-looking, too."

"She could be the most important foreign correspondent of her generation," Linc replied.

"And which generation is that?"

"Ours," Linc said, putting his feet up on the coffee table, perpendicular to Charlie's. "Almost."

"Almost: you wish." Charlie sat up, leaned forward and let the big one drop: "Linc, Nell and I are seeing each other. We're in love."

"What?" Linc seemed astonished by the news.

"You're surprised?" Charlie asked. "Really? I thought it was so obvious. You said I was half in love with her—"

"Disappointed," Linc said. "Hurt."

Hurt? "You're kidding."

"It's not about you and Nell," Linc said. "It's about you and me. I mean, it's over with Nell—that's obvious enough. She's fabulous, but we weren't right. She wasn't one for this life." Linc raised his arms, to encompass Spaso House. "Was it going on when—"

"No. Not until a month ago."

"She was with you that night I called—after *Nightline*. I knew it," he said, although it was obvious he hadn't. Linc stared at the fire.

"So?" Charlie said. But he knew: there was something unseemly about jumping in on a friend like that.

"So I'm disappointed in you."

"I'm disappointed in me, too," Charlie said. "In a . . . recessive sort of way—the dominant feeling is . . . just wild. I really do love her, Linc. It's a physical sensation I've never experienced before. It's—well, you saw it. I don't know what it is, but it's been there since the first night I met her. The Democratic convention." He felt an utterly ridiculous and inexplicable need to be absolutely candid. "I see her across a room and, before I'm consciously aware it's her, I'm smiling. I can't wait to find out what she's going to see, what she's going to say next. I know there's weirdness there. And she's difficult in all sorts of ways. She's got a temper. And she's got the kids, and I haven't had a chance to really get to know them yet. And there's Lucius, in-house. But it's worth all the—at least, I think it is. . . . Is this how you felt about her?"

"No." Linc looked at Charlie, making a final evaluation: he would never be president. "I didn't lose my head."

He said it quietly, without heat—but it was devastating, a clinical judgment upon a lesser person. They would remain friends. A clean break would be too violent, too drastic. Linc did like, and even admire, Charlie. But he wasn't sure that he respected him anymore. There was an emotional weakness, a debilitating romanticism—and the fact that Charlie had this odd tendency to pick up where he'd left off with women. They would be friends, but no longer quite equals. Not in Linc's mind.

The question of sloppy seconds bothered Charlie as well, but it was a peripheral concern. In that moment, sensing Linc's condescension, Charlie also understood the difference between them: what Linc saw as weakness was really the possibility of fresh air. What Linc saw as an admirable form of emotional restraint, Charlie now believed was a deficiency. It was a failing that he and Linc had shared: an inability to be unimportant—to submit, to make themselves disappear.

This seemed a simple enough human concept: the primacy of other-regard. Charlie had always paid his respects, and some dues, at the shrine of selflessness, but it seemed a rather grand and public thing, the essence of altruism, it meant being the way his mother was; selflessness didn't seem very intimate, and not at all humble; it was about giving, not surrendering. He imagined that the act of surrender—the opposite of success in war and politics—would not be easy for him. But surrender was essential: it was the only way out, the only escape from the strangulation of self-regard.

"Linc," he said. "I'm sorry. I'm an idiot. I'm going home."

And when he saw her again, in New Orleans, he found that he was able to forget about strategy and tactics, about Washington and Des Pointe. He forgot all about the Moderate Democrats, whose convention he was supposedly attending. He forgot about Linc, and Lucius, and the children, and—for a while—about himself. She was standing, waiting for him at the gate, smiling hopefully, holding a peach-colored rose. "I found this," she said, "for you."

"How lovely," he replied, without thinking about how unusual it was for her to have brought him a flower, without noticing what she was wearing and without reaching for a clever response. Without inflection or hesitation or nuance of any sort, he took the rose, which resembled the sunset he'd seen from her deck that evening in May, peach deepening to a rich maroon at the outer tips of the petals. How remarkably easy it all was.

*   *   *

"Do you think all the beds in New Orleans are this high?" she asked afterward.

"I don't know," he said. "More important, did I hear you say 'yippee' when we were, you know . . . ? I've never been with a woman who said 'yippee' at the critical moment before."

"It wasn't 'at' the critical moment." She stretched her arms straight out toward the ceiling, then clasped her hands behind her head, the sheet slipping off her breasts. He replaced it gently. She smiled, ran the back of her hand along his cheek. "It was after. And it was commentary rather than exclamation."

"After?" he asked, up on an elbow. He wanted to stroke her stomach with his left hand, which was the one available, but he was wary about breaking new ground and spoiling the moment. He could never be sure how a woman would react to his deformity, afterward. Afterward wasn't the same as "before" or "during." It was tougher. And, of course, it had to be the damnable hand that ruined everything, that brought him back to the world.

Nell noticed Charlie's uncertainty and thought it endearing. She wanted to take his sad hand, and kiss it, and put it wherever he wanted to put it—but that would require an untangling, a significant change in her position. She wanted the gesture to be right; it would be an action more intimate than making love, in a way. She rehearsed it in her mind: up on her left elbow, facing him; taking his left hand with her right, stroking it, holding it on her stomach. But would that be too obvious, now that she'd taken the time to think about it? She didn't want to embarrass or patronize him. The movement had to come naturally, artlessly.

"It's too bad about the room. I mean, look at this," she said, pointing a naked arm, a perfect beanpole of an arm, straight up at the ornamental Woolworth's-quality ceiling fan. On the other hand, it was wrong that they weren't touching each other, she thought. The air-conditioning, and the distance between them, raised goose bumps. "How tacky. And the chintz. I was hoping for something more decadent, more Tennessee Williams; more humidity, blowsy white cotton, a brass bed at least. . . . What I mean to say is, I'm so happy we're here." She made the move now: up, taking his hand, kissing it gently on what was left of the palm. He exhaled; she forced him onto his back and rested her head on his chest. "You were worth waiting for."

He circled her back with his left arm, the hand resting lightly on her ribs; she had slim, square shoulders and a wonderful back. Great women had great backs. He kissed her hair. "I told you," he said. "I had to get things straight with Linc."

Men say a lot of things, she thought, when they're having problems. But she didn't say that. "You got things straight, all right," she said.

"You want to go out and wander?" he asked. "We could hit the Acme Oyster House, get replenished before we meet the MoDems."

"Replenished, eh?" She asked. "Does that mean one needs a certain energy to meet the Moderate Democrats? Or merely that you've been depleted?"

"No way. I'm not done with you yet." He turned her over, kissing her full on the mouth, then moving down to her breasts. She felt him stirring—a witless, primal stirring—as he slid down her leg.

"Okay, cowboy," she said, pulling his head up from her chest with both hands. "That wasn't a challenge."

"Sounded like one."

They stared at each other, at close range. "So, it was okay?" he said, with a smile.

"Yippee," she replied. "I always knew we'd be fine, eventually."

"When did you start thinking that—you know?—we'd be . . ." he asked.

"Oh, early on, for sure," she said. "Maybe the time we were dancing, and you asked me what my kids were like, and actually seemed to mean it. And you?"

"The sound of one and a half hands clapping . . . and the perfume," he said. "That first night, at the convention. It wasn't quite love at first sight. But damn close. First and a half sight, maybe."

"You didn't seem that interested," she said. "You had the Asian child."

"You're fishing," he said. "You knew."

"A woman my age assumes that a man your age would be more interested in an Asian child than in a woman my age," she said.

"Well, she was pretty good-looking," he said. "But this sort of thing isn't just about looks."

"Thanks a lot," she said, pushing him away.

"I love the way you look," he said. "And you know that. You've always known that. Don't bullshit me."

"I've always *acted* as if I've known it because that's the way I act," she said. "But I didn't know it."

"Bullshit," he said.

"Then why didn't you call after the party?"

"Which party?"

"At my house. Last May. When we sent Linc off to Russia and I kissed you in the bathroom."

"I wanted to," he said. "But there was Linc. But that doesn't matter now. . . . Hey, listen: here's what I want. I want to get to know the kids."

"Thanksgiving's just around the corner," she said.

But there was only one possible place he could be for Thanksgiving: the Clarice Martin Community Center on the East Side of Des Pointe.

"What?" she asked. "No response?"

"Holidays are work days for a politician," he said. For the first time ever, his job seemed an encumbrance.

"Are work days holidays?" she asked. "When do you play?"

"Right now," he said, kissing her cheek and then, gently, her lips. She took his left hand, holding it easily, as if it were just a hand. "Whenever *you* want to play. Except holidays. And work days."

"Oh, brother," she said.

13

———

The calendar of the United States Senate proceeds unevenly, in fits and starts, but not without purpose. The winter and spring are spongy, with long recesses and vacant time. Not much happens until the midsummer, or early fall, when the members—a third of whom face re-election in each even-numbered year—erupt into furious activity and vote on thick, specific, often incomprehensible blogs of legislation. When approved, these bills enable the rest of the government to continue its business. Without the electoral spur—and, certainly, without the existence of the House of Representatives, whose 435 members must face the voters every two years—it is possible the debates and haggling would go on in the Senate forever; as it is, the schedule enables the politicians to approach their constituents immediately postpartum, flushed with the righteousness of belated productivity.

As a result, legislators tend to be ursine. In winter, they hibernate. In the spring, they stir. At least, some do. The more motivated members chug through spring expending great amounts of energy in committee hearings that produce the legislative monuments voted upon in the fall; the less motivated devote themselves to greeting constituents, raising money and appearing dignified. Spring is a curious time, when discipline is needed—if not necessarily rewarded.

For most of his career, Charlie Martin had been a diligent springtime politician. This began to change slowly, as the end of the cold war made Armed Services Committee business less compelling—and Charlie's presidential ambitions stirred, flowered and then sputtered. The first winter of the Stanton administration, the winter of the Parkinson debacle, had been a violent exception to the general trajectory of Senator Martin's waning political diligence. The second winter provided few such distractions. He would be facing reelection that fall, but his elections had never been troublesome—and this time it was assumed his opponent would be an antique Republican congressman, Porter Weingarten, who had volunteered to oppose Senator Martin as a valedictory kamikaze mission: a farewell tour in which the state's Republican party could celebrate the esteemed but profoundly unexciting congressman's retirement. Charlie Martin looked forward to a comfortable campaign. He'd begin to work at it when the snow cleared. In the meantime, he gravitated to New York. To Nell.

He had never been moved, one way or the other, by the immensity of New York. He was not particularly stirred by the worlds of publishing or finance, or particularly offended by the brusqueness of the locals, which seemed, to him, a logical consequence of the density of the place—if there were a million people on the street, it became impractical to say "Good morning" to each one you passed and the chances for civility devolved from there. But that winter, the city changed for him—became charming; at least Nell's part of it did. It was as if he were living in the Flats, back home, and the brick warehouses continued on for more than a handful of blocks; indeed, in New York, the Flats-like neighborhoods were endless. On weekends, he would jog down the West Side to the Financial District, which seemed ancient and empty, wrinkled with alleys. The wind rushed through the crevices, and Charlie enjoyed the acute discomfort of launching himself directly into the winter gusts: a fond legacy of his training as a snake-eater, where he'd learned to embrace privation—pain assaulted was pain obliterated.

It seemed remarkable to him that in Nell's immediate neighborhood, amidst the dense tangle of streets and buildings, there were the very same elements of community that marked Port Sallesby or Fort Dantrobet or any of the towns back home. There were shopkeepers, whom Nell knew by name. There were schools and churches, bake sales and Scout troops. There were block associations and ethnic festivals. Nell thrived in the midst of all this, her sensibility quite perfectly at home amidst the clutter. In Charlie's mind, she did not merely reside there: she was an institution—a business, a family, a retinue. There were the children, and Lucius, and the MerMaid employees, most of whom were Asian and Hispanic women (although there was also a great-grandfatherly Italian cutter named Nunzi, whose sense of the delicate Lycra calculus was impeccable and crucial). There were odd interminglings of functions. Lucius superintended the shop and the children. Nunzi sometimes came upstairs and cooked, as did a stooped Chinese seamstress from Guangzhou named Fou Zhi. MerMaid worked some Saturday mornings, and several of the women would bring their children—who played with the boss's kids (Pamela earned her allowance by supervising the mayhem). Nell managed all this with a calm intelligence; and more, with the graceful authority of a gifted field officer.

Soon, in ways that he scarcely imagined possible, the senator was absorbed into the neighborhood and the family. He learned to love the local customs, the syncopated ceremonies of Nell-enic domesticity, the rhythms of the loft; he established a comfortable place for himself in the household, assumed a useful role—he was an early riser (as opposed to both Nell and Lucius), and so he took control of the morning duties, which meant he was often the first adult the children confronted.

Robin was easy—dreamy, artistic, an unhurried and accepting soul very much like his father, with whom he was quite close. Robin and Charlie could sit quietly together in the morning, on the high bar stools surrounding the stainless steel kitchen island, munching cereal—Charlie reading the *Times;* Robin, a cereal box or Lego catalog.

On one of Charlie's first visits, Robin looked up from his Lucky Charms, all dark eyes and curls, his mouth a pinched little bow, and asked, "Is Daddy right? Did someone shoot your hand in the war?"

"Yup," Charlie said.

"Does it still hurt?"

"Sometimes, a little."

"Can I touch it?" Charlie nodded and Robin came around to his side of the table, and slowly pointed his right index finger toward the shiny pink stump, finally touching it lightly, then quickly pulling his hand back in horror. He looked up at Charlie, at once terrified and apologetic, as if his finger had been stung by the wound, yanking his hands behind his back and keeping them there, entwined.

"I'm sorry," he said.

"It's all right," Charlie replied, shaken. No one had ever approached him so—innocently, about his hand before.

"You won't tell Mommy?"

"No."

"I'm sorry," Robin said again, tears forming. "Y'know, I *hate* the . . ." He hesitated, unsure about the enemy in question. "The bad guys."

And he ran off to watch cartoons.

Pamela was more difficult, of course. She was prickly, defensive, fierce, skeptical. "I knew you were going to be Mom's next one," she said to Charlie one Saturday morning.

"I know you knew," he said. "You're a knower."

"I'm ADHD," she said, an acronym Charlie had never encountered before. He assumed that it had to do with some sort of precocity: most of his knowledge about Manhattan children had come from novels.

"Oh, yeah?"

"You don't even know what that is, do you?" She put her hands on her hips, screwed up her face, a mini Nell.

"Americans of Dangerously High Distinctiveness?"

"Attention Deficit Disorder, jerko. Hyperactivity. I'm hyper."

"Coulda fooled me," he joked. "You always seem so calm."

"Yeah, right," she said. "Mom says every kid in Manhattan either is gifted or has learning disabilities. Except Robin, he's average."

Charlie laughed.

"So Mom said," Pamela continued, "you could maybe walk me over to ballet? She's still in bed, of course."

"You woke her up? Where's ballet?"

"Someone had to. At the Y, Seventh and Twenty-third."

"Why did someone have to? She deserves a good long morning every once in a while."

Pamela shrugged. "So, you taking me or do I go wake up Lucius?"

They went out into the dull, chilly Saturday morning city, which still seemed to be recovering from its Friday-night revels, the streets smelling of stale beer and fast food. Pamela was wearing a multicolored sock cap with a long tassel on it—and suddenly, on the street, she was transformed from child harridan to little girl. She reached up to hold his hand, his left hand. She didn't think anything of holding it; her hand was tiny, precious in his. His eyes filled with tears.

"You're crying?"

"The wind," he said.

On several occasions, he was accompanied to New York by Hilton, who had a beau, an English professor at Columbia, on the Upper West Side. Hilton never introduced his friend to the boss, but he did spend a fair amount of time in Nell's loft—which he christened Mondo Nello. The official excuse was work on speeches and assorted nonsense with the boss, but he was also attracted to the intense domesticity of the place: it felt like a real home. He formed a natural, fraternal alliance with Lucius; they were Sancho Panzas to the two principals, Nell and Charlie. And Charlie noticed that Hilton seemed a somewhat different fellow in New York than the very professional Senate press secretary. He seemed looser, chattier . . . gayer. And he caused Charlie to wonder if the New York version of Charlie Martin was a different person, too.

Nell and Hilton got on from the first. She was quite taken by his almost mystical deftness as a shopper—for anything: food, appliances, airplane fares—but he was especially good in consignment shops, where she would buy secondhand designer labels for herself and the children. "Hilton, you are a human divining rod," she told him the first Saturday they went out together, as the three of them—Charlie, third wheel—had sandwiches in a Greek coffee shop on the Upper East Side after a particularly inspired gleaning of the Spence-Chapin thrift shop. "I can't believe that Bill Blass ball gown you found for me. You know, you could make a serious living as a shopper."

"Could I really?"

"No," Charlie interrupted. "Not a serious living."

"A good living, then," Nell said. "People would certainly pay cash money for your eye."

"No, the boss is right," Hilton said. "I'd run the risk of becoming so fey that I'd float off into the ionosphere. I do manly work now: tote that amendment, lift that press call. Get a little drunk and you land in subcommittee."

"You don't get weary and sick of trying?"

"Don't be such a showboat!" he said, pointing a long finger across the table at Nell, who laughed as Charlie groaned, leaving a tuna smear on her lower lip. Hilton handed her a paper napkin and said, "Remember, you've got to redo the zipper before you wear the Blass."

"Huge money, Hilton," she said. "You could come work for me."

"If you don't hush up," Hilton said, "he'll send me to the Des Pointe office."

"What's the shopping like in Des Pointe?" she asked Charlie.

"As if he'd know," Hilton sniffed.

"Why don't you come and find out?" Charlie asked.

"Here we go again," she said, rolling her eyes. "I'm as dreary as Des Pointe in December. . . ."

"Silly as Port Sallesby on a September noon," Hilton added, then stood, spread his arms and crooned, defiantly off-key: *"I can explain why you've corn on the brain: you're in love with a wonderful guy!"*

"Jesus H. Christmas," Charlie said, hiding his face behind a sleeve. "Both of you are such complete faggots."

In late January—and very much to Charlie's surprise—Calvin turned up in New York and stayed for several weeks. He was welcomed without much ado into Nell's snugly expandable universe, the loft always capable of including more. (Nell's life, Charlie realized, resembled her fabrics.) Like most musicians, Calvin was daunted and fascinated by the Big Apple; he haunted the Village jazz clubs. One afternoon, on a long father and son walk along Canal Street toward Chinatown, he asked Charlie, "Why didn't Buzz ever go for it, here or in Chicago—or maybe L.A.?"

It was a good question, the sort that Charlie would never have thought to ask his father. He wondered if Calvin was getting antsy in D.P. and thinking about taking a stab at the main chance himself. He wondered if he should offer a permanent spot in Nell's battalion; he was sure she could find room in the loft, sure that Calvin would be a welcome addition—and then the kid could explore the scene from a base of certainty. "Maybe Buzz didn't need to," Charlie finally replied. "Most people do. They want to test their chops against the best, see if they cut it. It's scary, but inevitable. Sort of like running for president in my business. But you know Buzz, he's easy."

"You were scared when you tried it?" Calvin asked. "Running for president?"

"Not scared enough," Charlie said. "Too dumb to be scared. It's something I learned belatedly: if you're not at least a little scared, you don't respect the process sufficiently. . . . And you? You thinking about the main chance?"

"I don't know. I'll get there. Kinda hard to leave Buzz and Edsy at this point, especially with—"

"Me spending so much time here?" Charlie asked.

"Sorta. Naw. It's not about you. But you know, Buzz and me—since I offered to back him a little on the traps, even Vern's rallying. It's interesting, the old guys are all technique now that the reflexes are gone. Gotta love it, the way they keep at it. Sad, maybe. But I'm learning from them."

"Buzz'd understand if you decided to try your luck," Charlie said. "He wouldn't want to hold you back."

"It's just . . . Dad." Charlie couldn't remember Calvin ever calling him "dad" before, certainly not with that degree of intimacy. But then, Charlie couldn't remember having so easy a conversation with his son before. "I couldn't do it to the old guy right now. Couldn't look him in the eye and say the words."

"I don't want to ruin our relationship," Charlie said, "but you're a hell of a guy."

"Yeah, well. Can I . . . like? . . ." Charlie waited for his son to continue. Calvin stopped, looked over at him, looked him in the eye and said, "I just want to say, you shouldn't worry. It's okay that you're here. I can handle the D.P. part of the program—and this seems to be a happening thing for you. I talked to Buzz and Edsy on the phone last night, told them about Mondo Nello. Everyone thinks it's about time. Buzz'd never say it flat out, but he's happy for you. And . . . and I am, too. It's even good seeing you get silly with her kids—I kind of imagine that's what you might have been with me, if you'd had the shot. And don't think it's not a temptation for me to stay. There is something addictive about this place. The other day, when you were in D.C., Fou Zhi showed me how to make dumplings. She was actually up in the kitchen, making them. . . . Anyway, don't worry. This is good."

Charlie still went home to Des Pointe for folk-poking many weekends, but when he went it was almost painful to be there, away from Nell and the kids. He spent the entire week of the February recess in New York— and remained, playing hooky there for several days after the Senate reconvened. He began to keep clothes in Nell's closet. He joined the New York congressional delegation on the air shuttles from LaGuardia to National Airport; by March, he was spending as many midweek nights in New York as in Washington. He called Lynn Thurston and told her that he'd fallen in love; she reacted with the tiniest of shudders. She had not harbored great expectations for Charlie, but she was surprised to have their stasis shaken by anything so violent as love. She said she was happy for him; she asked him who it was. When he told her, she said, "And Linc?" He told her about Marisa Carter. They chatted on a bit, then said good-bye. And that was that.

Actually, it was something more than that: Lynn had been his tether to the social life of the city, and now he slipped out, away, no longer constrained to the cocktail and dinner party circuit—and less of a presence in town as a result. There were things, bits of information, he didn't know now that he'd always known in the past. He'd always thought them trivial things—gossip about who was moving against whom in the White House and in the media; speculation about who had leaked what to the *Post* or the *Times*—but they were valuable in the way that information always is; they were the subtext of the business of the capital. The absence of Lynn combined with the absence of Linc had estranged him from both the society of power and the knowledge possessed by the innermost political circles. His status changed in Washington: from being a hot political property, a sought-after dinner guest, to a more occasional and enigmatic figure. The sense in Washington was that Charlie Martin's moment had passed. He found that he didn't much care: he had always imagined that he ran counter to the "sense" in Washington, and assumed he could turn the conventional wisdom around quickly enough, if he chose to do so.

But he chose not to do so. The central place in his life once held by the daily conversations with Linc—in which the topography of the capital was inspected and the tiniest calibrations of strategy adjusted—was supplanted by near-hourly conversations with Nell, and by the various concerns of Mondo Nello.

Mondo Nello was oddly hermetic. They didn't go out much socially. They brought movies in. They played charades, especially when Hilton or Calvin was around—there would be six of them then; three matched pairs of three—the pairs split into teams, which meant Charlie could come up with clues for Nell, things he could torture her with—like "The International Law of the Sea Treaty." He loved watching her act things out.

One Sunday afternoon, Nell came in from shopping and found Charlie and the two kids wrapped around each other in the television room, watching the end of *Close Encounters*—where the aliens come and turn out to be good guys—all of them rapt, unconscious, safe. Charlie looked up at her, woozy with domesticity. She wanted to pull him out of there, rip his clothes off, have at him: patriarchy was such a turn-on.

That night, in bed, she said, "I've got something for you." She opened the night table drawer and pulled out a small black box from Barney's with a golden ribbon.

He sat up and opened it. It was a keycase, of fine dark green snakeskin. "Open it," she said, her forearm resting atop his shoulder. Inside, there was a key—to the loft—and a charm: a mermaid. "The key to my heart," she said.

"I've never—" he started. She put a finger to his lips.

"Me neither," she said, reaching down for him. "I think, perhaps, you have something to give me, too."

*   *   *

One late March noon, Charlie found himself sitting in an Armed Services Committee hearing about the continued, torturous efforts to figure out a policy regarding homosexuals in the military when he remembered that Nell, who was off in Atlanta selling her line, had asked him to remind Lucius that Robin needed to be picked up at school and taken to the dentist. He rushed back to the committee office and called Lucius at MerMaid.

"Will you be home for dinner?" Lucius asked.

"I wasn't planning—"

"It's just that Nell's not around and the kids were hoping you'd be a fourth for Chinese checkers."

"The kids? Pamela, too?"

"She said she'd go pepperoni, onions, double cheese in your honor."

"We're doing pizza?"

"Cat's away." Nell hated pizza.

"Count me in," he said, reaching into his pocket for his schedule card, then dialing Donna. "D—that Hollowell Feeds guy coming in at five, you think we could move him to tomorrow afternoon? Tell him I was called over to the Pentagon. And tell Tam that we'll move the chemical weapons briefing to—I don't know. Soon."

"Ohhh-kayyy," Donna said. "We're going to have to move some stuff around tomorrow to fit Hollowell in and—this is an *important* meeting at the Pentagon?"

"Crucial," he said.

"I thought she was in Atlanta."

"I've been summoned by the kids," he said. "Pizza and Chinese checkers."

"Senator—" she began, then lost heart. "Do you want to assume the usual lecture?"

"Consider me suitably chastened," he said. "Look, I'll take the six-thirty shuttle back in the morning. See if the Hollowell guy would like to have breakfast. Tell Tammy to meet me in the office for the briefing after that. Have Rosemary order in some bagels and stuff. . . . Is Mustafa around? Can he give me a lift over to National about four-ten?"

"Yes, if you'll agree to put him on staff," Donna said.

"What?"

"He's never asked you for a thing—for himself. For the church, yeah. We've got a slot, with Alice McElvaine leaving. Don't you think it's about time we made it official with Moose?"

"I thought we'd done that," he said.

"We've temped him. We still share him, officially, with Goodwill. And you remember that kid, Jerry—the one he was training? Jerry's clean now, he can take the Goodwill slot and . . . Look, forget it. I'll handle it."

"No," he said. "You're right. Good idea. Let's do it."

Of course, the rearrangement of the boss's schedule didn't go as smoothly as Charlie assumed it would. It never did. Jack Carter, the president of Hollowell Feeds, was leaving town first thing the next morning and wasn't available for breakfast. Brendan Lofton, Hollowell's lobbyist, was furious: "I don't care if Charlie wants to blow me off all the time, but Jack Carter doesn't understand senatorial prerogative—Donna, he thinks *he's* more important than anything allegedly going on at the Pentagon. And he may be right. You know, word's getting around the ag community about Charlie not being quite so dependable as he used to be. Do I need to be more specific about that?"

"Brendan. First of all, fuck you." Donna understood that any sign of weakness would be taken as tacit agreement. "You know damn well we've always been right on ag. To a fault, probably. Second, how many times has he blown off Jack Carter? You couldn't count 'em on your thumb. And finally, we'll figure out a way to make this up. The senator's working home turf next weekend, maybe we can set him up with Carter out there—he can fly to Des Pointe via Minneapolis. Meet Jack, meet any folks out there Jack wants to impress. Okay?"

"Well," Lofton said. "Donna, everyone knows what's going on with Charlie."

"And what's that?"

"Never mind. You'll guarantee Minneapolis?"

"I'll give it my best shot."

Donna stood, stared out the window for a moment, then buzzed Hilton. "Summit meeting. Boss's office. Right now."

The office seemed chilly, embalmed. The television wasn't even on. Donna was astonished by its emptiness—which was, she realized, a direct consequence of the senator's distraction: a certain level of intensity had to be maintained or everything fell apart. That was true even for second-rate senators from low-maintenance states. But it was particularly true for someone like Charlie Martin, who'd been a real presence in the institution, a star—any change in his modus operandi was noticed immediately, sensed by colleagues and rivals, gossiped about by assholes like Brendan Lofton and eventually reported in the press.

"Okay, Hilton, we've reached a new level here," Donna said, when Devereaux ambled in. "He's going to New York even though she's in Atlanta."

"Lucky him," Hilton said, depositing himself onto the leather couch.

"Goddammit, Hilton," Donna said, still standing, pacing. "You're falling down. Your job is to watch out for him and instead you're a goddamn coconspirator. He should fire your butt, but he won't. If you had half a brain, you'd quit. You're not up to this."

"Whoa!" Donna had a temper, but she'd never loosed it on Hilton before. "Did something happen?"

"If something did, *you* wouldn't know about it."

"I don't understand—"

"Truer words were never spoken," she said. "You don't understand. He's in love. That's good. About time. It's great to see him so happy. But he's drifting—that's risky business, even if it weren't an election year."

"Just barely an election year," Hilton said, fending her off. "Some old fart doing a phantom victory lap."

"Goddammit, Hilton. That is one hundred percent the wrong attitude. Your job is to assume the worst, to keep on top of things, to protect him."

"From what?" he asked, knowing the answer.

Donna sat down. "From himself, in this case. I know that sounds harsh. But he can't go around blowing off the Jack Carters of this world because he wants to play Chinese checkers with Nell's kids."

"That's why he's going?" Hilton doubled over, laughing. "Cool. You ever stop to think, he might be a better senator—might get along with the folks better—if he goofed off every so often, just like normal people do? I gotta confess, I love working for a guy whose idea of fucking off is Chinese checkers with his girlfriend's kids. And you do, too, and you know it."

"It's just . . . it's just not *natural*," Donna said, and began to laugh. "You stop this, Hilton."

"Stop what?"

"Being insidious." She stopped, grew serious. "Hilton, I don't want to pry—but what on earth are you doing up there?"

"What *ever* do you mean?" he replied, very Blanche DuBois.

"I mean you. We know what the attraction is for him, what's going on with you?"

"And this is your business?" Hilton asked, miffed. "If I were hetero, would it—"

"Absolutely!" Donna said. "You're socializing with the boss. That isn't healthy."

"I'm not socializing with the boss," he insisted, startled, backpedaling. Donna was right, of course. "You should see the senator up there, D. He is so damn happy. We're playing charades last weekend and Robin—the little boy—has to act out the song *Happy Birthday,* and what does he do for 'Happy'? He points to the senator. None of us got it, of course. But you see what I mean?"

Donna got up, sat down next to Hilton on the couch, put her hand on his arm. "Look, I know your intentions are the best—and happiness, Lord knows I don't want to stand in the way of that. Not even your happiness, sweetie. But, Hilton, what you are doing is very, very wrong."

"Why?"

"Because your job, our job, is to keep him on the stick," she said. "He might not have been hurt by this yet, but he *could* be and that's what he has us around for—to cover his back."

"Even half-speed, even mailing it in," Hilton said, "he works twice as hard as three-quarters of the jerkballs in this place."

"First of all, that's not true. Second, even if it were, half-speed doesn't work for Charlie Martin. I can't explain why, I just sense it."

"D, he's not supposed to have a life?" Hilton was astonished by what he was thinking: maybe he was in the wrong job, and the wrong city. And then he had another astonishing thought: maybe the boss was feeling the same way.

"He's supposed to play it straight up," Donna said, standing now, ending the conversation, having figured out what she wanted to say. "Sure, he can have a life. Why not? But if *he* doesn't feel he's giving this job his all, there'll be consequences. He'll overcompensate, screw up somehow. He's got a conscience, Hilton. It's why we love him."

*   *   *

In politics, one should always look a gift horse in the mouth. Good fortune is earned; unearned fortune is suspect, bound to create unexpected consequences, gaps in the zeitgeist, opportunities to be seized. And so, when Patrick Dunn began to hear the gossip that Porter Weingarten might not run for the Senate against Charlie Martin, he began to worry. He called around, and gathered string; and then he called Charlie, who was in New York.

"Good news and bad news, Senator," he said.

"Bad news first," Charlie replied. "Always."

"Potsie Weingarten has angina, a sick wife, an iffy prostate and a daughter in San Diego who's married to a real estate mogul who's promising nirvana by the sea if Potsie doesn't squander the family fortune on a losing race against you. And I think Weinie's seen the light."

"Too bad." A race against Weingarten would have been paradise. Potsie would have pulled a safe 36 to 38 percent, mostly from the Scando-Teutonic farming communities like Hansen County and the religious wing nuts who never voted for Charlie Martin, in any case. More important, Potsie was old-school. Civil. He would flog safe issues like ag, taxes and defense spending. It was true that, in anticipation of the campaign and at the age of seventy-three, Congressman Weingarten had seen fit to become one of the only Lutherans in history to be "born again," but Charlie had assumed the conversion to be an election ploy, a device that gave Porter some breathing space with the wing nuts.

"So what's the good news?" Charlie asked.

"Chaos among the GOPs."

"That's not such good news. Didn't you teach me that certainty was always better than chaos?"

"Well, hold on a second," Dunnsie said. "You know that Jimmy Hapworth started off slow against Saunders." The governor's race. Hapworth was an attractive and impatient young Democratic congressman from the industrial towns along the river in the eastern part of the state; Arch Saunders was the popular Republican incumbent governor.

"Yeah, you've got me doing a round of fund-raisers for Jimmy," Charlie said. "So?"

"So Jimmy's doing better and Archie's doing worse," Pat said, with a laugh. "You want to know how much worse? A DWI worse."

"How on earth does a governor get bagged on a DWI?" Charlie asked.

"Well, if he commandeers a Pontiac Trans Am owned by one of the better-looking girls in the steno pool and drives it into one of those metal newspaper boxes at the corner of Fox and Second in downtown D.P., that probably wouldn't be enough, would it?" Dunnsie began, enjoying himself immensely. "Because the D.P. police might reasonably conclude that

the young lady was behind the wheel, and not even mention in the report that the governor was in the car. Unfortunately, the accident was the
third moving violation for the young lady in the past twelve months, and
the state police, as a matter of course, moved to lift her license. It seems
the governor felt a moral obligation to intervene . . . of course, not the
governor himself. But Tommy Duncan of the gov's office and Ingrasso at
the DMV."

Charlie whistled. "That's rich. How come the world doesn't know it?"

"The world does, sort of," Pat said. "If you'd been reading your *R-W*
carefully, you might have seen at the bottom of the front page a few days
ago an item titled 'DMV Commish Probed in Ticket Fix.' Ingrasso is as
far as it's gotten publicly, but the word is that it's going all the way to
Saunders—and the Republicans are way too caught up in that to be worrying much about a sacrificial lamb to put up against you."

"Well, that is good news, I suppose," Charlie said. "Unless some high
school civics teacher wants to take me on as a class project. Then it could
be trouble. You'd have to be civic. Debate him. Pain in the ass."

"Right," Dunnsie said, having maneuvered Charlie to the business part
of the program. "Anything that isn't Weingarten could be trouble of
some sort. And so you should make a couple of moves now, solidify your
position. Neutralize the civics teachers and assorted winkie-dinks."

"How?" But Charlie knew how.

"Do a fifty-three in seven Easter week."

Fifty-three counties in seven days. Every county in the state. It had
been one of Charlie's innovations when he'd first run for Senate. He'd
done two of them that year—to start and to end the campaign. He'd
done another when he'd run for reelection in 1988. It was silly, exhausting, twenty-four-hour stuff. He did it in a camper, and slept aboard.

"Oh, God. Aren't we getting a little old for that, Dunnsie?" Charlie
said. "Anyway, I've got plans for Easter week." He and Nell had talked
about taking the kids skiing.

"Plans?" Pat asked. "What about your Easter schedule?"

Charlie winced at the thought of so many bunnies and jelly beans, so
much honey-glazed ham, the flat kiddie colors of the season: yellow and
violet. Worse, he had done a stupid thing, leading Nell on—she'd already made the reservation at Killington—when he'd known that he
would never be able to get away for Easter week. He remembered warning her in New Orleans: politicians can't avoid holidays; they are human
greeting cards, famously festive. They must commemorate Arbor Day,

Flag Day, National Secretaries' Week. There was no way to get around a big one like Easter; a senator must preside over at least a half-dozen egg rolls and treasure hunts, and attend the Passover seder at the West Des Pointe Jewish Center, and be very, very well-dressed and public on Easter Sunday. He wondered why he had chosen to delude himself, and Nell: wishful thinking came to mind. But the strength of the delusion was perplexing.

"Okay, okay," he said to Dunnsie. "We'll beef up the schedule. I'm not going to do a fifty-three in seven, but we'll spend a nice, solid, high-profile week. Let's have Mary start working on it. A lot of civics classes—although school's out that week, right? Rec programs then, and media. We can do it in the Winnebago, give the appearance of a fifty-three in seven. You happy now, Patrick?"

"Delighted," Dunn said.

"You promised," Nell said.

"I lied," he replied. It was midevening. The kids had gone off to watch television. They sat at the dining room table, a raw March wind rattling the row of French doors.

"The kids'll be disappointed," she said.

"I'll be disappointed," he said. "Hey, you want to bag the skiing and everyone come out with me?"

"No."

"Why not?"

"Because they desperately want to go skiing." And because going out to the Midwest, and spending a week in Charlie's world—introducing the kids to that—seemed far too big a jump, too official, a formal announcement of something or other. Nell hadn't thought her way that far into the relationship yet, in part because he hadn't asked it of her. He seemed perfectly happy, drifting along in Mondo Nello; as happy as she was, as everyone was—all of them shocked by their sudden good fortune, as if a whole section of a very complicated jigsaw puzzle had suddenly fallen into place. The absence of tension in the household was astonishing.

"We could sneak in a couple days of Colorado skiing for the kids," he said. "Have you ever done that?"

"No," she said, refusing to give ground, annoyed that he was pushing this. Why did he want to change things so soon?

"Well, it's—"

"No."

"No?" He was surprised by her firmness. "Why?"

"Because I don't want to have to 'do pretty' on a vacation, and I certainly don't want the kids to have to. I want to vacate."

He could understand that. He didn't want to "do pretty" either. He was stunned by the emotional resonance of her point of view. It had all sorts of dire implications—for him. And Nell didn't seem to care about his career at all. "Look, I'd love to vacate, too. But I can't—"

"Why not? You said your opponent is dropping out. So why can't you celebrate?"

"You never celebrate," he said, "until after the election. When the tide's moving your way, you press your advantage."

"And when the tide's moving against you?"

"You press harder. Nell, look: I've got to do this. I've been goofing off enough—"

"'Goofing off'? Is that what you call this?"

"No, and you know that," he said. "This is the closest I've come to—" But he was too angry with her to concede how happy he'd been. She was being unfair, picking at his words. She knew how he felt and was pretending she didn't.

And he realized something else, the same thing—he now knew—that Linc had seen: Nell was entirely unimpressed by public service. It meant nothing to her that he was a United States senator. That was, of course, part of the allure: she loved him, not what he did, not his power or his potential; by doing so, she had freed him from both. This was both refreshing—and galling. He was used to being admired, not loved.

He looked at her; she conceded nothing. She was wearing a forest-green pocket T-shirt and blue jeans; he was amazed how long it had taken him to realize what a wonderful body she had—as if her unpredictable looks and clothes, and her even more unpredictable mind, had steered him away from his usual, banal male perceptions. He was desperate to make her happy now, and angered by his desperation. Why couldn't she indulge him, just a little? He understood why she wouldn't come out and campaign with him—he would have to nudge her toward that gradually. But couldn't she be awed, just a little, by what he did?

"C'mon," he said. "Let's go upstairs and goof off with the kids."

She stared at him, briefly, before moving—understanding that the honeymoon had just ended and that now the serious decisions and adjustments and concessions of making a life together would begin. It had been a fabulous honeymoon, the best she'd ever had, and she needed to tell him that, somehow. She stood before he did, leaned over him, slid her hands down his chest and nuzzled his ear with her nose. She felt him loosen, and he turned to kiss her: perhaps the honeymoon wasn't quite over yet.

"Oh, guck," said Pamela, from the top of the stairs. "Guhross."

"Oh, Shamela," Nell said, extricating herself. "That is such a wonderful observation! You are so gifted. That is so excellent." It was a game they played: Nell's Manhattan Mommy impersonation. "Isn't she just so . . . special, Charlie?"

"Moth-errr," Pamela said. "Can't we all do something . . . challenging together? It's been hours since I was challenged."

"Some mathematics, perhaps?" Nell asked. "Is there something *advanced* I could help you with?"

"Perhaps an advanced play date?" Pamela said. "You can bring *him,* if you want."

"Do you think he's gifted or talented enough?" Nell asked, tousling Charlie's hair. "He works for the government, you know."

"He's gifted enough—for you." And Nell chased Pamela up the stairs as Charlie watched, bright-eyed and tremulous, bedazzled and besotted with them both.

*   *   *

He went back to Washington the next morning, stopped in the office and then went directly to the Armed Services subcommittee meeting on force readiness adjustments—one of his specialties, a meeting he would chair. It was a sparsely attended affair: no other Democrats, Mike Rotello of Florida representing the Republicans, an under- and an assistant secretary representing the Pentagon, but Charlie was happy in the details of the work.

At about twelve-fifteen, Mustafa came in—through the committee office door, behind the senators. He put his hand on Charlie's shoulder and whispered in his ear, "Donna says you better come down to the office immediately."

"Why?"

"I don't know. Something back home, I think."

Charlie called a ten-minute recess. His office was two floors below the Armed Services Committee suite—a matter of real convenience: he could pop out of committee, go back to his office, greet local firemen and return without missing very much. Now he rushed downstairs with Mustafa, whose construction boots squeaked along the marble corridors, and into his office—where the two Ds had gathered. They both looked up as he came in: glum squared. "What's wrong?" he asked.

"Proctor just called from D.P.," Donna said. "Muffler Man opened his show this morning by announcing a week-long radio poll—a People's Poll, he called it—asking listeners to vote on whether he should run for the Senate . . . against you."

Charlie smiled. "Have you voted yet?"

"I've been on the phone with Pat Dunn," Hilton said. "He's going to start calling around, make sure that none of our people—the teachers, the choicers, the greens—do anything resembling an organized phone response to this. We can't appear to take it seriously. If we seem to be working this thing, it gives him more credibility right out of the box."

"He's got credibility, whether we work it or not." Charlie was torn between disappointment that he'd actually have to work the campaign and an intense desire to have at Lee Butler, to get back at him.

"Dunnsie wants you to call him as soon as possible," Hilton said, staring at Donna, who gave him an I-told-you-so look.

Charlie sat down on the couch, stretched his legs, dialed Patsy Dunn himself. "Okay, if I put you on speaker, Pat?" he asked. "I've got Donna and Hilton here."

"Fine," Dunn said, his voice a constricted, electronic echo in the high-ceilinged room.

"I guess," Charlie began, "we can assume the results of the People's Poll in advance. Did anyone see this coming?"

"No," Dunn said. "Phone calls I've gotten in the past fifteen minutes, everyone thinks it's nuts. Hamblin from the *R-W* says they've got a poll coming—mostly on the governor's race, but they threw in a couple of questions about you—that says your favorables are down slightly, but still pretty damn good, high fifties."

"You get any calls from Hamblin?" Charlie asked Hilton.

"I've gotten eighteen press calls from D.P. in the past ten minutes, including Hamblin," Devereaux replied. "What do we say to them?"

"We sing the praises of democracy, of course," Charlie said. "We welcome the boy into the race, if he sees fit to make it."

"Mr. Dunn, it's Hilton," Devereaux said. "Has Butler been lighting us up in any way these past few months? I figured Mary would give us coverage if there'd been anything."

"I haven't listened to *every* minute, but no—he had some fun with the Arch Saunders Safe Driving School yesterday. He'll mention Charlie from time to time, when he goes on one of his isolationist or antiimmigrant tears, but there hasn't been anything sustained since the 'Carlito Loco' bits after Charlie announced he was voting for NAFTA."

"Is there anything new with the Arch Saunders Safe Driving School?" Charlie asked.

"Mary says the current thinking at the *R-W* is they may have overrun the story. No one's stepping forward to place the governor in the car—"

"Figures," Charlie said: with Saunders safe, the Republicans could concentrate on unseating him. "How do you think the GOPs respond to Muffler Boy?"

"Well, they won't be thrilled—he's torched them often enough," Pat said. "But if he's really coming after you, and putting money behind it, they probably won't be disappointed either. . . . Senator, we're gonna need some help, working through all this. Media, polling, office staff."

"We've got Roy Branson," Charlie said. Hilton rolled his eyes: Roy Branson ran an advertising agency in Des Pointe and devoted most of his energy to inflating the egos of the local automobile dealers and their families—he'd turned them all into television stars.

"We're gonna need more than Roy Branson," Pat said. "Even if Muffler Man hires himself to do his advertising, he's five times slicker than Roy. Charlie, listen: if Butler runs, we're in the twilight zone. He's gonna run clever, and unpredictable. We need to take this very seriously. I don't have to tell you that, right? Hilton, I think you should call the D-triple-C and find out if there's anyone out there who's had experience doing oddball rich guy candidates. . . . Charlie, we want to start thinking big-league handlers, Washington guys."

"I don't know about that, Dunnsie." Charlie said, with a pro forma stubbornness. He knew Pat was right, but the prospect of big-league handlers raised awful memories: it reminded him of the presidential campaign. "I don't want to start bringing in high-priced talent from outside the state. We've never done that. I don't want people to think we're taking this pissant seriously."

"Fair enough," Dunn said, conceding the nuance, but not the argument. "Hilton will be very discreet as he begins to check around. Right, Hilton?"

"Muffle's the word," Hilton said. He looked over at Charlie, who sat on the couch scratching his sideburn with his index finger. His eyes were calm, as always; but his chin was down, tucked into his chest. A race against Lee Butler might prove easier than running against Porter Wein-garten—amateurs usually found a way to screw up—but the campaign would require effort and preparation, and a level of interest that might be a greater commitment of energy than the boss was prepared to make. One thing was certain, Hilton thought: Muffler Boy would cause the sus-pension of Mondo Nello. The boss knew that, and hated the thought of it.

"Patsy," Charlie said, "fuck you for being right—we'll do a real fifty-three in seven Easter week, okay? I'll bring Mustafa out to drive the Win-nebago—I don't want that kid, Barry, doing it. Hell, I don't want Mustafa doing it either, but he knows how to handle a truck. You think we can pry him away from the church for a week, D?"

"I don't know if we can put him on the campaign if he's on the Sen-ate payroll." Donna warned, all business, as always.

"We've got to worry about that happy horseshit again now, don't we?" Charlie said wearily.

"Actually, he can take a vacation week," Donna said. "He can moon-light the campaign, get double pay."

"Boss, I'll take a vacation week that week, too," Hilton said. "And I don't need the extra pay. And neither does Moose."

Charlie looked up at Hilton, and nodded. "Feeling guilty?" he asked.

"Always," Devereaux replied.

DES POINTE

———

14

Just after lunch on a thick, draggy afternoon in late August—about a week before the first debate of Charlie Martin's reelection campaign—a freckled, prematurely mature campaign kid named Anne Foster bounded into Hilton Devereaux's office and announced breathlessly, "We've got traffic."

"Okay." Hilton pretended to be calm. That was part of his job now. He had, over the past few months in Des Pointe, made the transition from junior to senior. He was the unofficial chaperon and leader of the Campaign Kids—the Den Mother, they called him. He was, in fact, the most accessible authority figure around, the most senior Martin staff member living in one of the standard-issue suburban ranch houses the campaign had rented for those who had come to do battle against the Muffler Man. And so, Hilton was determined to set a tone of cool efficiency (as he imagined the boss would)—especially now, with the battle about to be joined for real. "How much traffic?"

"All three networks, all three markets—prime fringe," Foster said. "D.P. cablevision. The U's. We're checking radio buys now. Looks pretty heavy."

"Okay, good stuff, Annie," he said, picking up the phone with one hand, jotting down a call list with the other. "You want to make sure we've got some doughnuts and coffee and amphetamines for tomorrow morning. Advance it. Make sure we're taping all three. Talk to Sonnenfeld, make sure he has a response team ready to research and refute anything that comes up, although I'm sure he does. Now, you go do that"—he smiled—"and let me spread the word. Just kidding about the amphetamines, by the way."

He called Mustafa in the van, who told him that the candidate was still in the midst of pie and coffee with the Itowaska Women's Bowling

League. "When he gets out," Hilton said, "tell him Muffler Boy is going up—and have him call in."

"He was asking about Nell," Mustafa said. "What flight's she on from the Apple?"

Nell had gone home for a few days, her second escape to New York since coming west in July, and was due back at any moment. Everyone close to the candidate was happier when she was around—Charlie grew testy, and often distracted, without her. Hilton told Mustafa he hadn't heard yet from Nell. He was concerned about that, always a bit worried that Nell would decide not to come back. She hated the campaign, and the heavy lifting hadn't even begun yet. But she felt bereft in New York, without Charlie. This time was worse: Lucius had a deep summer cold, or something. There was, as always, the terrible fear that it would be "or something," but his blood levels were stable. In any case, she'd had to park the kids, now home from camp, with Cousin Grigorii, who was between divorces, in West Hampton. "This is torture, Hilly," she'd said cellularly, the sound of a sea breeze ruffling the phone. "The kids are fine, beachin'—but me, I'm suffering from guilt, a junkie getting a saltwater fix. You hear that?" She held the phone up so he could listen to the waves. "I have to leave that, and go to the airport, and come out there and play Tennille to the Captain? Jeez Louise. Anything new, Hilton? Is there Muffler movement?"

"No, still waiting," he'd said. But that had been in the morning. A humid, premonsoon sort of anticipation had been building for weeks. Muffler Man and Charlie were out in their respective minivans, wandering the prairies—Hilton imagined the campaign as a video game, with the two minivans gobbling cornstalks from different ends of the state, never quite coming into contact but getting closer all the time. He wondered what would happen when all the corn was gobbled and there was nothing left to eat but each other. He wouldn't have to wonder much longer.

The Martin campaign had rented a bankrupt insurance agency's office, in the parking lot wastelands just outside the high-rise cluster of downtown Des Pointe: Hilton wondered if campaign karma was always so bad because the headquarters were inevitably located in the ruins of failed businesses. The air was awful in such places; it smelled like laundry bags. There was bad food and tension. They were hard on the complexion.

Hilton walked through the warren of sordid cubicles, past the main campaign kid area, to Patsy Dunn's office. "We've got traffic," he announced.

"Well, it's about time," Patsy said. "Sonny know?"

"I've sent word." Sonny was Paul Sonnenfeld, the director of research and a quiet power in the campaign: he was the personal selection—and unofficial representative—of Morey Richardson, the political consultant Charlie had reluctantly agreed to hire. Sonnenfeld was young, in his midtwenties, and drop-dead smart; very much a hired gun, a loner, aloof from the pizza-and-diet-Coke headquarters culture. But present, always—which was more than could be said for the rather mysterious and reputedly brilliant consultant, who had yet to make a single appearance in the campaign headquarters, or out on the stump with Charlie.

Pat buzzed Sonny as Hilton deposited himself upon the spare, ratty Danish-modern couch, cotton erupting from a multitude of threadbare rents in the fabric. This, plus several metal folding chairs, was the extent of the furnishings in the campaign manager's office. On one wall was a huge map of the state; on another were a series of oversized calendars: August, September, October, November. "Ten weeks out." Pat nodded, with admiration. He'd begun to look his age, in all that bad campaign headquarters air; his eyes sagged and his mouth quivered slightly. "I never thought they'd wait *this* long. Their discipline's been scary."

"So, what's your thinking?" Hilton asked. Even though they'd spent two months in close quarters, Pat Dunn still didn't trust Hilton completely—for all the obvious reasons. Patsy wasn't a moralist, but he was a campaign-elegance freak. He liked simplicity; the fact that one of Hilton's defining parameters—one that lurked in every transaction— had to do with sexuality was several syllables past simple.

"Who knows what they do?" Pat said. "Classic is, they open positive. Bio spot. But everyone knows Muffler's bio. The big question is, they open ugly or clever? Ugly we can handle. Clever, who knows?"

The words were familiar as a novena. Patsy's mantra: "Clever, who knows?" Clever was so threatening, so unpredictable, that Hilton was three-quarters convinced that it was the direction Muffler Man was heading: elect me, and be entertained for six years. There was one factor, however, that mitigated against clever: Ronny Bigler, whom Muffler Man had brought in to run his campaign. Bigler was young, chubby, apple-cheeked, religious and lethal: *The Washington Post* had called him a "natural born-again killer." At a time when other campaign consultants had taken to memorizing passages from Sun Tzu, Bigler stayed with the tried and true—the Book of Revelation (although, like most zealots, his gloss was inconsistent). When asked what his campaign model was, he answered, "The Crusades."

Bigler gave Hilton hope, and a serious case of the creeps. N-BAK (as the campaign kids soon acronymized "natural born-again killer," pronouncing it "in back") had not had much success in campaigns outside the South, and he wasn't subtle enough to be truly clever (although his candidate certainly was). The possible internal volatility of a Butler-Bigler campaign was promising. Hilton found Ronny Bigler a distressingly familiar type: he was every overweight, small-town adolescent who had ever exorcised his uncertain sexuality by whaling on guys like Hilton. Bigler's presence raised the prospect that this campaign would be as awful—as lonely and frightening—as adolescence had been. Which was why, in a way, the worshipful attention and respect Hilton got from the campaign kids was so reassuring.

But still, it was lonely. There was Charlie, and there was Nell. But the former was too wrapped up in business to be much fun; and the latter was even more scared and uncertain than Hilton was. "Mighty nice people out here," she'd say to him ritually, an acknowledgment of the all-vanilla diet they had imposed on their toffee-raisin-crunch sensibilities.

"The nicest people in the world," Hilton would reply.

In fact, their nice-offs had little to do with disdain—both Nell and Hilton were amazed, and touched, by the benign solidity of the locals; but there was a need to let off steam, to relieve the strain of always having to be on their best behavior. "You know why it's such a relief to go home, Hil? Because I don't have to think twice every time I open my mouth," she sighed, after returning from her first R&R in New York. "It's like speaking a foreign language out here. My jaw hurts."

"You're doing great, hon," Hilton bolstered her and, in fact, she truly was—Nell had a natural grace, an ability to connect with people, particularly women, that worked well on the stump. He sensed she'd be even better now that the real show was about to begin.

Paul Sonnenfeld walked into Dunn's office, short and intense, all five o'clock shadow, dark eyebrows and powerful forearms—Sonny's only known diversion, apparently, was to pulverize the Stairmaster and free weights at the D.P. Athletic Club—as Patsy was getting off with Mary Proctor. "Battle stations, huh?" Sonnenfeld said. He had a distinctive upper midwestern accent, with pancaked *a*'s and assorted glottal strangulations, a sign of the violent upward mobility—his father had owned a small-town shoe store—that fed his intensity.

"Yup. We've got traffic," Devereaux explained. "You heard?"

Sonnenfeld nodded, taking a chair.

"The response operation is ready to roll?" Dunn asked, though he knew he didn't need to.

"You bet," Sonny said.

"You think the boss'll come to headquarters in the morning to watch?" Hilton asked.

"No," Dunnsie said. "You don't want the staff to see the boss wincing, or pissed, or . . . whatever. Watching your opponent's first ad is too personal to be shared." Dunn was quiet for a moment. "It's smart. Going up now," he said, thinking aloud. "You figure they're going to lay down some themes for the debate, prepare the folks, mess with our minds. . . . We been keeping track of Muffles? Any sign of—evolution?"

"No," Sonnenfeld said. "If there were, we'd know about it. He's still doing essentially the same thing. 'Warshington' this, Stanton that, 'Where's Charlie?' Actually, Butler's been in the doldrums lately, waitin' for a second act . . . it's been downhill since he hired Bigler, in fact."

The start of the campaign had been amazing. A Memorial Day weekend cross-state Bible study tour by motorcycle. Lee Butler hit the trail wearing an American flag helmet and a brown leather bombardier's jacket. He and his entourage would meet a local minister at each stop, read some Scripture, and lead a discussion. The discussions were brilliantly opaque, well beyond partisan politics: about the importance of community, friendship, marital devotion, humility, humor. The closest Muffler Boy got to politics was an occasional reference to the corruption of the "sixties generation," which had gained control of the nation's capital. Butler was a member of the *Brady Bunch* generation, an afterthought at the end of the baby boom, and he had a different set of resentments: he was sardonic, not inspirational—a reaction to the pompous self-regard of Charlie's contemporaries. And he had a nice feel for politics. That was clear from the very beginning, when the Muffler Man campaign roared into Fort Jeffords—a tsunami of decibels—and Bob Hamblin asked him why a candidate whose family business was quieting down cars would run such a noisy campaign.

"It's a joyful noise, Bob," Butler had said, flashing what journalists would inevitably call a "boyish" smile. "It's a clarion call. Time to unmuffle ourselves. There are serious issues at stake in this campaign . . . but you want to get the folks' attention, get 'em in the tent so we can start the meeting."

He'd gotten the folks' attention, all right. *The New York Times* had run a feature—subtly sarcastic, of course, but front page below the fold—titled BIBLE BIKER TAKES ON FAVORITE SON. The national networks had each sent motorcyle-riding correspondents to spend a day on the tour. The *Register-World* ran a daily box: "Today's Butler Campaign Scripture," so that people could keep up with the Bible study sessions. The Bible Biking also proved a hit in the permanent parastudent community at University City, where the Butler campaign was seen as a kind of performance art, a satiric commentary on the banality of modern politics. A satiric fan club had been formed: the Ultimate Muffler Man Motorcycle Marauders. Black *UMMMM . . . ?* T-shirts had been printed. Calvin, whose sensibility tracked with that of the UMMMMers, showed up at Oak Street wearing one of them.

"You don't want to go too far with that," Edsy warned him, sipping sun tea out on the screen porch.

"It's a joke," Calvin said.

"Yeah, but—you haven't been through one of your dad's elections before: it's kind of serious, too. Right, Buzzy?"

"Squares won't get it," Buzz agreed.

"Dad's not square," Cal said.

"He's a . . . a missionary—to the squares," Buzz said, chuckling at his own creativity. "Son, you'd best trust Edsy on this one. Stow the shirt until this thing is over."

For Pat Dunn, the most impressive aspect of the motorcycle gambit was that Butler ended it before it grew stale. Or had that been Bigler's call? Bigler had come aboard in June, after which the candidate settled into fairly traditional minivan tracking, with a stump speech that reflected—lightly, calmly, without much heat—the conservative and populist themes that Butler had hammered on his radio show.

It was an odd campaign. A great curtain raiser, which had carried the Muffler Man into contention—indeed, slightly ahead in the horse race polls—but in a way that had little apparent impact on Charlie's standing with the voters. People still liked their senator. His popularity and trust numbers remained unaffected by the Bible Biking, which led Pat Dunn to suspect that the horse race numbers were a temporary phenomenon: the folks weren't sour on Charlie, they were intrigued by the other guy. And the senator continued about his business, the crowds no smaller or less enthusiastic than they'd ever been (although there were some modifications: Dunnsie made sure that Charlie hit traditional Wednesday night Bible study sessions in the home churches of every minister Lee Butler had showcased).

A second Bible Biking tour, from north to south across the state in July, proved less successful than the first—the most memorable moment coming when an enterprising state trooper pulled the entire Muffler Man entourage off the road on I-43 and ticketed them for speeding. Muffles apologized profusely, claiming they were late to a Fort Jeffords prayer meeting. The next day's *R-W* headline was: "Joyful Noise, Unlawful Speed."

"You're right, Paul. He hasn't had a second act," Hilton said, getting up, leaving Dunnsie's office. "Until now. Does he come after us, or what?"

"We'll see tomorrow," Patsy replied calmly. The first televised advertisements would air just before the early morning news, no doubt, and despite Dunn's "ugly or clever" mantra, which was a tactic to keep the troops prepared for any eventuality, he assumed there was only one direction that Ronny Bigler would take this campaign now: ugly. Charlie Martin was just too popular a politician. He would have to be taken down.

But Pat wasn't sure how. This was a new world, a campaign unlike any he'd ever experienced. Who'd have thought motorcycles would work? They were noisy and dangerous; they scared moms and senior citizens. But cycles muffled by Bibles—a brilliant move. The Reverent Outlaw— perfect for what Lee Butler was hoping to convey. And now the campaign was moving into territory Dunn truly didn't understand: media advertising, buys, points, traffic. He'd had the concept of "points" explained to him three different times, and he still couldn't quite remember what a ratings point was—was it the number of television sets, or the percentage of sets, turned on?

"Paul, you want to stick around while I call Morey?" Pat couldn't bear to call Sonnenfeld "Sonny," the way everyone else did: it made him seem even more of a codger. He phoned Morey Richardson's office in Washington. The secretary said, "One moment, I'll patch you through."

That was another thing: Morey's secretary always said, "I'll patch you through." What did that mean?

"Hell-ooo-ooh," Morey said.

"Hi, Morey, it's Pat Dunn. I've got you on speaker. Paul is here, too." "Yes?"

"We've got traffic."

"Paul, you'll have it covered?"

"Yes."

"And, Paul, you've checked with Sarah—we have scripts for response subpaths A, B and C?"

"Yup," said Paul. Dunn had no idea what they were talking about.

"And you know the rules," Morey said. "Research goes to candidate only. Call me after we see what they put up. Oooohkay, g'bye."

"Good-bye?" Dunn asked.

"I'm in the middle of dinner," Morey said.

"Isn't it early for that?"

"Not in Marseilles."

"You're in Marseilles?"

"At Luis Nicole's—best fish in the city. You should try it sometime, Pat. Buh-bye."

Even though Morey Richardson had been Pat Dunn's idea, the old man still wasn't sure it was the right one. You had to be careful when hiring consultants for Charlie Martin: he had a reputation, among the cognoscenti, of being a terrible client—a reputation well-earned during the presidential campaign. Morey was a genius, of course: all these media guys were lightning fast and inscrutable and informal and militantly unique—Charlie once told Patsy that if he ever found a media consultant who moved at the speed of sound rather than the speed of light, he'd hire him in a minute. But he didn't really mean that. In a close contest, speed was huge. Morey's real selling point, as far as Dunn was concerned, was that he'd made a specialty—indeed, a study—of beating oddball dilettante candidates.

The genius had come to Des Pointe exactly once, to Oak Street, to sell himself in May, as the word began to spread that Muffler Man had hired Ronny Bigler (and after Dunnsie—in one of the more dramatic moments of his career—literally got down on his knees before the candidate, begging him to at least consider taking on outside help). Richardson was wearing a blue blazer, a wine-red vest over a tattersall shirt with a navy polka-dot cravat, and blue jeans and low-heeled black leather boots with zippers. He was soft, grayish-pink, edgeless, with thinning black hair porcupined up and straight back; his hands shook slightly as he spoke. He was accompanied only by his wife, Louise—who was reassuringly unflashy and academic, with graying hair and wire-rimmed eyeglasses. She carried his charts.

"My first thought," Morey Richardson said to Charlie, who was sitting in Buzz's La-Z-Boy, "was fuck you. Life is too short for dingbats. I don't do dingbats. Anyone who refuses to do market research is a dingbat. You said no polling. Well, okay. We don't need to poll. We can test."

"No testing either," Charlie said. "We do this straight up, the way I've always done—the one time I didn't was the presidential campaign, and I'll never do that again."

"Do we dare, Lou?" Morey Richardson asked, turning to his wife—who almost responded. Morey plunged ahead, his voice thin, nearly falsetto, nasal, soft. "Well, I suppose . . . Senator, if it weren't for the fact that you are a certifiable, oops, excuse my Freud, certified . . . American hero—I wouldn't even consider this. But you are a hero . . . and this country can not afford to lose your valuable public service. We have too few veterans in the Congress now—"

"Did you serve?" Charlie asked.

"Ulcers," Richardson confessed, flinching at the thought. "A very severe reflux situation. . . . Anyhoo—Louise?"

Louise stood next to an easel and put up a flash card: RESPECT.

"That is what this campaign is all about," Richardson said. "That is what the citizens of this state feel toward you."

Louise put up a second flash card, which also said: RESPECT.

"That is how we will treat the public in this campaign. We will show them the things you've done for them. The biotech lab at the Agricultural College, the vet centers, the highways and water treatment facilities, the defense contracts that keep Singer Rapids singing, so to speak. . . . And this is how we will regard our opponent—"

Louise put up a third flash card, which said: RESPECT.

"We will regard him from a distance and from a very great height, as we might assay a buzzing insect, an inconsequential thing. We will not get down in the gutter with him. He sells noise control devices. You are an American hero!"

"And how much does all this respect cost?" Charlie asked, scowling.

"My standard rate is ten thousand dollars a month plus thirty percent of the buy," Richardson said. "But since you are an American hero, it'll be ten thousand dollars a month and thirty percent of the buy. . . . A little humor there."

"Get out of my house," Charlie said.

Richardson blanched.

"A little humor there." Charlie smiled. "Tell me about candidates like Lee Butler. And Louise, please sit down—no more RESPECT signs, I get the drift. . . . And Morey, please stop the American hero horseshit—and stop bullshitting me. I mean, does that sort of yak butter actually work with my colleagues?"

"You'd be amazed," Morey Richardson said, in a completely different sort of voice—still very soft, but more insistent, faster, with a more pro-nounced New York accent. "Ohhh-kayyy. You want to know the truth—really?—I'll tell it to you: I'm a lot more interested in Lee Butler than I am in you. You're plain vanilla. Butler is cutting-edge—we're seeing more and more of these guys, rich guys, celebrities, freaky-deakies run-ning for office. And winning. Butler is a new kind of hybrid freaky-deaky: a rich guy who is also a media celebrity—the radio talk show plus the family fortune: wow! You bring that combo into a state with big markets and . . . Eureka! Which is not to say you won't win. You'll win. He'll fuck up. But it'll be interesting to see how he fucks up. And whether we can find some way to induce him to fuck up. And it'll be interesting to see how these heartland folks respond to him—which is why I will be doing market research on this campaign. I was gonna do it without telling you—for my own purposes, on my own time, with my own money. But you want no bullshit, you get no bullshit. With me, Senator Martin, you get whatever you want—if you ask for it, specifically."

"What else do I need to know? Specifically."

"Only two deal-breaker slots in the campaign: press secretary and re-search director. You've got Devereaux—he's good, I know. So that's okay. I'll compromise there. The fellow I have in mind for research director is a graduate of Carlton College—a midwesterner, I figured you'd appreci-ate that. His name is Paul Sonnenfeld. He's paid seventy-five hundred dollars per month. He'll need six assistants—two to interface with your Senate staff, three on oppo, one on you. You can hire them and pay them whatever, but he has to approve."

"I'm not interested in opposition research," Charlie said.

"Then you are out of your skull," Richardson said. "Chances are, you don't need it. Chances are, he self-destructs and you breeze. But this is a guy who has been spending two hours in public making a fool of himself every day for the past year and a half. You're nuts if you don't catalog what he says. You're also nuts if you don't check out his business prac-tices. You want to know how we take down rich guys? We check out their business practices. You saw what I did in Massachusetts? The Golden GOP who ran for governor? He had a supplier who laid off thirty em-ployees in Framingham and took his business to Thailand. Ka-blam. Ratatatat. *Au revoir.*" He sang the *au revoir:* Ohhhhvwraa-ah.

"I don't know about this," Charlie said.

"That's right, you don't," Morey said. "And you won't. Nor will anyone else. In my campaigns, research stands alone. We don't share findings. You don't know unless we tell you."

"Why not?"

"Because you don't need to." Morey said. "You perform. You do your thing."

"I don't know. . . ." Charlie was appalled by this man.

"Yes you do," Morey Richardson said. "You may be many things, Senator, but you're not a virgin. Louise, let's fold it up. Senator, this is extremely late in the game. I make my campaign commitments a year in advance, but this is a special case. Call if you want to do business. . . ."

Charlie didn't. Until Butler launched with his motorcycle Bible tour and climbed the polls. And then, in late June—with Nell about to arrive in Des Pointe, and with Pat Dunn dialing and handing him the phone—he reluctantly asked Morey Richardson to take on the campaign.

"Smart boy," Richardson said, patched in from Bordeaux. "My guess: the Bible Biker bit was Butler, not Bigler. Bigler's too mean to be that creative. He'll be jealous now, Ronny. Work overtime to prove his stuff to the candidate—which means there's a good chance he'll overreact. This is going to be even better than I thought."

* * *

"You've got mail!" Nell said, unpacking at Oak Street, on the evening before Butler's first ads would appear. Charlie was stretched on the bed, making his way through several folders FedExed from Donna—line-item analyses of the appropriations bills the Senate would vote that fall. He looked up and saw Nell, in a white silk blouse and fitted blue skirt, waving a red envelope. He smiled and exhaled: as usual, his central nervous system reaction to her presence was joy.

"You're back!"

"You're surprised?" she said. "I like that."

"Who's the mail from?"

Robin. It was a single sentence, written in red crayon on lavender drawing paper: "Why can't we come see you?"

Charlie felt his chest go warm, his eyes get watery. Nell saw his reaction and sat down on the side of the bed, her hand on his knee. "You think it's time?" she asked.

"The state fair's a lot of fun for kids," he said hopefully. He'd been keeping up a correspondence with the children, especially earlier in the summer, when they were away at camp. He'd been shameless about it, surreptitiously sending them CARE packages filled with junk food. The bribery had even worked on Pamela, who had signed one letter "I MISS YOU" and drawn a little heart. And added, "P.S. Next time please, please, please send Cool Ranch Doritos!"

"I'm not talking about—" Nell started, then stopped, staring at him, tense and quiet, sucking in her lips, then exhaling. "About the kids. Well, in a way—of course . . ."

"Nell? What *are* you talking about?"

"Chuck you, Farley!" She began to laugh. "I quit." She flopped back on the bed. He sat up. "I can't fight both you and them," she said, staring at the ceiling.

"What do you mean?" he said with a half smile.

"You asshole! You reprobate!" She was back up. "You know exactly what I mean. You want me to say it? All right! Lucius and I began our divorce proceedings last week."

"About time," Charlie said, shaking his head. "You mean you *weren't* divorced? You always described him as you ex-husband."

"SO WHAT!" She reached for a pillow and began pummeling him with it. "Don't you understand anything? I'm asking you to marry me, you nitwit! That's what the kids want. That's why I went home."

"Marry . . . *you?*" Charlie replied, torturing her. Nell flopped on her stomach and covered her head with the pillow. Charlie reached over gently and pulled the pillow away, moved her left arm down so that he could snuggle next to her ear. "In a heartbeat," he said. "I've never wanted anything—anything—more in my life. I want to have your babies."

And she began to laugh again, and then to cry. "You want to have my babies? You're too old, buster . . . you know that, right? Our few remaining eggs are hard-boiled."

He pulled back, and looked at her, holding her by the shoulders. The tears had left her eyes opalescent. "I love your old eggs," he said, pulling her close, embarrassed now, because he realized that salt water was leaking horizontally out his own crow's feet. "And I love all the other things you bring to the table."

"You know," she said, "Every time I hear that expression about bringing things to tables, I think: *La plume de ma tante . . . est sur la table de mon oncle.*" He began to laugh and she sighed, "They had such idiot songs when we were growing up."

"It was the *bureau de mon oncle,*" he said, laughing harder now. "The song had nothing to do with tables."

"How do you know?" she said. "You don't speak French."

"But I do speak"—he paused for dramatic effect—"medleys!"

"Oh, no! Oh, no!" she said, doubling over, holding her belly. "Of course! How awful! Buzz's French medley! He couldn't resist: he played the accordion. Had to be, what? "La Plume de Ma Tante," the love song from *Moulin Rouge* and . . . and . . ."

"It's so easy," Charlie said, plopping his head in her lap.

" 'The Singing Nun'?" she said, and he gave her a thumbs-up. "If I do marry you, Charlie"—she slowed down, twirled his hair with her fingers—"you think there's some way we can get Buzz to stop—"

"In the name of love?"

"Help," she said, then saw him gearing up for the Beatles lyric. "Don't! Stop!"

"Don't . . . stop?" he said, pulling her down, feigning a shudder as her hair brushed his cheek. "Don't stop." He laughed. "Don't stop. Don't stop. . . ."

*   *   *

Annie Foster knocked on Hilton's bedroom door at four-thirty the next morning. They drove the five miles from West Des Pointe to headquarters silently, in the dark, the all-news radio station early-morning pristine—health news, sports scores, weather: hot.

The lights were on in the campaign headquarters, a row of cars—kid cars, Ford Escorts and Hondas—in the parking lot. And Hilton found himself moved by the sight of all of them, all the campaign kids, plus Sonny and Dunnsie, Mary Proctor and Mustafa, everyone involved in the campaign but the candidate himself—all of them there, and ready to get to work, the smell of fresh coffee perking, three televisions up and running in three separate corners of the room, each with a VCR attached and taping.

At 4:57 A.M. on NBC, and then at 4:58:30 on ABC and CBS, the screen went dark and the words—"The Friends of Charlie Martin"—appeared and then four faces, mug shots in a row. Hilton picked out several of the faces immediately—Stanton, Sly Parkinson . . . Lincoln Rathburn? He couldn't quite get the fourth. And now Jack Stanton's face was blown out to fill the screen—and a picture of Stanton and Charlie Martin shaking hands, Stanton smiling stupidly, Charlie sheepishly . . . and an announcer, a man's voice, deep and lush and countrified: "What's . . . so . . . darned . . . funny?" The photo began to shatter from jackhammer blows. "Higher taxes. A crime bill that doesn't fight crime. A trade bill that sends jobs to Mexico. Homosexuals in the armed forces. A blood tide of abortions. A government run by shadowy Hollywood executives, poisoning your children's minds . . .

"Jack Stanton's Washington . . . Charlie Martin's playground. A new generation of leadership—or the de-generation of America?"

And now bright color film of Lee and Joan Butler, and their two little boys, in blue blazers with open-collared candy-striped shirts (all four of them), standing in front of an American flag whipping, the camera moving along the family row up to the candidate, music rising, Butler turning, smiling at the camera, brushing his blond hair out of his eyes—"Hi, I'm Lee Butler. And I'm running for Senate . . . because it's time. It's time to make America—America again!"

And, gone. Replaced by ads for shower and tile detergent, cat food, milk. The headquarters erupted, nervous laughter and chatter. Hilton's cell phone was ringing. The candidate.

"Viva degeneration!" Charlie said. "Whatcha think?"

"Busy. I think he's trying to do too much," Hilton said.

"*He* looks good," Charlie replied. "Nell says he's grown from Troy Donahue to *Barefoot in the Park*–vintage Redford."

"She got in all right?"

"Yeah," Charlie said, barely controlling his urge to give Hilton the news. This wasn't the moment. "She's just thrilled to be back."

"So it's Stanton, Parkinson, Rathburn . . . Who's the fourth guy?"

"Oskar Millar."

"Why on earth?"

"He's rich. Muffler Boy is for capitalism but against capitalists. Or something." Hilton could see Paul Sonnenfeld on his cell phone—with Morey Richardson, no doubt. And Patsy Dunn with Mary Proctor, watching the spot replayed again and again, on the campaign VCRs.

"So what do you think?" Charlie asked Hilton.

"Relieved. They're gonna dredge up Parkinson? They're gonna do the Trilateral Commission stuff with Rathburn? And Stanton? Folks know that you've had your differences with him. It just seems lockstep, right-wing dumb. And confusing. Too many faces, images. It's impatient. What do you think?"

"R-E-S-P-E-C-T. Find out what it means to me," Charlie sang. "Morey was right. We ignore this shit. Run the spots we've got about the good stuff we've done. See ya, Hil. Miss Nelly and I are heading west, to the Bass County fair—if Mustafa's still over there, send him here."

Mustafa was gone. Hilton went over to Dunn and Proctor; Sonnenfeld joined them. "What does Morey—" Hilton began.

"Hey, guys," Annie Foster shouted. "Quiet down. We've got more."

And there, on all three networks, right after the local morning news and just before the network feeds, was a second Muffler Man ad. But different, softer this time. It opened with the original Muffler Man, the grandfather, in his straw hat, dandling a baby—who was Lee Butler, obviously—on his knee in smudgy black and white. Nice, slow, gently nostalgic piano music. Segue to more home movies, watery Kodacolor now. Lee Butler dressed as a little cowboy, dressed in a powder-blue tuxedo for his prom (with a *Brady Bunch* hairstyle—and with his high school sweetheart, Joan Emmons, his wife-to-be); segue to more recent videotape, Butler in the radio studio—the Muffler Man show—leaning back in his chair, laughing with a listener, then walking along a town square with his wife and kids, then sitting alone on a hilltop in the countryside, wearing jeans and a short-sleeved madras shirt . . . reading the Bible. And no words throughout. Leisurely, downright midwestern cutting between images. And finally, on a black slate: ISN'T IT TIME? [Fade] TO MAKE OUR FRIEND . . . [Fade] . . . OUR SENATOR? And back to Butler, looking up from the Bible, pushing his hair out of his eyes yet again and in that confident yet casual, very *professional* voice: "I'm Lee Butler. We've known each other a long time. Your support has meant the world to our family business, and now it's time to give something back. I want to help give you the country you deserve. Let's make America . . . America again."

The Martin headquarters was silent. This was a very effective ad, unexceptionable . . . except for the Bible part, which would have been laughable if most people in the room—virulent secular humanists all—weren't afraid that it might sell.

"What's the music?" Mary Proctor asked. "It's on the tip of my tongue."

"It's from a movie. It ran over the credits, I remember the sound of an old movie projector—a clicking sound. What was it?" Hilton said, then snapped his fingers. "Butch Cassidy. It was the incidental music, when they ran the old sepia-toned movies during the opening credits . . . or something very close to it. Jeez, Nell's right: they're running him as Redford."

"Paul?" Dunnsie grabbed Sonnenfeld by the forearm, as he was heading back to his office. It was an awkward move. "Do you know what country, what fucking time zone, our friend Mr. Richardson is in today? Is there some way we can reach him that doesn't involve a 'patch'?"

Sonnenfeld, wearing a plain white crewneck T-shirt—as always—with an effusion of dark chest hair curling over the collar, detached his arm from Patsy's grasp. Hilton had seen Pat Dunn angry on occasion, but this was something worse than anger: it was fear.

"You call Morey and tell him the senator would like to see him at Oak Street as soon as possible," Dunn said.

"I'll have to tell him why," Sonnenfeld said, in a way that made it clear that he considered Morey Richardson, not Charlie Martin, his boss in this campaign. But, Hilton thought, hadn't that always been implicit? Still, it was disappointing: a campaign needed to be cultlike, single-minded. Paul Sonnenfeld had divided loyalties.

"Because we need to game-plan how to respond to this," Mary Proctor jumped in. Hilton had learned that beneath her benign, midwestern butterfly-framed eyeglasses, there was an East Coast temper. "For ten thousand dollars a month, we rate something more hands-on than Marseilles."

"I'm sure that Morey will be happy to meet . . . with the senator," Sonnenfeld said.

"What the hell does that mean?" Mary put her hands on her hips.

"Response involves research," Sonnenfeld said evenly. "Research isn't shared with staff."

"Paul, you're a good kid. Smart as a whip. Hardworking," Dunn said, trying to cool things down. "But I want you to understand: this is Charlie Martin's campaign. Research will be 'shared' with who the fuck he wants to share it with."

"Of course, Mr. Dunn," Sonnenfeld agreed. "If, after meeting with Mr. Richardson, the senator wants to share our data with you . . . or you," he said, nodding to Mary and then to Hilton, "that's his decision. But there are sensitive areas here . . . areas that impact on—"

Pat and Mary looked at Hilton. Sonnenfeld saw that all of them understood. "It's standard operating procedure," he said. "Really."

*　*　*

"So, why Oskar?" Charlie asked, sipping a diet Coke in the Oak Street den—it was midmorning, which was usually respite and phone time between breakfast and lunch stumpings. The senator sat, jacket off, tie loosened, in Buzz's La-Z-Boy. Morey Richardson—shocking in a canary-yellow knit golf shirt, which bulged gently over his stomach—had pulled a dining room chair adjacent to him. Louise Richardson and Paul Sonnenfeld sat on the couch. The senator was there alone, as promised. Nell was off with Edsy, shopping.

"Preemptive." Richardson yawned, his smooth skin more gray than pink this day. "Jet lag," he explained. "Sorry."

" 'Preemptive'?" Charlie asked.

"Paulie," Richardson said. He had asked for, and received, a mug of boiled water and a slice of lemon. He dropped several pills and a package of NutraSweet into it, and stirred. Then he sipped it, gingerly—hands trembling slightly—and allowed his aide to take over the meeting.

"Senator," Sonnenfeld began, "our guess is that Bigler assumes the thrust of our research, and is trying to preempt it. Muffler Man Stores has two clear vulnerabilities—one is that franchisees are under no obligation to provide employment benefits to their workers. The stores controlled by Lee Butler and other Butler family members all give their employees reasonably generous benefit packages—although Uncle Bill Maloney's three stores in the eastern part of the state just added health benefits since the campaign began. Not a coincidence, I'd imagine. But some of the other franchisees give their employees nothing. Zip. And unlike McDonald's or any of the other major franchising networks, MMS doesn't write employment standards into its contracts with franchisees . . ."

"MMS?" Charlie asked.

"Muffler Man Stores," Sonnenfeld said.

"So?"

"So we can go after him on the way Muffler Man treats employees."

"Sounds once-removed," Charlie said.

"It wouldn't when we got done with it—we have six cases of workers injured on the job whose comp claims were challenged by Muffler Man franchisees," Morey said. "We've got a woman named Imogene Alvarez who can cry about her husband's mashed—uh, hand . . . at the drop of a hat." Richardson was not subtle. Charlie understood the detail had been added for dramatic effect. "But that's not all. Tell him, Paul—tell him where the mufflers are made. . . ."

"Monterey," Paul said.

"That's not Monterey, California, Senator," Richardson said with an infantile giggle. "So your opponent doesn't require that his franchisees provide health care, but he does require that they buy Mexican mufflers."

"The son . . . of . . . a . . . bitch. After the shit he gave me on NAFTA!"

Charlie said. "That's gr—" And then he remembered. "But what does this have to do with Oskar?"

But he knew.

"Oskar owns Monterey," Morey said, interlacing the tips of his fingers to control his jitters, which were a slight breeze across a pond. "Not literally, of course. I don't even know if he specifically has anything in Monterey. But he's holding significant positions in a lot of companies with major third-world operations. Sweatshops, in other words. Could I ask you something, Senator?"

Charlie nodded, feeling sick.

"Do you have any idea where he's invested your money over the years?"

"Not South Africa," Charlie said, with stubborn pride. "Nothing environmentally damaging. Nothing in defense—no conflicts of interest. That was part of the deal."

Morey laughed, ran a shaky hand through his hair. His halting tics, so much at variance with his intellectual certainty, were beginning to annoy Charlie. "That leaves a multitude of possibilities, doesn't it? And Bigler doesn't mess around. He can go the sweatshop labor route on you . . . or the vote-selling route."

"Vote selling? Get out of here."

"Well, let me put it this way. Has Oskar Millar ever asked you to vote a certain way?"

"Yeah, and I usually tell him to go fuck himself."

"But not always."

Charlie shrugged and Morey continued. "Oskar Millar was the finance chairman of your presidential campaign? And a significant packager of contributions for your other campaigns? Have you ever voted against any of his interests?"

"I'm sure I have." Charlie's tone betrayed his uncertainty. "But I'd have to check."

"We've checked," Morey said. "And apparently, you didn't tell him to go fuck himself as often as you think."

Charlie shivered slightly, imperceptively. "Oh, Christ, Morey, if I'd voted the way Oskar really wanted, I'd've had to change parties."

"NTP," Morey said. "Not the point. All you need is a couple dozen votes where the Big O benefits. You could do that in your sleep. In fact, you did. Last year's defense appropriations act, for example. There were contracts in there worth $632 million to various Millar operations."

"And every one of those contracts was awarded strictly according to price and merit," Charlie replied huffily.

"Uh huh." Morey leaned back, looked at the ceiling dramatically. "That means an awful, awful lot, Senator."

Charlie wanted to deck him, but he knew Richardson was right. "So that neutralizes our Mexican stuff?" he asked. "We don't go with it?"

"Oh, no," Morey said. "We'll go with it, if you say okay. The ads are made. Pretty creative, too, in a crude sort of way: Muffler Man's Mexican Hat Dance. We reference his old TV ads, use a clip of him ranting about NAFTA—then we stifle him with one of his red scarfs. We can have a screening after . . . but you're right, the Millar material does neutralize the thrust of our efforts. You know, I was flattered by their 'Friends of' bit: normally, you don't tip your hand in a campaign that way—giving us a preview of their entire first volley. But Bigler assumed we'd go after the business stuff, and he figured there was no harm in letting us know he was prepared. An act of pride, I'd say. He made that ad to impress *me*. He'll roll the Millar ads out—when, Paul? Next few days, I'd guess. Before the first debate certainly. That way, it won't seem a response to our ads, even if we go up tomorrow—which I'd recommend very strongly, by the way. In fact, this whole Bigler campaign is a tremendous show of respect: they know how devastating our stuff is. They're firing back with all barrels—the Stanton spot was the weakest, of course. The Rathburn spot, either you buy the International Commie Jewish Banker conspiracy stuff or you don't. Parkinson, we figure they go with the wife's line—"

"The wife's line?" Charlie asked. He felt light-headed. Tiny things, things he'd discounted or not worried about or not even noticed, were becoming huge.

"You remember, 'Charlie Martin has some strange ideas about the meaning of friendship'—don't you?" Morey said.

"I missed that," Charlie said, "in all the fun."

"Well, she said it. What we're wondering is whether Ronny just goes with the line, or if he gets her to say it live."

"Jesus," Charlie said. "I don't think Maggie would ever—"

"Doesn't make a difference, really," Richardson said. "Senator, you look surprised. Please don't tell me you're surprised. You're not going to make me utter the 'Politics ain't beanbag' line, are you? You knew this was coming."

"It feels different when it actually comes," Charlie said quietly, sitting up in the La-Z-boy, which was an effort, but he felt the need to push back against the force of the assault.

"Yeah, well." Morey made himself sound bored. "Could I have a little more hot water?" Charlie began to get up. "No, Louise—dear: you do it." Morey smiled again at Charlie, as Louise took action. "This isn't Stephanie Fetchit, Senator," he said, noticing Charlie's look. "Lou and I have a division of labor. I take out the garbage. . . . Anyway, where were we? Oh, right. You were being upset. But then, you knew we were going to check out Muffler Man's business practices. You don't think Bigler assumed the same thing? And Oskar's a slam-dunk for them. But . . . I understand: you feel as if the furniture's been rearranged."

"Uh-huh," Charlie grunted. He had hired Richardson because he assumed he'd have to go negative against Butler sooner or later, but the idea of actually doing it—of putting one of those raw, ugly advertisements on the air with his name attached to it—had always been blissfully theoretical. He'd never gone negative in a campaign before. Oh, there had been generic stuff about the "do-nothing" Republicans, but never anything personal, individual, about an opponent. He had seen respected colleagues get down and dirty, and he'd wondered how it would feel if one of his campaigns ever came to that. And now he knew: it felt perverse, amoral, crude.

"We can talk about your feelings, if you like," Morey said. "I can go into therapist mode. It's your nickel. If, however, you want to do business, vee can perhaps to beegin, yah? Can I walk you through the rest of the campaign?"

Charlie grunted defeat. "Let's see," Richardson said. "Paul: numbers?"

"Same as ever. Fave, fifty-eight. Honest, eighty-six. Hardworking, fifty-two. Cares about people like me, seventy-four."

"You know those numbers, right, Senator?" Morey said. "Your favorables. Very impressive. By the way, notice how the hardworking has slipped the last six months? The Arabella Factor. We'll talk about that later. But anyway, the numbers: if you're Ronny Bigler and you're facing a candidate with numbers like that, what do you do?"

"What your candidate allows you to do?" Charlie said, still stubborn about conceding that he was now, irretrievably, in another part of the political jungle.

Morey snorted. "If you're Ronny Bigler, you don't do the campaign if your candidate tells you what you're 'allowed' to do. . . . Senator, I think you know the answer to my question. In a situation of this sort, you've got to undermine your opponent's favorables. If you're Bigler, you've got to take Charlie Martin down, if he won't drop of his own accumulated baggage. Even if your candidate looks like Jesus Christ's younger brother—although the kid does have something of a sharp radio tongue, which is what that gooey sweetness-and-light positive bio spot is working to overcome."

Charlie was barely listening. He was kicking himself about Oskar.

"In a slime-off," Richardson was saying, "the theory is, the candidate with the greater reservoir of goodwill wins—you've got twenty years of service, of hugs and defense contracts and charity auctions here. They know you, sort of. That's why Butler's positive ads are so clever: they make him an incumbent, too. They make the mud you throw at him an attack on a beloved local figure: the original Muffler Man, his grandfather. Dat's not such a funny noise. But our response will be effective—at least *we* think it will be . . . at least, against the 'friends of' gambit."

"And the 'friends of' is just the beginning," Charlie said.

"That's what a gambit is: a first move," Morey said—mournfully, it seemed. "One doesn't only have friends. One has a staff. One has family."

"Family, huh?" Charlie said dully.

"Oh yes," Richardson said. "And a very low 'family' number. This hasn't been a very common polling question—at least, it wasn't until Jack Stanton came along. Local polls here, like the *R-W*, never asked it. So I had to go into the field. . . ."

"You went into the field?"

"Sue me," Morey said. "You want the result?"

"No."

"Paul?"

" 'Do you believe Senator Martin has a lifestyle similar to yours?' Eighteen percent, yes," Paul said.

"Fuck you," Charlie said.

"Tell him Butler's."

"Fifty-three."

"The fact that he's rich brings it down significantly."

"So he's going to—" Charlie began.

"Well, he's going to build toward it, whatever 'it' turns out to be. . . . He's got so many options. It'll have to be subtle. When he attacks you personally, he loses altitude, too. Usually, in these cases, they go through third parties."

Charlie understood that: independent, fly-by-night groups, not associated with the campaign—or leaks to the media. "What do you mean, 'so many options'?"

"Well, let's do a quick inventory," Morey said. "Your life, Senator, is practically an 'alternative lifestyles' theme park. Hell, even your father has an out-of-wedlock relationship. Your oldest adviser—your designated adult—grew up in a whorehouse and was the last master of a notorious political machine. Thank God, Oskar took care of Schollwengen or we'd have date rape—or whatever that was—to deal with, on top of everything else."

"Oskar took care of Schollwengen?" Charlie asked.

"Bought the old man a PharmLand franchise. Now, *there's* a franchisee who takes care of his workers, by the way."

Charlie looked at Morey; he failed to detect even the slightest flicker of empathy from his hired gun. This was his house, his den, Buzz's La-Z-Boy—and someone else's life. The room was vibrating with all the various ugly possibilities.

"Think of it this way, Senator," Richardson said. "If you weren't so popular, Bigler wouldn't have to dig up all this crap on you. It's a tribute, in a way, to your popularity."

"All right, you scumbag," Charlie said softly, evenly. "You are going to sit here now, and you are going to tell me everything you've dug up on my staff, my family and my friends."

"And what are you going to do with it?" Morey asked.

"Warn them. Give them a chance to get out of this cesspool now."

"All right," Morey said. "But you have to understand. This is confidential material. We're not certain that all of what I'm about to tell you will come out." He smiled again. "My research is better than Bigler's. It's the *best.*"

* * *

Charlie delivered his luncheon speech on autopilot two hours later, then canceled the afternoon schedule—fund-raising phone calls, for the most part. He commandeered a car and drove Nell to Crescent Lake. As they arrived, a day camp was finishing its afternoon swim, the counselors reeling in the kids, loading them onto a school bus, soaked and sandy, snapping towels and darting off in different directions, a flock of Nordic canaries.

Willows framed the beach area, an oak grove just beyond; Charlie and Nell walked along the shore, holding hands, gazing across at the Crescent Lake Casino, the place where Buzz had first wooed Clarice. The casino was an enormous log cabin–style building with forest-green shuttered windows above a long, screened-in porch—it punctuated a thin line of shacky beach houses dozing in the midafternoon shadows along the shore. Flies and microscopic, crazily spinning nits and tufts of nothing floated through the air. Nell took off her espadrilles, and walked along barefoot.

"Okay, Senator," she said. "What's up? You're not going to change your mind about marrying me, are you?"

"No," he said dully. "But I think we're going to have to put it off. I think you should go home."

Nell stopped. Her heart seemed to stop. He seemed quite serious. "Tell me why," she said.

He told her about the meeting with Richardson. Her first, visceral response was anger—at Richardson, and at Charlie, for hiring him. But she muted that, seeing Charlie so deflated—his eyes dead, sadder than she imagined possible.

"How are you going to handle it?" she asked. "Are you going to tell people what you know?"

"I guess," he sighed. "I already called Oskar and Linc, since those ads will come first."

"How did they react?"

"They were fine with it," Charlie said, proud that their support had been so vehement. "Oskar's in full battle mode. He is one tough no-legged fucker. He told Bob Hamblin that if he didn't stop calling for a comment about the ad, he would buy the *Register-World* and shut it down."

"That was probably helpful," Nell said.

"He doesn't care about helpful at this point," Charlie said with a laugh. "Although he did say he was going to raise a shitload more money for me and 'nuke that Butler pissant.' He said he'd do the nuking through independent committees, if I wouldn't go along."

But there had been an awkwardness about the conversation that Charlie didn't share with Nell: all the accumulated unstateds of a thirty-year friendship suddenly naked and public—the benefits they had tacitly exchanged, semitawdry and certainly pecuniary, but cleansed by the sense that the mutual assistance had its roots in the Philadelphia Naval Hospital and by the fact that neither of them ever talked about it. Charlie *had* bent his rules for Oskar. But he'd also trusted Oskar not to do anything that would hurt him. There was nothing he could do about that now. He was ashamed of himself, but he could live with it, sort of.

And Linc. "The Bible Biker is attacking *me*?" Rathburn laughed, from Russia. "I'm honored. I'll propose him for membership in the Council on Foreign Relations. You want to second? . . . You know, Charles, my first thought was that this guy was some sort of fund-raising gimmick on your part: everyone I know back in New York is opening his checkbook for you."

"He'll like that, Butler," Charlie said. "I'll have a who's who of the Tri-lateral Commission on my contribution lists."

"Charlie, come on. How many elections ever—ever—turned on inter-national banker conspiracy nonsense?" Linc said.

"True enough, but you're only a small, discrete lump in a giant pile of shit about to be dumped on my head," Charlie replied.

"You'll weather it," Linc said. "Everything else okay? Buzz? . . . Nell?"

"Fine," he said, acknowledging the gesture—he had missed Linc, too; at a certain point, too many memories are invested in a friendship, even a hurtful one, to let it lapse. "Hey, you know, it's great to hear your voice."

"Is there anything I can do?" Linc asked. "Aside from getting the Tri-laterals to send money? You want me to come out and lick envelopes?"

"Russia's that much fun?"

"Russia is . . . another conversation."

"And Marisa Carter?"

"A third conversation."

"Sounds like we have a lot of talking to catch up on," Charlie said.

Nell found she was quite relieved to hear this: she hadn't been com-fortable as the woman between. She remembered Linc's daily phone calls to Charlie when she'd been with Rathburn (the thought of being with Linc, and not with Charlie, seemed incomprehensible now). She had sensed his absence in Charlie's life the past nine months; she knew how important Linc's support would be now. A reinvigorated friendship seemed the perfect antidote to the impending assault—an asset re-gained, the fortress reinforced.

"Who are you most worried about?" Nell asked. "Hilton?"

"Of course," Charlie said, pausing wistfully, about to add something, then changing his mind. "But it's more than that."

"What do you mean?" she asked, trying to catch his eyes.

"Well." He hesitated a moment. "The experience this morning was just so strange. I was all alone. No support. None of my people, my *real* peo-ple, were there. Just Richardson and Sonny. And Sonny is, clearly, more his than mine. They were totally clinical. Peeling an onion in an operating theater—starring me as the onion. You know what they had? Back in 1981, when I was dating Sue Whitworth, we went to a party in Newport Beach. Sue was in her hyperzonked cokehead phase. That was one of the reasons why it wasn't going to work between us. One of several thousand reasons. But I was in a WTF mood . . . and I inhaled that night. Didn't like it much. Sexy, but too speedy, and I didn't need too much help in those areas. . . ."

"No kidding," she said.

"But Richardson *knew* about it," Charlie said, shaking his head in amazement. "He said it was just a coincidence. He's friends with Larry Foerbring, the producer, who remembered seeing me with nose engaged that night. Chances are Muffles will never find out about it. Or so Morey says."

"So why did he throw it in?"

"To intimidate me, maybe" Charlie said, sneaking a quick glance at Nell; turning away as she turned toward him. "To show that there are plenty of things out there. Too many things for even him to know."

"And what does he want?"

"Spend more money, I guess. Go negative."

"How negative?" Nell asked.

"Nothing personal. Apparently, there *is* nothing personal on Muffler Child."

"How sad that your fellow citizens would consider electing anyone so immaculate," Nell said. "It'd never fly in New York. . . . So: I don't suppose we could just forget about the campaign and blow this pop-stand?"

"I w—"

Nell looked at him, raised an eyebrow.

"Don't you dare," he said. "It was just a slip."

"Charlie," she said, softly, slowly, thinking. "What effect would it have on the campaign if we got married *now*?"

"You don't want to do that," he said abruptly. "It wouldn't be ours."

"Charlie, we had ours a couple of nights ago. I asked, you accepted. Or, I belatedly accepted your cornfield thing. . . . Whatever, we're there now. The rest is just details."

"Well, think of the kids," he said, refusing to play.

"Pamela would love the spotlight," Nell said. "TV cameras at Mom's wedding? Coo-ool."

He enveloped her then, hugged her tight. "Nell, God. You are so amazing." He paused. "And suddenly so political!"

"Face it, buster," she said. "I'm worth at least a couple of points. I could be a hell of a cross-tab."

"It would take that asshole right out of his campaign," he said enthusiastically, but not, she thought, very convincingly. "Still, this is the most important moment . . . and I'm really worried about bringing the kids in, next week, for the state fair. I don't know if I want them to see this."

Nell laughed. "Democracy in action?"

"Pretty fucking pathetic." He said. "You really want our marriage to be a public spectacle?"

"Not really," she said. "But WTF."

"Let's think on it," he said, stopped and kissed her. "You are remarkable."

"Let's sit down," she replied, wondering about his curious, distracted coolness: the meeting with Morey must have been really awful. "Let's sit down in the shade of this old oak tree—don't you like the way that sounds? Maybe we should just try to say soothing things to each other for a while."

He landed with a thud, leaned his back against the tree trunk; she put her head on his chest and curled an arm around his waist. "The lake lapped gently against the shore," he said.

She laughed. "The breeze wafted a whiff of pine needles."

"The last laughs of the summer campers echoed in the distance," he said. "You know, I do have this fantasy of the dreadful tykes at the state fair. Great rides for Robin. All sorts of wonderful things for Shamela to complain about. I don't suppose either of them has ever eaten a corn dog? In the universe of comestibles, a corn dog is the diametric opposite, nutritionally, of sushi."

"Actually, Senator, *there*'s an idea for you: you could launch a whole new home-state industry," Nell said. "Nutritional corn dogs, made of soy."

"This just sucks," he said, sitting up abruptly.

"Charlie, what is it?" She sat up with him, put an arm around his back.

"Nothing," he said firmly. Then, "It's just that we don't know what they're going to say, or how they're going to say it. Or what I'm going to have to say back."

"Just tell everyone that Butler's a little fart who doesn't deserve their attention." She looked up at him, wrinkling her brow and wondered what was really going on.

15

———

Hilton Devereaux assumed that Mexican mufflers would trump Martin "vote-selling" as a campaign issue. The public, unfortunately, didn't agree. Bigler's Oskar Millar attack was devastating: same format as the Stanton spot, but much rougher. It opened with a photo of Oskar, looking seriously Prussian (it was a head shot; not a hint of wheelchairs or amputations, of course). The same countrified announcer: "Who *is* Oskar Millar, anyway?" A question mark clanged over Oskar's face. Then fife and drum music, as a list of Oskar's assets marched down the screen: "Well. He controls forty-seven different companies. Worth twenty-three billion dollars. With operations in twenty-eight countries around the world." Full stop. Ominous music. "He also controls . . . Senator Charlie Martin." The announcer did a fabulous, ludicrous job with "Sen-a-tor Charr-leee Marrtin." More fife and drum music, more scrolling. "In fact, over the past ten years—according to official government records—there were one hundred and fifty-three provisions in Senate bills that affected Oskar Millar's business interests . . . and Charlie Martin voted for one hundred forty-eight of them. That's *one hundred and forty-eight* personal favors. *One point eight billion dollars* in tax breaks." Full stop. A slide of Charlie, looking slick (it must have been taken just after a shower, Hilton thought). *"Why* is Charlie Martin giving Oskar Millar *your* vote in the United States Senate?" Another clanging question mark. A series of photos of Charlie in WTF mode. "Because Oskar Millar is not only Charlie Martin's chief fund-raiser, he's also Charlie Martin's *personal* financial adviser. And, after twenty years in *public* service, Senator Charlie Martin has accumulated assets of seven million dollars."

And then, Lee Butler, looking up from his Bible on that hillside again:

"I'm Lee Butler. You know where my money comes from. It comes from hard work, not inside deals. Three generations of quality Muffler Man service. I want to give you back your vote in the United States Senate. I want to make America . . . America again."

Oskar hadn't helped matters any, nearly running down a television news crew from KDES just outside his Florida mansion on the day the spot appeared. His threat to buy the *R-W* had been duly reported in the *R-W*. It was, unfortunately, the only public comment he made on the subject of his assets.

Paul Sonnenfeld's research team did a rapid and effective job of taking apart the Millar tax break numbers—the $1.8 billion was foolishly bloated, the total value of the provisions in question; Oskar's companies' share was $142 million over ten years. A mere $142 million. He also didn't "control" the forty-seven companies worth $23 billion, at least not so it could be proven. He did hold "significant positions" in those companies, Sonnenfeld said, although Paul quickly admitted that the ownership point was too technical to even contemplate.

"Was the boss aware of this?" Hilton asked, disheartened, when he called Donna to let her know the senator was on a plane back to D.C. to vote on the first appropriations bill of the fall season. He knew there had to be an answer; he just wasn't sure what it was.

"Are you kidding?" Donna scoffed. "Oskar didn't ask for most of those so-called favors. They were just Christmas tree ornaments, gifts hung on those bills for some business interest or other—and Oskar benefited from it, collaterally. You don't get money bills passed without greasing them. Oh, come on: You know that, Hil—it's the way things work."

"Yeah, but—yuck," Hilton said. "Maybe it's just easier dealing with the press than with constituent industrialists. Maybe"—he paused for effect—"it is time to make America . . . America again."

"How's he taking it?"

"Well, you'll find out soon enough. He came out of Richardson's Magical Mystery Meeting looking like a Holocaust survivor. But he's rallied since then. Blood's up over this stuff. You've got him for how long?"

"I'll send him back to you on Friday."

"Early, we need to prep him," Hilton insisted. It was late in the evening, but the campaign office was bustling: phone bank volunteers making cold calls. Hilton sat with his feet up on the desk, pleased by the work going on around him. "Y'know, I know he has to go back there to vote—but it's kinda weird that he has to go back there to vote on goddamn money bills. This week, of all weeks. Have we scrubbed these things? Do we know what's in there?"

"Absolutely," Donna said. "Which is why he's voting against everything this fall except defense and ag and the Crime Bill. We've cleared our cowardice with O'Brien. He doesn't need Charlie's vote on the rest."

"Terrific," Hilton said. "The boss'll be feeling just great about all the health, education and welfare programs he's gonna stiff. He should be in a fabulous mood for the debate."

"It's on C–SPAN, you know—the debate," Donna said. "They love state fair sort of hoopla."

"Washington gets its first extended look at Muffler Boy?"

"We have seen the future," Donna said. "And it's clean."

* * *

There had been state fair debates for more than one hundred years. They were the ritual beginning of the general election campaign, a ritual now preciously ornate—having acquired all sorts of bogus Victorian frills over time, as if politics itself was a cute, though obscure, form of antique entertainment. The fairgrounds were located just north of Des Pointe. There was a series of brick and metal judging sheds with lapidary names—Poultry, Hogs, Produce—as well as a race course, an area for rides and lots of food pavilions. Each candidate's supporters were expected to march, brandishing placards, from the parking lot to the Big Tent, which was pitched in the fairgrounds infield. Both sides were expected to cheer wildly when both candidates were introduced. And both sides were expected to cheer both candidates again when it was over (this was, after all, a celebration of democracy—with the sweet, midwestern assumption that not only would the best man win, but that either man would represent the state honorably). Afterward, each candidate was expected to have a party for his supporters and for the general public. Charlie's parties were famous. A tent was pitched just behind the redbrick grandstand, not far from the debate scene. There was free bratwurst, corn dogs, hamburgers, corn on the cob, peach cobbler, beer and soda. The Buzzards provided the music, of course (with the candidate himself inevitably sitting in on the drums for a number or two). Indeed, the Martin parties were so good that, early on, several of Charlie's lamer opponents couldn't bear to miss the fun and dropped by to say hello—now each candidate was expected to pay a ritual call at his opponent's festivities. All of which was choreographed to a nanosecond.

Just after noon that Saturday, with a prematurely autumnal breeze from the north chasing off the late summer humidity, Hilton and Patsy Dunn drove solemnly to the fairgrounds. They had grown closer in recent days, especially after the Magical Mystery Meeting. Charlie had briefed the two of them, and Mary Proctor, at Oak Street soon after Morey Richardson had whisked off to wherever his next "patching through" would take place. Upon learning the gist of the meeting, Hilton offered to quit.

"No!" Dunnsie said, with surprising percussive force. "Absolutely not. I won't be intimidated by Muffler Boy. And I won't be intimidated by Morey Richardson, either. I know the people of this state. They might not be . . . comfortable with, uh, alternate whatevers—but they're not bigots either."

Hilton and Charlie glanced at each other, enjoying Dunnsie's decency and discomfort. "And anyway," Dunn concluded with a flourish, placing an awkward hand, defiantly, on Hilton's knee. "You're too damn important to this campaign. The kids need their den mother."

And now, tangled in fair traffic and nervous, Hilton asked Dunn, "Was the prep yesterday as bad as I thought it was?"

"Doesn't mean anything."

"I don't like the 'jobs' defense on Oskar's tax breaks. It sounds . . . defensive."

"Maybe," Dunnsie said. "But when he rattles off the local companies that were helped, I think people'll understand that. At least, well—who the fuck knows."

"Yeah," Hilton said. "I sure don't."

"I haven't told the senator this—and if you tell him, I'll kill you—but this is it for me: finito." Dunn said. "I don't understand half the things you people talk about anymore. I don't understand how TV works, how quickly you can turn ads around, how you buy time. And the other thing is, I just don't *get* Muffler Boy's appeal. In the old days, anyone showed up in a campaign toting a Bible, you'd figure he's got something to disprove. Guy like that doesn't get to first base in this state. But this guy starts with the Good Book and all that noise, and hits a stand-up double."

"Pat, you've forgotten things about this state the rest of us'll—"

"And I'm so damn old I'll probably never remember them," he replied, gruffly.

"What about the lawn sign?" Hilton said. A remarkable moment:

Dunn had been riding with the candidate through Singer Rapids one day and saw a Martin lawn sign in front of Frank Runkle's house—Runkle was a notorious repo man, everyone in town hated him. So Patsy had issued an edict: "All lawn signs go through me." (And made sure the Runkle sign disappeared.)

"Yeah, well—" Dunn pulled into the VIP lot. He and Hilton began the long walk across the infield to the Big Tent. "Ten years ago, that asshole repossessed my niece's husband's Dodge."

"Mr. Dunn, trust me," Hilton said, stopping, turning to the old man. "You are not what this campaign needs less of."

Patsy clapped him on the back. "Son—you just shut up now, and let's get to work."

Greenrooms for the candidates were set up in the lockers beneath the grandstand—the fairgrounds doubled as a stadium for occasional high school football games and the statewide track meet. Charlie was sitting, quietly, in the home-team locker room—reading that day's *R-W* sports section—with Calvin and Nell and Mary Proctor moving about the room. Nell, who like Charlie had just returned from a week on the East Coast, looked up hopefully when Hilton came in; he gave her a hug. "How's Lu and the kids?"

"Fine," she said, working at an equanimity that was betrayed by the nervousness in her eyes. "Lu's thing was just allergies, thank God. Hey, did Charlie tell you our news?"

"Hilton. Excuse us, Nell." Mary Proctor touched his elbow and nodded him out into the hallway.

"Don't tell the boss," Proctor said, squeezing his forearm, "but I have never seen anything like it. No one has. The parking lot is filled with church buses. There are so many people, they're never gonna fit them into the tent—it's already a news story: it's gonna lead the evening TVs. You didn't have the radio on in the car coming over?"

"No. What about our people? Did they show up?"

"We've got our usual couple thousand," Mary said testily—advance field coordination was her bailiwick. "That's always been more than enough. And it'll be okay in the room—the Butler people can't go over their assigned seats. If we're lucky, the senator won't even know about all the Bible-thumpers till it's over—but criminy, they sure brought out the flock for this one. I never knew there were so many damned . . . Christians in the state." And she smiled—a whoops-but-WTF grin.

"Maybe our boy'll win them over," Hilton said. "And you know what Dunnsie always says—"

"Crowd size means nothing," Mary said. "Except . . . sometimes."

A good politician doesn't need to be told. Charlie Martin knew that Mary Proctor—normally as even-tempered, in his presence, at least, as the four perfectly parallel wrinkles that creased her forehead—was flustered. He sensed an unusual buzz about the fairgrounds. He saw Mary spirit Hilton away. And he also noticed Paul Sonnenfeld—formal, in a jacket and tie for a change—approach Nell in the greenroom; he said something to her, she smiled, squeezed his arm and kissed him on the cheek. Charlie was distracted then, by Dunnsie, who wanted to review their Oskar Millar defense, so he didn't see what happened next.

"I'm glad you're going ahead with it anyway," Sonnenfeld said to Nell, having just congratulated her on the marriage. Nell had been surprised that the somewhat creepy research director, of all people, knew about the plans—and that Hilton clearly didn't—but she'd received his good wishes happily and made a mental note to ask Charlie just who else now knew, and so she was a beat slow catching up to the nuanced caveat that accompanied the endorsement.

"What do you mean 'anyway'?" she asked, pulling back.

"Nothing," Sonnenfeld said too quickly, knowing he'd screwed up, wondering whether to lie or distract or flee, but knowing, from the look in her eye, that sort of thing would never do—and amazed that Charlie hadn't told her about the contents of her dossier.

"Tell me," she said. "Now." Sonnenfeld looked around the room. "Or else we'll go over to the candidate," Nell added, nodding in Charlie's direction. "And he can tell me."

Sonnenfeld sighed. "I'm glad you're going ahead with the marriage, despite the research."

"What research?"

"Not here," he said and led her down a row of lockers, out of sight from the rest of the campaign team.

Charlie saw immediately that something was very different about Nell when she returned, just as he was about to be escorted onto the stage.

"Is everything okay?" He asked it seriously, hands on her upper arms.

Sure, she'd said, avoiding his eyes—meaning: let's not talk about it now. "What did Sonny . . ."

"Not now," she said, firmly, then she smiled and said coolly, almost dismissively, "I feel as if I should give you a handkerchief or something, so that you can wear my colors going off into the lists against Mordred."

"I've got my mermaid keycase," he said, trying to kiss her on the nose, but she pulled back. "That'll have to do. Wish me luck."

"Luck," she said, refusing again to look him in the eye.

Strange. Still, Charlie felt confident and comfortable as he entered the debate tent from the rear, shaking hands down the center aisle. The north breeze made the tent more tolerable than in stifling years past. The cheering for him from the Muffler Man section was, if anything, louder than in other years—a noticeable display of politeness that helped focus him on the challenge. His own supporters were not nearly so charitable: there were a couple of stray hisses—from the assorted civil servants, especially teachers, who made up the hard core of his base—at the tail end of their perfunctory applause for Lee Butler. The rudeness drew harsh looks from the members of the Des Pointe business and political establishment who anchored the vast center section of the audience.

As for the debate itself—it began affably enough. There was no reason for Charlie to attack his opponent, and Muffler Man was under wraps as well: Bigler had no intention of letting his candidate carry the assault. Hilton exhaled, along with the rest of the audience, and remembered: nothing happens in most debates. The rule of thumb is to take no chances, especially in a close race. Keep your core voters happy. Don't offend potential supporters. Don't try to overreach.

Charlie made some carefully scripted news early on by announcing that he wouldn't vote for the Stanton health plan, if it came to the Senate floor—cheap news, since it was clear that the Stanton health plan was quite dead and would never make it to the Senate floor. But it was always good for an incumbent to make news of some sort, lest you be accused of not saying anything new, and this might appeal to the uncommitted moderates who would decide the race.

Butler was creamy smooth, but slightly off his game. He shifted uneasily at his podium, searching for a natural place: he was making an effort to appear senatorial. The effort showed. Perhaps he was nervous. When he began to speak, his international conspiracy and end-of-morality riffs fell flat. Certainly, he was no match for the incumbent's charming calm. Charlie responded informally to the reporters asking the questions, calling them by their first names. Butler called them Mr. Hamblin, Miss Twomey (from KDES–TV) and Mrs. Blanchard (from AP Radio), and he seemed to draw himself in, and up—coiling tight—each time he spoke.

The questions were predictable. Charlie was asked about Oskar Millar, and didn't seem at all concerned by that: the scripted answer, which he delivered word for word, was almost irrelevant—in a debate, tone overwhelms substance and Charlie's was breezy, conversational but authoritative. Butler not only seemed younger than the incumbent, but smaller. His smile was forced, and occasionally inopportune. His hair was too neat, sprayed in place; it looked slick. More important, he clearly hadn't integrated his various personalities—the sharp-tongued radio host, the choirboy Bible Biker, the potential senator—into one credible package yet. He needed work. Pat Dunn, watching the show on television in the greenroom with the campaign team, began to feel better: class tells, he thought. His candidate was still the classiest political product ever to run the local track.

Hilton, meanwhile, was growing impatient, waiting for the next to last section, where the candidates asked each other a question. Usually, this was a dud. Most consultants don't like their candidates to appear prosecutorial—and they figure, correctly, their opponents will be well-stoked for every likely tough question. The standard tactic is to deliver an innocuous minispeechlet like: "With thirty-four million Americans needing health insurance, don't you agree with me that it's time we developed a low-cost, efficient form of universal health coverage?"

Charlie had come up with an interesting ploy—even Morey Richardson thought so. He would congratulate Butler on the high quality of the Muffler Man stores—and on the management's willingness to go anywhere, even to Mexico, to find the best mufflers at the lowest prices. And then he'd say, "Why do you think some people are opposed to free trade with Mexico, when free trade helps provide American consumers with the best products at the lowest prices—the way your family has for three generations?"

And it worked. Muffler Man, who had been prepped for a more direct assault on this issue, got all tangled up. His answer was incomprehensible. "Let me help you out a little," Charlie began his two-minute rebuttal. He turned to the audience, leaned a casual elbow on the podium: "See, folks, politics is more complicated than business. In business, there's a tried and true formula for success: the best quality at the lowest prices. In politics, it's tougher. There's always a trade-off. The lowest prices might mean importing your mufflers from Mexico . . . and closing down American muffler factories, costing jobs. Now, I've always believed that if you keep prices as low as possible—if you keep government from sticking taxes on imports—the economy'll stay strong and there'll be plenty of jobs for everyone. Which means more money in everyone's pocket. So I agree with what Lee Butler *does* as a businessman rather than what he *says* as a politician. Now, I know some folks—some of my strongest supporters in the labor movement, for example—disagree with me on this. And it's hard to watch factories close down, and we should help displaced workers all we can. But I also like what Lee Butler used to say on the radio: whenever a politician's telling you just exactly what you want to hear, it's time to check your wallet."

There was strong applause from the Des Pointe business establishment in the center section, a group that had done well off of farm exports and therefore loved free trade. Butler seemed to wince. He picked up his pen and, frowning, crossed out something on the sheet of paper before him. Later, when Pat Dunn tried to piece together how everything came crashing down, he would remember this moment—the moment Lee Butler rejected the Bigler-imposed debate pacifism. "Mr. Butler," the moderator, a middle-aged stalwart from the League of Women Voters, asked, "do you have a question for Senator Martin?"

"Senator Martin," Butler said quite formally, drawing himself up even tighter, it seemed, this time. He had just gotten his first full blast from a gifted professional politician. "Two years ago, you negotiated the release of Mustafa Al-Bakr from a Vietnamese prison. Could you tell us why the Vietnamese were holding him?"

What on earth? Pat Dunn thought: well, now we know. This is one of those dilettante candidates who, when you knock them down, they get right up and hit you back.

"Well, he had crossed into their country illegally," Charlie said, sensing that his opponent had, finally, figured out how to handle the podium—and at the same time, trying to figure out where this was headed.

"Is it true that the Vietnamese authorities arrested Mr. Al-Bakr because he was transporting heroin?"

Son of a bitch.

"It was a complicated situation," Charlie began, and immediately kicked himself: 'complicated' is a word politicians should never use, particularly in a debate. "Mr. Al-Bakr was feeling a good deal of remorse for things he'd done during the war and—"

"And he expressed that remorse by making a major heroin buy?"

"Both the United States and Vietnamese governments were interested in his release," Charlie said, frustrated that he couldn't explain—frustrated that the moderator didn't step in: this wasn't supposed to be a cross-examination.

"But *you* knew he was transporting heroin, didn't you?" Butler continued, buoyed. "Did you also know that he'd been arrested several times in the States for dealing drugs?"

Small quantities, Charlie thought. Linc had said small quantities. Morey, who was aware of both the busts and Mustafa's subsequent religious conversion, hadn't seemed very concerned—it was just another stop on the Magical Mystery Meeting scandal express.

"Senator, we can accept that you were acting at the behest of the government in this matter," Butler continued. "What I'm wondering about is why you made Mr. Al-Bakr, who was a known drug dealer, a member of your staff—not just a member of your staff, but a part of your personal entourage?"

Good question.

"Time's up," the moderator said. "Now we'll move to closing statements."

"Wait a minute," Charlie said. "Mr. Butler has raised a serious question and he's entitled to a serious response. Mr. Butler has also injected religion into this campaign, and I'd like to ask him what his Bible says about mercy and repentance? . . . That's just a rhetorical question, Lee. It says you should 'act justly and love mercy and walk humbly with the Lord.' There can be no question that Mr. Al-Bakr did some regrettable things in his life, terrible things. In the war, particularly." Charlie swallowed his perennial distaste, and distrust, and sold the Mustafa life story like a tent show preacher.

"When I first met him in that Vietnamese prison, he said that was where he deserved to be . . . for the killing he'd done during the war. Where he deserved to be. Can you imagine that? He asked me how to atone for it. I told him what my mother told me." He paused, lowered his voice in an intimate way. "You all remember Mom; she was almost as famous around here as your grandfather, Lee—anyway, Mom used to quote Gandhi: 'If you've harmed a child, save a child.' And since he's come home, that is what Mustafa has done. He's devoted his life to saving the devastated children of the inner city. You reporters who want to check this out, all you have to do is call Reverend Ronnie Deems at the Apostolic Community of Truth and Salvation in Washington. . . . Mr. Butler, you should have your negative research team check that out, too. Then you might check out your heart, and see if there's any room there for mercy. I don't defend the things Mustafa did in the past. Neither does he. But I'm proud of what he's done since his religious rebirth. And if this is what my opponent wants the campaign to be about, so be it. I'll be happy to stand for the principle of giving people a second chance. Maybe not a third chance . . . but everybody should get one opportunity to clean up their messes before the Lord. Lee, you want vengeance? Not just for Mustafa, but for all my generation's 'sins' of the past thirty years? I'll take my chances with mercy. That'll give the voters a pretty clear choice—vengeance . . . or mercy. I guess that'll do as my closing statement."

A total explosion of people, a wall of screaming and pushing and cameras and madness, hugs and handshakes, people grabbing his arm and knocking into him—then a protective circle formed, Hilton and Dunnsie and several of the campaign kids, and they were floating along, buffeted, bouncing like a bubble with an oddly thick skin on a flood tide. You okay? Hilton asked with his eyes. Charlie shrugged. He was lost, staggered in the rush. The last moments of the debate had been stunning; he wasn't sure what had happened. "Where's Nell?" he asked.

"The hospitality tent," Hilton said. "Where we're going."

Then out into the cool night air, a quick-step dash across the uneven grassy clumps of infield, the sense that he was pulling a crowd along behind him—although he continued to be assaulted from the sides and the front. Somewhere in the darkness, Bernie Hufsteter from the United Auto Workers stopped him. "Clever bit on trade, Charlie," Hufsteter said, seething. "Our members are gonna love the part about shutting down American factories. It might not send them all the way to Muffler Jesusville, but they sure ain't gonna make an extra effort to get out and vote for you."

"I—" Charlie said, and was shoved along. Dunnsie had warned him about the labor reaction to the Mexican bit. He'd decided to take an honorable WTF on it. Now "honor" just seemed defiant and stupid. And maybe his position wasn't so honorable, either. He was having trouble trusting his instincts. Nothing seemed right. "How d'you think the Mustafa thing played—" he asked Hilton breathlessly, moving through darkness.

"Great . . . great. You heard the applause." Well, no. He hadn't.

Just outside the Martin party tent, a tall figure stopped the senator. "We need to talk, Senator. I—" Mustafa said.

"Later," Charlie said.

"But—"

"Later." Charlie's eyes went cold. "Do you understand? That means *not . . . now.*"

And then someone handed him the flier. And someone else shined a fuzzy-edged circle of light on it, just outside the tent. It was black ink on pink paper:

CHARLIE MARTIN'S FUNNY FAMILY: THE FACTS

—HIS LIVE-IN "GIRLFRIEND" LIVES WITH ANOTHER MAN

—HE HAS AN ILLEGITIMATE SON

—HE MOLESTED A CAMPAIGN WORKER IN 1992

—HIS PRESS SECRETARY IS HOMOSEXUAL AND HAS AIDS!

—EVEN HIS FATHER IS LIVING IN SIN.

WHAT IS IT ABOUT MORALITY THAT SENATOR MARTIN DOESN'T UNDERSTAND?

[A Message from the Messengers]

"It's on every windshield in the parking lot." Mary Proctor was furious. "No one knows how they got there."

"Shit, Mary," Charlie said. "You know how they got there. . . . Where's Nell?" He craned his head, looking around. He wanted to see her before he went inside the party tent. "Hilton—find her. Bring her here. I'll wait. . . ."

An odd moment: after all the rush, he stood there—just outside the warm corridor of light extending out from his tent, protected by a circle of campaign kids organized by Barry Powter—silently waiting. He realized that he'd been sweating, his shirt was damp against the chilly wind; he shivered, shoved his hands in his pockets, stared down at his feet. He could hear Vern's sax droning from inside the tent—"Take the A Train": the start of Buzz's travel medley, to be followed by "Shuffle Off to Buffalo" and "Come Fly with Me." As it had been for forty years—forever. But held in place now by Calvin's quietly solid work on the drums.

Then several people penetrated the circle and began talking to him, but he wasn't listening. They were congratulating him. He was yanked from his reverie by Hilton—of all people—shouting, "Get away from him! Goddammit, Barry, I told you to keep a tight hold—"

"What?"

"YoGa Dems," Hilton said, when the congratulators had been hustled off: Young and Gay Democrats. "It's the last thing—"

"Senator—" A firm hand on his shoulder: Dunn.

"Dunnsie?"

"Senator, we've got a situation," Pat said.

"I'll say."

"Hamblin wants a comment on the flier."

"Hilton, what do you think?" Charlie asked.

"I don't know," Hilton said. "Obviously, Mustafa's the lead out of the debate. Hamblin says Bigler's furious at the Messengers for stepping on it. Butler's already issued a statement condemning the flier, of course." They stood, heads close together, Charlie's arms around both Hilton and Dunnsie. He saw Nell lingering, off to the side, but within the invisible cordon around the candidate created by Barry Powter and the campaign kids. He reached out for her; she eluded him. "You kind of wonder what's going on here," Hilton concluded. "It's really undisciplined. Out of control."

"Patsy, what do you think is going on?" Charlie asked.

"Well, I buy that Bigler's furious," Dunn said. "But I think he's more pissed at Muffles than at the Messengers, whoever they are—although you don't need three guesses to figure that out, right? I don't think Bigler wanted to break the Mustafa story yet. You watch Muffler Boy during your Mexican bit? He crossed out something, sucked his lip, set his jaw. My guess is, he slipped the leash. Bigler wanted his boy to be a sweetie pie—"

"And let the Messengers be the message?" Hilton asked, impressed: the old man was amazing.

"Maybe," Pat said. "Not impossible. Would've been clever. They figure, no real news out of the debate . . . and with half the state here tonight, the press won't be able to ignore the leaflet. The Messengers don't mention Mustafa among our transgressions, do they? They were probably saving that for October. So maybe that's a little piece of luck for us, in all this. Muffles stepped on his own dirty trick."

"Incredibly lucky." Charlie shook his head. He reached for Nell again, caught her by the wrist. She was struggling to break free. Why? "I just can't fucking believe our good fortune. So what do we say to Hamblin and the horde?"

"Nothing specific," Hilton said, but there wasn't time to say much more. Television lights were pushing in their direction, denting the cordon. It was Blake Dornquist, the male mannequin from KFYR.

"Senator?" Dornquist said. "Do you have a reaction to the leaflet? Do you have a comment?"

Charlie's right hand was behind him, still holding on to Nell's wrist—a good thing, since his first instinct would have been to use it to push Dornquist back. "A comment?" Charlie asked, collecting himself. "Blake . . . How's your mother?"

"She's—" And in that instant, Charlie slid past him and tried to turn toward the entrance to the hospitality tent, but there was Bob Hamblin talking to Hilton and Dunn. Charlie instinctively smiled to greet the reporter, then turned away: Nell had broken free. He felt the brightness of the television lights on his back. A boom mike snaked down between them. Someone—Hilton? Barry Powter?—pushed the mike away and moved behind Charlie, creating a wall between the camera and the conversation. "What's happening, Bob? Did you love the debate? You seem . . . concerned."

"It's pretty outrageous, Senator," Hamblin said, showing empathy but making a statement that could be interpreted any number of ways—a standard reporter's trick.

"What is?" Charlie struck, suddenly changing tone, ambushing his ambusher.

"The fact that someone would do this, of course," Hamblin said quickly, then tried to recoup by whispering in Charlie's ear, "I'm really sorry. This sucks."

"But he's still going with it," Patsy said, just behind them and close enough to hear.

Charlie was missing Nell; she had slipped his grasp. He looked around. She wasn't visible.

"Senator—"

"Excuse me?" Charlie said.

"Look, Hamblin, we've got nothing to say about this," Dunnsie was saying. "Jesus, Bobby, I knew your father—from the old days, from the Flats. He was management, but at least he was straight up. Is this the kind of work he'd want you to be doing? Stinks worse than the killing floor."

"Charlie." Hamblin tried to ignore Dunn. "You can't not comment. We're going to rip Butler a new asshole with this—"

"Sure you are." Dunnsie was suddenly angry. Charlie wondered if he was just doing it for effect. "You'll do it on the editorial page. Which no one reads. Think it through, Bobby. You told us Butler's reaction. He's outraged about the 'invasion' of Charlie's privacy. Just outraged. But he'll have the story out there now . . . courtesy of you."

"Not just me, Pat. They got this new invention—TV. Maybe you've heard of it. Pat, c'mon. You've known me forever. What the fuck can I do?" Hamblin pleaded, then turned to Charlie. "Senator, do you have a comment?"

"It's not the media, it's the Messengers?" Charlie asked, playing with the words. Hamblin raised an eyebrow. The senator seemed on the brink of another WTF. And Charlie was, indeed, contemplating the effect of saying, It's all true, Bobby. So the fuck what? But this wasn't just about him.

"Senator?"

"Bob, I don't think this sort of trash is worthy of comment and I'm willing to bet that you are so embarrassed to be in this situation that you won't have the stomach to ask me another question about it."

He turned, pleased with his discipline, and saw—to his horror—Blake Dornquist and several other TV crews sticking microphones in Nell's face. "Ms. Palmerston, do you have a comment? Is it true?"

"Get the hell away from me!" Nell flashed, knocking away a boom mike with her arm. Charlie reached for her wrist, but she knocked him away, too. "Goddamn you all!"

"Nell!" he said, grabbing her by the arms. "Stop!"

She looked at him then, blond hair exploding in the television lights. Her mouth was set, her eyes narrowed and dead fierce. "Get your hands off me," she said quietly, intently, looking directly at him. He was astonished by her vehemence and as he loosened his grip, she burst free from him, and slipped out, away, into the chaos of the crowd.

He tried to follow her, but his reactions were slow motion, as in a dream; he couldn't maneuver his way through the shouting, and then a path was cleared for him to enter the hospitality tent.

The pink flier had made its way inside now—and there was a furious reaction among Charlie's supporters: deafening roars as he entered, a fogbound boxer surrounded by his entourage. Too much light and heat, too much noise. Buzz stopped the music abruptly, then launched a raucous "Happy Days Are Here Again"—the ancient New Deal anthem.

Someone handed Charlie a beer. The plastic cup was frigid in his hand. He gave it to Barry, took a cheekful of lipstick from the chairlady of the Fort Jeffords Golden Agers. And he made his way up to the stage, where a microphone was waiting. "Nell come in, Pop?" he asked Buzz. He looked around for Hilton.

"No." Buzz hugged him tight and kissed him, to cheers.

"Dad, I'm so . . . fucking pissed," Calvin said, joining the hug with Buzz, making it three-way on the stage. Charlie buried his head amongst their shoulders, inhaled their performance perspiration. Buzz, he thought idly, was still young enough to work up a sweat. And Calvin was pissed. He squeezed the kid harder. But what had just happened? He needed a moment to think.

"Senator," Dunnsie was whispering in his ear. "Whenever you're ready, I think they want to hear from you. . . ."

Edsy wiped the lipstick off his cheek with a handkerchief she pulled from out of her scalloped cleavage. He looked around again for Nell. "Have you seen her?" he whispered to Edsy.

Edsy shook her head no.

All right. He tapped the microphone.

"We love you, Charlie!" a woman yelled, and there were more cheers.

"Well, this has been an . . . interesting evening," he began, to laughter. And suddenly there was a cascade of boos. Charlie looked up, toward the entrance to the tent—and saw Muffler Man and his wife, Joan Butler, coming in, both of them waving tiny American flags, flanked by a flying squad of white-bread security guards. Butler was smiling uncomfortably, the wife was grim-faced, swept along, embarrassed, perhaps. The ritual postdebate party visit seemed unimaginable given the circumstances, and yet unavoidable, from Lee Butler's point of view—especially if he wanted to convince the public that he had nothing to do with the Messengers.

"Hold on," Charlie said, raising both his hands—awkwardly, a gesture he never used, for obvious reasons—to tamp down the crowd. "None of that. None of that. Let him up. Let's be polite. . . ."

And there was utter silence in the tent. The crowd parted easily. Lee Butler came up to the stage, shook hands with Charlie. His face was unlined; his eyes were empty, he was concentrating on the moment rather than on Charlie. One way or another, this was news. Butler stepped to the microphone. "I just wanted to thank the senator, here, for a good debate and—"

Charlie was lost. Hilton was suddenly beside him, whispering in his ear. "She's okay. We put her in a car home. . . . What happened?"

"Where's Sonnenfeld?" Charlie asked.

"Dunno. Back at the headquarters, probably? Why?"

"Because I'm gonna fire his ass."

Muffler Man was finishing his remarks, which had been extremely brief and almost gracious; but the silence was brutal. And then someone pushed past Charlie and grabbed Butler by the arm, pulling him back, away from the view of the crowd. It was, remarkably, Buzz, who was seething: "You know who's illegitimate? You know who's illegitimate, you goddamn pipsqueak? Not my grandson! You are! You're an illegitimate scumbag!" Charlie moved to grab Buzz and pull him away before Butler's security guards moved in, but Calvin got there first, stepping between his grandfather and Butler, pushing Butler back—and receiving a retaliatory shove from one of the security guards. The crowd, which had only seen Calvin get shoved, surged toward the stage.

"Hey, hey. Hold it! Hold it!" Charlie had taken the microphone.

"Okay, okay," Butler said, hands up, trying to back off. The two candidates stood shoulder to shoulder, trying to quiet the crowd.

"Shove off, you little shit," Buzz snarled, leaning in from behind and making another lunge at Butler, giddy with anger, as if he'd discovered a fabulous new riff after seven decades of passive resistance. "Off my stage!"

"Dad," Charlie said, putting his hand over the microphone. "For chrissakes, chill." Calvin walked the old man backward toward Edsy's seat next to the synthesizer and sat him down. The guards, meanwhile, were hustling the Butlers off the stage—through chaos, shouting, screaming, a rush of television lights. But Charlie wasn't watching. He and Cal squatted in front of Buzz, cordoning off the crowd. "Jesus, Dad," Charlie said. "You almost caused a riot."

"Almost doesn't count," Buzz said, doing his mischievous left-eyebrow move. "Wish I could've popped him one. He's got one of those cutesy-pie kissers that needs to get smacked."

"Hell-lohhh, Buzzy," Edsy said, fanning him like a fighter between rounds. "What did you have for breakfast?"

"Wouldn't you like to know?" He stood, invigorated. "C'mon, Cal, Vern . . . let's make 'em happy." Charlie watched numbly as the Buzzards slid into the "Stranger on the Shore" medley, Vern's clarinet sounding mellow and almost in tune. People actually began to dance. He stood, staring, nonplussed, still reeling from Nell's on-camera explosion. He had a good sense now what that had been all about. He needed to get home and apologize.

*   *   *

As the car pulled into his circular gravel driveway an hour later, Lee Butler was still feeling dizzy. He'd been clocked in the head by a television camera on the way out of the Martin tent. There was swelling; he'd probably have a shiner in the morning. Worse, Joan had shut down on him again; she wasn't talking. He was glad she'd sent the boys home before the parties, glad they hadn't seen all that—but damn, he needed her to be strong now. She had turned the reading light on in the Lincoln Town Car and had found Micah, the prophet Charlie Martin had cited, on mercy, in the debate. She was reading him, as she always read the Bible, moving her lips silently with the words. It seemed an odd regression for a woman who had graduated with honors from State, with a master's degree in theology. But she believed that actually forming the Word in her mouth put her closer to the Truth.

One of the carriage lights was out, he noticed, giving a skewed aspect to the front steps. His legs were rubbery as Tom the driver opened the door for him and took his elbow as he stepped from the car on the far side. Joan was on the near side, moving up the stairs. Tom had followed Joan up the steps and was opening the front door when Lee Butler saw his wife's eyes widening. He turned and saw a tall figure emerging from the shrubbery. Joan either gasped or, perhaps, shouted, "No!" And Tom wheeled, drawing his gun.

"Whoa!" Mustafa said, raising his hands over his head. "Whoa now! Take it easy. Easy now." He was walking toward them, across the gravel.

"Hold it right there, buddy," Tom said. "You're trespassing."

"We need to talk," Mustafa said, still moving toward them, but slower now. "I just want to talk. You're a Christian, Mr. Butler . . . I'm a Christian, too. I need to explain. You got it right, part of it. I was a terrible sinner, a terrible, terrible man. I was looking to be punished, but I was hedging my bets . . . if I could make the score, I might be free. You see what I mean?"

Lee Butler couldn't understand a thing the man was saying, nor did he want to. But he told Tom, "Put away the gun."

"Vengeance is mine, sayeth the Lord," Mustafa intoned. Joan moved her lips: amen. "I was seeking out the Lord's vengeance. But you can't seek it, it comes to you. The Lord sent Senator Martin, and that changed my life. See, I can explain everything if you give me a chance." He had reached the foot of the steps. There were six of them, slate, up to the broad veranda. The breeze was playing tricks with the light, scattering it across the steps as it moved through the trees. "You're a Christian man, Mr. Butler. Will you take my hand?" Mustafa said, reaching out, moving to the first step. "Will you take my hand and pray with me?"

Lee looked at Joan, and at Mustafa. "Please go," he said. "It's been a long night."

"Pray with me!" Mustafa insisted. "After all the damage done, we need to find a way past the anger. . . . We need to find the way . . . please."

"No, not now."

"Please . . ." He came up another step, raising his arm, reaching out.

"No!" Lee Butler said, but not to Mustafa: to Joan, who had begun to reach out her hand. Butler moved across, trying to step between them—but still a bit dizzy, he missed the step, and began to fall toward Mustafa, who thought he was being attacked and stepped back, leaving nothing to break Lee Butler's fall against the stone banister, his head thudding against it dull and hard. Joan screamed, Tom pulled the gun again, but Mustafa was running and gone before Tom could find even a shadow of a target to shoot at through the maze of shifting light.

16

———

She was sitting in his black leather chair with a single light—the fluorescent on his desk behind her—casting ivory shadows across the room. Her hands were steepled in front of her face, supported by the arms of the chair; she looked leonine, regal, sitting like that. She glanced up as he came in; her eyes were bloodshot, puffy, but dry now and resolute. "Fuck . . . you," she said definitively, shaking her head.

A suitcase was packed, but open, on the bed. He slid it aside and sat down directly across from her. "I'm so sorry," he replied, putting his right hand on her knee, holding his left back.

"You should be. Asshole. That creep Sonnenfeld—"

"—is no longer with the campaign. He was just shit-canned."

"Why, because he *told* me what you were doing? You had them do *oppo* on me!"

"They did it without telling me."

"Of course," she snapped. "You had no control over anything, right? So, how did they find out we were getting married? Were they wiretapping us in here the other night? Or did you hire Morey to do the party planning?"

"A moment of weakness," he admitted.

The Nell section of the Magical Mystery Meeting had been stunning; his reaction to it, disgraceful. The list of men had been impressive, but not unexpected, and Charlie was disappointed by his jealousy, which seemed to erupt, biliously—a shameful, mortal ugliness—direct from his stomach, bypassing his brain. And then, there was the semilegal abortion Nell had gotten in Connecticut in 1968 (a friendly psychiatrist had certified her situation a medical emergency); and then, the treatment for herpes that Nell had received at the Cambridge Free Clinic in 1970. He was staggered. And furious at Morey Richardson—as much for the blithe equanimity with which he delivered the news as for the act of gathering the material in the first place. Morey seemed unimpressed by the quality of the dirt, although he noted carefully its blunt impact on Charlie—and thought that was a bad sign, an indication that he might be the sort of candidate who could be blindsided in a debate.

Actually, Richardson was more concerned about another aspect of Nell's past—a woman named Marianne Bowers, one of three roommates during the year Nell spent in Los Angeles after dropping out of Harvard in 1971. Bowers was a member of the Weather Underground, who had participated in the armed robbery and firebombing of a bank in Pacific Palisades, an incident that had resulted in the death of a security guard; she was now in permanent residence at San Quentin. Charlie, still reeling from the report of Nell's sex life, tried to mount a defense. "That was twenty-five years ago," he said to Morey. "She couldn't possibly have been involved. Not her style at all."

"She was living under the same roof at the time. She was hauled in. She was fingerprinted," Morey said, and then sighed. "And yes, she was cleared for lack of evidence, as were the other two roommates—an aspiring writer and a makeup technician. Bowers, it seems, was using the career girls as a cover. But that'll just be an inconvenient detail for Bigler."

"You mean, he'll use it? You're kidding!"

"I mean, he knows about it," Morey replied. "Any half-decent search engine will find any name associated with a bombing. I don't know how he'll use it. Or if. But I would."

"And the men? And the—"

"Disease?" Morey rolled his eyes. "Highly unlikely. But you sure can pick 'em."

"Fuck you," Charlie said, reflexively defiant. "By the way, we're getting married."

"You want me to say mazel tov?"

In retrospect, Charlie realized that his announcement had been as much a question as a statement. He'd practically asked Richardson to market-test his nuptials, which was Morey's knee-jerk response to *any* new information in the heat of a campaign.

And Charlie's moment of doubt—and revulsion—had passed quickly enough. Just seeing Nell, being with her, holding her hand as they walked along the shore of Crescent Lake that afternoon, had cleared his head. Her past was irrelevant; he was embarrassed by his reaction to the dossier. His own dossier hadn't been a picnic, either. That was why he'd told Nell the story about doing cocaine with Sue Whitworth. He'd been hoping—practically begging Nell to ask, So, did Morey dig up anything wonderful about me? But she hadn't asked. She'd been worried about Hilton. And Charlie hadn't had the courage to tell her. He was appalled by his cowardice. He was appalled by himself.

"I told Morey about the wedding because I was angry," he said now, not very convincingly. "I didn't want him to say another thing about—"

She looked at him, saw through him. "You're pathetic."

"You're right," he said, unable to meet her eyes. "Can you forgive me?"

"For which part?" She stood, hand on her hip, accentuating the curve of her waist. She was wearing the same white silk blouse and fitted blue skirt she'd been wearing the night that she'd proposed to him; she looked fabulous, he thought. "For having Morey do oppo on me? For having him do a—a fucking focus group about our marriage? Or for not having the guts to tell me about any of this—letting me learn about it from that geek Sonnenfeld?"

"I just fired him for that!"

"How decisive," she sneered. "Of course, if he hadn't blown it, I would never have known. Or so you thought. I *knew* you were holding back on me at the lake that day. I *chose* not to ask you. I figured: he loves me. I'll trust him. What a jerk I am: trusting a politician. You put on a good act, Charlie, almost human. But you're as full of shit as . . . the rest of them." She'd almost said Butler, but had restrained herself: a good sign, he thought. She knew he'd noticed the equivocation and quickly added, "I should probably congratulate you for not having Morey do oppo on the kids . . . or maybe you did that, too?"

She turned, zipped her luggage. He was stunned by the coldness, the absence of tears; it was as if a plug had been pulled. He had seen her angry, but never furious before. Her fury was as memorable as all the other things she did.

"Where are you going? It's the middle of the night," he said, standing, moving toward her. "And maybe I was thinking about the kids. Maybe I didn't want them to be out here if any of this . . . stuff came out."

"Get *away* from me," she said, picking up her suitcase, heading for the door. "You weren't thinking about the kids," she added wearily, over her shoulder. "You were thinking about you." She stopped and turned at the door, saw that her assault had had the intended effect. "You're a loser, Charlie," she said softly, definitively. "And you don't even know why."

The door slammed, and he stood there. A moment later—perhaps more than a moment—there was a knock, and Dunnsie came in. "Charlie," he said, "the police are downstairs. They're looking for Mustafa."

They stayed up much of the night, at Oak Street, answering questions for the police, who arrived about midnight; and watching as the television trucks arrived, and the D.P.P.D. established a roped-in area, a bull pen, for the reporters and camera crews who cluttered the street.

"What happened with Nell?" Edsy asked, bringing Charlie a brandy after the police had gone. Buzz was already upstairs, sleeping off his big night.

"Don't ask," Charlie said, collapsing onto the couch in the den.

"Must have been pretty good," Edsy said. "Sometimes you leave in tears, sometimes you leave in anger. She came through here looking like she was about to bomb Hiroshima."

"My fault." Charlie debated whether to tell Edsy the awful details. She was the closest thing he had to a mother, and she proved it now by sitting down next to him, wrapping an arm around his shoulder and kissing him on the forehead. "I blew it, Edsy . . . I really blew it this time."

"She'll be back," Edsy said, stroking his hair. "And if she doesn't come back, you'll go get her."

"I don't know," he said. "It was as if she suddenly decided I was a different person. It was so total, so cold."

"Look, it's been a tough night," Edsy said. "She'll figure that out, sooner or later. I've seen the way you look at her. Gal doesn't get that kind of look every day."

Edsy was first up in the morning—Buzz, recuperating from his heroics, had vowed to stay in bed all day—and, spotting the press mob outside, filled Clarice's old giant chrome percolator with coffee, then poured a tray full of Styrofoam cups and brought it out to the troops, wearing her red silk Chinese robe. "Will the senator have a statement this morning?" a young woman producer, who had drawn the lobster shift, asked.

"Honey, do I look like a politician?" Edsy replied. She noticed the fat Sunday *Register-World* flopped on the dewy front lawn with a banner headline—and as unobtrusively as she could, which wasn't very, she picked it up and brought it inside. After a quick glance, she went up to Charlie's room—he was asleep on top of his bed, fully clothed.

She knocked on his open door and said, "I'd say 'Good morning,' but there's this—" and handed him the paper:

MARTIN AIDE ASSAULTS BUTLER
by Robert Hamblin with Evan Cooper,
Caroline Adams and Mark Jones

Leland J. Butler, the Republican challenger in a suddenly vicious United States Senate race, was rushed to Otowulla County Hospital Saturday evening after a physical confrontation with an opposition campaign worker whom Butler had earlier accused of drug dealing, during the annual State Fair Campaign Kickoff Debate.

A hospital spokesman said Butler was in satisfactory condition after suffering a fractured skull in the struggle with Mustafa Al-Bakr, a member of Senator Charles Martin's campaign staff. According to witnesses, Al-Bakr, who was freed from a Vietnamese prison in April 1992 after intensive negotiating efforts by Senator Martin, disappeared after grappling with Butler on the front steps of the muffler magnate's West Lewis mansion.

The confrontation capped a memorable evening of charges, countercharges and physical scuffles between the Martin and Butler campaigns, including a shouting and pushing match that involved William "Buzz" Martin, the incumbent senator's father, and Leland Butler, after a leaflet accusing the senator of immorality was distributed throughout the fairgrounds. A spokesman for the Butler campaign said the Republican challenger had nothing to do with the leaflet and was "outraged by the invasion of Senator Martin's privacy."

The confrontation with Al-Bakr took place as the Butler family was returning from the state fairgrounds. "He came out of nowhere, just after we arrived," said Thomas McCormick, Butler's driver. "He was wild-eyed and talking gibberish. He was going for Mrs. Butler when Mr. Butler stepped between them. He said, 'Vengeance is mine, sayeth the Lord,' and he shoved Mr. Butler down the stairs. He ran off when he saw I had a gun."

Mr. McCormick said that he didn't fire the gun and didn't

pursue Mr. Al-Bakr. "Mr. Butler needed my immediate attention," he said.

Earlier, Butler appeared to surprise Senator Martin in the traditional state fair debate by charging that Al-Bakr had been
transporting a large quantity of heroin when he was detained by
the Vietnamese authorities. Martin neither confirmed nor denied the charges, and could not be reached for comment afterward. "We'll have a statement when there's definitive word from
the police about what happened last night," a Martin campaign
spokesman said. "Meanwhile, our thoughts and prayers are with
the Butler family."

The story drifted into an extended account of the debate and jumped
to a four-page spread inside the paper that included sidebars about the
Messengers' flier and the Christian turnout at the fairgrounds, debate
analyses by Hamblin and Lenora Cuttori, the *R-W*'s theater critic, and
distended swatches of verbatim transcripts. There was a front page photo
of the mayhem onstage at the Martin victory party: Buzz reaching an arm
across a knot of bodies—Charlie's, Calvin's, their faces hidden—trying to
get at Lee Butler, who was looking quite calm (although Charlie's eye, as
he scanned this, was drawn to Joan Butler, hands on her cheeks and
more than horrified—embarrassed).

Charlie read it all, in bed, sipping coffee Edsy had brought. Then he
called Patsy Dunn at home. "Have you seen it? What do you think?"

"Hard to tell," Dunn said. "There's so much of it. Do you want the
good news? Mustafa has pushed the personal stuff way down the paper.
He really trampled all over their story."

"Isn't that wonderful," Charlie said. "Dunnsie, I think we'd better call
off the schedule for today. And get Hilton, Mary and yourself over here
ASAP. We're not going to get out of this place without talking to the
press, one way or another. We need to figure out what to say."

As it happened, there wasn't much to say. Charlie emerged from the
house at eleven A.M., in a serious suit with a dark tie, and held a press
conference. "Good morning, everyone," he said. "I want to express my
concern and outrage about what happened last night after the debate,
and extend my sympathies to the Butler family. There's no place for violence of any sort in American politics—not the verbal violence that was

directed anonymously against my family last night . . . and certainly no place for the physical violence that occurred in West Lewis. I'm suspending my campaign activities for a few days, to give my opponent a chance to recover"—not a huge sacrifice, since Charlie was scheduled to get back to Washington for more voting that week, anyway—"and I also want to take this opportunity to make an appeal to Mustafa Al-Bakr: please turn yourself in to the authorities. You can only make things worse for yourself by staying away. I've spoken this morning with Reverend Deems at ACTS, and she is also asking you to come in—she wants you to know, too, that the congregation will pray for you, defend you and stand with you in your time of need. . . . Okay, I'll take some questions. Bob Hamblin?"

"Have you heard from Mr. Al-Bakr since the assault?"

"No."

"Will *you* stand with him in his time of need?"

"Well, Bob, I'm not going to defend violent behavior—or trespassing. But I'd like to hear what Mustafa has to say before we rush to any judgments here. In fact, we haven't heard yet from Lee or Joan Butler."

"Have you tried to reach Mr. Butler?" Mike Aaron from AP asked.

"Yes. But he's still recuperating. My staff is talking to his staff about how we proceed with the campaign from here, though."

"Could you tell us why you put Mr. Al-Bakr on your staff, given his history of drugs and violence?"

"Well," Charlie said, "I think I explained some of that last night. Some of the guys who came home from the war . . . some of us—came home and lost our bearings. Most didn't. But some did and while there's no excuse for criminal behavior, there are extenuating circumstances and—"

"But you knew about the heroin shipment?"

A shipment now? "Yes, and the Vietnamese authorities also knew that he was carrying a package of drugs," Charlie said. "Their feeling—and my feeling, by the way—was that Mr. Al-Bakr was emotionally troubled and that he was using the drugs as a ploy, trying to get himself arrested to pay for a crime he'd committed during the war."

"You didn't do a background check?"

"The government did. There were several minor drug infractions, I was told," Charlie said. "And I didn't give him a job immediately. He spent a year working for Goodwill Industries—with no problems. At the same time, he was doing volunteer work, of great value and dependability, around my office. He—"

Charlie allowed himself to be interrupted. The words he was saying were empty, meaningless. Mustafa had been a cipher in his life, a compelling story but a bland reality. His presence was not offensive; it was merely uncomfortable. Getting rid of him would have caused more anguish than Charlie was willing to expend. There were so many other, more important things to think about. He looked off to the left, to shake a fleeting memory of the scene with Nell, and fixed on the Fox house next door: once, when he was a boy, there had been a kitchen fire at the Foxes and Clarice, inevitably, invited the family to stay at Oak Street—for an interminable two nights—before they were resettled. The Foxes weren't friends of the Martins. Their presence overstuffed the house, and made even the most routine acts difficult. At breakfast, Dickie Fox had played with his cereal bowl and spilled it onto the floor, Mr. Fox yelling, "I'll give you a lickin' and you'll hop like a chicken. . . ."

Charlie began to smile, then remembered he was in the middle of a press conference. He had been talking all the while. What had he been saying? Nothing of substance, he surmised, gauging the boredom level of the reporters staring at him. There was a disconcerting wind, the sun was pounding Charlie's forehead. This was all bullshit—the questions, the answers, the situation. He looked around, to see which of his aides would step in to end the thing. Hilton was at headquarters. Dunn had gone back into the house to make phone calls. Charlie looked around for Mary Proctor, but he found Calvin first, standing at the edge of the press mob. The boy responded immediately and forcefully, saying, "Thank you, Senator." And the reporters, happily, began to pack up.

"Thanks." He squinted at his son, shocked by the kid's decisive action. "I needed that."

"It's okay, Dad," Calvin said, hustling him back inside the house. "What do we do now? What happens next?"

"We go inside," Charlie said. "And twiddle our thumbs morosely."

Proctor was sitting in the kitchen making a series of calls to Martin coordinators around the state. The initial reactions weren't good. The gut feeling was that Charlie had been careless to have Mustafa around, that he hadn't been taking care of business generally, that he'd lost his edge. She debated whether to share this news with the candidate, who sat in the breakfast nook, head back, eyes closed. "Senator," she said softly.

"What?" He lifted his head, looked up at her.

Proctor glanced at Dunn, who noticed something new and troubling in Charlie's eyes—the exact opposite of the playful confidence that had always been there: a glum, spiritless seriousness.

"Dad, excuse me," Calvin said, breaking in. "But do you think it's a good idea to suspend the campaign now? Don't you want the folks to see that despite all this you're still you?"

"I dunno, you might be right," Charlie said dully, not caring.

"I don't think so," Dunn said, concerned—and needing time to think through their moves. "Go up to your room. Look in the mirror, Charlie. I don't want you out there looking like you just got whipped."

"Is that what I look like?"

"Not just *look* like," Dunnsie said. "It's what you sound like, too. The real Charlie Martin would've just told me to go fuck myself."

"Go fuck yourself," Charlie said. "What do you think, Cal?"

"I think it's too early to give up."

Charlie looked at Calvin in wonderment. He had arrived that morning wearing a salmon-colored knit shirt with a collar—as opposed to his inevitable T-shirt—and khakis; he'd been wearing a blue blazer outside, during the press conference. "Cal, you dressed for this debacle?" Charlie asked—mischievously, Dunnsie noted with relief.

"I figured there'd be a lot of press," the kid said, slightly embarrassed. "After last night, probably a good idea for the Martin family not to seem like a bunch of fuck-ups."

"And you think I should do what?" Charlie asked, charmed, smiling now.

"Whatever it was you were gonna do today," Calvin said. "It's the first day of the rest of your campaign."

"Dunnsie, what was I going to do?"

Pat called scheduling. It was too late for church services, but there was a softball championship at the fairgrounds. He was supposed to throw out the first pitch.

"Some of the softball folks showed up at the tent last night," Calvin said. "With a hat and T-shirt. I think Barry put them in the back of the van. What's your policy on hats?"

"He never touches the stuff, Cal," Dunn said, thrilled—uplifted, actually—by the kid's timing: the campaign had needed reinforcement and Calvin was the Marines.

"Phew, that's excellent," Cal said. "Any other ground rules?"

"Cal-viiiiiiin, what's going on here?" Charlie asked. "You had a transplant or something?"

"Well," Calvin said, nodding over at Edsy, "Grandma said, 'Maybe it's time you give your father a little help.' "

"Don't lay it on me, boyo," Edsy said. "I've been saying that to you for months."

"Well, I figured that with Mustafa AWOL, I could drive," Calvin said. "I can see where this could be okay, maybe even *fun.*"

"Fun? You having fun, Dunnsie?" Charlie asked, making a conscious effort to appear sprightly in order to counter the old man's concerns.

"No, but it's nice somebody around here is," Dunn said. "It's something you might consider, Senator. Having fun." He saw Charlie's expression founder, and knew he had gone too far: the synaptic path associated with the words "having fun" led to only one place in Charlie Martin's mind. And Pat Dunn, who had spent the last two months worrying that Nell's presence would hurt the campaign, now had another thought: that her absence might destroy it.

* * *

"You did the right thing," Morey Richardson said as he and Louise breezed into Charlie's Washington office two days later wearing matching Burberry windbreakers. "Sonnenfeld breached security. A mega-no-no. He had to go. Have you thought about who—"

"I did the wrong thing, letting you get anywhere near Nell," Charlie interrupted. Richardson started to defend himself, but Charlie stopped him, "I don't want to hear about it. I should fire your ass, too."

But he couldn't. He wasn't sure why that was so. There was a perverse need now to see where Richardson would take him. He needed to know how deep into ignominy he would allow himself to fall: he wanted to be tempted. He wanted to be able, at some point, to say no.

"Proctor takes over for Sonny with research," he announced. He had made sure to receive Morey and Louise officially, sitting behind his desk. He didn't get up to shake hands, or help with their coats. He watched as the Richardsons fluttered over each other, in an elaborate arrival minuet: she took the coats, he took the charts; he squeezed her elbow, whispered in her ear. They sat in the wing chairs. "If you don't like Mary, tough shit."

"I can live with that, can't we, Louise?" Richardson sat bolt upright, uncomfortably. Gray light washed from the window behind Charlie's desk, the window usually hidden behind closed drapes—changing the room, making it unfamiliar, drearier, not quite Charlie's office anymore.

"So, assuming I don't fire your ass, what happens now?" the senator asked. "How do I run against a victim of campaign violence?"

"We-ell . . . Guess what?" Morey ignored the question exuberantly. "He hasn't voted! Ever. He has never cast a vote. Not once, so far as we can tell."

Charlie shrugged.

"You're not impressed?" Richardson asked. "This is our September surprise."

"The silver bullet?"

"He wants a silver bullet, Louise," Morey said, "if you can imagine. But then, they always want a silver bullet, don't they? They expect me to be the Lone Ranger. That would make you—"

"Tonto." They had done this before. Louise was wearing an olive sweater set, a calf-length Black Watch kilt, argyle socks and sensible shoes. The Richardsons were looking Scottish today. "Senator," she said now, "you've had a difficult time. You need to be patient."

"Louise had a distinguished career as a psychiatric social worker," Morey said. Before she was lobotomized, Charlie thought.

"Senator, let's review your situation," Richardson continued. "You are at forty-one, two points behind among likelies—still within the margin of error. A responsible journalist, if such a creature could be found, would call the race a dead heat. And he would be wrong. Why? Because you're the incumbent. An incumbent below fifty is in the twilight zone. An incumbent below forty-five should start thinking about which industry groups might hire him as a lobbyist after he loses. The rule of thumb is, seventy-five percent of undecideds will go against the incumbent." Morey paused, smiled; he had chubby teeth. "But there's still hope! We've got a MacGuffin in this race. An X factor: your opponent is a flake—a flake who made a mistake. That rhymes, doesn't it? Butler shot his wad at the state fair, like a good yokel. That's what they do, right? They come to the state capital for the big party and lose their heads?" Morey was thrilled with himself. "Had he saved Mustafa for the University City debate, he would have had his October surprise. On the other hand, of course, the skull fracture will be good for something when he reemerges—if I know Bigler, he'll milk it. You'll drop some. If you're still single digits down on October first, we might have a shot."

"By telling people Butler didn't vote?"

"It can't hurt," Richardson said. "Especially among sixty-five-plussers, a group that wasn't too keen on your hiring a heroin dealer, according to our cross-tabs. You'll have to carry it, of course. Shamelessly. Staring right at the camera: you risked your life, you gave your hand, for democracy—the right to vote! And this twerp doesn't respect this country, doesn't respect your sacrifice, enough to participate in our American democracy? Why"—Richardson paused and smiled, a boa digesting a rabbit—"it's enough to make my blood boil! Don'tcha think?"

It had possibilities, Charlie thought. It was one way to emphasize Muffler Boy's callowness, his fecklessness, his privilege.

"Morey, the women's angle?" Louise suggested.

"He doesn't need it, dear," Richardson said. "He's got the women. . . . What Louise is suggesting, Senator—when you get a challenger who hasn't voted, you can use suffragette footage spots: our grandmothers marched for the right to vote! But you're strong with women, we don't need to spend that money—unless you want to." Richardson smiled. "We want to save some ammo for October."

He is looking at me, Charlie thought, as if I'm dead.

"Donna, why are the curtains open?" he asked, when the Richardsons had left.

"I don't know," she said, sitting in one of the recently abandoned wing chairs. "I decided to let the sun shine in, for a change."

"It's a cloudy day." He was miffed with Donna, he realized—Mustafa had been her hire. She'd been his rabbi. "Has he called?"

"Who?" Donna asked. Charlie glared at her.

"Judge Crater," he said.

She nodded silently. "And?" He asked.

"He didn't push Butler down the stairs," Donna said. "Butler was moving on him and he stepped away—and Butler fell."

"And what was he doing there in the first place?"

"He was appealing to Butler, as a fellow Christian. For you. He didn't think it was fair that you should take the hit for his behavior. It was stupid. He felt guilty. He wasn't thinking clearly."

"And where is he now? I don't suppose he'd be willing to turn himself in and tell that story . . . ?"

"Do you think people will believe him?"

"No."

"Do you believe him?"

"Sort of."

"Does that answer your question?" Donna stared at Charlie and suddenly understood the odd, discomforting feelings she'd been having for months. This wasn't about Mustafa. It was about Nell. She'd been angered by Nell's impact on the boss: the woman had taken him away from his life's work, his true calling. Nell had put their relationship—Donna and Charlie's—on a different, more distant emotional footing. Had she latched on to Mustafa in anger? Didn't matter, really. But she knew then that, win or lose, she would have to start looking for another job, for a boss who took Washington as seriously as she did.

"Donna, I don't get this. I never have." He was up, pacing the room. "You are the most solid, sensible person—you've saved me from doing stupid things a thousand times. And yet—"

"And yet, I believe him?" she asked. "Yup, I do. Not that he's perfect, but he did take his obligations seriously. And wherever he is now—and I don't know where that is—he'll continue to take his obligations seriously. Because his 'rebirth' was real. He was grateful to you for that, even though he knew you didn't buy it. But he's gone now. He won't be back."

"How do you know it was real?" Charlie asked.

"It was real because Reverend Ronnie gave him a home," Donna said, and then paused for effect. "Just like Nell gave you—a home, I guess."

* * *

The pay phone on the corner of Tenth Avenue and Seventeenth Street refused to register Charlie's quarter. The coin just slid through, as if it weren't there. He was about to get angry, when he realized that he was carrying a cell phone. He felt the spiritual presence of Pamela Palmerston Belligio: "Well, *duh-uhh!*"

He called MerMaid. Lucius answered.

"Lucius, it's me. I'm downstairs, I need to see her."

"She's not here."

"Lucius—"

"Charlie, she doesn't want to see you. I wouldn't either, if I were her. You realize how far she had to go to agree to marry you. . . . Shall I tell you about the guy *before* Linc, very dashing, handsome—like you. An art dealer. She loaned him a hundred thousand dollars. Never saw it, or him, again. But I've got to say, this was much worse. . . ."

"Lucius—" He debated whether to get upset with Lucius for comparing him to a scumbag, thieving art dealer, and backed off: he had betrayed Nell, too. It was just a matter of degree.

"She's not here," Lucius repeated. "Which is a pain. Because the business needs her and the kids certainly need her."

"Where is she?"

"You think I'd tell you? Buh-bye."

Charlie reached into his pocket for the mermaid keycase, and raced across Tenth Avenue to Nell's building. He tried the door—she had changed the lock; he rang the doorbell. "Charlie, please," Lucius said, over the intercom. "Leave us alone."

He slumped down on the sidewalk, sitting with his back up against the wall. He called Des Pointe.

"Where are you, for chrissakes?" Hilton asked. "I thought you were coming straight home from Washington."

"New York, for chrissakes, locked out of Nell's loft. What's going on back there?"

"You saw the picture of Muffles 'emerging' from the hospital?"

"Yeah." With his head bandaged, looking like the Spirit of '76. They were both wounded war veterans now.

"There's talk of a big reemergence fiesta," Hilton said, "when Muff starts campaigning again. They may bring in Charlton Heston and half the Grand Ole Opry. . . ."

"H.D., I think I'm gonna take a couple days off, stick around here, see if I can find some creative way to make amends."

"Sir, you can't," Hilton said firmly. "You've got to be back tonight. In fact, you should catch the commuter out of Minneapolis to go directly to Singer Rapids. You're on Plant Gate duty first thing."

"Fuck that," Charlie said. "I'll do that Plant Gate six times between now and November, if I know Proctor."

"And the morning radio show?"

"I'll phone it in," he said, an unfortunate choice of words.

"Exactly," Hilton said. "Senator, ever since the state fair debate, everyone around here's been working double hard. The kids are just obsessed with Muff. They're calling in recruits. It's as if the future of the Republic were at stake . . . and you know what? It may be."

"And you're saying, I owe them my best shot."

"You owe it to yourself."

"No, Hilton. What I *really* owe myself is a good grovel. I've got to see if I can get her back. I won't be any use to you if I can't sort this out."

He hung up, feeling anxious and guilty. And frustrated and angry. He was angry at Nell, for walking out on him. He was angry at Donna, for being so resolutely Washington. He was angry at Hilton, for being right. He was angry about the election—he tried to imagine a voter, he pictured a middle-aged woman, confronted with his name and Leland Butler's in a voting booth. And actually *stewing* over that choice? Jesus! The hell with them all.

He called Hilton again. "Hilton, I'm a mess. I'm sorry."

"Sir, with all due respect—you can't afford to be a mess. Or sorry. And if you don't get on the very next plane here, I'm going to walk. I don't want to be part of this, live in a goddamned suburban ranch house, have my private life dragged out in public and hand this state over to a sociopathic charlatan, if you're not giving it your all . . . and I'm going to advise the kids to walk with me."

"All right," Charlie conceded. "I'm coming."

"Not good enough," Hilton pushed. "You've got to come back focused—and pissed."

"You're right," he conceded again.

"Stop agreeing with me, for chrissakes. Get pissed."

"A sociopathic charlatan?"

"Well, something like that."

"I'm on my way."

17

Once again, Patsy Dunn was impressed by the cleverness and discipline of the Muffler Man campaign. The candidate recuperated brilliantly. The doctors prescribed a month of rest before Lee Butler could resume a normal schedule, and a luxuriant month it was. The day after the assault, there was a thumbs-up-with-pained-smile photo from the hospital and the requisite Reaganesque quote: "The first thing he told me when he came in," said Dr. Lars Hansen at the next-day press conference, "was 'Joanie always said I should have my head examined.' "

A week later, Muffler Man was ceremoniously disgorged from the newly endowed Otowulla County Hospital (the Butler Family Charitable Trust had gratefully donated $1 million for a new pediatrics wing). A spray of nurses and assorted staff lined the path to the hospital's main entrance, applauding as their patient departed. A crowd of well-wishers stood behind police lines across from the hospital, cheering. The next day's *R-W* featured a Caroline Adams story about what a kind and thoughtful patient Lee Butler had been: " 'He was always over in the kids' wing, cheering them up,' said Susan McElvoy, registered nurse. 'And he gave each of us a lifetime gift of free Muffler Man service.' "

Another week passed, quietly. And then a Hamblin interview with the candidate in the *R-W*. The injury had been a "valuable experience," Butler said, arrayed in robe and pajamas—and still bandage-swathed—in his West Lewis study. "It was God's way of telling me to slow down and reflect upon the problems facing America, especially the legacy of drugs and violence."

An interesting word, "legacy." Hamblin asked him what he meant. "I think, unfortunately, the loosening of moral standards is what our older brothers and sisters in Jack Stanton's generation will be remembered for.

This is a problem that escalated in the sixties, one we've got to clean up now."

"Do you consider Senator Martin part of that generation?" Hamblin asked. "Is he part of the problem?"

"I'd rather not talk politics just now," Lee Butler replied.

Butler also said that he didn't remember the incident with Mustafa very clearly. He believed his wife had been in danger. He had tried to step between her and the intruder. "What do you think Mr. Al-Bakr's motivation was?" Hamblin asked.

"I'm not sure. He seemed angry and confused," Butler said mournfully. "I don't think Senator Martin had anything to do with it."

Truly impressive, Patrick Dunn thought. Butler seemed slower, deeper, more dignified; almost senatorial. The near-death experience had given him ballast. And now the injury could be used as protection from hostile questions about the Messengers and Mexican mufflers and his vicious ad campaign (actually, the negative ads had been suspended, leaving only the inspirational bio spots). It would have been unseemly for Bob Hamblin, and for the parade of local television anchors who followed him, to vamp on the recuperating candidate.

And Butler's recovery wasn't done yet. There was another week of preparation for the Grand Reemergence, which would take place during a monster rally in front of the state capitol, emceed by the hosts of Monday Night Football, with performances by an armada of country music stars. Each day a new crop of attendees was announced—crowned, eventually, by word that Sean Puckett, the revered coach of the state university basketball team, would break his long-standing policy of political neutrality and use the occasion to endorse Lee Butler for the United States Senate.

Throughout all this, Charlie Martin plugged away at his campaign. He worked twelve-hour days, crisscrossed the state, never complained. Patsy Dunn watched his candidate carefully, critically—and couldn't quite figure out what was missing. The performances were energetic, enthusiastic; there was a fair amount of anger, bubbling just beneath the surface, too. "What is it?" he asked Hilton. "What's not clicking? What's not there?"

"Mischief," Devereaux said, thinking: Nell, of course. The boss was in mourning. "He's not having any fun. He hasn't taken a WTF since Muffler Man got brained."

"Well, it's hard to run clever against a bandage," Pat said.

"I'm sure that's what the boss's opponents always thought, too," Hilton said. "You ever have a campaign where you didn't use a bio spot with the war hero pictures from *Life*?"

Cruel, Pat thought, but probably fair. "I'll tell you what I've never had," Dunn said. "I've never had a campaign where I had to tell so many people *not* to support us."

That had been a constant struggle since *The Washington Post* had run a piece using Charlie as the poster boy for incumbent Democrats in trouble across the country: all of a sudden the campaign was beset by professional liberals—gay rights groups, civil-libertarians, choicers, atheist anti-vivisection vegetarians, all of whom wanted to express their very visible support for Charlie Martin. Hilton had to beg the YoGa Dems not to run spots attacking Muffler Man for his opposition to "alternative lifestyles." There was fear that some of the other, more angry gay groups would disrupt Butler's campaign relaunch. "Why is it," Dunn asked, "that conservative extremists smile and liberal extremists snarl?"

"Why is it," Hilton replied, "that tank tops look so good on women and so awful on men?"

And yet, the Martin numbers held. The momentum seemed all Butler, but a stubborn 40 percent of likely voters stayed with Charlie Martin, and an even more stubborn 10 to 12 percent remained undecided.

"I think this is good for us," Dunn told his candidate one evening in early October, as the minivan traversed the barren, autumnal corn and soy fields between Fort Jeffords and Des Pointe, the first freshly fallen leaves eddying along the highway. "He's had all this great press and it hasn't gotten him anywhere."

"It's not bad for us," Charlie said. "But I wouldn't go so far as to say it's good. The most important thing happening is that ten percent of likelies—a disproportionate number of them elderly, addictive voters, people who always come out and usually vote for me—apparently can't stand either one of us."

"Does Morey have anything targeted at them?" Dunn asked.

"Muff's nonvoting stuff." Richardson had held off the new attack spots while Butler was recuperating.

"Almost forgot about those," Dunn said. "But they're not bad. Especially the ones with you talking straight to the camera. If you're trying to move World War Two guys, the notion that this kid has never exercised his right to vote might just work."

"What do you think, Cal?" Charlie asked.

"It's good," Calvin replied, his eyes fixed on the road.

"But?"

"But it's an ad," Calvin said.

"Calvin has a lot of sympathy for nonvoters." Charlie squeezed his son's shoulder.

"And for voters, too."

"Touché," Charlie said.

But it's an ad. There was something to that, and Charlie asked Calvin about it later, during one of the late night breakfasts at the Waffle House that had become a ritual for them. "What did you mean, 'It's just an ad,' Cal?"

"Ads suck, especially political ads."

"But they're effective." Charlie put grape jelly on a thick, spongy English muffin.

"I suppose, although it isn't the toughest sell to convince most people that politicians are assholes," Calvin said.

"But if he's busy convincing people I'm an asshole, what choice do I have but to convince people he is, too?"

"I don't know," Calvin replied. "I'm just driving the van."

"No fair," Charlie said. "You can't have insights and then not think them through."

"It just seems to me that the most memorable thing that happened in this campaign was Muffler Man getting brained," Calvin said immediately. "And the second most memorable thing was the Bible Biking. And neither of those were ads."

"And neither of them were things *we* did, either," Charlie said. "You got any ideas? Anything we might do?"

"You could skydive into Muffler Man's Reemergence Festival. . . ."

"Naked," Charlie said.

"Naked Came the Senator," Calvin said. "Good name for a band."

"No it isn't," Charlie replied.

*   *   *

The Reemergence Festival was unforgettable, but not quite memorable. It was enormous, and stupefyingly bland. It rained, and a sea of citizens filled the plaza in front of the statehouse, shivering beneath umbrellas. They sang "I'm Proud to Be an American" and "God Bless

America" and "America the Beautiful"—a medley Buzz would never have countenanced, but that couldn't be gainsaid—as American flags fluttered on giant screens that surrounded the stage. Lee Butler was introduced by Sean Puckett, the basketball coach who would have been called for a technical foul if politics were as orderly as athletics: "We've seen the sort of violence and immorality in this campaign that should never be a part of our American democracy," Coach said. "You have an opportunity—to say no to violence, to say no to immorality. You have a chance to bring order out from chaos. That's a slam-dunk in my book . . . and here's the most valuable player who'll make it happen: Lee Butler!"

Charlie took the night off. He and Calvin went to the movies. They saw *Quiz Show,* which was about a distinguished and apparently honorable academic—Charles Van Doren—seduced by celebrity. The next morning, on the way to a skein of church appearances in the western suburbs of Des Pointe, Charlie read the *R-W*'s account of Muffler Man's return, in which Butler patronizingly characterized Charlie Martin as an honorable man seduced by moral relativism. "I thank God for this injury," Muffles had said, with a catch in his voice. "I thank God for giving me the chance to meditate and reflect on my great good fortune. I thank God for revealing to me the importance of this campaign, the nature of the opposition, the need for an uncompromising, unrelenting and joyous sprint these last three weeks—a righteous dash: on to victory!" And the crowd took up the chant: "On to vic-to-ry! On to vic-to-ry! On to vic-to-ry!"

"Isn't chanting sort of Teutonic?" Charlie asked Patsy Dunn, with a smile. "Americans don't chant, they grunt—ooogah, ooogah. Right?"

"You like the way he slipped 'the nature of the opposition' in there?"

"Yeah, well," Charlie said. "I always sort of figured Muff was doing this as a hoot. Now it looks like he's a Blues Brother: on a mission from God. That should make him easier to beat."

It was, Patsy thought, the first time in a while that Charlie had actually talked about winning.

* * *

Morey Richardson descended on Des Pointe, unbidden, three days later. He met the candidate, at Oak Street, as before, with Louise and Mary Proctor, who had become a very enthusiastic research director, in tow. Everyone sat in the same seats. Charlie in the La-Z-Boy; Mary found Paul Sonnenfeld's spot, as if by radar, next to Louise on the couch;

Morey, wearing a bright baby-blue V-neck sweater over a white turtleneck this time, in the straight-back dining room chair next to Charlie—drinking his hot water with vitamins and artificial sweetener, as always. "All right," he said. "It's show time, Senator. It's time to win this. It's time for our October surprise."

"You mean, the nonvoting ads?" Charlie asked.

"Oh . . . yeah. Right. That was the September surprise," Morey said. Charlie gave him a look and he said, "There's always an October surprise. You know that. It's time to really take this turkey down. Mary?"

"She had an abortion," Mary said. "Joan Butler. In 1987."

"Oh, come on," Charlie said, laughing. "This is just too rich . . . and you just found out about it?"

"Well, we knew," Richardson said. "But we didn't want to bring it to your attention until the proper time."

"Until I was really desperate and willing to use anything?" He looked at Mary sharply; she was, quite wittingly, avoiding his eyes, staring at her notes. "Jesus, guys. . . . What kind of a slimeball do you think I am? Two months ago, I asked you to tell me everything you'd dug up."

"On your friends," Morey said. "You said, everything I'd dug up on your friends and family. You didn't ask if I'd gotten anything good on Butler."

"An abortion, Morey? Muffler Mom? I don't believe it. And I don't want to have any part of it."

Morey stayed him with a suddenly steady hand: "Tell him the rest, Mrs. Proctor."

"The procedure was done at twenty-six weeks. It was an intact dilation and extraction. The doctor was—"

"Whoa, whoa, Mary," Morey said. "Let's linger on the implications. First, twenty-six weeks. That's well into the second trimester. You have a baby on the very cusp of life. There are cases of children surviving ex utero—"

Morey was actually serious. Charlie was appalled. "Enough," he said. "This is disgusting."

"No, Senator," Morey said. "Not enough. Not nearly enough. Do you know what people like Lee Butler call an 'intact dilation and extraction'? They call it a 'partial birth' abortion. Mary?"

Mary flipped open a notebook and read, " 'The fetus is maneuvered into breech position and delivered into this world feet first—and then the head is crushed and the brains suctioned out to facilitate delivery.' "

"Mary's obviously reading from something," Morey said. "Can you guess what she's reading from?"

Charlie shook his head, but he could guess.

"The Muffler Man radio show. June eighth, 1993. 12:43 P.M.," Mary said. "I heard it myself. I remembered it. You never forget a thing like this."

"And read him the rest now. . . ."

"Well, after he gave the description of the operation, Butler said, 'There are those who would call this a "surgical procedure." But I think there is another, simpler term for it: murder. It is murder, pure and simple. And it is happening in this country, every day. By the thousands.' " Mary looked up from her notes. "He was off there. Not nearly in the thousands. But it does happen. It happened to Joan Butler."

"Why?" Charlie asked, frowning, amazed, grossed out.

"What do you mean, why?" Morey asked.

"There must have been a reason. They were married. This was 1987? They already had children," Charlie said angrily. He looked over at Proctor, who met his gaze coolly, steadily, as Paul Sonnenfeld would have: did Richardson have some sort of injection he gave to make his people moral zombies? "Why did she have the abortion? Mary? There must have been something drastic going on."

"Who cares?" Morey said. "You heard his words. He's a hypocrite."

"I don't know," Charlie said. "How'd we find out about this anyway? Aren't hospital records private? I don't think this is any of our business."

"I do."

Charlie looked up. Louise? She was standing, glaring at him, vehement—incomprehensibly furious. "If it's not your business, Senator, it's mine. It's my *body* he's talking about. It's my right. And it's extremists like Lee Butler who are the real danger to this country—"

"Louise has strong feelings on this subject," Morey said, with a patronizing chuckle. "As does Mary. As do many women. Including a certain anesthesiologist at Otowulla County Hospital, who was present for Joan Butler's surgical procedure."

"And other people have strong feelings on the other side," Charlie said. "My strongest feeling is that this is a private decision, and in this case, a decision that was probably very painful and taken for good reason. None of our business. Even when someone like Lee Butler is involved."

"Spoken like a true loser," Morey scoffed. "That's what's happening, you know. You're losing. A nice chunk of the undecideds fell into Butler's lap after that molasses-and-margarine festival the other night. He's at fifty-one now. You're down to thirty-nine—two points of yours moved undecided. Basketball fans, I'd guess. I figured Puckett was good for a point or two, and he was."

Charlie slumped—not physically, not so anyone could see. But he felt as numb, as devastated, as he had when Morey had unloaded on him about Nell. Morey had nailed him twice now, and there was a distant but familiar exhaustion that came with the territory. This was the emotional equivalent of sandbag drill. Carolina swamps, ninety degrees, humidity off the charts, a duffel bag filled with sand on his shoulders, two hundred pounds of dead weight. What did they call it? EUF drill. Extraction Under Fire. EUF sounded like vomit. He had EUFed, afterward; his arms, shaking with weakness in the heat; his hands numb, unable to grip. Another acronym for EUF: Exhaustion Under Fire. He was EUFed now.

"Muffler Boy's on a jihad," Morey was saying, "and you're playing badminton. I don't want to lose this thing. Bad for business. Senator, it's time to get real."

"What do you think?" Charlie asked. He had expanded the late night Waffle House ritual with Calvin to include Hilton, Dunnsie, and Mary Proctor. They sat in a booth, down the end; a few stray truckers, tight T-shirts, big guts and tattoos were scattered along the counter.

"Go with it," Mary Proctor said, without even a breath's hesitation.

"What if they had a good reason for the abortion?" Charlie asked. "I mean, a married couple, two kids. A very late-term abortion. There had to be extenuating circumstances."

"Let him explain it," Mary said. "It's probably good and complicated—like the reasons why you overlooked Mustafa's heroin. And this is far more relevant. It's an issue in the campaign. I, for one, *really* want to know what he has to say."

"Me too," said Hilton.

"I wouldn't believe a thing he said," Calvin said. "But I'd sure like to see him suffer."

"So you're with them?" Charlie asked his son. Calvin nodded. "Dunnsie?"

"It changes everything," Pat said, nursing a coffee. "Butler's been an express train. He just keeps picking up speed. This derails it. How does Morey want to do it?"

"Radio ad," Charlie said, leaning forward, speaking softer. "Pretty spectacular. A woman announcer says, 'The following is a political advertisement, paid for by Citizens *Opposed* to Lee Butler for U.S. Senate.' It's an out of state committee, solid citizens—OB–GYNS, women members of state legislatures from around the country. 'We want you to listen carefully to what Lee Butler said on June eighth, 1993.' Then you hear the partial-birth sound bite from the Muffler Man radio show. And nothing else. No explanation."

Dunnsie whistled.

"Yikes," Hilton said. "Devastating. It jumps to free media immediately. The TVs play it on the evening news. They ask Butler, what's this ad all about? It rocks Muff's world."

"And if he denies it, if he says he has no idea what this is about, there's a second ad," Mary Proctor said, smiling. "Right, boss?"

"Okay, the second ad," Charlie said hesitantly, glancing at Mary Proctor, still amazed by the vehemence of her transformation. "It opens with Butler speaking: his partial-birth sound bite from June eighth, 1993. And then the woman announcer says something like: 'According to records at the Otowulla County Hospital, Joan Butler had a pregnancy terminated by intact dilation and extraction on February eighteenth, 1987. The decision was a private one, made in consultation with a physician. Which is Joan Butler's constitutional right. Joan Butler's husband would like to eliminate your right to make a similar choice.' "

"Jesus Christ," Dunnsie said. "That seems pretty extreme."

"Extreme?" Mary Proctor said. "It's the plain truth."

"I agree with you, Dunnsie," Charlie said. "And, of course, Morey figured that's how I'd feel." He glanced at Mary uncomfortably; she was a spy. "The route he really wants to take is an anonymous drop—put the hospital records in Bob Hamblin's hands. Let him break the story."

"That's a lot better," Dunn said, exhaling.

"You think so?" Charlie asked, smiling: the airplane calm was back in his eyes. "Do you *really* think so?"

"Obviously," Hilton said, "you don't."

"Well, shit, I don't know," Charlie said, stirring the crushed ice in his Diet Coke with an index finger. "How'd you like it, Hil, when that Messengers leaflet mentioning your personal life fell into Blake Dornquist's sweaty little hands?"

"That was different. It was an invasion of—"

"Privacy?" Charlie asked. "Right."

There was silence around the table. Finally, Mary Proctor said, "Charlie, I've been out here working for you most of my adult life. If we allow this creep to beat us, it means everything we've worked for—"

"No it doesn't," Charlie said. "If we lose, it just means we lost."

"He's a bad guy, Charlie." Proctor seemed almost disdainful of her boss. "I don't want him to be our senator."

"You're not the one who has to pull the trigger, Mary," Charlie said softly.

"Then we're not gonna go with it?"

"I didn't say that," Charlie said. "It just means that I'm the one who has to take ultimate responsibility for this decision. And I'm not sure yet how I want to go. But here's what I'm thinking right now: we've rejected the radio ads. Too harsh. We're uncomfortable with the anonymous leak to the press. That's something *he* would do. On the other hand, I think we all believe this is a remarkable bit of information—I assume that there were excellent reasons for whatever Joan Butler decided to do. The fact that Muff would go through whatever that experience was, and then take such a hard-ass cruel position, denying other people a similar choice, speaks directly to his hypocrisy. The fact that Lee Butler is a slimy, hypocritical piece of shit is the big issue in this campaign—and this is our very best evidence of that. It's why he should lose." Charlie paused.

"So?" Mary Proctor asked.

"So, if we agree that this is a subject worthy of debate," Charlie said, "then we shouldn't beat around the bush. I should raise it directly—face-to-face, during the University City debate."

"Jesus," Dunn said. "That is the stupidest idea I've ever heard."

Charlie smiled, crinkling his eyes. "Oh?"

"You'll lose. He'll be outraged, and most people will be outraged along with him."

"But if the issue is hypocrisy," Charlie said, "if we think Muff is a phony and a turd, shouldn't we be the exact opposite? Shouldn't we raise this issue forthrightly . . . honorably?"

"It won't seem honorable. You'll look low. No one'll understand the moral distinction," Patsy said. "They'll just hear the words. You think you can actually say those words, talk about his wife's abortion, in public?"

"If we agree they're worth saying, why shouldn't I?"

"Because this is *politics*," Hilton said—and everyone around the table laughed nervously. "In politics, you never say anything real—you just give the appearance of saying things that are real."

"You really believe that?" Charlie frowned and then smiled.

"Think about it," Hilton said. "And see if you don't agree. Seriously, what would you actually say? Let's hear you do it right now—pretend I'm Muffler Man."

"Mr. Butler," Charlie said, squaring his shoulders, "you've taken some extreme positions on a lot of complicated issues. Positions that don't allow much wiggle room. For example, on June eighth, 1993, you said this about late-term abortions . . . And then I'd read the transcript. And then I'd say . . . I—I-ayy-ayy-ayy . . ."

More laughter.

"I could say, didn't you and your wife have a decision to m-m-mmaay-ayy-ayy . . ."

"Very clever," Mary Proctor said. "You're just trying to show us how sleazy bringing this into the campaign in *any* way would be."

"Sleazy but worthy," Hilton said.

"I'm not ruling it out," Charlie said. "Let's mull it. What do you think, Calvin Coolidge? This qualify as nude skydiving?"

"Well," Calvin said, "it wouldn't be an ad."

*   *   *

Francesca Warren, the junior senator from California, had offered to come in and campaign for Charlie. Morey Richardson was opposed—her flashy, West Coast feminism would do the Martin campaign absolutely no good and quite possibly some harm, with the elderly and the blue-collar populists who would decide the election. But Charlie believed it would be rude to turn down a colleague's offer of help (he'd received precious few others); more to the point, he was lonely. The silence from Nell had lasted more than a month and seemed irrevocable. He had sent notes; he had sent flowers; he had called and called. In late October, the Mer-Maid phone line was suddenly disconnected; Nell's new private number was unlisted. Over time, Charlie found his self-loathing seeping toward anger. He had made a terrible mistake, but Nell's abrupt exit—her utter unwillingness to forgive him—seemed extreme and irrational and thoughtless; another amputation, almost. Worse, in a way: there was no sane reason for so destructive an act. There was only pain.

And so, he decided, for sanity's sake, to have a run at Senator Warren, who came in two days before the University City debate. She had cut her hair—it was dark and short and bouncy now—and she was the rarest of elected woman office holders: one who eschewed the heavily shoulder-padded linebacker look. She was sleek, and she was fun; she traveled in the van, meshed easily with Dunnsie and Hilton, gave rousing introductions for Charlie as they moved from event to event. She worked a rolling debate prep with Dunnsie in the van on the day before the University City event. Charlie asked her what she'd do about the Muffler Mom abortion issue, even though he assumed—correctly—that she'd go with it (not in the debate, though; she was adamant that it be raised, as Morey wished, through a press leak).

"Char-lie," she said, as they picked up their keys to identical suites, a floor apart, at the University City Crowne Plaza on the afternoon of the debate, "I know what's going on in your head on the abortion thing. I've seen this before. . . . Remember Jessica Mahon?" She smiled remorsefully and punched him gently, awkwardly, on the arm. "You're delaying now, same way you did then. You're trying to be a nice guy, hope it'll go away."

"I don't want to think about it right now, unless you have some clever, painless way I can bring it up in the debate," he said.

"The debate's a cover. You don't want to use it at all."

She was certainly right about that. Morey Richardson raised the abortion question and Charlie shut him down during a final prep consult late that afternoon, the prep team—Dunn, Senator Warren, Hilton and Calvin—gathered in the candidate's suite. "All right. You're right. Forget about the abortion thing now. Concentrate on the business at hand," Morey said, patched in from Paris. "But you've got to promise me, we make a solid go/no-go decision on Muffler Mama tomorrow. We need this out now. Any later looks too tactical. This is it, boys."

Afterward, Francesca asked, "Why'd you hire Morey? He's so un-you."

"Because Muffler Man is un-me, too," Charlie said, surprising himself with the insight. "If we're going to have these geniuses around advising us, might as well pick them to match our opponents."

She offered a high five. "All right!" she said. "You just made the trip worthwhile. You've given me a rationale to hire a scumbag in '98." She smiled, touched his cheek. "Actually, I was looking forward to coming out here, seeing how you reacted . . ."

"Under duress?"

"Or perhaps . . ." She paused, about to say "underdressed," but she noticed Calvin, slouched on a couch and testing the local cable system, raising a Buzzy eyebrow.

———

The debate was held at the Parkman Theater on the state university campus. There was a broad slate patio out front—which, that evening, was the site of a "pee-in" staged by members of ACT UP, who used poster-sized photos of Muffler Man for target practice. They were quickly hustled off by police, but the event would be reported prominently—more bad news for the Martin campaign.

Morey had launched the spots relating Muffler Man's "nonvoting" record a week earlier, and Charlie had been prepped to add his needle to the surprisingly brutal press assault that the ads had occasioned—Butler's belated reemergence and his lead in the polls had liberated Hamblin and the others to start treating Muff more critically: this nuanced gyroscopy was one of the more subtle rituals of political reporting. Front-runners were treated tougher; the press was inevitably biased in favor of a closer race.

Charlie figured the debate would be his last real shot at changing the momentum of the campaign. He wasn't sure how he'd do that; he was going to improvise—take whatever Muff gave him, and run with it. He had sleepwalked the prep, going through the motions to keep the staff happy (and to impress Francesca Warren). He knew that the passive-aggressive hazing—the battery of difficult and embarrassing questions from the staff, the attempts to get him riled—was completely irrelevant. He couldn't predict what he would say or do when Lee Butler walked onstage.

At the same time, he had decided not to use the abortion material. Ever. He wasn't going to allow it to be leaked and he certainly wouldn't approve the radio ads. He'd probably have a fairly memorable confrontation with Morey over that. He'd probably have to fire the guy (although his impromptu rationale for hiring the jerk stayed with him, giving him second thoughts); he might even have to part ways with Mary Proctor: she was Mary Zombie now. But this was his career, and his reputation, and his home. He had invested twenty years in not being a scumbag; he would have to spend the rest of his life looking these folks in the eye. He didn't want to be remembered as someone who would do *anything* to get elected.

And then Lee Butler walked out onto the stage, and everything changed. The kid was ready for his coronation. He was all puffed out and glowing, barely able to control his smile. He'd been flying, ever since the Mustafa incident; everything he did, every interview, every ad, every public appearance, seemed to be working. Charlie had never known that feeling, the adrenaline rush of having a hard-fought campaign break his way—he'd always been a heavy favorite—but he could imagine how it felt, seeing Butler bounce onto the stage, all gassed up, his feet barely touching ground. The light-headedness of the moment was heightened by the presence of the audience, steeply banked from the pit of the orchestra to the balcony—a receding wall of people, a visual effect Charlie had enjoyed in the past. But the emotional surge when Butler entered, a few seconds after he did, was as if a large wave had crashed onstage, creating a rolling displacement, causing the audience to float higher in the theater, as if it were levitating. Charlie had to squeeze his lectern to keep his balance.

Butler moved toward him now, abruptly. He crossed the stage, jazzed with his power, to shake hands—a winning move: he had taken the nice-guy initiative . . . but then he took it a step too far and actually tried to hug Charlie, as if they were comrades in some grand and memorable shared experience. Charlie braced Butler, pushing him back with his handshake, and rolled his shoulders away from the hug; Muff looked surprised, and then slightly hurt. "How *dare* you?" Charlie whispered ferociously, through clenched teeth.

Butler glanced at the senator sharply before turning away—and saw something far more terrifying than anger: an assassin's look, a snake-eater's fury.

Muffler Man glanced again, nervously this time, at his opponent—then moved into his opening statement and lost himself in the swollen, gassy wonderfulness of his oratory, a celebration of God and the greatness of Our Country and the wisdom of Our People . . . and how he'd tried, in this campaign, to lay out a new path of righteousness, to turn Warshington back to the people's business. He was wearing a red, white and blue striped tie and American eagle galluses; he hooked a thumb in one of the braces and seemed to swivel as he spoke, full on his heels.

And then, it was Charlie's turn. "I want to congratulate Mr. Butler on this sudden burst of public spirit," he said. "But I'm curious, Lee. What was it about democracy that you found so . . . uninteresting in all those other election years?"

"Is that your opening statement?" asked the moderator, Thurston Frame, the president of the state university.

"Yes," Charlie said.

"Well—" Frame began, scanning his list of questions.

"Actually," Charlie said, "I'd kind of like to know what Mr. Butler's answer is. Lee, what were you doing all those election days when everyone else was out voting—selling mufflers?"

Frame looked to Butler, who put his hand out, palm down, willing to answer: he'd taken the bait. "I made a mistake," he began, hitting his talking points straight on. "But—"

"I mean, weren't there any Republicans worth voting for all those years?" Charlie interrupted him—calm, smiling; completely composed.

"I should have—"

"What about your running mate, the governor?" Charlie pressed. "You never voted for him. You never even voted for the Otowulla County school board, for your kids . . . why not?"

"I guess," Butler huffed, but with a country smile, "I was like a lot of folks. I saw a lot of Warshington politicians giving tax breaks to their friends, and making fortunes and dating movie stars . . . and so I just turned off on politics. If I'd looked more closely, I'm sure I would have found a lot of good people, like the governor, to vote for."

"But that would have involved taking some time, and you were a very busy guy . . ."

"Excuse me, Senator," said Frame, who saw his evening slipping out of control. "But I have a question for Mr. Butler now, about taxes."

"I'm against the Stanton tax increases," Butler said, without waiting for the question, "which my opponent voted for. I'm against tax increases, period."

"Another carefully thought-out position," Charlie said, smiling slightly. "You know, the thing that really impresses me about you, Lee, is how much *thought* you give these issues. I mean, you spent more than a year on the radio, every day—taking extreme, uncompromising positions on some really complicated issues. Positions without much wiggle room . . ."

Hilton snapped to attention in the holding room. He remembered this line.

"You must have an awful lot of confidence," Charlie went on firmly, "an awful lot of moral certainty, to just go and haul off on this and that and everything else—I mean, really sad and difficult issues like abortion . . ."

Hilton grabbed Pat Dunn's sleeve. "What's he doing?"

"I think he's taking a WTF," Dunnsie said.

"Senator Martin," the moderator began.

"President Frame, with all due respect, I'm sure Mr. Butler is anxious to explain the sources of his moral certainty. Aren't you, Mr. Butler?"

"Well, of course," Butler said, uncertain—but proud. "That's not a difficult question for a person of faith to answer, Senator. Taking a life is wrong."

"Period," Charlie added. "You were about to say that, weren't you? Like 'I'm against raising taxes, period.' "

"Senator Martin—" the university president tried.

"President Frame, I know you have lots of really terrific questions—and I'll cede my closing statement and promise to keep my answers short so we can get to everything you want to know. But this is something I want to know: I want to know how Mr. Butler gets to be so certain. I guess that's a difference between us. A very important one, the folks should know about. We come from different parties . . . and from different punctuations. He has periods and I have question marks. For example, on abortion. I think most folks have question marks on that one . . . I mean, it is murder, isn't it? You are snuffing a life, right, Mr. Butler? Or maybe I should say, snuffing a life—period."

"Absolutely," Lee Butler said. "And I guess if we're asking questions, I should ask you: if you know it's murder, Senator, how can you vote for it? Not just vote for it, but for outrageous, late-term procedures like—"

"Gentlemen, gentlemen," President Frame tried.

"Aw, c'mon, Mr. President," Charlie said, shoving his hands in his pants pockets, extremely aw-shucks. "We're havin' fun. Discussing the issues. We're not even interrupting each other too much. Let us keep going . . . what do you folks out in the audience think?" Thunderous applause. Frame shrugged and exhaled. "So, Lee," Charlie asked, "you were saying . . . ?"

"I was saying that you've been willing to vote for the most outrageous late-term pregnancy termination procedures. . . ." Butler hesitated a bit on the last few words. The audience didn't catch it, but Charlie did. Now the hard part.

"Reluctantly, I did," Martin said. "Very sadly and reluctantly . . . but I'm . . . I don't know. I guess I just don't know enough, medically." Hilton thought: he's faltering. "There are rare cases, when such rare and awful procedures might be appropriate—I'm sure if you checked the records of the local hospitals here . . . maybe even your local hospital, Lee, Otowulla County. . . . Go back ten years. Less than ten years, even . . ."

Butler looked at Charlie. He did this slowly, evenly, "you might find that friends and neighbors of yours, maybe even married friends—with children . . . I've heard of cases like this . . . people who for one reason or another found it necessary to terminate a pregnancy in some rare and unfortunate way. Sadly. With terribly mixed feelings . . . with the consent and advice of their physician . . . but that's none of our business, really. Their decision."

"I don't see what this has to do with anything," Lee Butler said curtly, as if Charlie were proposing a truly irrelevant hypothetical.

"You *don't*?" Charlie asked. The question hung in the air interminably—and Charlie found himself admiring the Muffler Man: the sucker had called his bluff, and paid him a compliment, all in the same moment. He had made the calculation that Charlie Martin wouldn't pull the trigger. Never, ever—

"Well, maybe you're right. . . ." Charlie said. "Maybe this doesn't have anything to do with anything." He paused, and gave Butler a sly smile—a reflex covering the reality that he had just collapsed internally, that he had just conceded defeat. "I just wanted to point out that sometimes good people face complicated decisions—even on something so clear-cut as life and death. I just wanted to let the folks know why I haven't been so *certain* a senator as you, apparently, would want to be. Why I've found an awful lot of question marks in public life, and not so many periods. Anyway, President Frame, you've been waiting patiently—next question, please."

Hilton saw Mary Proctor flip out her cell phone as soon as Charlie flinched. He looked at Pat Dunn, who shrugged; and at Francesca Warren, all done up for the occasion—in shoulder pads, even—but staring down now, arms crossed, studying her Ferragamos. "Excuse me," he asked Dunn, "but what just happened?"

"I'm not sure," Patsy said, "but we may have just lost."

That certainly was Morey Richardson's sense. He called Charlie in his suite an hour later. "Do you realize what you've done?"

"What," Charlie asked, snagging a green apple from the inevitable fruit basket on the table in the dining area, "have I done?"

"You blew it!"

"Says who?"

"Oh come *on*. You may be a dingbat, but you're not a dope."

"Thanks."

"You've made it fucking impossible to use this now."

"Did I?"

"Near impossible, maybe. We put the radio ads up and everyone says, So that's what Charlie Martin was hinting at in the debate." Morey's voice was distant, transoceanic; there was a slight metallic echo. "We leak it to the papers, everyone knows where it came from."

"And they wouldn't have known otherwise?" Charlie took a bite of the apple, aiming the crunch directly into the phone. "Who's kidding whom, Morey?"

"But you had plausible deniability." Even Morey knew how ridiculous that sounded. "And now, you know what we have? Nothing!"

"Hey, More . . . don't be so hard on yourself. The voting stuff was great. I think it really worked." Charlie smiled over at Francesca Warren, curled on the couch like a cat, shoes off. "But then, what do I know?"

"We'll talk about it tomorrow, after we get numbers," Morey said. "I need to think."

Hilton and Dunnsie returned from the pressroom, exhilarated. Spin patrol had been a breeze. The general feeling was, Charlie had won. He had stung Butler on the voting issue. His abortion hypothetical was seen . . . as a hypothetical. And as another question Butler couldn't answer. For most observers, Butler's "I don't see what this has to do with any-thing" had been extremely damaging: an acknowledgment that his posi-tion on abortion was simplistic. Bob Hamblin thought Butler had been subdued, unnaturally deflated, after that. The reporters were gleeful, coltish, charming; they had the possibility of a horse race again. There was a rush of requests to spend the next day traveling with Charlie.

"Boss, you think that's right?" Hilton asked. "Was Muff deflated after the abortion thing? I thought so, sort of."

"It doesn't matter. The pressies are happy. We're happy," Charlie said, trying to recall what had happened after Butler called his bluff. He wasn't sure. The bluff-calling had been so spectacular, such a clean kill. Charlie Martin, R.I.P.

And no one knew. Not even Hilton, not even Patsy Dunn. They knew that Charlie had whiffed on the abortion material; they weren't close enough to understand that Butler had made the calculation, called him on it—and Charlie wondered, is it possible that Lee Butler and I are the only ones who know what actually happened tonight?

The suite filled with supporters, and then it slowly emptied. The mood was festive, but quietly so. The assumption was the debate had gone well, but the election was still a problem. Charlie was heartened: these were pros. He looked in each face and saw a town, or a county: Port Sallesby, Singer Rapids, Nebble Forks. He'd given them something to work with. They'd go home, get on the phones, plug away the last ten days—instead of just going through the motions. When the last of them had gone, he sighed, shed his jacket and collapsed on the couch, next to Francesca Warren—and realized, suddenly, that it was just the two of them there.

She had dark, bright eyes—and she narrowed them now, seductively, and moved confidently across the couch and kissed him on the mouth.

"Mmm," she said. "You're a good kisser . . . Charlie?" she asked, tickling the back of his neck with a finger. She kissed him again. Then she pulled back, and looked at him: "This isn't going to happen, is it?"

He laughed, remembering the day in Bartle Bramlette's office when she'd read his body language. She saw everything; too much. She lacked Nell's inspired languor. "Senator," he said.

"Am I out of order?" she asked.

"No," he said. "You seem to be in perfect working order. It's just that—"

"Two alpha-plus senators equal a minus?"

"Something like that," he said, giving her a squeeze. "You're something else, you know that?"

"You're thinking about someone else, you know that?" she said. "If I were Lee Butler, I'd undoubtedly add: period."

He nodded sadly, then started—there was a sharp rap at the door.

"The morals cops!" Francesca said, laughing, putting on a cockney tabloid announcer's voice: "Liberal senators caught in love den!"

They were both laughing giddily—relieved that their moment had passed—as Charlie moved to the door, opened it, and saw Lee Butler standing in front of him. His first impulse was to laugh harder: the morals cops, indeed.

Butler still had makeup on, too much of it: his face looked like one of those old color-tinted black-and-white photos that portrait studios displayed in their windows. His American flag tie was loosened; he seemed tired, played out. "Can I come in?" he asked. "Am I disturbing you?"

"No . . . no," Charlie said. "You know Senator Warren?"

"Yes . . . no, hello, Senator. I'm Lee Butler." Charlie ushered him in, offered him a diet Coke; he refused. Butler's physical presence was every bit as discordant as his televised image. He was, quite clearly, exhausted from the evening's exertions, but his blond hair was astonishingly fresh and glowing as if charged by some internal power source, especially when compared to his matte skin; his eyes were hazel—a brownish green—and not nearly vivid enough to suit the hair. He didn't seem quite so young up close. "I haven't brought anyone with me for a reason," he said to Charlie. "I think we need to talk, just the two of us."

Francesca stood and said, "Well, I was just about to go down to my room—"

"Senator, I'm sorry," Butler said. "I didn't mean to be impolite."

For a moment, Charlie considered asking Francesca to stay: the rule of three and all. He could set the rules now. Butler had come to him. . . . Then again, he'd always known that there would be a moment when it would be just the two of them—of course, he'd assumed that *that* moment had already come, and gone, earlier in the evening. He walked Francesca to the door, gave her a peck on the cheek. "See you in the morning," he said.

"We have the University City five-K run at six," she reminded him.

"Gawd," he said. "All right. Six it is."

He closed the door and turned to Butler, who had taken a seat—a club chair, covered in awful purple, green-and-gray-checked fabric, facing the mauve couch where Francesca had been. "You know why I'm here," he said, absentmindedly—nervously—twirling a lock of his brilliant hair.

"Tell me," Charlie replied, taking a seat on the couch, leaning forward, elbows on his knees.

"Because, you know." Charlie didn't say anything. Butler seemed uncertain about how to proceed, and Charlie let the silence hang: he was delighted to make this as difficult as possible.

"There were good reasons for it," Butler began again. Then stopped, realizing that he'd been playing with his hair, looking for something else to occupy his hands. "I think I could use that diet Coke. . . ." Charlie stood, crossed the room to the minifridge and Butler began to talk again. "I could even make a 'life of the mother' argument. The baby was a breathing corpse. It was deformed, hydrocephalic and—and other things." He faltered. Charlie handed him the Coke, but didn't sit down. He leaned back against the window frame, at a suitable distance.

"The brain was so filled with fluid that it was pushing against Joan's innards—but that wasn't it: she was hysterical. She couldn't take it. We had her sedated, but still—she'd fight it. She didn't want to be sedated. She was almost delusional. She was giving birth to—to a child of . . . Satan.

She was convinced of that." Butler looked up at Charlie, his eyes bleary—
but there was no emotion in them, or in his voice; the story was so embarrassing that it beggared any possible emotion. "All her guilt about the
bad things she'd done in her life—and she hasn't done very many, Senator, Joan is a *good* person. But that child was a judgment on her, for all
the bad."

"You don't have to—" Charlie interrupted, violating his game plan
and thinking: what a wuss I am. Let him suffer.

"No, she became convinced she had to get rid of the child before it
was born. She had to do it by killing herself—because"—he laughed—
"because God would never countenance her having an abortion. She
used a kitchen knife, one of those serrated bread knives, on her wrist.
She didn't do much damage with it, but it was bloody and we rushed her
to the hospital . . . and the doctor, Shaughnessy—do you know him? His
kid played basketball at—who cares about his kid? But Shaughnessy, he
sedated her and he's strict Roman Church—and even Shaughnessy was
saying, this baby has no chance to live. Not a chance in the world. And
maybe we should take care of it, since Joanie's here anyway—and she
wasn't sure what we were consenting to. But I was. I was. I didn't ask how
he was going to do it. But I guess with the hydrocephalic, they had to re-
duce the size of the . . . head. And that's why, I guess—but I didn't know
at the time. If he had used the words 'intact dilation and extraction,' I
wouldn't have known what he was talking about. And ever since, for
whatever reason, we haven't been able to have babies. She's convinced it
is God's judgment upon her. She's carried that with her; it's a terrible
burden on our . . . marriage. And I didn't know. I knew that we had terminated the pregnancy. But I didn't know . . ."

"Didn't know what?" Charlie asked.

"About the procedure. The exact procedure. What it was," Butler said.
"Until tonight . . . I put it together while we were up there. It's funny,
how slow everything can get. I don't even know what happened, except
that after the words were out of my mouth, 'I don't see what this has to
do with anything.' Then I knew."

"And all that bloviating on the radio?" Charlie asked. "You never
thought about it then?"

"Oh, I thought about it—generally, not specifically," Butler quickly admitted, digging the sharp edge of the aluminum pop-top into his thumb.
"But that wasn't real. That was showbiz. And with my audience, I had no
choice: I had to say it was murder. In their minds, abortion is all those

girls wearing too much makeup and too little clothing getting themselves into trouble. That's what they believe. And they have a point: it's convenience murder. You even said that tonight."

"You know what the penalty is for murder in this state?" Butler's easy acknowledgment of hypocrisy was infuriating.

"Death."

"By lethal injection," Charlie said. "Though I seem to recall you saying that that was too civilized. You favor a public spectacle—hanging with a crowd. Beer and balloons and hot dog vendors. You said that on your show, right? I'm trying to remember whether that was before or after you came out for public castration of convicted rapists."

"And that's what you're planning for me, a public spectacle?"

Charlie was about to say no, but stopped himself. "I'm curious," he said. "You had this horrible experience. A life and death experience. And you had this microphone. And you had this audience. Probably more than a couple of people who had faced similar moments, who felt guilty . . ."

"And I should have used what I knew to help them?" Butler leaned back, laughed. "You really *are* a do-gooder, aren't you!" He turned his voice mock-serious. "There are two kinds of people: the very few who 'face similar moments'—incredible crises like Joan's—and then there's everyone else. Most people just drift on through. They have heart attacks, and get pacemakers. Their mom goes in for chemo. Nothing you can poll, no *policy* implications. Those people are my audience: the great, slightly pissed off but largely untroubled multitude. They don't need crisis counseling."

"And if you win this?" Charlie asked. "Who's the audience then?"

"Well." He smiled and slowly spread his arms to incorporate the multitudes. "I'll become a statesman! I'll moderate! I'll compromise, trade my vote for the greater good. Isn't that what you guys do? But I don't get it," Butler said, impatient, getting back to the main topic. "Why didn't you just leak the story? Why'd you tip your hand tonight?"

Charlie shrugged, remained mute. He was not going to tell Butler the truth: *Well, I was really pissed at you . . . but then I chickened out.* He considered the rather remarkable possibility that Butler wasn't aware that he had successfully called Charlie's bluff.

"I wasn't going to come over here," Butler said proudly. "But Joan insisted. She said she would if I didn't. But I guess the question is, were you trying to send me a message tonight? Some sort of deal? You don't go with Joan's abortion if I don't go with something else?"

"Something else?" Charlie asked. *"What* something else? What else you got on me? That I once jacked off in a baseball glove? What is it with you, kid? You need to be a senator that badly? I don't get it."

"Then there's no deal you're willing to make?" Butler said, plunging ahead, not answering the question.

"What something else?" Butler looked up, startled. Charlie realized that he was shouting. "Do you have any idea of the pain you've caused me and my family? Do you have any fucking idea of the damage you've caused?"

"I'm sorry." Butler retreated, hands up, in front of his chest. "We don't have anything else on you. I was . . . bluffing."

"Were you now?" Charlie said. "Well, I'm not." But, having said that, he wasn't quite sure what he meant. And then he had an idea: "Okay, here's my price. I won't use your partial-birth abortion"—he emphasized the words—"but I want you to fire Bigler, and I want you to take all your ads off the air. Tomorrow."

"Unconditional surrender?"

"You think that's a white flag?" Charlie asked. "Jesus God. It's just firing your consultant and pulling your ads. Hell, I'll do the same. I was going to do it anyway. Last ten days of the campaign, it's just you and me—man to man, the old-fashioned way."

"And you won't use the abortion material?" Butler squinted at him. Charlie nodded, arms crossed on his chest. "How do I know that?"

"You have my word," Charlie said, thinking about how archaic a formulation that was. Butler would never have offered *his* word—and Charlie would never have accepted it.

"And that's what you want?" Butler asked. Charlie had a twinge of a second thought: Muffles was ahead. His ads had already done their damage. He didn't have much to lose by pulling them. There was a good chance Charlie was pouring concrete, settling the race where it was. Dunnsie, Mary Proctor—everyone would be pissed at him, and rightly so, for acting unilaterally. But he was sick of the whole business now, and this way, at least, the end of this horror of a campaign would be tolerable, familiar. He would do a fifty-three in seven and let the chips fall. WTF.

Butler stood, reached out to shake hands. No more questions? Was it going to be that easy? But then he hesitated. "How do we explain this to the press?"

"Any way you want—you can say you were disgusted with the un-Christian tenor of the campaign. I don't give a shit."

"I have to talk to Bigler. . . ."

"No you don't," Charlie said, smiling slightly. "You're a big boy. Use your gut. Now or never. Go or no."

"All . . . right," Butler said. Neither of them had any idea what to do next. It couldn't be as easy as this, Charlie thought. And then he had another thought. "Wait a minute, Lee," he said. "I just thought of something else I want."

"What?" Butler turned, exasperated.

"What really happened that night with Mustafa?"

"I . . . I don't remember too well." Butler looked down, ran a foot back and forth on the wall-to-wall carpet. Charlie saw that he was lying.

"You don't remember? You said he attacked your wife."

"Well, he was trying to . . . he was moving up the stairs, I went down to stop him and fell, somehow."

"Somehow," Charlie said, leaning against the back of the couch. "You mean, it's possible he never pushed you, or even touched you?"

"It's possible . . . but he was on my property."

"Why was he there?"

"I don't know," Butler said.

"What did he say?"

"I don't remember," Butler was drawing himself up, stiffening. "What difference does it make?"

"All the difference in the world to Mustafa. It means he can't go home to his life in Washington, to his church." Charlie stopped, laughed. "You know, he has the same position on abortion that you do . . . I mean, the one you pretend to have. How does it feel to have ruined the life of a Christian?"

"A drug dealer," Butler said.

"Perhaps, in a former life," Charlie said. "But apparently not a mugger."

They stared at each other. Butler made another move to leave, but something was holding him—he was still thinking through the deal, trying to figure the angles. "So anyway," Charlie said, tempting the odds, "I want you to make that right, too."

"What?"

"Admit you were 'confused' about what happened that night. Drop the charges. Let Mustafa go home. That's part of the deal, too."

"Another thing for me to explain? 'Oh, and excuse me, folks, I was just kidding about being attacked by the drug dealer?' "

"Tough shit," Charlie said. "After all the baloney you've been slicing, don't you think it's time this campaign got just a little bit real? Maybe the price of a United States Senate seat should be to tell the truth about something difficult at least once, publicly."

"Yeah, sure. You go first," Butler said, eyes narrowing—he had been pushed too far. "I mean, *you're* what passes these days for a profile in courage? I don't think so. You're just another politician. What have you ever done that's . . ." His voice trailed off as his eyes locked on Charlie's left hand, which hadn't moved, which was resting, absurdly truncated, on the top of the couch.

"Oh, I've done a few things—and no, not just the stuff in the war," Charlie said quietly. "I've done some things in politics I'm proud of . . . and other things I'm not so proud of. That's how it goes. No one gets to be a full-time hero in this business. . . . The best you can do is try to take it seriously—and I get the sense, Lee, that you don't."

Butler was quiet, distracted; he seemed to be thinking about something else. "Senator," he asked, "how many people on your staff know about Joan?"

Charlie shrugged.

"The information came out of Richardson's research operation?"

He nodded.

"Did you share it with your staff?"

"In a limited way," he lied, and Butler knew it.

"You think your people—the rabid feminists and all—you think they're gonna be able to keep it quiet if we make this deal?"

"If I tell them to," Charlie said.

"I don't think so, now that I think about it," Butler said, shaking his head, staring at the floor, disgusted. Everyone was going to know. There was no way to avoid it. His sons would know. And Joan: dealing with Joan was going to be extremely difficult.

"If this gets out, deal or not, it won't be because I had anything to do with it," Charlie said, firmly but not very convincingly. "I don't traffic in this sort of stuff."

"You don't, huh? That's a good one," Butler said quietly, staring directly at Charlie for what seemed the first time. "How stupid of me. Deal's off, Senator . . . no dice. In fact, if it's possible, I'm going to double my ad buy." He shook his head, moving toward the door again. "You act as if I'm some lower life-form. But what about you? What about this? It doesn't get much lower than this, Senator. You hired Morey Richardson, just like I hired Bigler. You gave him clearance to look into my private life—"

"No I didn't," Charlie said.

"Sure you didn't," Butler said, confident now. For a moment, Charlie almost admired him. "We didn't have to *tell* them to check these things out, did we? I didn't tell Ronny Bigler to put a tail on you and check out your girlfriend's history. You were smart, by the way, to get her out of town. If she hadn't left, Ronny would've found a way to educate the public about her choice of roommates, past and present." Charlie sagged, and Butler continued, "Face it, Martin. Neither of us has an excuse, here. If my poor, sweet churchly supporters are right, and there is such a thing as hell—we've both got tickets to ride."

* * *

Butler was right about the inevitability of the abortion story. It broke, with sickening force, on the Friday before the election. Charlie had given strict instructions to his inner circle: anyone who said a word about Joan Butler's abortion would be fired. He'd had, as expected, a terrible fight over that dictum with Morey Richardson—who said, in a climactic and perfectly solipsistic moment of pique, that it was *his* reputation for taking down freaky-deaky dilettante creep candidates that would suffer if the material weren't put in play. "I've got an *international* reputation to protect," he said.

"Tough shit. You're fired," Charlie said, getting far less enjoyment out of this epiphany than he'd expected.

Of course, it was Mary Proctor who dropped the dime on Lee Butler. Charlie had seen it coming. He had ordered her, then pleaded with her, not to do it. She quietly resigned from the campaign, before Charlie could fire her, on the day the story broke. But it all made perfect sense: Mary was close to the higher-ups at the *Register-World,* especially the publisher, Marvin Kimmel.

And, as it happened, a week before election day, the name of a certain anesthesiologist at Otowulla County Hospital was passed from Marvin Kimmel to his executive editor, Jack Davis . . . who passed it on to staff reporter Caroline Adams, who'd once had an abortion—a horrible emotional experience, one that she still thought about and almost, but not quite, regretted—all of which made her incensed by the blithe simplicity of Lee Butler's position on the issue.

Adams worked the story throughout the last week of the campaign. It was a very dramatic job of work, straight out of Woodward and Bernstein: the anesthesiologist confirmed the story—though not on-the-record, of course. Adams needed another source. Dr. Shaughnessy wouldn't budge. And the anesthesiologist couldn't remember who else was in the operating theater that day. Adams was able to get a roster of nurses working the operating room at Otowulla County Hospital in 1987. She dragooned three other reporters into locating every operating-room nurse who could be found. On the Thursday before the election, she found one Kelly Lister—who confirmed, off-the-record, that she had been present for Joan Butler's surgical procedure. She could not violate the patient's right to privacy, but she would not deny that such an event had taken place. It had been, in fact, an evening that Kelly Lister would never forget. She had joined Otowullans for Life as a result, and refused to be involved in any such procedures ever again.

The story—which led the paper, but with a demure two-column headline—WIFE OF CANDIDATE HAD LATE-TERM PROCEDURE—broke too late and too huge for all the nuances to be plumbed; like, for instance, the possible role of the Martin campaign in making it available to the *Register-World*. There were a variety of other angles to be covered: the Joan Butler in seclusion angle, the furious reaction of prolife pastors across the state, the Muffler Man Campaign-in-Disarray story. Butler didn't regain his sea legs for forty-eight hours, until Dr. Arthur Shaughnessy reluctantly held a press conference, on the afternoon before the election, to say that the procedure had been performed because the life of the mother had been at stake—reluctantly, because his patient, Joan Butler, had said, "No no no no no. No!" when he asked if she favored her husband's request that the information be released. Dr. Shaughnessy would never learn why or how Joan Butler's mind was changed. He never spoke to her about the decision. On Sunday morning, he received a handwritten note: "Dear Dr. Shaughnessy, You may release the information. Sincerely, Joan Butler." When he checked the signature, it was shakily approximate—but he was no handwriting expert, and Lee Butler was very insistent.

Shaughnessy's press conference stopped Butler's bleeding, but the race had tightened considerably again—according to a KDES poll, released on the evening before the election—back to a two-point margin for Butler, with 10 percent undecided.

———

Charlie watched all this transpire from a very great distance. He was deep into his last fifty-three in seven—and quite exhausted, in every conceivable way. He would spend the last forty-eight hours of the campaign going nonstop in a rented Winnebago, his throat raw and his bones aching, as if the campaign itself had become a dreadful case of the flu. Calvin and Barry Powter took turns with the driving; Donna came in from Washington for the last run; and Pat Dunn was on the bus, too.

Butler had gone ahead with his massive advertising buy, blanketing the state during the last few weeks of the campaign. Charlie had done the same: Morey was gone, but his Mexican Muffler ad and "nonvote" ads were forever—along with the earlier, blander, "Charlie Martin works for you" series, featuring the biotech lab and ed funding and vet centers and all the rest. . . . The campaign picked up steam—witlessly, inertially—during the week before election day, and then it seemed to explode when the abortion story broke. Charlie thought about calling Joan Butler to apologize: the trajectory of her humiliation was nauseating and familiar. All political scandals, he thought, were the same scandal.

On Monday afternoon, as the Winnebago traversed the northern tier of the state, from Fort Jeffords to Fort Dantrobet to Port Sallesby, Dunnsie got the news, from the field operation, that Lee Butler's last maneuver had been targeted at organized labor—a flier detailing Charlie's mediocre votes on issues of interest to union members. For higher taxes. For taxes on social security (for wealthy recipients, but the flyer didn't say that). Against Protecting American Jobs. Against the Stanton Health Plan.

"As if Muff would support the Stanton health plan," Charlie scoffed.

"It's not a get-out-the-vote-for-Butler thing," Dunnsie said. "It's a don't-get-out-the-vote-for-Martin thing. They took a hit with their base when the abortion story broke. They're trying to hit ours. I wouldn't be surprised if they're spreading walking-around money in the labor precincts—to get people not to show up for our phone banks, and GOTV ops. You know how old that trick is? I learned it from McManus Mulvaney in the 1948 Dewey-Truman. Mac gave me a wad of bills and said, 'Patty, m'lad, why don't you take a walk around your precinct, and see if you can disinterest some Republicans in going to the polls.' "

"Didn't Mulvaney end up in jail?" Charlie asked.

"Not for that," Dunnsie said. "That was just politics. Isn't it strange, after all these consultants and television and polls, an election can still turn on walking-around money."

"Let's hope not," Charlie said. They were pulling into Fort Dantrobet. A mildly impressive clump of people had gathered in front of the courthouse—crunching a carpet of fallen leaves—for a midafternoon Martin for Senate rally. Charlie noted two overweight women at the edge of the crowd: the quilters Nell had chatted up at the burrito festival in July. He went over to them, half-expecting they'd have news of her. But they shook his hand, with cool and distant respect, as if he were just another politician.

*   *   *

Late night, on back roads from University City to Des Pointe—where Charlie's traditional last rally would be held at daybreak, at Clarice Martin Park: a flowery island in the ghetto, an unprepossessing memorial to his mom, across from the East Side Community Center—Charlie sat up front in the van with Calvin, letting Donna and Dunnsie snooze in the back. Calvin fingered the "seek" button, looking for acceptable music. He had his brights on, occasionally illuminating a farmhouse or gas pump or a billboard promising McDonald's down the road. America at night in early November: nothing more desolate than the night before an election.

"I've been thinking about what you asked the other day," Calvin said. "You know, the question about what I'm going to do next?"

"And?"

"And I was thinking, I'll bet no one ever asked Buzz that, what he was going to do next."

Charlie chuckled at the thought. "You might be right."

"Everybody always knew what he'd be doing next," Calvin said. "The next gig. The next medley. He had something to carry him through, something that was all his—the music didn't depend on anyone else."

"Right," Charlie said. "And so?"

"Grandma was that way, too—according to Buzz," Calvin went on, making the argument at his own speed. Charlie was surprised that Calvin and Buzz had talked about anything so personal as Clarice. "For her, it was the poor people thing. Buzz told me, 'If she'd lived past being mayor, she would have gone right back there, to the East Side Center.' That was what carried her through. I guess what I'm saying, Dad, is that's what I want for me, too: something to carry me through. I'm hopin' it'll be the music, like it's been for Buzz. But we'll have to see about that."

"Calvin, seems to me you're doing just fine," Charlie said, warmed by the easy intimacy of the conversation. If nothing else had happened in this awful campaign, he thought, I've actually become a father.

"Yeah, but—" Calvin said slowly, debating whether to say the next thing. He hit "seek," found heavy metal and grimaced.

"But?" Charlie asked.

"No buts . . . it's just—forget it." He hit "seek" again, found country music; hit "seek" again. He was down the low end of the dial now, and fixed on the state college radio station—there was a subtle, stunning, perfectly calibrated saxophone glissando into a slow, sexy big-band number. "Wow, Dad, what's that?"

"I think it's Ellington," Charlie said. "The song is, 'I've Got It Bad (And That Ain't Good).' " But he hadn't remembered the fabulous saxophone. He and Calvin listened, together, intently, in the darkness; his son's face illuminated only by the reflection of the dashboard lights. The station was playing an Ellington set.

"What is it about late-night radio when you're driving?" Cal observed. "Either it's all crap or total genius."

"Calvin?" Charlie pressed gently. Listening to the music together was, in a way, the closest they'd ever been. "You think I'm actually gonna let you off the hook? Tell me what was on your mind before Duke came on."

"Well, I was just thinking: maybe 'What are you going to do next?' is a better question for you."

"You mean, you're not convinced politics is something that will 'carry me through'?" Charlie asked, with a self-deprecating laugh. "Yeah. Me either."

"God, listen to that," Calvin said. It was "Take the A Train," with a live audience. "Listen to the way he has the brass and reeds pulling against each other. It's so out of sync, and yet it works."

Charlie allowed his son the rest of the song, and listened to it carefully himself, for the first time really, thinking: So that's why Ellington's so great. When the stereotypical, soporific public radio announcer came on, Charlie turned down the sound and asked, "Cal . . . okay. So tell me, if it's not just politics for me, what do you think it is?"

"Well," Calvin said, without the slightest hesitation, "when I was in New York last winter, I kind of thought you'd found it."

THE END OF
THE CAMPAIGN

18

———

"WE LOVE YOU, CHARLIE!"

Always that strange, forlorn cry, through twenty years of victory parties—and he wondered: had it always been the same woman, with the same immaculate sense of timing, able to discern the precise moment the applause waned and the audience began to settle in, the semisilent beat before he began to speak. He had vowed never to exercise the cliché, "I love you, too." And now he simply smiled and nodded, as the crowd laughed.

He liked them a lot. But love? He looked back over his left shoulder at Buzz and Calvin and Vern, and Edsy sitting proudly off to the side. They had played "Hail, hail, the gang's all here . . . what the heck do we care," when he'd come in. Played it with tears in their eyes, but smartly, appropriately. And then there was nothing left, but to do what he had to do.

"A few minutes ago," he said, "I called Lee Butler to congratulate him on his victory." Boos now. Predictably. His role here, according to the handbook of Standard Political Practice, was to remind them to be gracious. But the hell with that. "Yeah, that's right," he said, with a mischievous smile. "Boo! But no boo-hoos. Okay? We've had a very good run. We've done some terrific things for this state, and for this nation. And I want to thank you for standing with me, and working so hard—for the right things, for all those years. We may have lost tonight, but we've got nothing to be ashamed of. . . ."

"He does!" A different voice this time. Charlie let it go.

Actually, the phone call to Muffler Man had been almost civil. "Lee, it's yours," he'd said. "Congratulations."

Silence on the other end, as if Muffles didn't know what to say. "Thank you," he finally said. "It was a tough race. No hard feelings."

Yeah, right.

"How's Joan?" Charlie tried, but immediately regretted it.

"Not good. I'm not sure I'm gonna be able to get her out onstage with me tonight. . . . I'm counting on the kids to—well, you don't want to know the gory details."

"Lee, I'm sorry," Charlie said. "You were right. Once the cat was out of the bag, it was out of the bag." An idiotic thing to say. He considered asking Muff if the experience of voting, for the first time, had been . . . *fun*. But the campaign was over. He didn't feel like taunting the sucker.

Happily, Butler hadn't asked him directly to make his concession speech a resignation speech, a long-standing local tradition—in order to give the new senator a few additional months of seniority, to put him a leg up on the other arriving freshman members. In fact, Charlie had received a specific request from Jack Stanton not to do that. The President had called, just as Charlie was about to concede. "Crummy night," Stanton said. "We're getting creamed all over. I feel so bad for Donny O'Brien: he's gonna have to move his office to the minority suite, after all those years." He paused, long enough to notice that Charlie wasn't amused. "It's me. It's my fault. I'm sorry I wasn't stronger for you, Charlie."

"Well, Mr. President, I'm sorry I wasn't stronger for you," he said. It was remarkable, in the end, how little Jack Stanton had had to do with this.

"Could I ask you a favor, Charlie?"

"Sure, Mr. President."

"I know your state has one of those early resignation things, but don't do it—we're giving the Congress over to the Republicans soon enough. I may want to call y'all back and get some things done while we're still in charge."

The thought was appalling. Charlie never wanted to go back there again. And, what manner of things would Stanton want done? But he went along. It was the President of the United States making the request. "I appreciate that, Charlie," he said. "And I know this is a little too early to think about the future—I remember how it was the time I got my butt whipped for governor—but when the smoke clears, I'd like you to come on in here, and maybe we could talk about a spot for you somewhere. Something diplomatic . . . or over across the river, at Defense. I'm gonna need all the help I can get."

"Thank you, Mr. President," he said. "I'll do that."

As he spoke with Stanton, Charlie looked around the suite at the Barberry, his sad, ancient "victory" hotel. There was a table with cold drinks, trays of fruit and vegetables, cubes of cheese. He saw Donna, dry-eyed, on her cell phone. Dunnsie, hands in his lap, beaten. Hilton, hugging a stream of desolate campaign kids.

He had watched the figures roll in, knew almost from the start that the numbers in his counties were lower than normal. He didn't even need to do the math. Nor did he care to know how badly he would have beaten Muffler Man if his troops, especially the labor folks in Singer Rapids and Port Sallesby, had come out in their usual strength—if half of them had voted, as opposed to a little more than a third. "Dunnsie, what was it that Reagan used to say?" Charlie asked. Dunn looked up at him. "Passadena? You were right. About labor. They took a pass on this one."

"I was wrong bringing in Morey," Pat said.

"No you weren't. Morey was an asshole, but he was good," Charlie said. "And you were right about the big one: we could have survived everything if I'd tended to the base. . . . Donna, the Prez doesn't want us to resign yet, so you've got a job through the end of the year. Unless someone else wants to hire you sooner."

"I'm with you to the bitter end, *muchacho,*" she said, coming over to him and giving him a good hug. "Can't imagine having as much fun with anyone else."

Donna would have plenty of offers; no doubt, she'd get another chance to work for a serious player or a rising star. D2 wouldn't be so lucky—not in politics, now that his "orientation" was public. But Hilton had decided he was ready to leave the business, anyway: he could handle snarling, snarky fashion reporters instead—or film critics, or foodies. He was going to New York.

As was Charlie, of course.

* * *

Past midnight at Oak Street, Buzz sat in the La-Z-Boy, the synthesizer resting across the arms of the chair. Calvin was on the floor, noodling his guitar; Charlie was stretched out on the couch, his head in Edsy's lap, staring at the ceiling. "Anyone got a good loser medley?" he asked.

"I'm a loo-oo-ser . . ." Calvin began to sing.

"They're all about love." Edsy sighed. "Loser songs."

"There's 'Mood Indigo,' " Buzz offered, "And 'Deep Purple.' "

"That's a color medley," Charlie said. "Depressing colors, I'll grant. . . .

A depressing color medley. Actually, that's pretty cool. The third would be 'Paint It Black.' "

The phone. Linc from Russia. "How about this one, Rathburn?" Charlie said. " 'Mood Indigo,' 'Deep Purple . . .' "

"And 'Paint It Black'?" Linc laughed. "You're so obvious. . . . You should throw in something optimistic, like 'When the Red, Red Robin Comes Bob Bob Bobbin' Along.' "

" 'Live, love, laugh and be happy'?" Charlie asked. "Is the sun shining over there, or something?"

"In November?" Linc asked. "Are you kidding? So what happens now that these lunatics have overrun the fortress? Do we get concentration camps for Trilateral Members on the Mall?"

He was trying not to be morose. Charlie was grateful for that. But the mood wouldn't be sustainable for very long. "Linc, thanks. I don't think it's hit me yet. Stanton called. He thinks it's all *his* fault."

"That would count as gracious," Linc said, "if it weren't for the fact that if things had gone the other way, he probably would have taken credit for your victory. Did he offer you a job?"

"Almost," Charlie said. "Why? You been conspiring?"

"Oh, I was just talking to Coleman today. You'd make a perfect sec—def, if there's a second term."

"Thanks for the plug." Charlie assumed Linc was just trying to boost his morale. "But a second term? That's pretty hilarious."

"You never know," Linc replied. "Two years is a long time, or so they say. So what are you going to do?"

"First of all, find Nell."

"Have you lost her?"

"She walked out on me the night of the state fair debate."

"And she hasn't come back since?" Linc said carefully, "You must have done something wonderful."

"Linc," Charlie said, "I really blew it. Richardson did oppo on her, just as he did on me and everyone else in our campaign."

"And?"

"And she found out about it."

"He found something . . . interesting?"

"He found that she'd lived through the past twenty-five years," Charlie said vehemently, "just like the rest of us."

Linc had the choice of pressing the issue, or finding a graceful way to let Charlie off the hook. "Well, I guess it's understandable that she was pissed about being investigated—by your own guy. She does have a temper, I recall. But I'd imagine the anger would pass."

Charlie didn't like this at all, talking to Linc about Nell. He tried to find a way to divert the conversation, but where else could it go? "She's changed her phone number," he said, depressed by his lack of discipline. "And I think she closed down the business. The line's been disconnected. I don't know how to get to her, except to go there."

"The business was always iffy," Linc said.

"I was thinking about trying Gwyn."

"Lord," Linc said, laughing uncomfortably. "I'd all but forgotten about *her*. You must really be desperate." But he heard Charlie not laughing on the other end of the line. "Well . . . hey, you need a place to stay in the city? My flat is empty. In fact, I could use a house-sitter. Take it."

"Thanks, Linc. That's very kind."

"Shut up. And anyway, if you decide to hang around, it puts you in the right place when Marisa and I come in for Christmas. CNN's moving her to D.C.: chief diplomatic correspondent. I'm gonna help get her settled . . . and . . . if I can get the courage—"

"Ask her to marry you?"

"There are so many obstacles. I'm here in Moscow, she's gonna be there. There's the color thing. The age thing . . . but what was it you said about Nell? Remember? 'I look at her across the room and before I'm conscious of it, I'm smiling.' Thank you for that, Chas."

"Uhh." Charlie grunted and thought: ouch.

"You'll use the flat, right?" Linc asked. "And prep me for the big proposal?"

"All right." Charlie was working hard not to let Linc know he'd just dissolved, his eyes brimming, imagining Nell across a room—the night of the inauguration, the dinner at the Mayflower, chatting, with whom? Lanny? Coleman? Moving her hands as if she were mixing something, the brown and turquoise shawl slipping off her shoulder.

"And if I succeed," Linc was saying. "If I can get her to say yes, you'll be best man?"

"Of course."

"Charlie," Linc said, sensing the anguish on the other end of the phone. "You were right—the things you said when you came to visit—and I wasn't a very good friend."

"It was awkward," Charlie replied. "I could have found a more elegant way to tell you about Nell. And you were right: it was unseemly, my poaching that way."

"No, *you* were right!" Linc said, laughing.

"No, *you* were! Jesus, Linc, we really are a fine couple of coconuts."

"Especially when it comes to women. Look, Charlie, here's what I know about you: You're a stubborn son of a bitch. You'll turn her around."

But he knew how stubborn Nell could be when her mind was set, and as that thought occurred to Linc, it also occurred to Charlie.

*   *   *

He went to New York two days after the election. Linc's flat was a triplex in a brownstone in the East Seventies and Charlie hibernated there, disconsolately, unable to make a move. He tried to make himself at home, but the place wasn't even vaguely domesticateable. Linc had formal, mahogany furniture—and delicate chintz couches and chairs that some unknown decorator had once decided would brighten the life of an extremely busy corporate lawyer; there were elegant, Matisse-like Indonesian batiks on the walls and thin, subtle silk and wool carpets from central Asia—Rathburnian globe-trotting trophies; there were blue velvet drapes, and venetian blinds, and the windows were locked shut against the soot-encrusted air. Like Charlie, Linc obviously paid very little attention to where he lived; unlike Charlie, he tried to keep up appearances.

Charlie found himself behaving like a guest: limiting his activities to the den, the kitchen, the bathroom. He slept on the fold-out couch in the den. He seemed to be sleeping an awful lot, in front of the television, drifting off two or three times a day. He tried to rationalize the paralysis: he needed some time, a few days, to get over the lost campaign and prepare himself for Nell. He tried reading Trollope—*Can You Forgive Her?*, the first of the Palliser novels. His mind wandered. All the characters were either inexplicably prissy or ridiculously passionate; Trollope only made Nell seem less accessible. He made tentative forays into Linc's neighborhood, shopping in the shoeboxes that passed for supermarkets in Manhattan, filling the refrigerator. He went to the movies. He went to the museums, tried to slow his eye, think as she thought, see as she saw.

A week passed. Rathburn would call at about five each afternoon, which was one in the morning in Moscow. And they'd talk about . . . nothing. Linc didn't ask Charlie how the Nell campaign was proceeding. Charlie was cheerful, but not very chatty; he was impressed, and rather grateful, that Linc was making the effort to keep tabs on him. He began to take longer walks, and then afternoon runs, uptown—and then down-town, to the general vicinity of Mondo Nello. The physical exercise began to revive him. One afternoon—the sun was setting early now, throwing sharp, strident shadows west to east; the wind off the river gritty with cinders, funneling down the cross streets, rattling the street signs—he rang the doorbell at the corner of Tenth Avenue and Seventeenth Street. There was no answer.

"All right," he said, shouting up at Nell's window. "It's official. I've been a fool for a week. But no more dithering. I'm coming to get you!"

Fifteen minutes later, after a flat-out sprint downtown through a mile of stalled commuters hoping to achieve New Jersey via the Holland Tunnel, he pushed the G. Coxley button at 57 Mercer Street and was buzzed in with an alacrity to match his mood.

"My word!" Gwyn said, opening the door upstairs. "It's the sneaky senator. Did you run all the way from the Midwest?"

"Hello, Gwyn." Charlie was still puffing steam, his cheeks burning, his eyes watery. "Will you invite me in? I won't bite."

"I might," she said coolly, not opening the door. She was wearing a plaster-splatted blue flannel shirt. She seemed more prim and middle-aged, not nearly so melodramatic as she had the night of the party at Nell's; she was more attractive without the heavy makeup, her dark page-boy pulled back with a chartreuse scarf. "I try not to track shit into my studio," she added, thickening her accent, mocking him. "You really devastated my poor cousin."

"I devastated myself, too."

"We cheered your loss," Gwyn said evenly, figuring the loss was what Charlie was referring to; he winced in reply. "Ted and I did. I don't know how Arabella felt; it's not the sort of thing we talk about anymore. She's been very down, you know."

"I'm sorry," Charlie said, sagging in the foyer, leaning on a narrow sideboard with a vase that stood between Gwyn's flat and the apartment across the hall.

"Quite so," Gwyn agreed. "You are one sorry senator."

"Please, I've been trying to reach her. Gwyn, you may not believe this, but . . ."

"You're sorry."

"Goddammit, Gwyn." He slammed his fist down on the sideboard.

"And violent, too."

"Mostly sorry," he said, shaking his right hand, which hurt. "Pathetic," he added. "Lost, without her . . . Gwyn, would you please, please, have a cup of coffee with me?"

She stared him up and down, sighed, closed the door, then reopened it, toting a brown leather bomber jacket and a clutch of keys. They took the elevator—which was tiny, too intimate to talk in—downstairs, and out, into the wind, and now, frigid rain, pelting like bullets. Gwyn dashed across the street to a place called the Blue Canoe; Charlie followed, his legs tightening after the run. The coffee house was dark, self-consciously Bohemian, draped in Indian fabrics with newspapers and magazines strewn about. They sat at an oak table. He ordered a diet Coke; she, a cappuccino.

"First thing you should know," Gwyn said. "She told me everything." Charlie began to speak. "Every thing," Gwyn interrupted. "Of course, I knew most of it already. We lived through it together. She had an abortion; I had two. We both had spectacularly felonious roommates. Mine was a boyfriend who dealt drugs; I testified against him. Not my finest hour, but the early seventies were *such* fun . . . and," Gwyn added, arching her eyebrow suggestively, "she told me all about you."

"I did a terrible thing," Charlie admitted.

"Which was?"

"Well, I . . ." He found that he couldn't succinctly explain what it was that he'd done wrong. His initial sin had been an insinuation, a tacit flicker of a communication with Morey Richardson: I haven't said that you are explicitly forbidden from checking out how the marriage will play. The moment had been so subtle, so insidious, that he'd almost been able to convince himself, later, that it hadn't happened. His more obvious sin had been not telling Nell about her dossier immediately, that day at Crescent Lake.

"Why didn't you tell her that the guy was looking into her past, too?" Gwyn asked.

"I didn't—"

"Trust her, obviously. She thinks you were freaked by her report card. She thinks you got cold feet and didn't have the guts to tell her."

"She's right," Charlie said. "For about fifteen minutes, I had cold feet. But as soon as I saw her, I remembered, this was *Nell* that asshole had been talking about. . . . And then I bet that she'd never learn about the dossier. We'd just go ahead as planned, and she'd never find out. But you always find out. Everyone always finds out everything."

"Two points for honesty," Gwyn said, stirring the steamed milk into her cappuccino, adding more cinnamon from a shaker on the table. "But you're still in the hole."

"Tell me about it," Charlie said. "Why didn't she just blow up at me as soon as Sonnenfeld gave her the details, before the debate?"

"Maybe she's more honorable than you are," Gwyn said. "Maybe she didn't think it was fair to obliterate you before the debate."

Charlie put his head in his hands. "What can I do?"

"I don't know," Gwyn said. "She's very proud, and this hasn't been her best season. She didn't have the energy for much of anything when she came back—and that business of hers demanded too damn much, from her and from her trust fund, even when it was going well, which was just about never. After she shut it down, she spent two weeks finding jobs for every one of those women who worked for her. Then she spent a few weeks out in Bridgehampton—alone. Thank God for Lucius, with the kids. Cousin Grigorii finally retrieved her. She hasn't been much fun since. Won't go out. Keeps getting the flu, or so she says."

"Would you give me her phone number?"

"No," Gwyn said.

"I'm going to—"

"Get to her anyway?" Gwyn smiled. "I assume that. You wouldn't have done something as desperate as corral *me* if you weren't fairly intent about this. The question is, how do you do it in a way that doesn't cause more pain? In a way that might even lead to success? My guess is you go through Lucius—he's the gatekeeper—and the kids. If you can't win over Lu and the kids, you don't have a shot with her."

"You want me to succeed? Why?"

"Well, she's no damn use to anyone moping around. And besides"— Gwyn paused, drained her cappuccino—"we were all watching the debate that night on C–SPAN. You were right about second chances, and mercy as opposed to vengeance." She stopped, and smiled. "Even a perfidious shit like you deserves a second crack."

"I am grateful to you, Gwyn," Charlie said, standing, dropping some money on the table, reaching across to shake her hand.

"A handshake instead of a kiss?" she asked, playing the flirt. He flirted back, gave her the crinkly eye, leaned over, and pecked her cheek. "Folks in your state are fools," she added.

*   *   *

Two weeks passed before he could begin the Nell campaign in earnest. He had promised Donna that he would spend the week before Thanksgiving closing down the operation in Washington, saying good-bye to all his people, packing his office. Then he went home to Des Pointe for turkey at the Clarice Martin East Side Community Center and the beginning of the Christmas gift drive for the kids. He moved through these events crisply, truly grateful to his Washington office staff, especially Donna; happy, as always, to spend Thanksgiving as it was supposed to be spent. But he was antsy, ready to get back to New York and make his move.

On the Monday after Thanksgiving, Charlie was waiting on the corner of Tenth Avenue and Seventeenth Street at seven-forty-five in the morning as Lucius emerged with Pamela and Robin, bundled against the cold, for their morning trek to school. Robin immediately ran up and hugged Charlie, who squatted down and held the boy very tight. He looked up and saw Lucius and Pamela eyeing him warily.

"Hey, Lu—" he said, breezily. "I've got an idea. You take Robin down to PS–41, and I'll escort Miss Pamela over to Grace."

"I don't know," Lucius said.

"C'mon, Lu—you've got enough to handle, and Miss Pamela and I have some catching-up to do." He looked at Pamela. This was going to be her call.

"All . . . right," she said. "But who's going to pick me up at ballet this afternoon?"

Charlie and Lucius exchanged a glance, and almost smiled. "I will," Lucius said.

Pamela gave Charlie her hand. They strolled down Tenth silently. "You want to take the bus across Fourteenth?" Charlie asked. "It's cold."

"All right."

They sat in the very back. Pamela took the window seat. "Aren't you going to ask me about Mom?" she finally asked. "I mean, where have you *been?*"

"I didn't—" But an explanation would have been silly. There was no explanation.

"How could you dump her like that?" Pamela glared at him.

"Dump her? She dumped me!" The words exploded out of him. Several passengers turned and smiled: another New York moment.

Pamela folded her arms and stared out the window. He reached over, put his right hand on her shoulder; she shook it off.

"Pims, look at me." She wouldn't. He leaned over and whispered in her ear. "Okay, we had a . . . misunderstanding. It was my fault. But she has a temper."

"Well, du-uhh."

"But it was my fault," he added quickly, not wanting to sound even vaguely critical of Nell.

"What was?"

"It's . . . complicated."

"You had her investigated."

"Yes," he said, heartsick: even Pamela knew.

"Why? What did you think she'd done wrong?"

"Nothing, it was just politics," he said, regretting that. Pamela would now associate "politics" with intrusiveness and mistrust and ugliness. He remembered his own first serious consideration of "politics," via his mom: he had watched the 1956 Democratic Convention with her, and while Clarice was, of course, smitten by Adlai Stevenson, the nominee, Charlie was immediately attracted to the lithe young senator from Massachusetts making an unsuccessful run for the vice presidency. John Kennedy had defined "politics" for him—and the words he had associated with it, when he was Pamela's age, were honor and heroism and style.

The girl looked at him skeptically, disappointed that he had seemed to drift off. "Well, you can't blame her for dumping you," she said.

"No," he agreed. "You can't."

"Then why did you do that? You ruined her life. She cried and cried." The little girl's eyes filled with tears. She gulped, trying to hold it in.

"Come on, let's get off," he said.

They were in Union Square. He squatted down, put his left hand on her shoulder, used his right to tuck stray hair under her hat. "Pims, I made a bad, bad mistake. The worst I ever made. I've missed you all so much. I need to find a way to apologize, and have your mother forgive me. I really do love her. I need your help."

"Oh, Charlie," she said. "It's been so yucky!" And she burst into tears, deep racking sobs—the sort of crying that children do, that adults can't. He envied her the catharsis.

It was freezing, but he didn't feel the cold. He led her over to the stone wall at the edge of the park, lifted her up onto it. She put her arms around his neck, and held on tight. "It's okay, honey," he said. "It's okay . . . I'm here now. I won't go anywhere. Unless you all decide to send me away."

She quieted, and he pulled back. "You're a mess," he said, smiling. "We need to clean you up, before I deliver you to school."

"And if she decides to send you away?" Pamela asked, sniffing.

"I'll cry and cry," he said. "Pamela, would you help me?"

"How?"

"I don't know yet," he said. "For starters, give her this."

He handed Pamela a note he'd written in Des Pointe on plain white stationery. He'd used Senate paper first, but ripped it up—that part of his life was over. The note was simple:

Dear Nell—

I just want you to know that I'm here, in New York, and I'm not going to go away. I'll help Lucius take the kids to school every day, if that's okay, and anything else that needs doing. I've missed them so much. I miss you, too. I know I've apologized—how many times now? I'm sure you got the cards and letters and flowers and gifts. But the pain, the emptiness, just won't go away. I love you beyond anything I can say in words. I'm here for you, whenever you're ready.

Love, Charlie.

Pamela took the note and put it in her backpack. She looked at him, warily again. "What did you say in the letter?"

"I told her I loved her, and I love you, and I'm not going away."

"I'd like to go away," she said.

"And where would you go?" he asked, taking her hand, walking her down Broadway toward her school.

"Not Russia," she said. "Someplace warm."

He didn't really expect a reply from Nell when he showed up the next day to help Lucius take the kids to school, and there wasn't any. Actually, this was a good sign: she hadn't told him not to come. This time he took Robin, promising Pamela that he'd pick her up in the afternoon and walk her home.

He fell easily into the routine, and soon augmented it: bringing coffee for Lucius and doughnuts for the kids each morning. After the first week, he gave Pamela another note for Nell—a chatty note, about books he was reading, museums he was visiting, movies, music. He tried to do Nell-ish things: he plugged away at Trollope, he went to a display of nine-teenth-century English wallpaper at the Cooper-Hewitt Museum. He told her that Hilton had landed a communications job at the Fashion Institute. Charlie helped him move into a closet-sized flat in the West Village; they'd had lunch, gone to a movie—an awkward, postemployment attempt at friendship. But then, Charlie was feeling awkward with everyone, and all the time.

The initial exhilaration of seeing the kids, being part of their lives again, slowly began to curdle: he wasn't making any progress. He tried to approach Lucius, at the beginning of the second week of school patrol. "I'm not gonna get in the middle of this," Lucius said.

"But you *are* in the middle of this," Charlie insisted.

"Look," he whispered, exasperated, not wanting the kids to hear. "I tried to talk to her about it, but she just won't."

He called Gwyn. "You made your move," she said. "It's her turn. Be patient, if you can. I know her: she's going to test you."

"I'm too old for tests," he said. "This isn't a game."

"Of course it is, honey," Gwyn said. "And you're playing . . . by her rules. Approaching her through the kids, rather than banging down the door, or posing as a UPS man—that told her you were willing to do it her way. . . . It was a *good* move, Senator. She's got to respond. And she will."

Christmas was approaching. Linc and Marisa were coming in for the holidays, but he wasn't looking forward to seeing them in his current, bummed condition. And Buzz called, asking about his plans: "The folks over at East Side are wondering why you aren't working the holiday drives, like usual."

"I'll be back," Charlie said. "But not this year, Pop. You can explain it to them, can't you?"

Buzz grunted. "Listen, son, I'm sending Cal East for Christmas goose with youse," Buzz said—the goose with youse was an ancient formulation.

"Not necessary, Pop," Charlie said.

"You're right. It's not necessary. It's voluntary. Kid insisted," Buzz said. "He wanted a Brie and freezy X-mas. Had some stuff we wanted you to get for the holidays anyway . . . Christmas pastries, and assorted Edsies."

"Thanks, Pop, but—"

"You making any progress out there?"

"Hard to tell."

"Hang in there, boy."

"Hey, Buzzmeister," Charlie said. "I love you, too."

Calvin's arrival meant arrangements. Linc had insisted that Charlie stay on at the apartment, even after he and Marisa arrived, and that Cal could sleep on a couch—but Charlie figured that would be too cramped by half and, anyway, he wanted to do something memorable for his son, so he booked rooms for them at the Plaza and checked out the music listings for the week. He figured a night at Seventh Ave South with the Brecker Brothers, and another at S.O.B.'s for Milton Nascimento. He bought Calvin a very cool leather jacket for Christmas and a boxed set of Ellington; he bought toys for Pamela and Robin, and a sweater for Lucius—but he was having trouble figuring out something for Nell . . . until he saw the garnet earrings in the elegant Russian antique store, diagonally across from the Plaza.

He walked in and said, "I'll take those."

The saleswoman couldn't help but laugh. "You know what you want," she said. "They're four thousand dollars, by the way."

"Then you better put them in one of those nice satin boxes," Charlie said.

And then, two days before Christmas vacation, there was a breakthrough of sorts. Lucius emerged from the loft door that morning smiling broadly. "What?" Charlie asked. *"What?"*

"She wants to know if you can take them to the Big Apple Circus on Tuesday," Lucius said.

"I don't want to go to the circus," Pamela said. "Circuses are for kids."

"Shhhh," Charlie said, squeezing her head in the crook of his elbow. "You go to the circus with me, I'll do whatever you want."

"Buy me a pony?" Pamela asked. "Take me to Morocco?"

"Morocco? Tell you what—maybe you and Robin can spend a night with me and Calvin at the Plaza. We can go ice-skating and—"

"Yay yay-yay-yay," Robin said. "The Knicks, the Knicks, the Knicks—too?"

"If they're in town," Charlie said. "But, kids, let me talk to Lucius for a moment." He pulled Lucius aside as the kids swung around parking meters on Fourteenth Street. "She actually asked if I would do it? That's progress, right?"

"I think so," Lucius said.

"Lucius, what *is* it with her?" he said, glancing over to see if the kids were listening. They were swinging around a light pole. "What do I have to do to break through?"

"You're doing fine. You know, her dad was a very charming guy. Like you, only not quite so stable. . . ."

"And he betrayed her? She never talked much about—"

"Ignored her," Lucius said. "You know she's a high-wire act. Things go crash sometimes."

"So what do I do?"

"Rock steady," Lucius said, leading Pamela off to school.

"Can we talk some more?" Charlie yelled. He stopped, picked up Robin to hold him in place. "I need to know everything."

Lucius nodded, and went off. Charlie marched Robin down to Twelfth Street and then across, exhilarated: he knew now he was going to win.

Which made Christmas more tolerable. Actually, that Christmas would have passed for terrific most years. Dinner was at Linc's. He and Calvin helped Marisa put together ham and mashed potatoes and greens and black-eyed peas. Hilton showed up, with a date—a shortish Latino named Reynaldo with dark, sweet eyes—and with dessert, a Sacher torte. Calvin had brought his guitar, and they sang Christmas carols.

"Are you okay?" Linc asked, when he could get Charlie alone in the study for a minute. "You look like shit."

"I'm fine, exhausted, frustrated—but fine," he said. "Lucius thinks I'm doing okay. She *is* stubborn, and high-strung."

"That's why she's a lot better suited to you," Linc said, "than to me."

"Marisa being flexible and low-key?" Charlie asked.

Linc laughed. "Well, at least Marisa's interested in the same things I am. I never could get into Nell's effete, visual . . . whatever. And I saw, right away," he quickly added, "that you could. She taught you a lot, didn't she? You must have been teaching her something, too?"

"How to trust a politician," Charlie said, staring at the nonknuckles of his left hand. "This is hard, Linc. There isn't a day that goes by when I don't say, This is ridiculous. What are you doing here?"

"And the answer is?"

"Penance, obviously. But I'm getting penanced out."

Linc deposited himself between piles of government briefing papers he had unpacked and stacked on the couch, leaning an elbow on one of the piles. "I always thought you got frustrated when things seemed too easy. You always tried to make everything harder. Like running for—"

"That wasn't real," Charlie said. "This is. You know, I just barely look at the newspapers these days." He nodded at Linc on the couch. "Things like that pile of cables you're leaning on? Used to love reading 'em. No interest now. I haven't even asked you about Chechnya, or what's happening in D.C. I haven't talked to Don O'Brien, and I know I should. I know I should be concerned about a Congress full of Muffler Men. But then, we weren't too terrific either. I wasn't too terrific. Friendship or no, I should have told Oskar to go fuck himself religiously, all the time, just to be sure. I took the job for granted; I deserved to lose. Just not to that twerp."

Linc smiled, and then began to laugh.

"What's so funny?" Charlie asked.

"You love penance. You're a penance junkie," Linc said. "You got anything else you want to apologize for?"

"The Madame Nhu rumor?"

"Now, *that* was a truly dastardly act." Linc stood, crossed the room, put a hand on Charlie's shoulder. "Did you ever consider the possibility that maybe she's waiting for you to stop apologizing?"

*   *   *

Dear Nell—

Thank you for the donation of the kids. We had a wonderful time, mostly because I said yes to almost everything. I realize this may make your job harder now that they're back, but—too bad! It's the price you pay for excluding me.

Anyway, the circus was fine—better for Robin than for Sham and me. Circuses are like Santa Claus, I think: after a certain age, you just stop believing in them. I had the distinct impression that the Bulgarian jugglers and Romanian acrobats were mailing it in, in any case. And clowns are a bit much, don't you think? The kids scarfed Cracker Jacks and cotton candy (I have noticed that actual mealtimes are when they do their least eating), and I did buy them those things that glow in the dark, but drew the line at a giant fake-sponge thumb.

Another thing I noticed: when they get tired, they don't want to do anything so rational as rest—they just get noisier and nag more. Not that they really want anything. They just need to keep their nagging reflexes in fighting trim. After the circus, I was wiped, ready to let them veg out in front of the TV at the Plaza. Happily, Calvin was around—a strange "guy" bond has developed between him and Rob—and they played some sort of game, involving traffic (don't worry: they were standing at the window, watching it), while I made some calls and shagged a break.

Then we went skating in the park. Pamela only cried once. Did I ever tell you how much I hate skating? It's the slippery part of it that I really don't like. But Calvin, again, a revelation! Have you ever seen a six-foot-tall Vietnamese-American who could skate like Hans Brinker, arms clasped behind his back, long diagonal strides, the world's most placid smile. . . .

I won't tell you anything about what I did with the kids for dinner, since what we had was the sort of thing you never let us have.

Putting them to bed was easier than expected. They fell asleep watching White Christmas *on TV—which, I've always believed, is all the attention* White Christmas *deserves. After they went down, Cal went out to hear some music and I settled in with Harold Acton's* Memoirs of an Aesthete, *which you were raving about all last summer—if you recall. Well. Several questions: when do we get to the good part? And, why is it that no English boy ever had fun in "public" school? If every last one of them is an outcast and hated by the masters and forced to take cold showers, who rules the roost? Or, did just the nerds write memoirs? I know you think the books I like are 3D—dour, dense and depressing—and that the "reality" of the twentieth century (all those unhappy endings, all that angst) is every bit as unreal as the sunshine of the nineteenth, and there may be something to that. But why on earth did Alice Vavasor decide to marry her asshole cousin George, and then immediately change her mind again? (Yeah, I'm still working my way through Trollope, too.)*

Anyway, room service this morning. Pamela was born for room service. They are watching cartoons now, as I write this. I've given them a choice: taxi, bus, subway or walk downtown. You'll be shocked to learn that the verdict is split: Rob, subway; Sham, taxi. How does one get out of these situations? Will they live with Flip a Coin?

I hope you are well. Whenever I do anything with the kids, I imagine you there and think about the way you see things, how you'd react to this or that. Whenever I don't do things with the kids, I do that, too.

Love, C.

* * *

On the Tuesday after New Year's, when Charlie arrived at the loft for school-walk duty as always, Pamela came out the door with a mischievous smile and a light-blue envelope. "Only if you tell me what she says," Pamela said, dangling the note in front of Charlie, then pulling it away. "Promise."

"I promise. I promise," he said. "Even though it's none of your goddamn business."

"Yes it is. Promise?"

"Give it to me, or no doughnuts again, ever."

She handed it to him. The sight of Nell's messy scrawl was exhilarating. He tore open the envelope:

C—

    Harold Acton? No heterosexual male should be forced to read Harold Acton in order to impress a woman. Thank you for helping with the kids, but the more I think about this, the more I think our time has come and gone. It's very sad, I know. But I think what's best for me would be a fresh start.

I'm sorry, N.

Lucius, Robin and Pamela were staring at him, on the freezing street. He looked at them sadly, shook his head.

"What's the *matter* with her?" Pamela said.

"It's her choice," Charlie said. "And I don't want you arguing with her about it."

"But—"

"No buts." He looked over at Lucius, who had an odd smile and was holding up his right hand in a fist, a gesture that resembled an ancient black power salute. "What?"

Lucius dropped his arm and opened his fist, offering Charlie the key to the loft. "Lucius?"

"She's being a jerk," Lucius said.

"When should I—"

"After you take us to school," Pamela said.

"All right," Charlie said slowly. "Maybe I'll go home first and get cleaned up, think this through."

"What are you going to wear?" Pamela asked, taking his arm, starting the trek to school.

"What am I going to *wear*?"

"Not a politician suit, okay?" she said. "Blue sweater, those dark green corduroy pants. I don't want you to screw this up."

"Any other advice?"

"Don't be a wimp."

*   *   *

Don't be a wimp was excellent advice. His instincts were all adolescent, jittery. What to bring? Not candy. Flowers? Oh, come on. He had the garnet earrings, but he needed something in his hands. He went down to Patel's magazine rack and got her the latest *Italian Vogue* and *World of Interiors*—and then he nearly tossed them in a litter basket.

The key was an extra, and needed to be coaxed into the lock. For a moment he was afraid he wouldn't be able to figure it out, but he wiggled it around and then pushed harder, there was a grudging click and he was inside. He rode the elevator. The door was open. There was an unusual silence to the place: he had been expecting the hum of MerMaid sewing machines. He thought about her note: "our time has come and gone." True, in a way: a time certainly had come and gone. MerMaid was gone, politics gone. But those had been encumbrances, hadn't they?

"Lu—?" She had heard him.

He turned the corner and found her in the living room, sitting in one of her rattan deck chairs—an original of the sort that began to be copied and sold egregiously in the 1970s—wearing a navy watch cap down over her ears, a forest-green bathrobe with cream piping over silk pajamas, an afghan spread up to her armpits. Her eyes, which picked up the bathrobe green, were rheumy; her skin was pale, except her nose, which was an angry scarlet; there was a cold sore on her lower lip.

"Shit," she said.

"Boy," he said, laughing, "do you look great!" There was a box of Kleenex on the table next to her, within the cone of weak amber light cast by the art deco lamp, the only illumination in the room. She had been reading *House & Garden;* a copy of *World of Interiors*—the issue he'd just bought for her—was sitting on her lap.

"Did you break in?" she asked. "Can I call the cops?"

"Lucius gave me the key. He didn't tell me you were ill."

"He's fired," she said. "Can't seem to shake this thing. Now please leave."

"No way. Not until we talk this out."

"There's nothing to talk about." She pretended to be interested in her magazine, an effort so transparent and ridiculous that it seemed, for a moment, to undercut her resolve. But she refused to budge. "These things have their seasons. Yours passed."

"You look like a passenger on the *Titanic,*" he said, trying not to be a wimp; achieving nincompoopdom instead.

"You've gotten gray," she replied. "Losing hasn't done much for your looks."

"Losing you—" Well, there was no way to get around that. "Losing you was not fun. Losing the election wasn't terrific, either. But losing you was worse."

"You should have thought about the possible consequences more clearly," she sniffed, straining for hauteur, "at the time."

"It was the middle of a fucking election campaign!"

"Campaign mode," she said, singsong. "Everything was so public, even when we were private."

"Not for me," he said.

"You let that asshole invade . . . us!" She tossed the magazine across the room and glared at him. "Was that keeping things straight? I was a novice. I was counting on you—to know where to draw the line. To protect us. To protect me. But you couldn't do it. And now it's gone, buster. So leave."

He sat down on the coffee table, impaling himself on the sharp corner of a photo book about Italian hill towns, and quickly stood up again. "I—"

"You can't even figure out where to sit, can you?" she said, the anger receding. He peered at her in the dark room, trying to understand where she was headed. He was blind, but hopeful.

"I—I'm not leaving," he said, sensing an opening, remembering her way. "Until I can figure out where to leave from."

"I didn't plan the room for a moment like this," she admitted, fighting a grin, joining his deliberations. "You could try the couch, but that's way over on the other side. The armchair has a restricted view. If you sit in the deck chair next to me, our feet are close together, but our heads are off in different directions, and we have to snake around the big lamp to get a good look at each other—if you want to look, which I wouldn't if I were you."

"I like the hat," he said. "So you."

"You're sweating," she noted.

"Well, it's a tough decision," he said, doffing his coat. "Where to sit."

"There's . . . tea," she said, angry at herself for the concession, but the offer of tea was an involuntary reflex. "If you must. I don't want to be inhospitable as I send you packing."

"That's okay," he replied, trying to think his way through the game: to play by her rules or not? "I'm fully caffeinated. Can I get you some more? Milk, two sugars?" He didn't wait for a response, but eased his way to the end table and took the mug there, picking up a whiff of her—Vicks Va-poRub; she smelled like childhood. He took the mug, walked the long acre over to the kitchen silently; prepared her tea; returned it to her silently.

"You are sitting there," he said, "waiting for me to do something clever, win you over yet again, jump another hoop."

"No, I'm—"

"This is infantile. Nell, I am all apologized out. I did a stupid thing. But it was in the middle of a campaign. There won't be any more campaigns. And you're doing a stupid thing now."

"And what's that?"

"You're wasting time."

"*What?*"

"We're not getting any younger. We have only—I don't know—forty more good years left?" She began to smile, involuntarily. "You already blew the holidays this year. That leaves us only about thirty-nine Thanksgivings and Christmases and New Years. . . . I mean, I had plans for us: a last official act as senator. A junket. An investigation of how Italy's dealing with Most Favored Nation—"

"Charlie, you *are* trying to be clever," she interrupted. "Feebly."

"You're right," he snapped back at her. "My cleverness is as pathetic, and transparent, as your stubbornness. Nell, I gotta say, this is the *stupidest* charade."

"I'm not going to be able to get rid of you, am I?" she mused. "You're still standing there, uncomfortably, hands in your pockets . . . and you really can't figure out where to sit, can you?"

"It's just a strategy—to buy time." He gave her his crinkliest eye. "I mean, what would happen if I just came over and—"

She was shaking her head no, but he ignored her and squatted on the floor next to her and, leaning over, put his arms around her waist; she put her arms around his neck and sighed.

"Well, at least we got that out of the way," she said, running a hand through his hair, sliding over, making room for him on the deck chair.

"Hello," he said, kissing her cheek, his nose nuzzling her ear. "I love the smell of VapoRub. It's so elementary-school."

"Hello," she said, taking his left hand in hers, stroking it. He kissed her on the lips this time, softly. "You're going to catch my flu."

"I certainly hope so," he whispered, and kissed her again.

"Could you hand me a Kleenex?" she asked. He did, and she blew her nose. There was still a distance to go, he thought.

"You scared me to death, walking out like that."

"Good," she said, too breezily. "You needed scaring."

"No, I did not." He stood abruptly. She looked up at him, surprised. "Comeuppance, definitely. A poke in the mouth? I would've understood that. But scaring? Walking out on me? I didn't need that at all. Nell, for chrissakes. You can't live a life where every argument is a cataclysm."

"That wasn't just any argument," she said. "And I don't live a life where every argument is a cataclysm. What I can't do is live with someone who doesn't trust me enough to tell the truth."

"I was wrong," he admitted, but quickly added, "and I said so immediately. And vehemently. That night. You're too smart not to understand what happened. I had a moment of weakness in the middle of a campaign. . . ."

"Sounds like you're admitting to an affair," she sniffed again.

"And I've been moping around, wringing my hands like Alice Vavasor, ever since," he said, ignoring her. "What a great title! The story of my life: *Can You Forgive Her?*"

"I can't remember what Alice Vavasor did that needed to be forgiven," she said. "And I can't believe you're giving me Trollope!"

"She jilted John Grey, the good guy, and agreed to marry her cousin, the bad guy," he said, proving that he'd done his homework. "She wised up less than a chapter later. And then she spends the next three hundred pages assuming—wrongly—that Good John Grey will never forgive her."

Nell began to laugh. "This situation isn't like that at all, you clunk!"

"Well, the title applies," Charlie said, still serious. "The question is, Can You Forgive Me? And I don't have three hundred pages to wait around and find out."

"Thirty-nine years, you said." Nell sat up, and motioned him toward her. Charlie stood his ground.

"Only if we put this behind us," he said quietly. "Nell, I love you, but it's time for this particular game to end. So: can you forgive me?"

"All right! All right!" she said, banging the deck chair with both fists. "I forgive you! Jesus, what a pain in the ass you are!"

He was awakened by her sneezing. She had an incredibly loud, melodramatic sneeze. He reached over for a Kleenex, checking his watch as he went: it was just past noon. They had fallen asleep, snuggled together, Nell on top of him, her head on his chest, on the deck chair.

"You want some more tea?" he asked.

"Charlie," she said, ignoring the offer, "if we do this, if we're going to be together, where are we going to do it?"

"Right here," he said. "Where else?"

"And what are you going to do with yourself?"

"There's plenty of time to think about that," he said, sitting up, trying to unkink his neck. "I think I'll get myself some tea."

"I know there's time, but let's start—right now," she said.

"Okay, how about this," he said, standing. "Linc's coming home from Russia in six months. He and Mike Coleman are floating the idea of having me replace him—that would be tons of fun, wouldn't it?"

"It could be—"

"Oh, come on, Nell," he said. "Russia? Would you come? Would Pamela? 'Moth-errr, what's there to *do*?' "

"Pamela," she said, standing for the first time, "would follow you anywhere."

"She would?"

"Uh-huh," Nell said, leaning against him—and looking up insidiously: that old Nell look. "But I have another idea."

"What?"

"Why don't you make me some tea, I'll go freshen up and then we'll reconvene and I'll put my alternative on the table?"

Five minutes later, they had resumed their positions on the deck chair. It wasn't very comfortable, but it had the advantage of continuity and the proximity of Kleenex. Nell was freshly doused with VapoRub, but she'd shed the watch cap and brushed her hair. She rested her head on his chest for a moment. "All right," he said. "What's the alternative plan?"

She twisted sideways, up on an elbow—which rested on his shoulder—and said, "We go back to Des Pointe, and you could run for governor next time."

"Get out of here," he said, laughing. "We do so well together in campaign mode. And Pamela in Des Pointe? I don't think so."

"I think she'd like Buzz and Edsy," Nell said. "And I don't think I'd mind it, being so far away from the beach anymore. I'm out of the swimsuit business now. We could buy a farm, like Tom and Leah's. Or a loft building in the Flats. But most important"—she paused—"I think all those Future Farmers deserve a really good governor."

"Come on, Nell—politics? In the immortal words of your daughter: Oh, guck. I don't know if I have the stomach for it anymore," he said.

"And one thing I do know now: you have to really, really want it. You can't want much of anything else in life. You can't *have* much of anything else. And you've got to figure, a lot of other people are gonna want it more than me. I'd be a long shot, at best."

"Not if we went back and started working it now," she said, tapping his nose with her index finger.

"We?" He looked at her.

"We could sort of do it together."

"Two for the price of one?" he said. "I think I'll throw up."

"I keep thinking of those quilters in, where was it, the place with the burrito festival?"

"Fort Dantrobet."

"What about skirts?" Nell said, looking him in the eye now, very serious. "Made from quilting like that. Down jackets, too—that might be even better. Don't you think? I could set up a network of quilters. Lucius could work the business end, from here."

"Nell," he said, putting a hand to her face. "What is going *on*? Why can't we just settle in here for a while, get used to each other again?"

"Because, if you're going to have any hope of winning, you have to send a signal right now. You have to show everyone you're not going to go away. Just like you did with me."

She was right, of course.

"Face it, Charlie: you're a politician," she said mournfully, turning her head, kissing his hand. "You need to go out and politick. If this relationship is only about you walking the kids to school and reading Trollope and making me tea, I'll suffocate. And you'll wither on the vine. You'd be a terrific governor."

"I don't know," he said, pulling back. "I'm not sure politics is what I want anymore. And I'm sure it's not what you really want. There'll be other jobs, maybe some good ones—maybe ambassador to Ibiza will come up." He stopped. "But you do realize, if we did run for governor and you did come back to Des Pointe with me, we'd probably have to—"

"Get married?" she asked, arching an eyebrow. "Oh, dear me. Of course we would. Sonnenfeld said it polled really well—despite the roommate and the herpes and everything. So are you asking?"

"What?"

"If I'll marry you. It's your turn to ask." She looked up at him. "You're hesitating?"

"If I ask, does that mean that we have to go back to Des Pointe and run for governor, because I'm not sure—"

"I'm not so sure, either," she said. "In fact, this is the biggest thing I haven't been sure about—I figured I could forgive you for the other stuff easily enough, but then what? That's what I've been stewing over. I mean, face it, Charlie: we need a second act. We need a new place to live. The loft is extraneous now: no more MerMaid. And isn't it about time you stopped living with your parents? In any case"—she paused thoughtfully—"I think you may be more the executive . . . than the legislative sort."

"Get *out* of here." He was laughing. "How the fuck would you know?"

"And the job does come with a mansion. That would be fun." She shifted then, turned on her stomach to face him directly. It was a provocative move; their hips were locked, his hands found the swell of her back; he pushed upward gently.

"Char-lie," she said, "what on earth are you doing?"

"Nothing."

"I can feel you," she said. "You're getting hard. . . . That's *sick*. We're having an important conversation."

"Well—don't you think it's important to find out if we're still compatible?" He moved his hands under her robe, beneath her pajamas, to the small of her back, which was very warm—feverish, perhaps—but her skin was so remarkably soft. He nuzzled her ear, stroked her back. "I mean, it's so implausible: you and the kids in Des Pointe. I'm touched, but I have to think . . . and of course, I'll be able to think more clearly if you—"

"Martin, you're pa-*thetic*. I'm sick as a dog. I'm dry as the Sahara down there."

"I can lubricate you," he said, working to slip her pajama pants off her hips. "You said I was good at that."

She shoved back, planted her elbows in his chest, which had the unfortunate effect of grinding her pelvis against his; he smiled and moved to pull her legs apart, to straddle his. She looked at him and shook her head. "God, Charlie," she said, beginning to laugh—and then dissolving in tears, but still laughing, rolling on to her side, shaking with laughter.

"What?" he asked. "What's so funny?"

She turned back around, taking his head in her hands, shaking it back and forth, putting her fingers on his mouth, tears rolling down her cheeks, but still laughing, too. "Oh, Charlie—you're such a *boy*."